CORNER WINDOWS
AND CUL-DE-SACS

CORNER WINDOWS AND CUL-DE-SACS

The Remarkable Story of Newfoundland's First Garden Suburb

C.A. SHARPE AND A.J. SHAWYER

MEMORIAL
UNIVERSITY
PRESS

© 2021 C.A. Sharpe and A.J. Shawyer

All rights reserved. No part of this publication may be reproduced, stored in a retrieval system, or transmitted in any form or by any means, without the prior written consent of the publisher.

Library and Archives Canada Cataloguing in Publication

Title: Corner windows and cul-de-sacs : the remarkable story of Newfoundland's first garden suburb / C.A. Sharpe and A.J. Shawyer.

Names: Sharpe, Christopher A. (Christopher Andrew), 1947- author. | Shawyer, A. J. (A. Joyce), 1940- author.

Series: Social and economic studies (St. John's, N.L.) ; no. 90.

Description: Series statement: Social and economic studies ; no. 90 | Includes bibliographical references and index.

Identifiers: Canadiana (print) 20210344644 | Canadiana (ebook) 20210344822 | ISBN 9781990445019 (softcover) | ISBN 9781990445026 (EPUB) | ISBN 9781990445033 (PDF)

Subjects: LCSH: Suburbs—Newfoundland and Labrador—St. John's—History—20th century. | LCSH: Housing—Newfoundland and Labrador—St. John's—History—20th century. | LCSH: Housing development—Newfoundland and Labrador—St. John's—History—20th century. | LCSH: City planning—Newfoundland and Labrador—St. John's—History—20th century. | LCSH: Municipal government—Newfoundland and Labrador—St. John's—History—20th century. | LCSH: St. John's (N.L.)—Social conditions—20th century. | LCSH: St. John's (N.L.)—Economic conditions—20th century. | LCSH: St. John's (N.L.)—History—20th century.

Classification: LCC HT352.C32 S75 2021 | DDC 307.7609718/1—dc23

Cover images: Car and cul-de-sac: F.P. Meschino; corner window: C.A. Sharpe; street sign: iStock.com/mphillips007
Cover design: Alison Carr
Copy editing: Richard Tallman
Page design and typesetting: Julianna Smith

Published by Memorial University Press
Memorial University of Newfoundland
PO Box 4200
St. John's, NL A1C 5S7
www.memorialuniversitypress.ca

Printed in Canada
27 26 25 24 23 22 21   1 2 3 4 5 6 7 8

Funded by the Government of Canada | Canadä

CONTENTS

Acknowledgements ix
Prologue 1

1. St. John's before 1888: A Town Unplanned 7
   Transition from Fishery to Industry: New Jobs,
   More Workers, Increased Burdens on the Town 8
   A Haphazard Collection of Buildings 10
   Who Owned the Houses? The Leasehold Property System 16
   Absentee Landlords 18
   Public Health: A Desperate Situation 21
   Water Sources, Sewer Systems, and Nuisance 22

2. The Fledgling Municipal Council Faces Reality 29
   Launching the Municipal Council: Straight into Debt 30
   Improving the Water Supply: "Waste Water" and
   Fire Protection 31
   Expanding the Sewer Network: Not an Easy Task 32
   Public Health Becomes a Priority 39
   Public Health: The Public Becomes Engaged 41

3. The Municipal Council Seeks "A Cure for Housing Ills" 47
   What Was the Urban Reform Movement? 48
   Thomas Adams: An Influential Town Planner 51
   Land Speculation: An Obstacle to Planning 54

	The City Charter: The First Planning Document	
	for St. John's	55
	Mayor Gosling's Initiatives	58
	Building Houses for Workingmen: Quidi Vidi,	
	Cavell, and Merrymeeting	61
4.	**The 1920s and 1930s: Difficult Times**	**67**
	Mayor Tasker Cook (1921–29)	68
	The Rotary Club Investigates	69
	Arthur Dalzell: "Is All Well?"	71
	Mayor Charles J. Howlett (1929–32)	74
	Frederick Todd: "Though Slums Are Bad the	
	Cure is Simple"	75
	The Unimaginable: The Arrival of the Commission	
	of Government (1934–49)	77
	Mayor Andrew Carnell (1933–49)	78
	Housing: "Shacktowns," New Houses, and Old Tenements	79
	Councillor Meaney's Proposal	88
	The Commission of Government Examines	
	Councillor Meaney's Proposal	92
5.	**War and Modernity Come to St. John's**	**95**
	World War II, 1939–45	95
	The Municipal Council Copes with the	
	"Friendly Invasion"	97
	The War Opens a Window on the World	100
	The Municipal Council and Town Planning	102
	The Municipal Council Pursues Councillor	
	Meaney's Proposal	104
6.	**"A Humiliating Catalogue of Facts"**	**109**
	The Commission of Enquiry on Housing and	
	Town Planning	110

	Introducing Brian Dunfield	111
	The Six Reports of the CEHTP	115
	The Public's Reaction to the Report: "A Humiliating Catalogue of Facts"	123
7.	"A Bold Scheme for Doubling the Living Space of the Town"	125
	Properties: Expropriation, Compensation, and Cost of Acquisition	131
	What Kind of Houses? How Will They Be Financed?	135
	The St. John's Housing Corporation	137
	The Public's Reaction to the Proposal	138
	The Fourth and Fifth Interim Reports	140
	Sixth Report: The Commission Resigns	146
	From Dream to Reality: Filtering Out the Poor	147
8.	Dealing with the Opposition	149
	Selling the Project to the Dominions Office in London	151
	A Sharp Reminder	157
	The Leasehold Question	159
9.	Shovels in the Ground	162
	The Trunk Sewer	162
	Turning the Sod	167
	"The Housing": Owner-Occupied and Detached	169
	Paul Meschino Joins the Team	170
	Meschino Brings House Styles from "Away" to Newfoundland	173
	Inside Meschino's Houses: A New Style of Living	178
	Inside Meschino's Houses: Retaining Newfoundland Tradition	180
10.	Mr. Dunfield's Folly?	187
	1945: The Rising Cost of Construction	187

	Construction Begins: "Citizens Enthused Over	
	New Houses"	190
	Unexpected Demands: The "Widows' Mansions"	
	and the "Soldier Emergency"	193
	1946: The Changing Landscape	199
	Who Could Afford to Buy the Corporation's Houses?	
	The SJHC Tries to Economize	201
	The SJHC Begins to Lose Control of the Project	210
	The Housing Area Gets a Name	214
	1947: The Axe Falls on the SJHC	215
11.	Canada Enters the Discussion	219
	1948: Phasing Out the SJHC	219
	The Central Mortgage and Housing Corporation	220
	1949: Brian Dunfield Leaves the SJHC	223
	1950: Loose Ends, and a Tangle of Financial Troubles	224
	1951–81: A New Mandate and a New Philosophy	
	for the SJHC	227
	The Residents of the Inner City Are Finally Rehoused	229
12.	Churchill Park: A Daring Experiment	235
	The Two Mandates of the CEHTP	236
	The Three Villages	239
	Life in Churchill Park	243
	Brian Dunfield and His Passion for "The Housing"	249

Appendices ... 253
Bibliography ... 322
Index ... 357
About the Authors ... 363

ACKNOWLEDGEMENTS

This story takes place over a period of 100 years and it has taken us 20 years to collect the material for the story! We have relied on many sources: archival material; conversations with individuals who have shared their memories with us; discussions with experts to clarify our understanding; and our own fieldwork. We are grateful to all those who helped us along the way and who contributed their skills and memories so generously.

The City of St. John's Archives provided access to the Minutes of St. John's City Council from 1897, which we have used extensively. Neachel Keeping and Alanna Wicks guided us through their holdings: maps, photographs, and municipal archival material. At The Rooms Provincial Archives of Newfoundland and Labrador, Melanie Tucker and Larry Dohey and their staff were unfailingly helpful. Joan Ritcey and Linda White and their staff at the The Archives and Special Collections at Memorial University answered many questions, suggested new materials for us to study, and found a picture that we badly needed. Ken O'Brien, chief municipal planner for the city of St John's, provided copies of city maps.

The Smallwood Centre of Memorial University gave us the grant that enabled us to bring Paul and Phyllis Meschino to St. John's in 2000 to discuss Paul's role as architect, more than 50 years earlier, for the original 244 houses and 92 apartments in Churchill Park.

Many individuals generously contributed information to this book: Stanley Pickett, urban planner for St. John's, 1952–56; Joe Ryan, director, St. John's Branch Office, Central Mortgage and Housing Corporation, 1953–60; Paul Power, former corporate secretary of the Newfoundland and Labrador

Housing Corporation (NLHC), and Janette Loveless and Marjorie Gaulton of his staff, who provided us with a copy of the entire set of the Corporation's Minutes; Clarines Rincón, who was in charge of the Resource Room of NLHC and gave us access to many documents and photographs; Paul Meschino, his wife Phyllis, and daughter Martha; Robert Mellin, architect; and Jane Lewis and Mark Shrimpton, who first realized the story behind Churchill Park and blazed the trail for us.

We are particularly grateful for the talents of Charles Conway, cartographer in the Department of Geography (retired), who has provided us with wonderful maps over the years, and David Mercer, former departmental cartographer, now in the Centre for Newfoundland Studies of the Queen Elizabeth II Library of Memorial University, who provided us with maps and photography. Wanda Murrin-Davis and Hogarth Clauzel shared with us their expert knowledge of property and leaseholds. We talked sewers with archaeologist Blair Temple. And we talked house construction details with cabinetmaker and furniture restorer Ralph Clemens, who demonstrated them to us as we toured his house. We turned to Hilda Murray for knowledge of the agricultural footprint in the northern valley prior to the expropriation of land for Churchill Park.

We are very indebted to David Whalen of the Property Services Division of the Newfoundland and Labrador Housing Corporation, who discovered a cache of 437 Searles and Meschino blueprints in the basement of Elizabeth Towers in the spring of 2000, and called to offer them to us. That telephone call gave us access to vital material that we could never have found on our own, and we couldn't have told the story properly without it.

We enjoyed many conversations with people who had stories to tell: about life in the inner city (Mary and Bill Skinner, Gerry Owens, Wayne White), and about the early days of Churchill Park (Robert Halliday, Phillip Hiscock, George Garner, Joan Bantleman, Nathan Penney, Judge Rupert Bartlett). Some people told us about their fathers (Elizabeth Parker, daughter of Eric Cook, and Dorothy Dunfield, daughter of Sir Brian Dunfield) or about their employer (Carrie Toope, maid to the Dunfield household). We were fortunate to meet and talk with His Excellency Gordon Winter, Q.C., the second chairman of the St. John's Housing Corporation and later lieutenant-governor of Newfoundland. Conversations with colleagues of Brian Dunfield (Mr. Justice John Mahoney, Chief Justice Alex Hickman, Judge Rupert Bartlett) helped us to understand his persona.

We owe a large debt to Janet Rowe, who provided astute editorial advice on the manuscript, and to Doug House, who read the draft manuscript and discussed it with us.

Memorial University student employment programs (SWASP, SCP, and MUCEP) provided us with useful research assistance over a period of years. The students extracted material from voters' lists, assessment rolls, city street directories, and the Registry of Deeds. They prowled the streets to take photographs and to check archival data "on the ground." They played a vital role in the research and we are grateful both to the university student employment programs and to the many students who shared the fun of research with us. They included Emily Hobbs, Jodi Sturge, Carolyn Pelley, Kimberley Dymond, James Maloney, Darrell Kennedy, Susan Windsor, Claire Rillie, Janesta McCarthy, Alec McNab, Julie White, and Christina Tizzard.

Dr. Fiona Polack, academic editor of Memorial University Press, provided encouragement and expert guidance in the early days as we worked to refine the final manuscript. We are very grateful for her support. Managing Editor Alison Carr then guided the final production process with the assistance of her excellent team. We thank Richard Tallman who made sure that our sentences were perfect, and Julianna Smith for her attractive book design.

And finally we thank all our colleagues in the Department of Geography at Memorial University of Newfoundland — past and present. They provided encouragement over these many years, and the academic home in which we were able to carry out this research.

Abbreviations

In the book, we refer to a variety of public bodies using these abbreviations:

CEHTP: Commission of Enquiry on Housing and Town Planning in St. John's
CMHC: Central (now Canada) Mortgage and Housing Corporation
LAC: Library and Archives Canada
MUN: Memorial University of Newfoundland
NLHC: Newfoundland and Labrador Housing Corporation
TRPAD: The Rooms, Public Archives Division
SJHC: St. John's Housing Corporation
SJCM: City of St. John's Council Minutes

PROLOGUE

In 1945 Newfoundland was a bankrupt country, governed by a Commission appointed by the British government. The St. John's Municipal Council was the only elected body in the country, with limited powers and a crippling debt of a million dollars (SJMC 1937, 491). It had no zoning ordinance, no planning department, and no system of building inspection. Much of its population was desperately poor because of a long-standing reliance on casual, seasonal employment. Many of the households living in the inner city suffered from the combined effects of two principal problems: overcrowding, even in houses of reasonable quality; and too many houses that were deemed unfit for human habitation.

A chronic shortage of housing made matters worse. It was so acute that many people were building their own houses on the outskirts of the city, wherever they could get a piece of land. Like many Canadian cities, St. John's was hemmed in by peripheral accretions — on Signal Hill, in the Battery, around Mundy Pond, and along Blackhead Road. City councillors and compassionate people in the community were well aware of the housing problems these informal neighbourhoods posed, but they were powerless to do anything about them.

The roots of the inner-city housing crisis go back at least as far as the Great War. Newfoundland raised and maintained a full battalion of infantry that served at Gallipoli and on the Western Front. The cost of this contribution in terms of human casualties and money was huge. By 1933 the people of the country, fewer than 280,000 of them, were facing a public debt of about $100 million, which included the cost of the war and the $23 million spent on the trans-island railway. Debt repayments absorbed about 65 per cent of current revenue (Mayo 1949, 505).

The St. John's Municipal Council, the leaders of various labour organizations, the Board of Trade, the Rotary Club and other philanthropic groups, and several of the city's mayors (Gosling, Howlett, and Carnell) were well aware of the need for housing reforms and better planning for the city. They sought the advice of some of the most prominent planners and social reformers of the day, including Arthur Dalzell and Frederick Todd. But the plans those experts prepared were impossible to implement. Eradication of the dilapidated housing in the central city and the provision of badly needed water and sewer services required much more money than was available to either the municipal or national government. Medical officers of health routinely identified housing so badly deteriorated it needed to be demolished, but since there was nowhere for the poor inhabitants who would be dispossessed to go, the buildings remained standing. And then came the Great Depression.

The national economy depended heavily on the export of salt cod and the Depression decimated the market for this product. By the end of the 1920s the country was bankrupt. In 1934 the Dominion agreed to relinquish responsible government in exchange for British assistance in staving off a default on the debt. Consequently, between 1934 and 1949 the country was governed by a Commission of Government consisting of an English governor and three British and three Newfoundland commissioners, all appointed by the British government. For 15 years the St. John's Municipal Council was the only elected government in the country. Its limited sources of revenue and the inability, or unwillingness, of the Commission to provide the funds necessary to tackle the long-standing problems of the capital city meant that the quality of life in inner-city neighourhoods continued to decline.

But in 1939, an extraordinary convergence of circumstances made a solution possible. An energetic, albeit controversial city councillor, a deputy mayor who wanted to make up for what he thought were his father's missteps during his mayoralty, and a justice of the Supreme Court of Newfoundland with a well-developed social conscience and time on his hands all contributed to a grandiose scheme to solve the inner-city housing problem.

As improbable as it now sounds, the Commission of Government and the St. John's Municipal Council embarked on a joint project to build a new suburb of 1,000 houses on 800 acres of expropriated land on the northern fringes of the city, while the world was at war. Churchill Park, as the development became known, increased the footprint of the city by a third and represents the first application of modern urban planning principles in Newfoundland. Indeed, it was the first post-war suburban development in Canada (although Newfoundland wasn't part of Canada until 1949).

What pushed the country and its capital city into such a huge undertaking? The root of it was an old city, unplanned, mostly wooden, dating from the eighteenth century. A succession of fires had forced a continuous process of rebuilding, but the new buildings repeated the same pattern of narrow streets and lanes, irregularly placed buildings, and high-density living in tenement blocks. St. John's suffered from a social profile comprised of a small group of merchants and a very large proportion of everyone else often living on only a few months' wages each year. The latter generally worked on the docks and in the factories and lived nearby, affording the cheap rents in crowded buildings. Many of these tenements had landlords who had failed to keep the buildings in good repair and had failed to install sanitary facilities when the water and sewer lines reached their streets. Many buildings were condemned by the City Council as "not fit for habitation." Public health statistics for the city were worse than they were for elsewhere on the island. Cholera, typhus, tuberculosis, and infant mortality stalked the streets. The situation became untenable. Churchill Park was one of the responses.

Churchill Park is unlike any other neighbourhood in St. John's. It stretches the length of Elizabeth Avenue from Freshwater Road in the west to Torbay Road in the east, and from Empire Avenue north to Prince Philip Parkway. The central hub is Churchill Square, a cluster of shops and commercial services surrounded by apartment blocks. Around it is a network of quiet, tree-lined streets and cul-de-sacs neatly set out with a mixture of bungalows and one-and-a-half storey, and two-storey dwellings. The houses are rather plain, lacking external decorative features or vibrant colours, but are built on generous lots with front, side, and back gardens. The distinctive corner windows found on many of the houses are a signature feature of the architect who designed more than 200 of the houses in the development. Beyond the houses and gardens are quiet streets; the main street diverts through-traffic away from the residential sections. The houses were built to include the "modern" features of built-in kitchens, central heating, and full bathrooms.

The landscape of Churchill Park is very different from that of "old" St. John's below LeMarchant Road. Here, houses in the style of the nineteenth century, two and three storeys high, are often built in ranges with shared party walls. These form an unbroken façade flanking the narrow streets. The houses are brightly coloured with decorative trim framing doorways, windows, corner posts, and eaves. They have no front or side gardens; their walls edge the sidewalk. The Churchill Park landscape also differs from that lying north beyond Prince Philip Parkway. That area is dominated by one-storey modified "ranch style" houses and bungalows, a legacy of Confederation and the immediate arrival of "mainland" house designs promoted by the Central Mortgage and Housing Corporation (CMHC).

Several episodes in the history of Canadian suburban development can be considered exceptional. They include the redevelopment of the north end of Halifax by Thomas Adams after the 1917 explosion of the *Mont Blanc* (Weaver 1976), the development of Mount Royal by the Canadian Northern Railway in the 1920s (McCann 1996), and the creation of the Cité-jardin du Tricentenaire in Montreal in the 1940s (Choko 1989; Gilliland 2000). Each is part of a continuing tradition of experimentation with an evolving form of townscape, and all are important not only locally but nationally.

Don Mills, built by E.P. Taylor on 2,000 acres of land north of the city of Toronto, has pride of place in the Canadian suburban literature. It has been described as the hallmark of Canadian suburbia, representing the epitome of modernist garden city principles: separation of uses; low-density development and a hierarchy of streets, with shopping concentrated in retail malls and strips; loops, crescents, and cul-de-sacs, with buffers of green space to protect single-detached from high-density housing and plenty of open space (Grant 2000, 449; Sewell 2020, 24). Churchill Park can be described in precisely the same way, except for the high-density housing. The first house was built in Churchill Park in 1944; in Don Mills, not until 1953.

But for all its local and, one might argue, national significance, there are almost no published references to Churchill Park. A book "about the coming of age of modern planning ideas to Canada" (Sewell 1985) makes no mention of it. Nor do works by Rose (1980), Perks and Jamieson (1991), Gerecke (1991), Bacher (1993), McCann (1999), or Harris (2010). To be fair, it must be admitted that Churchill Park has no local fame either. Neither the *Encyclopedia of Newfoundland and Labrador* nor the only published history of the city (O'Neill 2003) refers to it. Obviously, we think the story is interesting for what it tells us about politics and urban planning in the capital city of the Dominion of Newfoundland during the waning years of World War II and the beginning of the post-war era. Those responsible for the creation of this suburban development were obviously *au fait* with the current trends in urban planning elsewhere and this small development remains as a tribute to their valiant efforts to bring it to Newfoundland.

Every town, no matter how small or large, rich or poor, young or old, has its stories. This one took over 100 years to unfold. There were many actors. All had hopes and faced setbacks. This is their story. We have tried to tell it fairly, recognizing that history isn't a single narrative, and that by constructing this one we have excluded others (Harari 2015, 205). We have heard the voices of the many actors through a variety of sources: municipal and government legislation, minutes of the participating agencies, assessment rolls, voters' lists, conversations with participants, memoirs, photographs, and more. And we walked through the city, observing the layout of streets, the siting and design of houses, and the distribution of open space. But Churchill Park is the end, not the beginning, of this story. We begin with the inauguration of St. John's Municipal Council in 1888.

ST. JOHN'S BEFORE 1888: A TOWN UNPLANNED

This is a story about housing in St. John's. It is the story of a time when some families lived in crowded conditions because there were too few houses. It is the story of a time when some families lived in houses condemned as unfit for habitation. Yet these families had no other place to live. How did such a situation come to be? How long did it last? What attempts were made to solve it?

Figure 1.1. A view across the harbour of St. John's from the South Side, c. 1890 (City of St. John's Archives [CSJA] 01-20-001).

On 9 May 1888 St. John's was incorporated and acquired its first municipal council. Twenty-nine years later, Sir Edward Morris (Newfoundland's prime minister, 1909–17) reflected back on that time:

> We had no civic government. The control and the management of the civic affairs of St. John's were managed by the Water Company and the Board of Works. . . . we had but a

very limited sewerage system, the most important of all civic services; we had no sidewalks on our principal streets; we had but a limited supply of water; we had a Fire Department that went to pieces the first time it had to grapple with a serious conflagration; we had no parks or gardens, which in other cities are the lungs of the people; we had no light, save a few old-fashioned gas lamps that tended to illuminate only the darkness; no permanent Health Officer; no telephone service and no pavement in our principal street. (Morris 1907)

In his brief description Sir Edward touched on many of the features of the town that made it a less than an ideal place to live: limited sewer service, limited water service, the lack of parks or gardens, the danger of fire in a wooden town, and the lack of a municipal council. The combination of these factors had given rise to a serious lack of quality of life in St. John's, which was particularly expressed in its lack of decent housing.

Transition from Fishery to Industry: New Jobs, More Workers, Increased Burdens on the Town

St. John's was settled in the seventeenth century and engaged in the migratory fishery through much of the eighteenth century. It then transitioned, with flushes of immigration, into a mercantile town with a settled population, the centre of the colony's government, and increased engagement in international trade. Towards the end of the nineteenth century the town had begun to transition yet again with the advent of its industrial growth. "It is clear that the 1880s is an important benchmark in Newfoundland's economic history. The traditional economy reached a limit to its extensive growth and further development was perceived as a function of the emergence of modern resource industries" (Alexander 1976, 65). Industrialization went beyond the resource industries to the development of secondary manufacturing and brought new patterns of wage employment.

Figure 1.2. On the wharf: the cod fishery, early twentieth century (CSJA 01-13-011).

The 1880s were an exciting time for residents of St. John's. Jostling against the blacksmiths, sailmakers, cooperages, shoemakers, bakers, located in their traditional workshops in sheds and houses scattered throughout the town, were now large factories employing dozens of labourers. There were shoe factories, clothing factories, furniture factories, biscuit factories, and iron foundries. Gaden's Ginger Ale factory helped to quench the thirst of local residents, and Archibald's Tobacco employed 120 people to produce Newfoundland plug tobacco (Alexander 1976). That product would later give rise to an anti-spit bylaw. The largest factory of all was Colonial Cordage on Ropewalk Lane, which employed almost 200 "hands" (*ENL* Rope making). A new dry dock was completed (*ENL* St. John's). Electricity (Baker, Pitt, and Pitt 1990) and the railway arrived (*ENL* Railways; Hiller 1980).

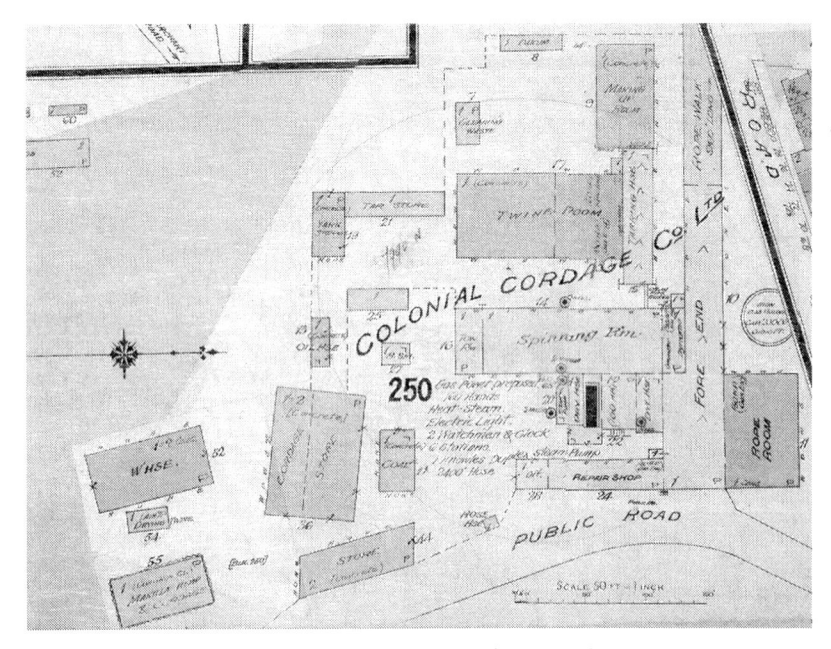

Figure 1.3. The Colonial Cordage Company (City of St. John's Insurance Plan 1893).

In 1858 the labour force in secondary activities was 5 per cent of the total; by 1891 it had risen to 22 per cent (Alexander 1976, 68). These new industrial activities and the need to accommodate the workers placed an increasing strain on the town's already inadequate local services, water, and sewerage. This resulted in conditions that were described by the Medical Society as "filthy and disgusting . . . [and] would lower the vital powers of the community, so as to make it succumb more readily to any epidemic that may arise" (JHA 1879).

A Haphazard Collection of Buildings

The layout of the streets and lanes of St. John's had never been planned. In some other British colonies, for example in Upper Canada, the British government had been determined to establish settlement and did so by surveying large tracts of land into plots, together with a road system, and assigning a particular portion of land in a specific location to every settler. But Newfoundland belonged to the fishery. It was acknowledged that "the right of the soil rests in the King ... but in this island it has been conveyed away to the exclusive rights of the fishery" (Newfoundland Law Reports 1819). The land was in the governor's gift to give and was granted at will to important men in town in the military and in the fishery. Houses were sited and streets were developed in an ad hoc fashion, "all out of straight," on these estates (O'Neill 2003). Admittedly, to make a plan would have been difficult, considering the very steep hill that flanked the town and the presence of rock outcrops such as the one on McBride's Hill, which confined Water Street to a width of six feet in 1809 (Fey 1956, 156).

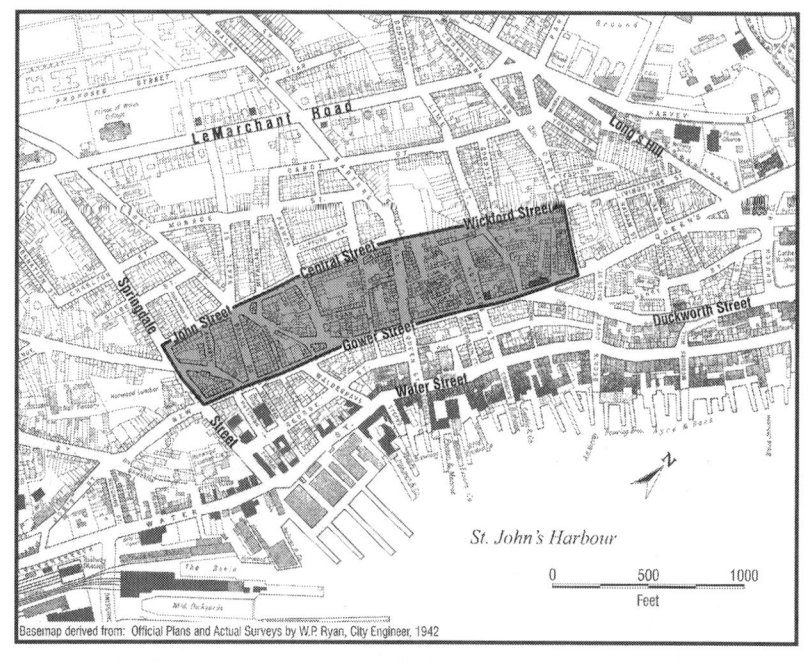

Figure 1.4. The "Inner City," 1942 (Charles Conway, based on Ryan 1942).

Only the experience of successive fires provided any encouragement for planning: the widening of a few specific streets to serve as fire breaks.

Sir Richard Bonnycastle, a career soldier serving in Newfoundland in 1842, commented: "Take St. John's altogether, with its 15,000 inhabitants, it has made great progress of late years; and every fire, although entailing much individual loss and suffering, has improved it" (Bonnycastle 1842, 234). Table 1.1 outlines the damage caused by major nineteenth-century fires in the city. Figure 1.5 illustrates their extent.

Table 1.1. Major Nineteenth-Century Conflagrations, St. John's.		
Date of Fire	Houses Destroyed	People Made Homeless
1816	120	1,000
1817	300	2,000
1819		1,000
1846	2,000	12,000
1892	Unknown, but "2/3 of the city"	11,000

The worst houses were located immediately north of New Gower Street between Carter's Hill and Springdale Street. They were concentrated on Codner's and Dammerill's Lanes, James, Notre Dame, and Simms Streets, the area now occupied by St. John's City Hall. A long-standing explanation attributed the presence of these dilapidated houses to jerry-building in the aftermath of the 1892 fire (Horwood 1997, 7). This is a misconception. Many of these houses predated even the 1846 fire — James Street was reported to be "thickly settled" in 1845 (JHA 1845, 52; *The Newfoundlander* 4 Jan. 1847). They weren't burned in 1846 because that fire destroyed only a few houses north of New Gower Street. Then the Great Fire of 1892 stayed east of Carter's Hill. Ironically, the very poor quality of housing in the area was because the area hadn't been burned, and the houses, now at least a half-century old, had never been properly maintained.

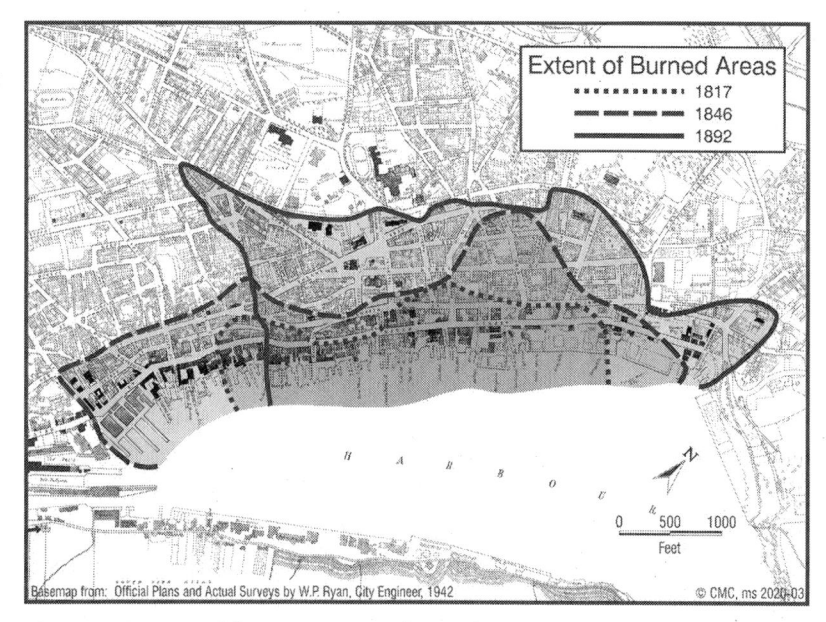

Figure 1.5. Map of the Great Fires of St. John's (Charles Conway).

There was very little straightening or realigning of streets in the windows of opportunity given by the nineteenth-century fires. Property owners were loath to give up land for street widening without meaningful financial compensation. However, they did acknowledge the danger of fire in another way. In the commercial area between Duckworth Street to the harbour, rebuilding after fires was required to be in brick or stone to protect the merchants' premises, the economic engine of the town (Legislation 1851, 1852). As the town grew, wooden houses and tenements were built by landlords on their estates farther away "in the western suburb," which developed beyond the end of Duckworth Street on New Gower Street and on the flank of Barter's Hill. These houses were not built to any particular plan. The 1846 Road Report entry for James Street noted "no regard being paid in laying down the sills of houses in this street, it is difficult to make satisfactory improvements on it, without having several steps descending to some houses and ascending to others" (JHA 1846, 228).

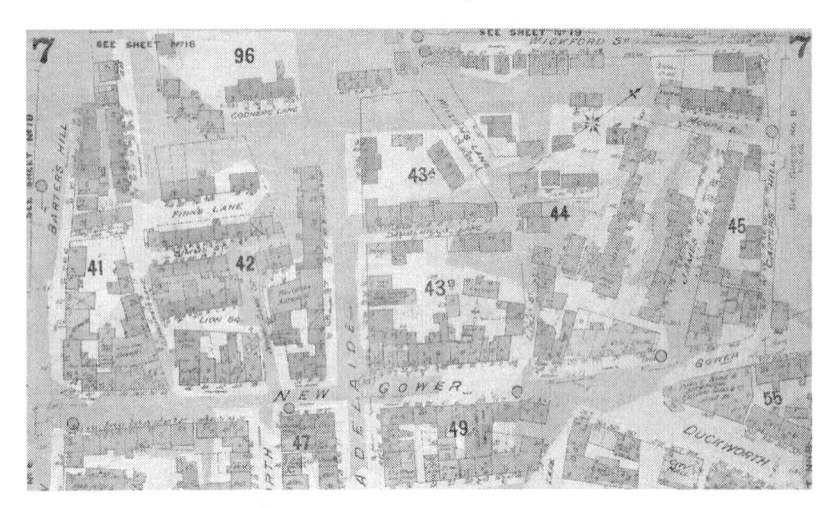

Figure 1.6. Lion Square and Dammerill's Lane (St. John's Insurance Plan, 1893).

Figure 1.7. Looking up Lime Street from New Gower Street, c. 1950 (CSJA 01-13-014).

Houses continued to accumulate on the flank of Barter's Hill for the next 40 years, and by 1888 the area had become a proper neighbourhood. There was both casual and wage employment, and shopping on Water Street had become unnecessary because a neighbourhood shopping area had developed on New

Gower Street: butchers, bakers, grocers, milliners and tailors, a notary public, a watchmaker, and liquor dealers. There were also churches and schools (Sharpe 1885). The houses were often crowded with large extended families and with lodgers. It was usual for children who were able to work to remain in the household well into marriageable age (Oliver 1983; Baker 1983b, 1984c).

Figure 1.8. Looking up Notre Dame Street from New Gower Street, early 1900s (CSJA 04-19-002).

Figure 1.9. Whiteway's Grocery Store, 71 Casey Street at the corner of John Street, 1910s (CSJA 01-11-023).

Who Owned the Houses? The Leasehold Property System

The United Kingdom had a long-standing tradition of investing one's wealth in property. A saying — "Safe as Houses" — referred to the growing need for workers' accommodation in the industrializing towns and cities and the presumed safety of real estate investments (Shaw 1934). Investment in the construction of dense rows of tenements for rent could see a good return. A significant proportion of the land in the UK, both urban and rural, was held by large estates, and "entailed," meaning that it could not be sold. But owners could sell the leases and extract ground rent from those who built on the land. Leasehold tenure was exported to Newfoundland and became significant in determining the type and quality of urban development. When the merchant landlords in St. John's leased their land for development they generally did so with the proviso that the lessee "erect

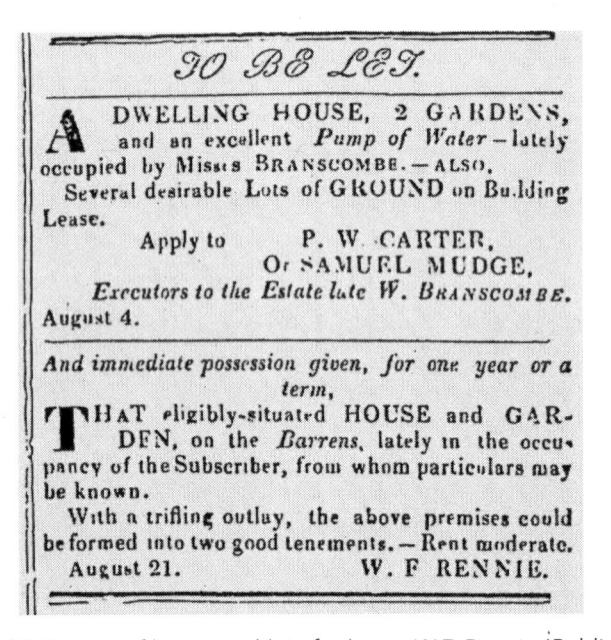

Figure 1.10. Notice of house and lots for lease, W.F. Rennie (*Public Ledger* 1 Sept. 1840, 2).

buildings compleat and in a Workmanlike manner . . . and maintain them" (Job 1818). The leaseholder, in turn, could rent the houses he had built to subtenants for his own rental income during the period of his lease. Some leases were for periods as short as 30 years, others for as long as 99 years. The interests of the landowner were secured by the fact that any buildings erected by the lessee reverted to the landlord at the end of the lease.

In 1903 only 38 per cent of the assessed properties in St. John's were freehold, most of them concentrated south of Water Street where merchants' premises predominated. Elsewhere in town leasehold was endemic (Rolfson 2003). Under this system, landlords could increase the value of the property for the benefit of their descendants by accumulating houses on it. The system worked well for the land-owning merchants. It also benefited the leaseholder by giving him security of tenure and protection against increases in rent during the term of the lease. It isn't hard to understand why landlords were happy to permit groups of closely packed dwellings on their land. To take one local example, the Stripling Estate included the entire east side of Cochrane Street and a considerable length of Gower Street. The rent roll from that estate in 1916 included 207 names (Squires, MUN Coll 250).

This medieval form of landownership was criticized because of an assumed relationship between leasehold land and poor-quality housing. Reformers argued that the quality of urban working-class housing could not be improved until the great entailed estates were broken up and the land tenure converted to freehold (Reeder 1961; Baumann 2000; Cox 2008; Dixon 2009; Home 2009). Critics implied that leasehold land was almost universal in the UK and almost absent in North America. This dichotomy is false, as is the assertion that leasehold tenure was responsible for dilapidated housing. Cannadine (1980) demonstrates that "slums" existed on both sides of the ocean and occurred on both leasehold and freehold land. It is now generally accepted that the continued existence of poor-quality housing and the great difficulties involved in trying to eradicate it are functions of poverty. But this was not understood in the nineteenth and early twentieth centuries, and the appalling, overcrowded conditions of the inner city of St. John's were commonly blamed on the "rapacious exactions of landlordism"

(*Newfoundlander* 25 Oct. 1855). The real estate markets of many major cities in the UK continue to be dominated by landed estates (Tichelar 2018), but the last vestiges of this system in St. John's disappeared in 1990 when leasehold tenure was finally abolished (Legislation 1990).

Figure 1.11. Duggan Street in the 1950s (CSJA 11-02-105).

Absentee Landlords

The leasehold tenure of so many properties in central St. John's was criticized not only because of the perceived intrinsic deficiencies of the system, but also because so much of it was held by absentee landlords (Baker 1986c). Considerable numbers of wealthy merchants with property in Newfoundland, not just in St. John's, had traditionally retired back to the United Kingdom to live off their Newfoundland rents (*DCB* MacBraire). Their affairs on this side of the Atlantic were left in the hands of agents, often lawyers. As long as the flow of rent continued, many landlords ignored what was happening to their properties in St. John's. Newfoundland-based revenue became integrated into the lives of the recipients in the UK. A Newfoundland plantation might be inherited, or used to provide a marriage portion, and could be bought and sold in Devon as well as in Newfoundland (Hardy 2021).

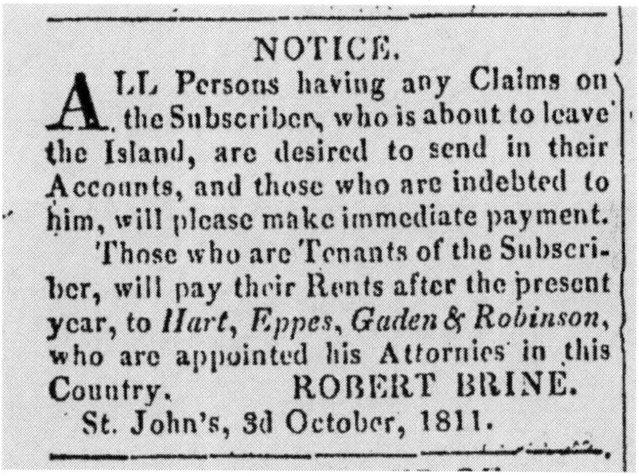

> **NOTICE.**
>
> ALL Persons having any Claims on the Subscriber, who is about to leave the Island, are desired to send in their Accounts, and those who are indebted to him, will please make immediate payment.
>
> Those who are Tenants of the Subscriber, will pay their Rents after the present year, to *Hart, Eppes, Gaden & Robinson*, who are appointed his Attornies in this Country. ROBERT BRINE.
>
> St. John's, 3d October, 1811.

Figure 1.12. A notice from Robert Brine regarding his return to Britain as an absentee landlord (*Royal Gazette and Newfoundland Advertiser* 24 Oct. 1811).

The fact that large portions of downtown St. John's were owned by absentee landlords need not have been a cause for concern, as long as the local agents discharged their duties responsibly. The problem was that, almost to a man, the absentee landlords doggedly opposed the imposition of any form of taxation and so contributed nothing to the Newfoundland government for the expenses of the colony. When the government instigated an inquiry into land tenure in 1882 it discovered that 41 locally owned estates on the south side of Water Street received annual rents totalling $40,390 while 34 absentee-owned estates in the same area yielded $65,610 (JHA 1882, 1883). The absentee landlords either ignored their legislated obligation to pay a variety of taxes and assessments or chose to ignore the government's repeated exhortations that they not pass these assessments on to their tenants who could not, or would not, pay them. In many cases no money was spent on repairs and maintenance, and as time passed many fell into disrepair. Many attempts were made to correct this problem, but they were always successfully resisted by the landlords until St. John's was granted the right to create a municipal government in 1888.

Figure 1.13. Duggan Street and Fergus Place, c. 1950 (CSJA 11-02-034).

Generations passed. Complications arose. Property owners died, and long-term leases of 30 or 40 years became lost in time, perhaps forgotten. In other cases, a multiplicity of heirs claimed a portion of the estate: "On the north side of St. John's harbour, Squarey's Plantation, long occupied by Brophy, was divided by inheritance into three to provide income for a gentleman and his wife in Ashburton, a surgeon in Bideford, and a druggist and his wife in Salisbury" (Hardy 2007). The estate of Nicholas Gill, who died intestate in 1855, was not settled until 1985 when 14 descendants claimed an interest (Newfoundland Law Reports 1985). The leasehold system was finally done away with by the provincial government in 1990, but not before it had caused generations of families to live in terrible conditions that the city was virtually powerless to improve (Legislation 1921, s. 94; Legislation 1990).

Public Health: A Desperate Situation

"Public health" is a nineteenth-century concept that developed in response to the growth of cities and the rise of industrialization in Europe and North America. The rapid movement of people into the cities put a strain on housing, water, and sewerage, all of which impacted the safety, cleanliness, and health of the population. Insanitary conditions and overcrowding became a breeding ground for infectious diseases. In the nineteenth century the Newfoundland government passed a number of Acts dealing with the general promotion of public health, for example: "The speedy abatement of Nuisances" (Legislation 1833); "To provide for the performance of Quarantine" (Legislation 1834a); ". . . respecting the Sanitary Improvement of the Town of St John's . . ." (Legislation 1879). Eventually, a Board of Health, district surgeons, and hospitals were put in place (*ENL* Health; *ENL* Hospitals; Baker 1983c).

In addition, the Legislative Assembly passed several Acts specifically designed to promote healthy conditions in St. John's. For example, burial grounds within the town were closed (Legislation 1849), butchering within the town was banned (Legislation 1860), and inspection of households' sanitary arrangements was decreed (Legislation 1879). There was inspection of food for sale — fruit, vegetables, bread, butter, and milk — "that it not be diseased or unsound" (Legislation 1880). And both the supply of adequate and pure water (Legislation 1859) and the construction of a sewer system (Legislation 1863) were legislated for St. John's.

Also important within the broad compass of public health was the long tradition of the government taking responsibility for the poor and indigent (Baker 1982d). This expressed a concern for those under extreme economic or social stress: lack of work, lack of shelter, lack of family support, lack of fitness. There was also provision for illegitimate children and deserted wives (Legislation 1834c, 1834d). The poor were classed as "casual," that is, those who were able-bodied and could be employed on casual work such as road-building, or "permanent," those who were disabled and unfit to work. A chronic problem, arising from the structure of employment and the seasonality of the fishery, was that "the Operative Population attempt to live for twelve months on the labour of three or four months" (JHA 1855, 259).

Water Sources, Sewer Systems, and Nuisance

The unhealthy environment of the town was clearly recognized in 1860 when the area from Carter's Hill to the Flower Hill firebreak was described as:

> An extensive collection of wooden houses closely huddled together, without either sewerage or a sufficient supply of water. . . . Almost entirely occupied with labourers, fishermen and mechanics, persons of limited means, who cannot possibly provide these indispensable requisites for themselves and whose families are exposed to the attacks of disease, owing to the filthy state of the narrow lanes by which these dwellings are separated from each other. (*Newfoundland Express* 5 Nov. 1860)

In 1859 the General Water Company was formed to bring water from George's Pond on Signal Hill to the town (Legislation 1859). The water was piped to the older, eastern section of the town; the rest of the town continued to depend on public wells. In the 1860s, with heroic effort, a tunnel was blasted and pipes were laid from the town to Windsor Lake to access an endless supply of pure water. In the western section of the town beyond Duckworth Street, on the flank of Barter's Hill, 17 fountains were provided for use by the poor (Penney 2010; Baker 1982c). Some of these fountains, commonly called "tanks," remained in service until the end of World War II.

Figure 1.14. Fetching water from the fountain (*Montreal Standard* 23 Nov. 1946).

"Nuisance" has been part of the Newfoundland vocabulary for a long time, referring to "all the Filth, Rubbish, and other offensive matter or things, which may have been deposited in any Street, . . . Lane, or Cove" (Legislation 1833; Story, Kirwin, and Widdowson 1990, 354). Some residents provided their own private sanitary arrangements. Others, the majority, deposited "nuisance" wherever convenient — a privy behind and near the house, under bushes, or into a brook. The many brooks running down the hill above the town and emptying into the harbour had been the first sewers in town. They were handy for depositing waste of any kind. In the early nineteenth century many of these brooks were diverted underground. Some were enlarged and lined with plank or, later, ceramic tile imported from the UK. It seems that the larger ones were used by the public for both drainage and sanitary purposes. "There is much filth &c. thrown on this street, which ought to be prevented. It is, perhaps, owing in a great measure to the want

Figure 1.15. Looking north on James Street to the back of 2-18 Moore Street, 1950s, showing a woman hanging laundry, a dog, a hydrant on the left beside power pole, a "tank" or water fountain to its right, and an open drain (CSJA 11-02-028).

of back yards to the houses on the North side [of Water Street]" (JHA 1841, 178). The many horses that pulled delivery carts throughout the town also contributed to the deposit of "nuisance" in the streets.

Meanwhile, across the Atlantic, the rapid pace of industrialization in the UK and the consequent burgeoning of urban population outstripped the provision of accommodation for the increasing numbers in wage employment at ever-larger work sites. Officials began to recognize the special needs of the changing urban spaces. This led to an urban reform movement that sought to provide local oversight for towns and cities. The UK Municipal Corporation Act of 1835 (5 & 6 Wm. IV c 76) allowed them to apply for incorporation in order to add a layer of government at the local level to deal with their specific needs. These municipal councils would oversee city growth and its ramifications: provision of water and sewer infrastructure, planning of streets, fire protection, and sufficient housing.

At the same time, Newfoundland Governor Sir John Harvey (1841–46) presented the House of Assembly with a list of suggested "improvements" for the town: a regular and abundant supply of pure water for the city — for shipping, and for fire protection; a "commodious road" to connect the east and west ends of the city; a surveyed map of the town; and even a town clock (JHA 1843, 66). Some of these suggestions were adopted. Gower Street was properly extended west beyond Duckworth to open the area of Barter's Hill for development. Surveyor William R. Noad produced an excellent map of St. John's (TRPAD MG 93), but municipal incorporation and sewerage infrastructure were not pursued at this time (*DCB* Harvey).

When Governor LeMarchant (1847–52) arrived in St. John's in the immediate aftermath of the 1846 fire, he was dismayed to find that the city had no system of drains or sewers specifically for sanitary purposes. All that existed was a privately built patchwork. Residents could and did throw their filth, garbage, and wastewater into drains that flowed down the hill to the harbour. But by mid-century the government began to discuss the institution of a proper system of daily scavenging to collect "night soil" set out on the street by individual households (JHA 1851b, 244–46). LeMarchant hoped to create a system that would give St. John's the same benefits already enjoyed by the citizens of the larger towns in England after passage of the UK 1848 Public Health Act (11 Victoria c 63), which empowered local boards to pave streets and install sewers where necessary. Unfortunately, the long-standing opposition to the imposition of any property assessment by landowners made it impossible to introduce similar reforms in St. John's (Baker 1983c, 28). LeMarchant observed that the strong prejudices against direct taxation were a principal reason the legislature was afraid to establish municipalities that could raise money through local assessments (*DCB* LeMarchant).

Cholera is a virulent bacterial infection of the gut, most commonly caused by the ingestion of fecal matter from an infected person by means of polluted water. It was one of the most feared afflictions of crowded eighteenth- and nineteenth-century cities. A combination of the paving of streets, the disposal of human waste by means of enclosed sewers, and the provision of potable water eventually brought it under control, although it has never been eliminated. In the summer of 1854, an outbreak of cholera ravaged the town and, according to Governor Keir Baillie Hamilton, left 500 people dead (*ENL* Health). An urgent report on the state of sewerage and drainage in the town put the problem squarely:

> The caution to avoid any scheme involving great expense has a paralysing influence when the total absence of any sanitary provisions is borne in mind — no drains — no pavements — ... no places for the deposit of filth and ordure excepting the surface of unpaved alleys, and a total want of privies; the absence of all these things renders a considerable outlay necessary, particularly when it is remembered that the whole area of the Town is in the same lamentable condition. (JHA 1854 vol. 2, 12–13)

By the 1870s sewerage had become an important element in the legislative conversation and some progress had been made in improving the state of public sanitation. A system of night carts was now in place to collect the household buckets and to transport them for dumping in the fields at the edge of town. For liquid waste — the household slops — gratings were put at the entrance to old drainage sewers so that the slops could be emptied into them. In Stephen Street (north of New Gower) "a grating ... at the entrance to this sewer ... is a receptacle for all the liquid nuisance that was heretofore thrown broadcast over the surface of a square of unoccupied ground ... so likely to breed epidemic amongst our inhabitants" (JHA 1875 vol. 1, 1007).

Public health reform, and the improvements in sanitation it would eventually bring about, was hampered in St. John's not only by the aversion to taxation but also by the absence of a municipal government. In 1879 a Joint Committee of the Legislative Council and House of Assembly was appointed "to take into consideration the sanitary condition of the town of St. John's." But no matter how obvious the need for a sewer system was and how many people decried the lack of one, its creation was a formidable task and expense. A Scottish firm was invited to come to St. John's in 1879 to propose a new sewerage scheme and submitted a detailed report. St. John's replied to them that there was "little probability of local contractors undertaking sewerage; large cost causing hesitancy of adoption" (JHA 1880; Baker 1982d, 68). The problem, as always, was the lack of revenue. Until 1888 St. John's, by far the largest town in the colony with a population of 30,000, was completely dependent on the colonial government for the provision of all municipal services except for water supply and fire protection (Baker 1986a, 21)

By the 1880s the deplorable state of public health could no longer be ignored. In 1886 the government engineer reported startling statistics about the ineffectiveness of the poorly designed sewerage infrastructure: "Several drains opened were found filled to the covers with solid material; others had been blocked for years. The house drains, however, continued to discharge even the contents of the water closets into the soil . . . the soil saturated with sewage" (JHA 1886a, 982). He noted that medical opinion considered consumption (tuberculosis) to be the most common disease in the town as a result, and that a new British survey had supported the argument that the incidence of consumption could be reduced by better control of sewage.

> Twenty-four towns, sewered by the modern system, were examined. It appeared that, while the general death rate had diminished, it was strikingly evident in the smaller number of deaths from consumption. The scientific world accepted the theory that the purifying of the atmosphere, and the drying of the soil, as an incidental effect of sewerage, had led to the diminution of that disease. (JHA 1886a, 985)

In his address to the Legislative Assembly that same year, Governor Carter observed that "The time appears to have arrived when municipal regulations should be established in the town of St. John's. The particular form which would best adapt such a measure to local circumstances invites your careful reflection" (JHA 1886b, 13).

Finally, on 9 May 1888, St. John's was incorporated as a town and given the authority to "carry into effect an improved system of Sewerage . . . and to make provision therefor; [and] . . . to make further provision for the improvement, repairs and maintenance of Streets, Sidewalks and Drains, for the lighting of the Town." The new municipal government was also given the power to raise revenue by charging assessments for water and sewer services, fire protection, and, ultimately, to impose taxes on property (Legislation 1888).

2

THE FLEDGLING MUNICIPAL COUNCIL FACES REALITY

> The importance attached to property by the ordinary man aroused violent opposition to any proposal which might permit taxation on real property and so led to a hostile public opinion against the creation of municipal government. (Crosbie 1956, 333)

The new Municipal Corporation of St. John's inherited all the problems that had plagued the Newfoundland government's oversight of St. John's for years: lack of water for domestic consumption and fire protection, inadequate sewerage, crowded and poor-quality housing, and the uncompromising attitude of the landlords, particularly absentee landlords, towards any form of property tax. The creation of the Municipal Council, armed with the power to levy taxes, was perceived by many as an act of betrayal.

The new Municipal Council experienced a difficult birth. It was the first municipal government in Newfoundland and would remain so until the incorporation of Windsor in 1938 (*ENL* Windsor). This was new administrative territory for both the government and the Council: the structure of the Council had to be decided and its responsibilities described. These discussions were often contentious. The Council was even suspended from 1898 to 1902 (Baker 1976, 1986a, 1984b). It was finally settled that St. John's Municipal Council would have a mayor and six councillors (Legislation 1902, s. 3). Fortunately, enough residents of the town had sufficient interest in this experiment in democracy to offer themselves for election. The members of the early councils were representative of commerce and industry in

St. John's and this set a pattern that would be typical for years to come. For example, the 1902 Council included a shipping agent, a brewer, the owner of a marble works, two building contractors, and two commission agents. And several members of this Council had political experience in the House of Assembly.

Launching the New Municipal Council: Straight into Debt

The newly created Council needed funds. The 1888 Act set out a budget, and much of this remained unchanged for years. The government gave the Council a 50-year "start-up" loan of $607,000 (Legislation 1888, s. 50). This was quickly spent on assets that now came under municipal jurisdiction: the purchase of the private General Water Company, which serviced the town; the payment of debts owing on the town's infrastructure of streets and sewers; and expenditure on the development of Bannerman and Victoria Parks and $100,000 dedicated to "the carrying out of an improved and effective system of Sewerage and the cleaning of the town" (Legislation 1888, s. 50). To put it plainly, the new Council began office with a debt of $607,000. It haunted the city's fiscal landscape for years.

Sufficient money had to be set aside to run the Council's affairs until revenues accrued from assessments on water and sewer service and fire protection. The government promised other revenues, including the duties collected on all coal imports to St. John's, the water rates on shipping that passed through the Customs Office, and all the rents from Crown property within the town limits. In addition, the government promised several annual stipends to help pay for lighting and sanitary arrangements, streets, and bridges (Legislation 1888, s. 52). In future years, the withdrawal of some of these stipends in times of economic stress would become a bone of contention between the town and the government. The Council was required to submit to the legislature an annual balanced statement of revenues and expenditures and to seek the government's approval for any proposed tax increase or loan.

With reference to assessment due on property, a recent Act had made it clear that landlords were expected to pay the assessments on their properties and not to pass that responsibility onto their tenants: "taxes or assessments shall be declared to be landlord's taxes, shall be payable by the Landlord, and in no case shall the Tenant be liable therefore" (Legislation 1887, s. 1).

The Council's debt soon grew to $1 million, in part because of the expense of rebuilding infrastructure after the 1892 fire, and, more ominously, because of the reluctance of residents and landlords to pay their assessments and taxes. Worrying, too, was the attitude of Council, although it expressed an element of compassion. When the Attorney General urged the Council "to take any steps necessary" to recover arrears from Crown rents, the councillors decided that no orders to that effect would be issued "as many people were doing their best to pay" (SJCM 1 Apr. 1898, 397).

Improving the Water Supply: "Waste Water" and Fire Protection

The Council quickly turned its attention to the state of the town's water supply. The Windsor Lake system was now 40 years old, and since its inception the population of St. John's and the number of industrial establishments had grown considerably. There was no longer sufficient pressure at the higher levels, north of LeMarchant Road, to provide for simultaneous domestic and emergency use. This situation was exacerbated in cold weather by the amount of "waste water" generated by householders in uninsulated houses who left their taps running to prevent their pipes from freezing. As a stopgap measure, a 2,800-gallon reservoir was built on the hill above the town and 18 additional hydrants were ordered (SJCM 11 June 1901, 263).

The government rebuffed the city's request for a loan to finance a more permanent solution. But when the merchants were threatened with a 20 per cent increase in their fire insurance premiums and spoke to the government about it, the government changed its mind and promised to issue a loan of $100,000 (SJCM 20 Dec. 1903, 98; 28 Dec. 1903, 101). The

Figure 2.1. Fire hydrant on Stephen Street, 1952 (CSJA 01-46-012).

Council then called in John Galt, an engineering expert from Toronto, to design substantial improvements to the Windsor Lake system. The resulting project was completed in 1906 at a cost of $200,000, improving the city's water supply but adding to its debt (Foran 1937, 18; Baker 1984c; SJCM 28 Dec. 1903, 101).

Expanding the Sewer Network: Not an Easy Task

Another important mandate of the newly incorporated municipality was to upgrade and expand the sewerage system. The 1902 Municipal Act (s. 81) required that new buildings must be erected with a sewer connection and imposed a financial penalty for failure to comply. This was the ideal, but achieving it would be a herculean task.

A year after the city was incorporated in 1888, a collector sewer more than two kilometres long was constructed beneath Water Street. It flowed east from Queen Street to a small cove below the Battery, and received sewage from the numerous smaller mains throughout the downtown area.

Made of more than 830,000 bricks, it measured about 0.87 metres across at the top and 0.57 metres at the bottom. The ovoid structure was wider at the top to provide extra capacity to handle excess flow during heavy rain and narrow at the bottom to constrict and therefore speed up the flow, to help prevent blockages. Junction boxes, made by Daulton and Co. in Lambeth on the south bank of the Thames in London, were built into the side of the sewer to permit the connection of clay pipes from smaller sewer lines along the street. Most of those that have been excavated are still sealed, indicating they were never used.

Figure 2.2. Archaeological exposure of the cross-section of the Water Street interceptor sewer and a sealed junction box (Blair Temple Associates Ltd.).

Many of the old, smaller sewer pipes in the eastern part of town were burned, smashed, and buried by the 1892 fire. Some were repaired but apparently never connected to the new collector sewer (Penney 2010). But these piecemeal repairs did not solve the serious problems with the water supply system. In the burned district most of the water pipes in Water Street were corroded and the hydrants were deemed "quite useless" (SJCM 4 Aug. 1892, 18; 23 Sept. 1892, 29). And the western part of the town, especially in the vicinity of Barter's Hill, where sanitary sewers were planned for the first time, was an engineer's nightmare. The flimsy wooden tenements, untouched by the 1892 fire, were now the oldest houses in town. They were scattered, built in blocks, unevenly spaced, sited on narrow lanes and cul de sacs, underlain by bedrock, and frequently flooded by water draining down the steep slope from the higher levels. Progress on the construction of sewers west of Carter's Hill was slow and piecemeal because of the irregular street pattern. Each landlord had planned within his own estate, placing his blocks of tenements where he chose, coping with obstacles like steep slopes and rocky outcrops on an ad hoc basis. It was expensive to build sewers across empty patches of ground to serve only a few buildings in a block some distance away (SJCM 9 Nov. 1933, 410). Construction of an integrated sewer system to serve the huddles of houses on Stephen, Sebastian, and Cuddihey Streets, Notre Dame, Dammerill's Lane, and Lion's Square seemed impossible (CSJA Map H080, 1900, Map H132, 1918; SJCM 9 Nov. 1933, 410).

Figure 2.3. Cuddihey Street, 1950s (CSJA 11-02-176).

Figure 2.4. Stephen Street, Sebastian Street, and Burke's Square, 1950s (CSJA 11-01-219).

Nonetheless, it was a task that had to be undertaken. The city engineer, who was concerned with the "unparalleled uncleanliness" of the city, reported that "the stench is almost unbearable and if it were not for the constant use of disinfectants [by the city staff] and the strongest winds which prevail, an outbreak of sickness would be sure to take place." He enumerated three causes of the difficulty of the situation:

> 1. The erection of houses by persons of small means instead of them being erected by the owner of the land;
> 2. The insufficient power given to the council to govern the erection of such buildings and the means of drainage of the same; and
> 3. The still lingering prejudice against the putting-in of water closets. (SJCM 2 Jan. 1894, 184)

Every night the "sanitary men" visited 109 streets in the town and emptied 2,910 night soil buckets (SJCM 2 Jan. 1894, 183).

Building the sewer lines was going to be a difficult task in and of itself. Persuading people to connect to them from their houses posed a different, and unexpected, problem "of pressing necessity and importance." Sir Edward Morris touched on it:

> Until we do away with our present night-service [sanitary carts] or largely reduce it, we can never hope to have a healthy city. It is, in my opinion, a most serious state of affairs. We have laid down a most expensive and splendid sewerage service [in some parts of town], and yet we keep alive in many streets the night-service *because certain people will not connect*.... It is quite true that many of the poorer people in small and cheap houses will not for some time be able to connect with the service, but there are hundreds of well-to-do people in the city, and on streets where the property is valuable by reason of city improvements, who can and ought to connect immediately with the main sewers. (Morris 1907, 7; emphasis added)

The city engineer reported to Council that only 16 of the 49 houses on Cabot Street wanted water services. On Munroe Street, only 8 of 22 houses wanted it. And of 22 houses on lower Barter's Hill, no one wanted the service (SJCM 8 Mar. 1906, 303). The installation of a sanitary facility — toilet and basin — and its connection to a public sewer line was a significant expense for a householder. According to the prices listed in the Minutes of the Municipal Council, a plumber would charge as much as $80 to install sanitary facilities in a house, an unaffordable amount if your income was only $300 a year, the contemporary wage of the men working on the waterfront (Calahan 1914; McGrath 1914).

At the same time as Sir Edward was expressing his concerns, the new mayor of St. John's, lawyer Michael Gibbs (1906–10), was looking for solutions

(Baker 1986b; *ENL* Gibbs). He tackled the public non-compliance to hook up to the sewer mains by realizing that at least part of the problem must be the expense. He devised the Small Homes Sewerage System by which householders could pay for the installation of sanitary facilities over time, on an instalment plan for a period of years (Legislation 1910). The government helped to fund this scheme with a sinking fund to the value of $30,000 repayable in 50 years (Baker 1984c). Applicants were vetted as to income and whether there was room in their house to install the sanitary facilities. The scheme was in use until the 1940s (the names of applicants were recorded in the Council Minutes).

Figure 2.5. Mayor Michael P. Gibbs (1906–10) (CSJA 06-01-012).

But Mayor Gibbs's plan did nothing to help the tenant whose landlord refused to pay for a sewer connection and the installation of sanitary facilities. The Barter's Hill area had hundreds of tenements belonging to many different landlords. Some of the tenements were so dilapidated as to be classed as "unfit for human habitation" by the city engineer and the health officer (SJCM 1911, 335). The Council tried to get both local and absentee landlords to upgrade their tenements or remove their dilapidated ones (SJCM 9 Mar.1907, 201; 11 Mar. 1907, 203). There was little response from the landlords other than to plead that if they removed one or two houses in a range, the others might fall down (SJCM 26 Jan. 1907, 172).

The Council met with K.R. Prowse, agent of the Hutchings Estate, located west of Springdale Street, on the south side of New Gower Street, to discuss the Small Homes Sewerage program. Prowse said that he had met with the owners of the Estate, who decided they could not install sanitary appliances in their properties because that would cost more than the value of the rental income. The Estate simply didn't generate enough money to do the required work (SJCM 27 June 1912, 338) and rents could not be raised until the end of the leasehold period, which could be years ahead. Consequently, many of the old tenements began to fall behind the rest of the city, which gradually modernized.

Some of the tenements in the inner city, which were condemned as unfit for human habitation, lingered on and were occupied to the 1950s. While many of these houses were occupied by the very poor, others, according to the self-identification of occupational skills as listed in St. John's street directories, were occupied by tradespeople. Duggan Street, for example, in 1904 listed 14 occupants as labourers and 14 others with trade skills, particularly carpentry (McAlpine 1904).

Figure 2.6. Notre Dame Street, c. 1950 (CSJA 11-02-107).

At the same time as some people in town were declining the opportunity to install water and sewer services, a group of 46 others petitioned to have it:

> Petition from the householders and residents of the district of Flower Hill and Munroe Street asking that a public tank [fountain] and a lamp be placed as near as possible to the intersection of the above named streets as great inconvenience is caused in having to carry water up Flower Hill at night owing to the darkness. The Petitioners also called attention to the fact that they were without Sewerage Conveniences and state that the state of things is extremely dangerous to the health of the residents. (SJCM 12 Aug. 1904, 284)

But the Council, strapped by lack of funds, was unable to respond to such requests.

Various officials — city engineer, the councillors, the MHAs, the health officer, and even the police constables — brought to City Hall lists of dilapidated houses, houses that lacked water and sewer, and observations of incidence of nuisance — the latter often on vacant ground or even in the public places. City inspectors responded to these complaints as well as to flooded drains, dirty stables, broken railings on the many steps in town, and spills from the night carts, which created cesspools. Even paper was a nuisance and shopkeepers in particular were warned against letting it blow in the wind, with a penalty not exceeding $25 and imprisonment for 30 days (SJCM 26 Oct. 1906, 111). However, the general citizenry seemed not uncomfortable with the high incidence of nuisances.

Public Health Becomes a Priority

Sir William MacGregor, governor of Newfoundland (1904–09), had trained as a medical doctor (*ENL* MacGregor). By foresight, or by happenstance, he was the right appointment at the right time for the colony. The health of the population of St. John's had become a major concern.

In 1890 the Newfoundland government established the position of medical officer of health for the colony. In 1905 the government, worried about the crowded living conditions in St. John's and fearful of epidemics, supported the town's hiring of its own medical officer (Baker 1984a). This addition to the city staff brought the lack of public services and the careless sanitary habits in St. John's into startling focus.

Dr. Robert Brehm's initiation (*ENL* Brehm) to the standard of public health in St. John's was a visit to Wills Range off Pleasant Street, where "The privies there drain into the wells which supply the water for drinking purposes" (SJCM 26 May 1906, 350). He quickly summed up the situation in town: that out of 624 deaths in the town for the year ending 30 September 1905, 208 of them had occurred among children under one year of age (Baker 1982a, 31). He opined that the problem lay not only in the ignorant and careless methods of feeding among the poor, and their lack of a milk supply, but also in crowded living conditions and their lack of sanitation and decent shelter (JHA 1917, 523).

These alarming findings were not unique to St. John's. Dr. Charles Hastings, Toronto's new medical officer of health, released his scathing report of The Ward, a crowded immigrant section of Toronto, in 1911: "The people of Toronto . . . thought they were free from the slum problem, which besets many American cities. The facts . . . prove that Toronto is not a whit better than other cities of the same class." The report argued that the proliferation of overflowing outdoor "privies" and filthy, unventilated apartments could be

Figure 2.7. Dr. Robert Brehm, medical officer of health for St. John's, 1906–36 (*Newfoundland Quarterly* 4 [1917], 9).

implicated in high levels of infectious diseases, including typhoid, cholera, and tuberculosis (Lorinc 2015, 91). In many Canadian cities it was assumed that the insalubrious housing and sanitation conditions in the inner city were the result of a concentration of recent immigrants there, in the only housing they could afford. This was not the case in St. John's. The contemporary condition in the central area of town was an expression of endemic poverty, caused in part by access to only casual employment opportunities, which provided only intermittent income. Poverty, poor-quality and often subdivided houses, and lower rents than those prevailing elsewhere in the city, although by no means necessarily "low," were the joint causes of the deprivation and misery that characterized the area (Mannion 1986; Matthews 1988).

Public Health: The Public Becomes Engaged

Dr. Brehm's observations brought the unsanitary conditions of the city into the realm of morality because it was evident that so many needless deaths could be prevented by public education. In 1908 Governor MacGregor chaired a public meeting in St. John's to discuss how the public might be encouraged to campaign against the dread disease, tuberculosis. The outcome was the creation of the Newfoundland Association for the Prevention of Consumption, of which the president was the Hon. John Harvey and the vice-presidents William Gosling and Dr. Herbert Rendell. This initiative met with marked success and within months the association had more than 1,000 members with branches across the island, all of them engaged in educational programming (*ENL* Health; *ENL* Tuberculosis; Nolan 2004, 105).

That same year the registrar-general issued a report comparing the death rates in the various districts across the island between 1902 and 1908 with those of St. John's and its suburban areas. In every year, the suburbs had the lowest death rate, the districts the next highest, and St. John's the highest of all. In 1908, for example, the rate in the suburbs was 11.26 deaths per 1,000; in the districts, 22.95 per 1,000; and in St. John's, 27.06 per 1,000. More shocking than the numbers were the underlying

Figure 2.8. Hon. John Harvey, president of the Newfoundland Association for the Prevention of Consumption, 1901 (TR-PAD 01-56-003).

factors. The leading cause of death among adults was consumption (tuberculosis) and the largest single cause of death for the whole population was infant mortality. In large measure, both were the inevitable result of poor levels of public health (JHA 1909, 454–55).

The dreadful statistics revealed by the registrar-general, together with the governor's personal interest in tuberculosis, stirred the Newfoundland government into action. In 1910 it commissioned a *Report on Public Health in the Colony*. The Hon. John Harvey chaired the Commission. Harvey's Commission confirmed the registrar-general's findings and he used them to urge the Council to make use of its power to inspect domestic premises "in certain parts of town" as fumigation was required if there was incidence of tuberculosis (JHA 1912, Appendix: 594–604). Among the recommendations suggested by health-care workers to combat tuberculosis was the call for an anti-spitting law. In the meantime, DON'T SPIT cards were widely distributed (JHA 1912, 589, 626–27).

When these statistics became public knowledge, the volunteer community was galvanized into action. A delegation from the Imperial Order of the Daughters of the Empire called on the Council in 1910 to urge the Council to stop the clandestine disposal of night soil in public spaces and to improve the system of routine collection of night soil by the city's horse and cart sanitary system (SJCM 1 Nov. 1910, 225). The I.O.D.E. extended their concern for the health of the town by opening a camp for consumptive women near Mundy's Pond on the outskirts of the city that same year. This led to such an improvement in the health of the patients that the Jensen fresh air camp was opened on the west side of the city and in 1917 the government opened a hospital for tuberculosis patients (SJCM 1 Nov. 1910, 225; *ENL* IODE; *ENL* Tuberculosis).

Figure 2.9. Mayor William J. Ellis (1910–14) (*Newfoundland Quarterly* 10, no. 1 (1910), 10.

Typhus is a bacterial disease commonly found in areas characterized by poor sanitation and overcrowding. In early 1911 typhus struck on Pope Street in the heart of the inner city. The outbreak caused agitated discussion in the press. Dr. Brehm wanted the affected tenements destroyed. St. John's third mayor, William Ellis, a stonemason whose construction business rebuilt several of the major buildings destroyed in the 1892 fire, objected because, he argued, there was nowhere else for the tenants to live. The moral dilemma posed by this familiar problem was to haunt the Council for the next 40 years. The Pope Street houses were fumigated and cleansed but the residents remained there, with the underlying causes of poor health unresolved (SJCM 18 Sept. 1911, 67; 5 Jan. 1911, 260; 11 Jan. 1911, 264; 13 Jan. 1911, 266; *Evening Telegram* 1911a to 1911h).

The Harvey *Report on Public Health* showed that although there had been a gratifying decline in deaths due to consumption, St. John's continued to have the highest rate of infant mortality in the colony: "The Commission again emphasize: *the need of grappling with the housing problem, and they submit that the rebuilding of the poorer part of St. John's is urgently called for*" (JHA 1912, 589; emphasis added). It was estimated that 4,500 to 5,000 residents were living crowded in 900 to 1,000 tenements (Baker 1982b, 31). Clearly, there was pressure on the City Council to take some action in the face of these appalling statistics. But what could they do? And how could they pay for it?

The outbreak on Pope Street moved Hon. John Harvey to address the Council with a speech that was reprinted in the local press (*Evening Telegram* 1911a). He commented that the rate of tuberculosis had declined by one-quarter during the period 1906–09 for the colony as a whole but had remained stationary in St. John's; that the death rate for the colony as a whole was 15/1,000 living and for St. John's it was 22/1,000. He identified housing as a big part of the health problem and opined that the condition of housing was getting worse. He illustrated this with a map showing that 90 per cent of the incidence of consumption was located in an area west of Long's Hill, where the worst houses were located.

Harvey recommended that the Council act on the provisions of the 1910 Municipal Act, which provided for legal inspections of houses: "The Council shall have the power to direct the Municipal Supervisor or any other official or person on behalf of the Council to enter into and inspect every part of any house or building used as a dwelling for the purpose of ascertaining its condition as regards fitness for habitation" (Legislation 1910, s. 12). He also expressed his support for the anti-spitting bylaw, remarking that the expectoration on the sidewalks was picked up by women's skirts and carried into the houses.

Harvey expressed his concern about poor housing with a new suggestion, that a Building Society might construct a few modest houses to explore the economic feasibility of housing people in need. There were already several examples of industrial employers who had built houses for their workers: the Colonial Cordage Company in St. John's near Mundy Pond, the Iron Ore Company on Bell Island, and the Anglo Newfoundland Development Company at Grand Falls. Could other employers be encouraged to do the same? Harvey and the Council resolved that industrial concerns should be encouraged to build houses for the workingmen. This was wishful thinking. They discussed their resolution with the prime minister but had no success (SJCM 18 Sept. 1911, 67). There was no profit to be made from such provision of housing. If the mayor and Council had hoped the great men of industry would put aside their entrepreneurial habits for the sake of the workingman, they were disappointed. We can find no record of any such houses having been built.

The Council was having difficulty meeting the expectations of the Municipal Act. By 1915 the municipal arrears had grown to $98,000 in a budget with estimated revenues of $237,567.72 and expected expenditures of $234,875.00 (SJCM 5 Feb. 1915, 291–96). A significant element in this situation was the continued refusal of landlords to pay rates and taxes. The problem was exacerbated by the number of others who could not afford to pay. Did the government show an interest in these municipal problems? The legislature, traditionally, was dominated by merchants whose business affairs did not, in general, include concern for the plight of the Municipal Council other than being assured that there was sufficient water for fire protection.

The reality was that whole sections of the Municipal Act were a mockery. For example, the requirement for a person to include functional sanitary facilities when building a house within the city limits made no sense when the city could not provide water and sewer lines to the site for lack of funds. In practice, instead of refusing a building permit, the Council, sympathetic to the housing shortage in town, allowed a person to build his house on the promise that if and when water and sewer pipes were extended to his street, he would connect. This led to houses being built on new, privately established streets in unsurveyed, unserviced fields that often had only one entry to the street: Franklyn, Gear, and Beaumont, north of LeMarchant Road; McKay and Warberry west of Sudbury Street; Summer and Rankin off Merrymeeting Road. Something else was happening, too. People were building on unserviced lots at the edge of town — Mundy Pond, the Battery,

Signal Hill, Blackhead Road — beyond the reach of the Municipal Act, thereby escaping from assessments and taxes.

Clearly, there was a disconnection between the Municipal Act and the reality the councillors faced on a daily basis. The initiative to review this situation came not from the Council or from the government but from the president of the Board of Trade, William Gilbert Gosling.

3

THE MUNICIPAL COUNCIL SEEKS "A CURE FOR HOUSING ILLS"

> The common people are in the great majority, and their proper accommodation is the greatest problem. (*Canadian Municipal Journal*, quoted in Van Nus 1975, 175)

William Gosling was born in Bermuda. He came to St. John's in 1881 to work with Harvey and Company and eventually became a director in the firm. Harvey's was a long-established company that traded salt fish to the West Indies. However, in Gosling's time, it modernized its activities to include manufacturing, trade in a range of natural resources, and the adoption of new technologies (*ENL* Harvey Group of Companies). Gosling, too, seemed to be a man interested in new and better ways of doing things, a thinking man. Widely read, he researched and published several books, one on Labrador (1910) and one on Sir Humphrey Gilbert (1911) (*ENL* Gosling; A.N. Gosling 1935).

As Gosling's business travels took him to England, the Continent, and the United States, he was able to visit some of the great and lesser cities of the time — St. Louis, Chicago, Des Moines, New York, London, Paris. This experience served to further his interest in how cities functioned. In her memoir of his life, Gosling's wife noted that "for years he had been making a study of city requirements and of the various methods of civic governments . . . because the subject fascinated him" (A.N. Gosling 1935, 64). He was intrigued by the new urban reform movement that promoted town planning and "best practices" in civic administration.

Figure 3.1. Mayor William Gilbert Gosling (1916–20) (*ENL* 2, 571).

Gosling lived at a time when their rapid growth had led to the study of cities: the concept of urban reform was born and professional urban planners emerged to undertake that reform. St. John's may have been a small town in an impoverished country but it faced the same problems, although perhaps on a different scale, as the large mainland cities: the security of revenue and concern for proper planning to provide a healthy town and adequate shelter. Gosling applied his knowledge of urban reform to the city of St. John's. He led an inquiry into the city's civic administration.

What Was the Urban Reform Movement?

In Canada, between 1880 and 1920, the urban population increased from 25 per cent of the total population to 50 per cent. St. John's, too, had experienced industrialization during this time and had grown to be the largest centre of both population and economic activity in Newfoundland.

The urban reform movement of the nineteenth century was born of the urgent need to improve sanitation and public health in order to mitigate the terrible effects of infectious diseases like cholera and typhus that thrived in the noisome, crowded living conditions of the industrial cities (Johnson 2006). The approach to viewing these problems had turned from horror and dismay to positive action. The emerging profession of town planning offered hope "as a cure for housing ills" (Bacher 1993, 52). Thoughtful planning could create urban plans that could increase housing stock and regulate greater access to space, light, and air. Gosling brought an awareness of these discussions to St. John's.

There were two different approaches to the art of urban reform: the American "City Beautiful" movement extolled at the Chicago Exposition

Figure 3.2. James Street in the 1950s, looking north to Moore Street (CSJA 11-02-043).

of 1893, and the British "Garden Cities" movement exemplified by the creation of Letchworth Garden City in 1903.

The American City Beautiful movement fostered the belief that civic harmony would be best promoted in a city characterized by monumental architecture and formal landscape design. Frederic Law Olmstead and Calvert Vaux were two of the best-known practitioners of this vision, and Central Park in New York City (1858) was their most important joint project. They believed in the big city. They took for granted its continued existence, and they were inspired by the need to improve its total visual environment (Simpson 1985, 73–74).

The British Garden City movement, on the other hand, was fundamentally anti-urban. The idea behind it was outlined in *Tomorrow: A Peaceful Path to Real Reform*, published in 1898 by Ebenezer Howard (Howard 1898). This slim volume is the only thing Howard ever published, but is still celebrated as "the most important planning response to the Victorian city" (Hall 2014, 7). It had an impact far more profound than Howard could ever have imagined. He believed that the major problem facing industrial cities was the inexorable deterioration of living conditions for the working class (Hodge 1991, 49). As an alternative he proposed the creation of community-controlled, decentralized, self-contained towns circling major industrial centres but separated from them by a green belt. He didn't attempt to prescribe the details of their internal structure, saying only that they should combine the best attributes of town and country in order to promote healthy living based on a spirit of communal co-operation (Osborne 1946; Birchall 1995; Bowie 2017). The most prominent planner of the early twentieth century described Howard's idea as "the keynote of the revival of English town planning that has taken place in the past 20 years ... [involving] nothing less than an attempt to alter the method of growth of large towns by splitting off portions of them and forming new nuclei in the country, with limited possibilities of growth, at the same time securing full municipal ownership of land" (Abercrombie 1909, 88).

In the first half of the twentieth century, urban planning in Britain, the United States, and Canada developed as a "scientific discipline" practised by professionals who were principally devoted to improving the living conditions of the urban poor, most of whom lived in congested inner cities (Simpson 1985, 74). The creation of the federal/provincial Canadian Commission of Conservation in 1909 provided an important opportunity for Canadian urban reform pioneers and municipal leaders (Stein 1944b). The Commission's mandate was to "investigate, enquire, advise and inform the nation" on how best to use science to develop its natural resources, including human resources (Girard 1991, 27). The Commission's chairman was Clifford Sifton, whose career as federal Minister of Immigration had included the settlement of the prairies. This experience gave him an intimate knowledge of natural resources and their relation to human settlement, especially the importance of clean water and improved sewerage technology (*DCB* Sifton). The Commission asked for laws to enforce all municipalities and industries to clean up their fouled water and effluents. It distributed information on existing sewage treatment facilities to Canadian municipalities, promoted the use of water meters, and hoped to establish national standards for water and air quality.

The influence of the early practitioners was profound. Henry Vivian was a leading light of the urban reform and town planning movement in early twentieth-century Britain. A carpenter by trade, a trade unionist and Member of Parliament by avocation, his involvement in several co-housing projects in England led to an invitation from Canada's Governor General Earl Grey (1904–11) to undertake a Canadian lecture tour in 1910. Vivian argued that nothing affects the life of people more than their housing, by which he meant "not merely the . . . house . . . but its setting and the whole atmosphere in which people live." His principal message was that town planning and housing reform were not just a passing fancy or the "mere opinions of a few cranks" but a real national movement that deserved universal support (Vivian 1910, 401).

Figure 3.3. Joy Place with fire hydrant (left) and water fountain or "tank" in foreground, 1930s (CSJA 11-01-102).

Thomas Adams: An Influential Town Planner

One of the most prominent early urban planners was Thomas Adams, who was appointed the first full-time secretary of the Garden City Association in 1901 and then became the principal administrator of Letchworth Garden

City between 1903 and 1905 (Simpson 1985, 68–69). When he attended the Canadian Commission of Conservation's national conference in 1911 he made such an impression on those present — the Canadian Manufacturers' Association, National Council of Women, I.O.D.E., and Canadian Public Health Association — that he was pressed to join the Commission so he could provide advice on how to plan proper suburbs for workingmen. In 1914 he accepted the position of town planning advisor to the Commission. His important years in Canada were contemporary with Gosling's own studies of urban reform (Simpson 1982; Stein 1944a).

Contemporary town planners generally subscribed to the view that planned workers' suburbs should solve the housing problems of the inner cities. However, in his opening address to the Conference, the Commission chairman, Clifford Sifton, made a prescient remark: "the people who are moving to the suburbs are not those from the congested districts, but from the well-to-do districts, from districts where the people, before they moved, had no particular fault to find with their circumstances" (Sifton 1914; Rutherford 1974, 216). This remark would become a cautionary tale for future planners, including those who promoted planning initiatives in St. John's.

Adams eschewed the City Beautiful fixation with its aesthetic effects, and instead advocated practical statutory planning, which he said would stimulate the building industry, create new jobs, and facilitate the elimination of slums. He advocated owner-occupancy. In his view, slumlords should be required to maintain and repair their properties, and if they did not the municipality should demolish them without compensation. He particularly railed against those landlords

Figure 3.4. Thomas Adams, c. 1921 (Simpson 1985).

and landowners who had a stranglehold on land, arguing that it was a "menace to the health, morality and well-being of the race." He attributed the Canadian housing crisis to the tendency of Canadian cities to regulate urban development primarily to ensure maximum return to land speculators. Critical of this, Adams asked: "Is it not time to pay more regard to human life and less to the sanctity of that kind of property that injures it?" (Simpson 1985, 78). He believed that through careful design and control of land speculation, suburban house prices would decline and that would give competition to slum owners, forcing them to lower their rents and improve their properties (Bacher 1993, 53). We will hear an echo of this argument in planning discussions in St. John's.

By the time Adams left the Conservation Commission in 1923 he had made an indelible impression on the fledgling planning profession in Canada. He left behind a collection of published articles on Canadian housing and planning (Adams 1916, 1917, 1918a, 1918b). He also left a small legacy of completed projects that includes the garden suburb of Lindenlea in Ottawa (1918), the rebuilt Richmond District in Halifax with its Hydrostone houses (1918), and the Townsite in Corner Brook, designed in 1923 for the Newfoundland Power and Paper Company (L. White, 2007a; Symonds 2001; Mellin 2011). But his most important legacy was the impact he had on fostering the planning profession in Canada and popularizing the idea of town planning among the business and political leaders of the country. He left behind a cadre of dedicated professional planners, some of whom he had trained personally, some who were inspired by his work and publications, and others who found employment in the profession that he had almost single-handedly created, nurtured, and made an unquestioned sector of the Canadian establishment. Two of his protégés were Horace Seymour and Arthur Dalzell, who formed a Toronto-based partnership and became prominent members of the small cohort of Canadians devoting themselves full-time to city planning. Dalzell was to make an important contribution to the debate about planning and slum clearance in St. John's.

Land Speculation: An Obstacle to Planning

Land speculation was one of the many concerns of urban reform, and was an important topic of discussion on both sides of the Atlantic. In the late nineteenth century the American reformer Henry George argued that the economic value derived from land, including natural resources, should belong equally to all members of society (Tideman 2004). The "People's Budget," drafted by UK Prime Minister David Lloyd George in April 1909, proposed a taxation on land, in a nation of historically embedded large landowners. It was described as "a war budget ... for raising money to wage implacable warfare against poverty and squalidness" (Lloyd George 1909).

This discussion resonated in St. John's, where a small number of landlords owned the land on which were housed a great number of tenants. John Slattery, secretary to St. John's Municipal Council, mused upon the People's Budget:

> Here in St. John's in a smaller way but with the same effect or results, the unearned increment is a proper subject for public consideration. The landlord — absentee or otherwise — the former particularly, has not or is not doing anything towards forwarding the city or paying a fair contribution towards the Municipality which gives protection to his land and by the expenditures for sewerage, streets, drains and other public improvements, gives the land a value it otherwise would not have. The landlord has simply to make out a lease as he has done, draw the rental, make a covenant in the lease for "the tenant to pay all present and future taxes", sit idly by and watch the land grow in value and at the end of the lease all the buildings and improvements fall to him. In other words, the buildings on the land, the result of the industry of the tenant, become entirely the property of the landlord, without an item of expenditure or contribution on his part towards public improvements in any shape or form. (Slattery 1909, 14)

The prevention of land speculation was an important goal that was incorporated in the planning of what became the Churchill Park garden suburb.

The City Charter: The First Planning Document for St. John's

In December 1913 a reform group within the Board of Trade, led by President William Gosling, persuaded the government to sanction the creation of a Citizens' Committee to explore a revision of the Municipal Act. This committee became known as the Charter Commission. Its members were chosen both by public consultation and by appointments made by the government. Chaired by Gosling, it included prominent merchants and owners of private businesses as well as representatives of labour unions and the press. Several members had previous experience as municipal councillors or members of the government.

The Municipal Council stood down and the Commission administered the city for two years while it developed the Charter. New Council elections were held in 1916. Gosling was elected the mayor of the city and in that same year the Commission submitted its Charter to the government for review and approval. Many of its principal recommendations were included in the 1921 Municipal Act, which awarded "city" status to St. John's and provided it with broader powers and greater independence from the legislature (Baker 1981, 1982b, 1984c, 1985c; *ENL Government*):

> The Council shall have the power to control the development of land within the City limits, by the opening of new streets, by the widening, diverting, closing or improving existing streets and lanes, by the laying out of building lots, and by the provision of fire breaks, parks and recreation grounds, *so that same shall be well ordered*, and arrangements made to meet the future needs of the locality in so far as can be reasonably anticipated. (St. John's Municipal Act 1921, s. 74; emphasis added)

The detailed Charter drafted by Gosling and the Charter Commission attempted to address many of the chronic issues plaguing the city in a way that was appropriate to its needs and resources. The Charter embraced some of the essential aspects of contemporary town planning: the need for maps and land surveys, and better administrative control of revenue and expenditure. A Municipal Arrears Commission was recommended to bring some control to the collection of taxes.

Sanitation was all-important. There would be stricter rules and regulations for handling night soil, by both the householders and the sanitary men who were frequently accused of splashing and spilling material. In 1914 "hoppers" had been installed to aid in disposing of liquid waste (SJCM 18 Dec. 1914, 253). These looked like upended pipes into which the household slops could be poured to disappear down into an old drainage sewer. They were much praised by Mrs. Gosling, who mentioned "about forty catch-basins — hoppers — were installed in sections of the city where houses were not connected to the [sanitary] sewer and where the inhabitants were wont to hurl their waste water into the [surface] gutters" (A.N.

Figure 3.5. A street fountain ("tank"), child, and slop hopper (Dalzell 1926, 6).

Gosling 1935, 71). She noted that the death rate began to decline after 1914 and attributed this to the innovation.

The 1902 Act had said that no house could be erected without its plan having been approved by the city engineer. Now, the Charter demanded much more detail. Any house or building erected without permission would be declared a "nuisance" and possibly demolished. Regulations for construction were greatly expanded to include method and quality of construction techniques and materials used and, with an eye to the future, location with reference to access to water and sewer lines. The 1921 Act (s. 167) would now require that "every house within the City situated within fifty feet of the public drain or sewer shall be connected with the general water and sewerage system . . . to every such house there shall be constructed and maintained one or more proper and sufficient water closets." There were also specifications with reference to light and ventilation. Overcrowding was defined by stipulating cubic space per person: floor area and ceiling height of main rooms and bedrooms (ss. 358–64).

All these concerns were combined in a section in the 1921 Act that defined a house as being "unfit for Habitation": "dangerous to life or health by reason of want of repair or of defects in the drainage, plumbing, lighting, ventilation, or construction of same" (s. 365). In addition, section 90 of the Act gave Council the power to regulate and control the opening of new streets and the building of houses within one mile beyond the official city limits. This provided a mechanism for controlling land speculation and the further development of unserviced residential developments beyond the city limits. Also, the Act weakened the traditional leasehold system by stipulating that at the end of a lease, the leaseholder should have the right to purchase the freehold. The amount due to the landlord was the equivalent of 20 years of rent on the property (s. 94). This right to purchase the freehold remained in effect until the final abolition of the leasehold system in 1990 (Legislation 1990).

The 1921 Municipal Act extended its purview beyond issues of structural safety, regulations, and leasehold arrangements. Section 92, for example, authorized the appointment of a Town Planning Commission "to make recommendations ... annually to the Council ... generally for beautifying the City and developing it with a view to its future expansion." Section 8 broadened the electoral franchise to include female property owners, and more than 1,000 of them qualified to vote for the first time in the 1921 municipal election. The fact that Gosling's wife, Armine Nutting Gosling, was a strong supporter of women's suffrage may have had something to do with that (Duley 2014; A.N. Gosling 1935).

Mayor Gosling's Initiatives

In addition to his Charter work, Gosling continued to work towards improvements in the city. He saw a strong connection between inadequate housing and the dreadful health statistics. Inspector O'Brien of the Police and Fire Services told him that 369 houses in town were absolutely unfit for habitation and yet were fully occupied. He also told him that 2,000 houses were without sanitary appliances (sink and toilet) of any kind. And many cellar tenements lacked fresh air and light (A.N. Gosling 1935, 90). Gosling tried to ameliorate this situation with two approaches. He created a public health service and initiated a program for repairing houses identified as "unfit of habitation." The aim was to make them habitable and to extend their life in the housing stock.

Gosling's fledgling public health service had the full support of Dr. Brehm, the Council's officer of health. The service was initiated in 1917 and the following year several nurses were employed to do home visits, improve sanitary conditions, and set up milk stations. All these were points of concern for Dr. Brehm. The nurses were largely paid for by Gosling's own salary as mayor, with grants from the government and the voluntary support of the Women's Patriotic Association (WPA). In 1921 the government acknowledged the importance of this work by opening a children's ward in the General Hospital. At that time the WPA disbanded and reorganized as the Child Welfare Association to carry on with the same volunteer work, supported by both municipal and government funding (Baker 1982a; A.N.

Gosling 1935, 89–94; Bishop Stirling 2020, 42–50). The Child Welfare Association grew out of this initiative (Smallwood 1937a, 309–10; Baker 1982a, 31–32; *ENL* Child Welfare).

Gosling's second initiative was "Roofs and Walls." Asked by the press for a New Year's Eve message for the beginning of 1915, he said:

> I do not think St. John's people understand the miserable condition of the houses in which so many of our poorer classes are compelled to live. . . . There are hundreds of houses which are neither wind-tight nor water-tight, that are decaying and in every way unsanitary. There are many houses on the hillsides under which and through which drainage from the houses above continually trickles. There are dozens of families living in the basements of other houses on these hillsides, which are open to light and air on one side only. (quoted in A.N. Gosling 1935, 74)

The Council had the authority to enter and inspect any house to ensure that it was "fit for habitation" (Legislation 1910, s. 12). Although Gosling wished that they could include "water and sewer" in this definition, it was not possible. However, he did order inspection of tenement houses "with a view of having the roofs made staunch and tight and the houses fit for habitation" (SJCM 1 Aug. 1918, 353). Tenants were invited to complain and landlords were obliged to make repairs — if they did not, they would be subject to a fine (CSJA RG01-13). This scheme remained in effect until at least 1940, and many dwellings were successfully rescued from dilapidation. However, some landlords ignored repair orders, recognizing that the threat of condemnation was not practical because of the chronic shortage of alternative accommodation. Other owners decided to tear down the houses rather than repair.

The records of the city's house inspectors, with reference to "walls and roof," provide graphic illustrations of the miserable conditions in which many families were forced to live because of the scarcity of decent, cheap accommodation:

Figure 3.6. Rear of a house on Duggan Street, early 1950s (CSJA 01-46-020).

On Larkin Square, 1919: a double house with 5 tenants. "2 skylights admit rain and snow. The house is above ground in the back and the dampness soaks through, also the back door is loose. The owner explained the tenants owe 6 months' rent and he wants to get them out."

On Southside Road, 1920: "Two story and attic V roof. House old and in very bad shape. Shingles off. Plaster falling out practically all over the house. Owner threatens eviction unless the rent is paid which is excessive considering the state of the house."

The reports list houses located across a wide area of the city. In 1918, for example, 30 houses were inspected and reported on, and many of these were revisited to make sure the work was done. Of these, eight houses were located in the inner city. Many owners did the repairs, under repeated inspections.

While the city's inspectors did what they could to improve the quality of life for inner-city residents, some new houses were appearing in the area north of LeMarchant Road and west of Patrick Street. Two hundred people applied for building permits between 1914 and 1921, although we don't know how many permits were applied for more than once, or how many of the approved dwellings were actually built. However, the number of applications shows that those who could afford it wanted to have a house of their own.

Building Houses for Workingmen: Quidi Vidi, Cavell, and Merrymeeting

Mayor Gosling for some time had been focused on the need for workingmen's homes. "Nearly all the evils which beset the City can be referred back to the poor condition of so many of the houses. . . . Quite a number of houses have been pulled down recently and a great many more can be described as tottering. Houses must be found for the people thus turned out and there does not appear to be any prospect of these being provided by ordinary commercial means. The same problem . . . has confronted a great many communities . . . *to provide . . . the cheaper class of dwellings has become a recognized duty of cities*" (SJCM 23 May 1918, 307; emphasis added).

Gosling was aware of tenanted housing projects in other cities, whether run by the local councils or by the state (Pooley and Irish 1993, 193–219; Peabody Trust). However, his knowledge of the situation in Newfoundland made him hesitant to emulate them. When a tenant defaulted on rent, the owner of the house could not evict him in less than six months. And then, in many cases, the overdue rent couldn't be collected because the tenant had no valuable possessions that could be claimed by the owners in lieu of the missing rent. Gosling understood that anyone who offered to put money into a housing project would have to be protected against tenants who might default on the rent.

Gosling asked James McGrath, president of the Longshoremen's Protective Union (LSPU), for advice. McGrath replied:

> I beg to point out that in order that a family be able to pay fifty dollars a year house rent, it will be necessary for the head of the family to be earning at least ten dollars a week, and *as there are very few even skilled workmen earning that wage in this city*, the housing problem becomes all the more serious. . . .Take the more numerous classes of our people, namely, the men working on the waterfront, their average earnings do not exceed three hundred dollars a year. (McGrath 1914; emphasis added)

The final decision of Council was to build houses rather than tenements. Gosling convinced the government to add an enabling clause to the existing Municipal Act permitting the Council to construct low-cost housing "for the working poor" five years before the new 1921 Act was passed (Legislation 1916, s. 4; Baker 1982b, 37–39). As far-sighted as this initiative was for its time, the cost of taking on the purchase of a house put the city's project out of the grasp of most of "the working poor." This would become a familiar obstacle in future attempts to provide housing for the wage earner.

Gosling now had to find a suitable site for the Council's housing project. Harvey's Estates had earlier deeded a piece on a possible site for workmen's dwellings. But the site was near Campbell Avenue and too far out of town to permit the installation of services. The city engineer said it would require a new road, 430 feet long, and 1,600 feet of water and sewer pipes to develop the site. There were also worries about the wells in the area being affected by further development (SJCM 28 Aug. 1917, 154). So the Council chose a more suitable site on Connor's farm, at the base of Signal Hill on Quidi Vidi Road. The nearby General Hospital was already provided with services that could be extended to serve the project.

Gosling persuaded Council to proceed, and architect Jonas Barter, who will reappear later in the story, was commissioned to draw up the plans of the houses. The next challenge was to find the necessary funds. Gosling convinced the government to provide a $50,000 loan, to which he added some Council funds, and by the summer of 1919 construction had begun.

Figure 3.7. City of St. John's workmen's houses on Quidi Vidi Road and Cavell Avenue (C.A. Sharpe).

The plan was to build 12 six-room, semi-detached houses on Quidi Vidi road in 1919, and 10 more on Cavell Street in 1921. The first houses were completed by January 1920. "There was to be nothing jerry-built about them. They were to be lathed and plastered throughout and only good and durable materials used. Though small, they were comfortable and convenient, and ... with water and sewerage" (A.N. Gosling 1935, 87). When the houses were advertised for sale at the cost price of $1,950, they quickly sold

(SJCM 24 Jan. 1920, 245). The successful buyers were those who offered the highest down payment and shortest pay-back time — not those who lived in the worst houses in the city. However, a few had lived in the more difficult parts of the town, on Sebastian, Brine, Plymouth, and Power Streets (*St. John's City Directory* 1919, 1924). Most were skilled tradesmen, including a draper, a tinsmith, and a machinist, and the remainder were clerks, hospital employees, and an accountant.

This was a small project, considering the size of the need, but it set an important precedent for the Council. The government was sufficiently impressed that it considered exempting duty on materials to be used in the future construction of houses by the Council (SJCM 24 Jan 1920). Unfortunately, the city built no more than these 22 houses, in spite of Council's stated intention to continue building "until the demand is satisfied" (*Daily News*, 1920a).

Gosling was not the only person who took positive action to create some workingmen's houses. His friend Hon. John Anderson was told by James McGrath, president of the Longshoreman's Union and, like Anderson, a former member of the Charter Commission, that his members were complaining about the shortage of accommodation in the city and the consequent high rents. In an effort to improve the situation Anderson founded the Dominion Cooperative Building Association with the goal of building 900 workingmen's houses over the next decade (Legislation 1920). He raised money by selling shares to businesses, labour groups, and churches. The government agreed to help by waiving the import duties on all materials and machinery used by the Association (*Newfoundland Magazine* 1920; Commercial Christmas Annual 1919; Baker 1985a; Ellis 2019).

The Association secured land on the north side of Merrymeeting Road, east and west of Mayor Avenue. Here it built 30 houses, all with water and sewer, before being forced into liquidation in 1924 because it was unable to raise sufficient funds to build more (Baker 1982b, 40–41; Ellis 2019). As in the case of Gosling's houses on Quidi Vidi Road, the occupants of the Anderson Range houses were clerks and tradesmen, not labourers (*St. John's City Directory* 1919, 1924).

Figure 3.8. The Dominion Cooperative Houses on Merrymeeting Road in 2013 (C.A. Sharpe).

These successful housing projects yielded 52 houses, but they were too few to make any significant impact on the housing problem in the inner city. However, they clearly demonstrated that without substantial grants and loans, it was going to be impossible to do more. Meanwhile, the scale of the problem continued to grow. The assessment rolls show that in 1897, on the 32 streets in the inner city, there were 396 civic units. They belonged to 57 property owners, who owned between one and 45 units each. There were 197 leaseholders, many of whom owned more than one lease, and 123 subtenants. By 1915, there were 522 civic units in the same area, with 70 property owners, 251 leaseholders, and 261 subtenants and their families. It was a crowded place. But, facing a depressed economy, carrying the huge debt created by the building of the Newfoundland Railway, and with the cost of raising the Royal Newfoundland Regiment during the war, there was little the Council could do to solve the housing problem.

4

THE 1920S AND 1930S: DIFFICULT TIMES

The euphoria that accompanied the end of the Great War in 1918 quickly turned to despair as Newfoundland entered the 1920s. Political instability, economic hardship, and relentless unemployment gripped the country. The problems grew more severe through the 1930s as the industrialized world suffered the Great Depression and Newfoundland yielded her elected government to government by Commission from the Dominions Office in London. The St. John's Municipal Council, perilously short of funds, continued to agonize over its inability to assist citizens who were living in deplorable conditions. The weekly Council minutes painted a bleak picture: inadequate sanitation, houses "unfit for habitation," dilapidated buildings, wells polluted, uncontrollable flooding, increasing unemployment, and mounting tax arrears.

The scale and nature of the problems faced by City Council as it struggled to provide services to the inhabitants of unplanned residential areas on the fringe are illustrated by a report on sanitary conditions in an area northwest of the city, near Mundy Pond and Upper Pleasant Street (now Campbell Avenue):

> 75% of the wells ... are affected by surface drainage. Sections of this place are somewhat thickly populated with all the houses occupied, and the locality is noted for the lack of sewerage or drainage facilities. The soil must be full of foulness which would affect wells. Under these circumstances it

is impossible to estimate the value to the city of the sanitary results growing out of the maintenance of health ... by the convenience of pure water. At present time there are 8 deliveries of 110 gallons daily. This quantity serves about 100 families and the cost is $38.00 a week. (SJCM 5 Jan. 1928, 305)

Mayor Tasker Cook (1921-29)

Gosling was too ill to seek re-election in 1921. He returned to Bermuda where he died in 1930. He was succeeded by Tasker Cook, a prominent businessman and director of several local companies (*ENL* Cook).

Cook and his Council were the first to have the One Mile Area outside the city boundary under their jurisdiction. Council didn't authorize the building of any new suburbs, but they grew anyway, unplanned and unserviced, in the fields at the edge of town. In the inner city, attempts to repair properties and to install sanitary facilities continued to be stymied by the obdurate refusal of the landlords to comply with exhortations from City Hall. Meanwhile, some citizens tried valiantly to hold Council to account. A deputation from the Child Welfare Association, including Lady Crosbie, Miss Southcott, who had founded the St. John's General Hospital School of Nursing in 1903, and Miss Anderson, head of the Community Nursing Service, addressed the Council (*ENL* Southcott; Government of Canada, 1998). They spoke of the

Figure 4.1. Mayor Tasker Cook (1921–29) (CSJA 06-01-019).

high rate of infant mortality brought about by unsanitary conditions and submitted a long list of suggestions for improvement, including cleaning the hoppers and acquiring lids for the sanitary carts. They also suggested that the sanitary inspector should read a highly recommended book, *Hygiene and Public Health* (SJCM 19 Sept. 1924, 73; Whitelegge and Newman 1908). By the early 1920s the Council's revenues were nearly exhausted and it was on week-to-week budgeting (SJCM 1922, 115). The Council requested help from the government but it was equally strapped for money. The chronic lack of money made it very difficult for the Council to act on the new regulations and plans for the town, which had been enshrined in the 1921 Municipal Act. However, in the midst of these trying circumstances, an unforeseen event reopened the discussion about housing.

The Rotary Club Investigates

A branch of the Rotary International Club, which had been founded in Chicago in 1905, was organized in St. John's in 1921. Its first major undertaking was a survey of "the life of boys" in the city — focusing on boys who lived in difficult circumstances (Hunt 1937). The Rotarians were shocked when they became aware of the appalling conditions in which the boys lived, lacking proper sanitation and warm and weather-tight houses. Better housing, they argued, would be a first step to a better life for these children, and they invited a number of prominent local men to give them the benefit of their experience.

Local engineer F.W. Angel, president of United Nail and Foundry (*ENL* Angel), stressed the magnitude of the housing problem in the city when he addressed the Rotary Club. He reported that in the inner city immediately north of New Gower Street there were 900 unsewered houses, 80 per cent of which were unfit for habitation because they had no basements and therefore could not protect water and sewer pipes from frost. Highlighting a contemporary problem common to many North American cities, he referred to the One Mile Area where uncontrolled building had occurred before the area came under the city's jurisdiction in 1921. He noted that "houses were built haphazard and without regard to levels, street lines, or anything else. It will now cost double or treble the amount to water and sewer these areas which an inexpensive survey might have avoided" (*Evening Telegram* 1925a).

When his turn came to address the Rotarians, Mayor Cook gave a detailed account of the revenues and expenditures of Council. Like Angel, he referred to the large number of unsewered houses in the city, the majority of which he claimed were unsuitable for the installation of water and sewer. He challenged the members to consider whether they would be willing to consider replacing these houses with new ones that would likely cost $1,500 each: "Now, I ask you, are you or any of the taxpayers prepared to tax themselves with this object in view?" Referring to the Biblical account of how Pharaoh increased the burden of the captive Israelites who were making bricks by demanding that henceforth they bind the clay together without straw (Exodus 5:1–11), he concluded by saying, "give us the money and we'll give you a city; we cannot make bricks without straw" (*Evening Telegram* 1925b).

A third principal speaker to address the Rotary Club was Major Leonard C. Outerbridge (*ENL* Outerbridge). Because of his wife's involvement with the Child Welfare Association and his work in organizing the Charity Organization Bureau in 1925, he was already very familiar with the economic and social problems facing the city (Smallwood 1937a, 1937b). Like Angel and Mayor Cook, Outerbridge deplored the continued occupation of condemned houses, the lack of sanitary facilities, and the financial inability of the Municipal Council to remedy the situation. Recognizing that "the whole matter is bristling with difficulties, legal and otherwise," and beyond any local ability to solve, he proposed that the town "call in an expert in slums and town planning to tell us how best to gouge out the rotten core which exists in the centre of our city." He suggested town planner Arthur Dalzell, "regarded by some as the greatest expert in his line living today" (*Evening Telegram* 1926).

The Rotarians were no doubt much better informed of the problems facing the city after hearing from these men, but they were as powerless as the city was to solve them. There simply wasn't the money to do anything. The Council could not raise taxes without government approval, and it had no authority to raise loans even if it could, whether from the financially strapped government or from some other source. Although Cook was adamantly opposed to increasing the Council's debt in order to solve the housing situation, Council did at least agree to bring Dalzell to St. John's for discussions (SJCM 14 Jan. 1922, 350).

Arthur Dalzell: "Is All Well?"

Arthur G. Dalzell had trained as an engineer and sanitary inspector in England before moving to Canada in 1919 to work with Thomas Adams, who was then the town planning advisor to the Canadian government. In working with Adams, Dalzell came to believe that because private enterprise had failed to address major planning issues, the state should get more directly involved in the housing market (Lewis and Shrimpton 1984, n. 13). For Dalzell, "shelter means more than the protection from the elements; it implies all that is essential for the physical, moral and intellectual development of the individual" (Dalzell 1926, 4). He believed that the ideal home was a single-family dwelling, preferably owner-occupied. This reflected the view of urban reformer Henry Vivian, who told the Canadian Club "I trust that in Canada you will avoid the tenement as far as possible" (Vivian 1910, 403).

Dalzell visited St. John's during September 1926. His report to Council was fair and measured, with the realization that the present city had laboured under a lack of planning in the past. However, he gave Tasker Cook's Council no excuses for their lack of initiative in solving some of the city's endemic problems. He praised the work of Gosling's Charter Commission: "If the provisions of the 1921 Act were lived up to and enforced, a very great improvement of conditions would soon be seen" (Dalzell 1926, 10). He decried the fact that many unserviced houses were located on streets that had both water and sewer services. He dismissed the idea that many houses

Figure 4.2. The cover of Arthur Dalzell's report to the citizens of St. John's, 1926.

were unsuited for water and sewer services because they were inadequately heated. In his view that could be corrected with little expense. He lamented that the medical officer had the authority to close unsanitary houses but could not do so for lack of alternate accommodation, and concluded that purely as a business proposition no modern community can afford to neglect the element of health: "A community can *buy* health *if it wants to*, but it *has* to pay the deficit on poor health, *whether it wants to or not*" (Dalzell 1926, 9).

Dalzell recommended that the city appoint a Town Planning Commission under section 92 of the 1921 Act because "the housing problem is a town-planning problem. Houses require sites; sites require streets to serve them; and these streets must be provided with water and sewer services which should be carefully planned" (Dalzell 1926, 11). He noted "there is nothing exceptional in the fact that private enterprise in St. John's will not now provide homes suitable for the poorer classes" (Dalzell 1926, 14). So he recommended that the Council ask the Newfoundland government for funds so the city could use its power to expropriate land, build houses, and give financial assistance to those willing to build houses for workingmen. He pointed out that the Canadian government, most of the provinces, and many municipal governments loaned money for house building. His final point was a telling one: that the St. John's housing problem was a national problem, not a municipal one, because one-fifth of Newfoundland's population lived within the city of St. John's. A decade later this argument would be used, with some success, by those advocating the creation of Churchill Park.

There was little or nothing in Dalzell's report that the councillors didn't already know:

> While every resident was aware of the deplorable housing conditions, no one has yet found a solution to the remedy other than that they should be removed and more modern and up to date workmen's homes erected which should be sanitary from every viewpoint but the question of finance was the answer to the whole situation and when this is forthcoming it will not take long to remedy the conditions. (SJCM 25 Jan. 1927, 58)

But funding was not forthcoming, and until it was there was nothing Council could do. It couldn't demand the demolition of the dilapidated houses that had already been listed by the medical officer because there was nowhere for the displaced inhabitants to go (SJCM 4 June 1926, 433).

However, heeding the entreaties of Major Outerbridge, the Charity Organization Bureau, and the Rotary Club, and recalling a recommendation made by Gosling's Charter Commission in 1921, Cook took Dalzell's advice and created a Town Planning Commission (TPC) in 1928 (SJCM 26 Apr.

1928, 339). The mandate of the TPC was " to make recommendations for the improvement and extension of existing streets, reservation of land for firebreaks, parks and playgrounds, for the laying out of building lands, for the planting of trees, and generally for beautifying the city and developing it with a view to future expansion" (Legislation 1921, s. 92).

Justice James Kent of the Newfoundland Supreme Court was appointed chairman of the TPC. During its short life (1928–34) the TPC worked diligently to discharge its duties. It requested surveys of proposed new developments and laid out new streets in old congested areas, working with developers to design the layout of their proposals. The TPC's Housing Committee, chaired by Major W.F. Ingpen, inspected many of the older houses and concluded that because of a "mutual apathy," neither residents nor landlords were willing to spend money on connecting to water and sewer services. In a prescient statement that foreshadows by more than a decade the position adopted by the Commission of Enquiry on Housing and Town Planning, the report of the Housing Committee said that the only possible remedy was "to construct better homes elsewhere to house the inhabitants of these slums, so that by relieving congestion the worst homes might gradually fall into disuse and be demolished" (*Evening Telegram* 1930a). But this was not considered a practical solution. Mayor Cook was quick to point out the houses built by Gosling's Council at Quidi Vidi had been purchased by people "in fairly comfortable circumstances" and were of no help to those who lived on the poverty line (SJCM 23 Aug. 1928, 438). The Council didn't have the funds to act on the TPC's enthusiastic recommendations and the Commission slowly faded into obscurity.

Mayor Charles J. Howlett (1929-32)

In 1929 dentist Charles Howlett foiled Cook's attempt to win a third term as mayor (*ENL* Howlett; Baker 1984d). During his campaign, Howlett railed against what he referred to as the "twin evils" of St. John's: overcrowded houses and gaps in the sanitary system that allowed tuberculosis to flourish and kept the death rate high (*Daily News* 1929). Once in office Howlett was able to secure several government grants that had been owing to the Council for some time. He successfully applied for permission to seek a $500,000 loan, initiated a Civic Relief Committee, and invited the TPC to speak to Council about their work. Then, in one more demonstration of the fact that there was in St. John's an understanding of modern town planning practice and the need to emulate it to the extent possible, he arranged for the renowned town planner Frederick Todd to come to St. John's (SJCM 31 Jan. 1930, 59; Cuff et al. 1990, 164–65).

Figure 4.3. Mayor Charles J. Howlett (1929–32) (*ENL 2*, 1092).

Frederick Todd: "Though Slums Are Bad the Cure Is Simple"

Frederick Todd (1876–1948), like Arthur Dalzell four years earlier, brought his knowledge of cutting-edge planning practice to St. John's. Todd had been in Newfoundland previously, after having worked with world-renowned landscape designer Frederick Law Olmstead. Todd, like Henry Vivian, was a firm believer in the benefits of garden suburb design (Jacobs 1983, 28; McCann 1996, 268; Asselin 1998). In 1921 Sir Edgar Bowring commissioned Todd to plan Bowring Park in conjunction with Rudolf Cochius, the Dutch-born landscape artist who was then working in the city.

Recognizing the influence of the Rotary Club, Todd took the opportunity to explain why a town plan could help solve urban problems. He assured Rotarians that:

> The adoption of a comprehensive city plan need frighten no one. Town planning is a practical thing and may be defined as the scientific and orderly disposition of land and buildings with a view to obviating congestion and securing the economic and social efficiency, health and well-being of the community. It means the exercise of such prudence and foresight as is necessary to ensure the success of any undertaking which deals with future events. (Todd 1930, 1)

Todd gave some pragmatic examples from his observations of St. John's: "In one case, if the streets had been properly laid out it would have saved one third of an acre of land, 15,000 feet of street and 300 feet of sewer pipe" (Todd 1930, 3). Eschewing diplomacy, he argued that "any city which does not try to improve such conditions [as the slum in St. John's] is morally guilty of criminal neglect against a very considerable number of citizens" (Todd 1930, 2).

Todd concluded that the most pressing matter for St. John's was the elimination of the dilapidated houses on inner-city streets such as Duggan, Wickford, Stephen, and James. He called for the complete redevelopment of the flimsy, haphazard neighbourhood. However, he cautioned that clearing the ground might be counterproductive, making it too valuable to be for workmen's dwellings.

Todd's prescription was undoubtedly correct, but local conditions made it impossible to fill it. Architect Jonas Barter, a member of the TPC, calculated that Todd's clearance plan, if workmen's housing was built on the site, would replace 490 crowded buildings with only 200 new buildings. He estimated the cost of the project would be $1,732,500 and concluded that "this proposition is too ridiculous to be considered seriously" (Barter 1930).

Between 1921 and 1934 the city of St. John's enjoyed the benefits of new municipal legislation and the best professional advice of the day. The Council was not ignorant of current "best practice" but was unable to implement much-needed reforms because of the lack of adequate financing and other contributing factors — the untimely death of Mayor Howlett in 1932, the election of Andrew Carnell as mayor in 1933, and the imposition of the Commission of Government in 1934.

The Unimaginable: The Arrival of the Commission of Government (1934-49)

Newfoundland's political confusion and dire financial situation led to its acceptance of a Commission of Government in 1934 (Amulree 1933). Newfoundland's responsible government was replaced by a Commission appointed by the British government. The Commission was to remain in power until "the country is again self-supporting [when] responsible government, on request from the people of Newfoundland, would be restored" (Neary 1988, 34). Three of the six commissioners and the governor were British, and three commissioners were Newfoundlanders. The Commission's mandate was "to give Newfoundland a rest from politics" and to provide economic and social reconstruction. However, the budget of the Commission was limited and tightly controlled by the secretary of state for dominion affairs in London. This hampered the well-meaning efforts of the commissioners, and they had little immediate effect on Newfoundland's economy. The number of people on relief increased during the 1930s. The Commission continued until Newfoundland became a province of Canada in 1949.

Some historians have said that the forfeiture of independence was Newfoundland's greatest political disaster and a more important inflection point in Newfoundland history than Confederation with Canada (Jackson 1986, 60; Major 2001, 404). Although the Commission's economic impact may have been insignificant, the impact of these 15 years on Newfoundlanders' self-esteem was not (Johnson 2009; Malone 2012). The legacy of the Commission years played an important role in the arguments advanced to convince the government, and the people, of the necessity for the Churchill Park development.

Mayor Andrew Carnell (1933-49)

Andrew Carnell was the manager of his family's carriage-building and undertaking business. During his years as mayor, Newfoundland was governed by the Commission of Government and he had to work under the constraints that it and the Depression imposed. When first elected to St. John's Municipal Council, his was the only elected government in Newfoundland. His steadfast defence of his Municipal Council in the face of the authority of the Commission of Government won him strong support from the electorate (*ENL* Carnell; Baker 1985d, 17).

In the fall of 1935 the financial situation was so desperate that the city could not meet its payroll. Temporarily, all casual labour was discharged, all ongoing work was closed down, and no new work was authorized (SJCM 15 Nov. 1935, 643). The immediate crisis was averted after Carnell was able to convince the Commission of Government to restore some of the subsidies that had been granted to the city in 1888 but later withdrawn. And his successful attempt to have the municipal debt reduced from $1,648,904 to $1,000,000 eased the city's expenditure on debt service (SJCM 27 July 1937, 491).

The 1921 Act (s. 246) authorized the creation of a Municipal Arrears Commission empowered to collect outstanding taxes. One was finally established in 1937 but it wasn't very effective because of Council's ambivalent attitude towards its mandate. On the one hand, Council desperately needed the landlords to pay what they owed. On the other, there was concern for poor property owners. The compromise was that the city solicitor was permitted to make every effort to collect overdue taxes while trying to minimize the imposition of undue hardship on those who were really incapable of paying (SJCM 27 Aug. 1935, 549; 18 Oct. 1935, 609).

Figure 4.4. Mayor Andrew G. Carnell (1933-49) (TRPAD E 11-45).

A long-standing bone of contention between the municipal government and the Commission of Government and its predecessors was the question of who was responsible to provide housing for those of very limited means. Mayor Gosling believed that it was "the recognized duty of cities to provide the cheaper class of dwellings for the workingman." Carnell, on the other hand, firmly believed that the *national* government was responsible for housing, not the city. He was ahead of his time in understanding that the principal underlying cause of poor housing is poverty, and the city was virtually powerless to do anything about that. He told the Council that "the present deplorable condition of many of our citizens and the prevalence of disease and increase in mortality is due not to housing conditions, but to malnutrition and to the fact that family wage-earners are given no opportunity to earn a living" (SJCM 28 Feb. 1935, 361).

The lack of progress in St. John's under Carnell's watch with reference to housing led Frederick Todd to write to the commissioner of public health in 1941 offering his help if the commissioner thought it might be useful (Todd 1941). His offer wasn't accepted, and it would be another quarter-century before the clearances advocated by both Dalzell and Todd finally began, and a further 40 years before the last of the old dilapidated dwellings in the central area of the city was demolished. And yes, as Todd had predicted, when that happened, the land did change in value and the land use changed from residential to commercial and institutional with the construction of a new City Hall, Mile One Stadium, Cabot Place, and the Delta Hotel.

Housing: "Shacktowns," New Houses, and Old Tenements

"Shacktowns"

The history of Canadian suburbanization began long before the arrival of the widely criticized post-war tract suburbs. The first large-scale examples of development outside the formal boundary of cities date back to the late nineteenth and early twentieth centuries when unplanned, unregulated suburbs were created by owner-builders of small means in areas where they would build quickly and cheaply in the absence of municipal regulations and building standards bylaws. Such developments, often pejoratively referred to as "shacktowns," were a feature of almost every Canadian city (Harris 2004, 99). The inhabitants were too poor to afford a house built by speculative contractors. Their only route to homeownership was to become an owner-builder, substituting sweat equity for waged labour (Harris 1996, 223). This type of suburban development was very common, and played a significant role in easing the housing shortage in many Canadian cities until the end of the 1930s when increasing state regulation of building standards made them both too expensive and illegal (Harris 2004, 7).

Such developments had appeared in St. John's by the 1920s, if not earlier. They grew in number during the 1930s as desperate families left the outports and came to St. John's looking for work. These in-migrants were joined by people evicted from the houses in the city that were so obviously "unfit for habitation" that the Council had them demolished, in spite of the lack of affordable alternative housing in the central city. The largest concentrations were near Mundy Pond, on Campbell Avenue, in the Sand Pitts area near Long Pond, in the Battery, on Blackmarsh Road, and on Signal Hill (House 1964; Williamson 1971; Outer Battery Neighbourhood Association 2012).

The 1921 Municipal Act gave Council the power to enact regulations that would have prohibited such development. But the Council made no such regulations, nor did they extend water and sewer services to that area. Mayor Cook had said "it was practically impossible for the Council to prevent people from erecting homes to shelter their families, owing to the shortage of available land in the city ... also the prohibitive prices of building sites" (SJCM 10 Dec. 1928, 497). Carnell's Council was the first to draft regulations for the One Mile Area where some of the shacktown growth was located. These regulations became law in 1936, 15 years after the 1921 Act created the One Mile Area (SJCM 6 Aug. 1936, 209–11).

Families who built their houses on unserviced lots shared the same goal as families who built on serviced lots: to own their own house. It was a point of both pride and necessity. Using city directories and the 1937 municipal electors list we tracked some of the owner-builders in the Mundy Pond area and other households in the new and properly surveyed and ser-

Figure 4.5. Pearce Avenue pre-1964 (CSJA 01-82-001).

Figure 4.6. Blackhead Road, 1950 (CSJA 11-01-002).

viced streets north of LeMarchant Road. The majority of the house owners were tradesmen — butchers, carpenters, bakers, mechanics, plumbers, and a few clerks. In both areas the labourers were in the minority. The number of houses in the Mundy Pond area increased from about 30 in 1915 to 173 by 1936; in the Battery, from 122 in 1915 to 183 in 1936; on Signal Hill, from 63 to 74; and along Blackhead Road, from 6 to 100.

Assuming Harris (2004) is right in his categorization of the stages of Canadian suburban development, these shacktowns represent a normal phase in urban growth, and they played an important part in providing much-needed housing during a time of great distress. Despite the negative connotation of the epithet applied to them and the rough living conditions that characterized their early days, owners gradually enlarged and upgraded their small houses. And eventually they all acquired services, although it took the urban renewal projects of the 1960s to accomplish this (Project Planning Associates 1967 [(Blackhead]; Canadian-British Engineering Consultants 1966 [Mundy Pond]; British Consultants Limited 1978 [the Battery]).

Figure 4.7. The Battery, undated photo (Department of Geography, Memorial University of Newfoundland, Coll. 137, 03.07.005).

New Houses

As the grip of the Depression eased towards the end of the 1930s the city engineer convinced the Council that the extension of services, in spite of the initial cost, would encourage new construction and lead to an increase in residential property tax revenue (SJCM 6 Aug. 1936, 213). The profitability of new construction was enhanced by the city's insistence that developers pay a frontage charge to allay a portion of the cost of the new services. Sensibly, the Council also began to collaborate with various trade organizations to adopt and enforce higher building standards. The result was the development of good-quality houses by commercial

> **BUILDINGS ON SIGNAL HILL**
>
> The shack menace which has already converted several localities in the vicinity of St. John's into potential slums is at present threatening the open spaces of Signal Hill. Not all the buildings are of this type but there are already on this area several approaching that class, and unless steps are taken promptly, it may not be long before George's Pond will have a village on its shore and much of the area which for generations has been used as public grounds will be occupied.

Figure 4.8. "Buildings on Signal Hill" (*Evening Telegram* 2 Oct. 1936).

Figure 4.9. New houses north of LeMarchant Road, late 1930s and 1940s (A.J. Shawyer).

builders on Glenridge Crescent, the Comerford and Carpasian Estates on Allandale Road and Empire Avenue, and the McLea Estate north of St. Clare's Hospital. Then the Railway Employees Welfare Association built 124 "railway" houses for its members on Craigmillar and Topsail Roads (Kennedy 1996).

Tenements

None of these new initiatives affected the tired landscape in the inner city. One former resident, recalling the neighbourhood he grew up in during the 1920s and 1930s, described it as Dickensian: "Row houses, with broken windows, leaking roofs, rotting front steps, and two or three families . . . in tenements . . . the whole area seemed to be just waiting for another fire. The fire never happened" (Horwood 1997, 7).

Such conditions notwithstanding, it is a mistake to conflate such graphic descriptions of houses that were known to be badly dilapidated with the perceptions of those who lived in them. Generations of families lived, worked, and played here. Reformers came up with euphemisms for the pejorative terms by which poor areas were commonly referred to: "unhealthy areas" or "blighted areas" rather than "slums" (Toopalov 2014). This may have mattered to them, but not to the residents, who didn't necessarily think of themselves as poor slum dwellers. James Street might have been rough "but not to us who lived there" (Owens 2001). "We never thought of ourselves as poor, had no sense of that growing up. We had everything we needed. Our mother made sure that we had new clothes for school, and Christmas, and the Regatta. Our mothers and the Nuns and Brothers at school made us keep to high standards — clean and tidy, well mannered, and respect for the elders" (Skinner 2006).

Jack Fitzgerald, who grew up on Flower Hill in the 1940s and 1950s, wrote that "our playgrounds were the dusty unpaved streets. . . . we played in the horse stables and on the jetty wharfs of the old harbour front. We cut seal meat, shovelled coal, and sold splits and bottles to make pocket money. We lived in houses built for the nineteenth century, most with no water and sewerage, poorly insulated. . . . We lived in a time when disease and

Figure 4.10. Two schoolgirls on Barron Street (Accession no. 04-117, Jack Fitzgerald manuscripts and photographs, Archives and Special Collections Division, Queen Elizabeth Library, Memorial University of Newfoundland).

malnutrition were common . . . [but] despite adversity and the hardships we experienced, most of us recall our childhood downtown as a memorable and a happy experience" (Fitzgerald 1997, x). Robert Hunt wrote about the fun of living on Brazil Street: "we could walk Water Street blindfolded: we knew every nook and cranny of it. Besides doing errands for stores, we were always at Job's, Steer's, or Baird's Cove when the fishermen brought in their catch . . . they would give us tongues from the cod to sell. We sold them by the bagful for pocket change" (Hunt 2011, 14).

These are the voices of men whose lives as children were much less constrained than those of girls, who didn't have the freedom to be out and about on the streets and the wharves. They stayed closer to home, nurtured by their mothers, aunts, and grandmothers in the domestic arts, and moving in the social circle of church events and school activities (Porter 2011).

The girls did not expect a life of paid employment, as the boys did, but anticipated a life of homemaking. "I left work when I married William. By that time I was twenty, tired of working at the factory, and glad to be making a home for us" (Forestell 1995, 76). Such a life experience was typical of the 1920s and 1930s in St. John's. For girls, full-time paid employment, if there was any, was just an interlude between school and marriage.

There has been a great deal of debate about the issue of slum clearance, both historically and in more recent times. Most Canadian slums resulted from either an influx of immigrants or a concentration of what would now be called racialized minorities (James 2010), neither of which was provided with accommodation or other assistance in adapting to their new circumstances. The residents of the inner city of St. John's, however, were different. In many cases they were families who had lived in Newfoundland for generations. Their situation was characterized by poor-quality

Figure 4.11. A range on the south side of Duggan Street, 1950s (CSJA 11-02-064).

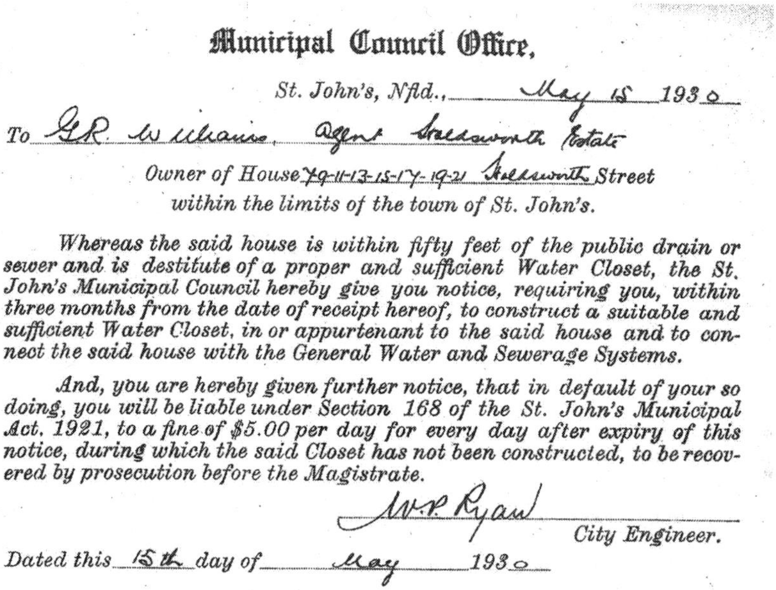

Municipal Council Office,

St. John's, Nfld., *May 15 1930*

To *G.R. Williams, agent Holdsworth Estate*
Owner of House *7-9-11-13-15-17-19-21 Holdsworth* Street
within the limits of the town of St. John's.

    Whereas the said house is within fifty feet of the public drain or sewer and is destitute of a proper and sufficient Water Closet, the St. John's Municipal Council hereby give you notice, requiring you, within three months from the date of receipt hereof, to construct a suitable and sufficient Water Closet, in or appurtenant to the said house and to connect the said house with the General Water and Sewerage Systems.

    And, you are hereby given further notice, that in default of your so doing, you will be liable under Section 168 of the St. John's Municipal Act, 1921, to a fine of $5.00 per day for every day after expiry of this notice, during which the said Closet has not been constructed, to be recovered by prosecution before the Magistrate.

W.P. Ryan
City Engineer.

Dated this *15th* day of *May* 1930.

Figure 4.12. Notice to the Holdsworth Estate, 1930 (CSJA Coll RG 01-13 Misc Series).

and overcrowded housing. The planners who came from away — Todd and Dalzell — called the area a slum, but if it was a slum it had its own character and wisdom. As much as the residents might have wanted to improve their situation, they were condemned to live as tenants, not property owners, and left to wait until the civic authorities roused and decided their future for them. Cabbagetown, on the east side of Toronto, was described as "the largest Anglo-Saxon slum in North America" (Garner 1971, 7). But, as the doyenne of Canadian urban reformers pointed out, Cabbagetown (and one might add downtown St. John's as well) was the type of slum that harboured the potential for regeneration. Nonetheless, the neighbourhood was condemned by paternalistic planners who couldn't understand this (Jacobs 1961, 271; Mayne 1993).

    Outsiders had a very different view of the inner city, which did not inspire praise from visitors. Soon after her arrival in the spring of 1934,

Lady Hope Simpson, wife of the commissioner of natural resources (*ENL* John Hope Simpson), described St. John's with disappointment and distaste:

> ... a horrid little town really. ... It might be a beautiful little capital of this beautiful island. But it is just a dirty, foul-smelling slum. ... The dirt and carelessness are preventable. ... It is a town without self-respect. No one seems to have cared enough for it to think and plan and spend for it. (Neary 1996, 78)

Robert Jones, a young Nova Scotia doctor passing through on a medical ship in 1937, described the city as:

> The city of a thousand stinks . . . . millions of flies, dirt, squalor ... chronic malnutrition ... very little middle class here, people being either very poor or very rich ... most of the city lives in miserable shacks and only about one third have plumbing or sewerage I am told. I suspect that is an under estimation ... sewerage in pails which is put outside at midnight . . . . A modern hygienist would go crazy here. (Jones 2000, 214)

The municipal councillors knew all this, and as we have seen, previous councils had done what little they could to find solutions to intractable problems. Although the condition of inner-city housing was much the same in 1939 as it had been for decades, and the state of the country's finances as desperate as always, one councillor bravely proposed a new strategy.

Councillor Meaney's Proposal

The minutes of the Municipal Council provide a fascinating account of the sequence of events. On 6 April 1939, Dr. Brehm condemned four occupied houses on Carter's Hill as dilapidated, insanitary, and unfit for habitation (SJCM 6 Apr. 1939, 398). On 20 April 1939:

> The City Clerk stated that he had been furnished by the Medical Officer with vacation orders to be served to the occupants of [four houses] on Carter's Hill, in accordance with the instructions of the Council. As it meant putting some twenty people out of their present homes, he thought it advisable to mention the matter again to Council before serving notices. A lengthy discussion followed in the course of which some Council members expressed the opinion that the Public Health and Welfare Department should take the responsibility for such action, and not the Council. It was pointed out, however, that under the Municipal Act, the City's Medical Officer is required to notify the occupants of unfit dwellings to vacate the same, and the owners to destroy or repair, as the case may be. It was finally agreed to let the notices be served, as originally ordered. (SJCM 20 Apr. 1939, 418)

At the next meeting of Council, on 27 April 1939, Councillor Meaney outlined his proposed plan for the elimination of the city's slums (Meaney 1939; SJCM 27 Apr. 1939, 421). John T. Meaney was first elected to the Municipal Council in 1937 after an ill-fated appointment as chairman of the government's Liquor Control Department and then a period of working as a journalist. Energetic and proactive, his skills in journalism, both as a researcher and writer, were to be put to

Figure 4.14. John T. Meaney, municipal councillor (1937–43) (*ENL* 3: 489).

good use in his short-lived career as municipal councillor (*ENL* Meaney; Elliott 1980).

Meaney's eloquent and impassioned address noted that about half of the houses occupied by low-income workers were below acceptable Canadian habitable standards and that the scale of the problem was such that even if the private sector was willing to try and solve it — which it was not — sufficient capital could not be found (*Evening Telegram* 1939). So:

> If the individual cannot, and the capitalist will not bid to meet the normal requirements of decent housing, then the state and the municipality must take cognizance of the situation and make available the use of public funds or public credit to enable others to build for those who cannot build without assistance. . . . I am not an alarmist. I have unbounded faith and confidence in the courage, ability and industry of my fellow citizens to surmount every obstacle that lies in the path of their industrial and social progress. But, gentlemen, I am firmly convinced that they cannot, without material aid, emerge from their present unfortunate plight, nor break the paralyzing strangle-hold of this seven-year-old depression which is stagnating the stream of industrial enterprise, debilitating our manhood, and pauperizing our citizens. . . . The plan I am proposing . . . is to arouse our city from its deathlike apathy, from its reproachable lethargy, from its slumber of industrial and social death. (Sharpe 2000, 54)

Meaney proposed that 500 houses be built, and offered on a monthly rental-purchase basis to industrious, wage-earning citizens. He had in mind those who could not afford to make even a minimum down payment but would be able to make the regular payments necessary to pay for the house over time. For those whose earnings were too low to enable them to commit to such a scheme, government and municipal financial assistance would be necessary, and "weighty and cogent reasons will have to be advanced to justify the refusal of assistance." He was astute enough to recognize that his proposal was not a panacea for the problems of the inner city. He also knew that there would be no support for housing built on a charitable basis, So he stressed his proposal "is not paternalism. It is not socialism. It is not commercialization. Philanthropy does not enter the picture."

The scheme would only work if the Commission of Government agreed to raise a loan of $1,250,000 at no more than 3 per cent interest. This would make possible the building of houses that cost $1,800 for those in blocks of four and $3,500 for single houses. The monthly payments required to retire the loan would range from $16 to $30, much more than the city's poorest inhabitants could afford. The proposal also required that the city reduce the 1.6 per cent tax rate on low-cost houses to 0.6 per cent. Over the projected 15-year amortization of the loan, the city would have provided a subsidy of $112,500.

The proposal contained two important caveats. The first was that neither the government nor the city undertake to build the houses. To do so, he said, would be "calamitous." Meaney argued that there would be no need to set up a new organization because the city's existing philanthropic and co-operative house-building organizations had all the knowledge and experience to carry out the proposed project. The second was that the project should be undertaken within the existing city limits, and "under no consideration beyond the reach of such water and sewer services as at present exist" (Sharpe 2000, 59). Both of these caveats were to be ignored in the development of Churchill Park.

On 4 May 1939 the Council unanimously adopted Meaney's proposal and, together with a set of accompanying resolutions, sent it to the Commission of Government for approval (SJCM 4 May 1939, 430). The commissioner of finance, John H. Penson, referred it to a committee consisting of himself and the commissioners of public health and welfare (John Charles Puddester) and public utilities (W.W. Woods) (Penson 1939a).

The Commission of Government Examines Councillor Meaney's Proposal

While the Commission didn't acknowledge receipt of the proposal, its members did discuss it privately. Penson acknowledged that "the slum problem in St. John's is one of the most pressing which we have to meet" and that "building new and better houses for men in regular employment would eventually bring abandonment of the worst houses." However, he argued that Meaney's assertion that the plan is economically sound could easily be discounted because it wouldn't provide houses that even the most affluent families living in the slum areas could afford to rent (Penson 1939b).

Penson argued that rehousing the poorest inner-city families could only be done through charity because the Commission of Government could not spend public money to build houses in Newfoundland. At the same time, he cited the 1929 report of Major Ingpen's Housing Committee of the Town Planning Commission (*Evening Telegram* 1930a), which argued that by providing new and better houses for men in regular employment:

> we should not only be benefitting them and their families, but also indirectly the other occupants of the congested areas. The tendency would be in the course of a certain time that the worst houses would be abandoned. Indeed, if a few hundred houses were erected for those able, in part at least, to pay for them, it should render possible putting into operation a policy of condemning the worst dwellings on health grounds and thereby gradually improving the general state of housing from the bottom. (Penson 1939b)

Employing an argument that would later be used to justify the construction of houses in Churchill Park, he said that this policy would have a "knock-on" effect. Although he didn't support the Meaney proposal, his intervention did bring the rehousing of the poor into the discussion.

Commissioner Woods agreed with Ingpen and Penson that a "move-up" or "knock-on" effect was a possible solution. Public Health and Welfare Commissioner Sir John Puddester's view was that "it is not within the realm of practical purposes to build houses for everybody, but the problem of finding accommodation for the poorest classes is usually solved by wealthy and middle-class people acquiring new and better homes. This results in a general move-up on the part of the lower classes" (Puddester 1944; *ENL* Puddester).

For governments opposed to the idea of building new, subsidized housing for low-income households, a reliance on "filtering" was an ideal way to solve an otherwise intractable problem. Governor Sir Humphrey Walwyn disagreed. He argued that the proposed program, if it worked at all, "will do little to benefit the slum dweller for many years ... as houses are vacated in St. John's by those people moving out to the 'garden city' ... that the slum dwellers will move up to, say, Circular Road and Military Road houses. This I do not agree with, as the latter houses are far beyond their standard and whatever type of house they moved to would become foul and verminous in another few months" (Walwyn 1944h).

The Council's request to the Commission of Government for help in solving a housing crisis was not unusual. Well-known success stories from other jurisdictions told of the provision of houses for the workingman by government and charitable organizations. In England, the Liverpool Corporation (Dockerill 2016) and the Peabody Trust, London, had been building homes for the poor since the 1860s (Pooley and Irish 1993; Peabody Trust). Norway, Sweden, Denmark, France, and Germany all had help from the government to alleviate the housing shortage for workingmen after the devastation of World War I (Sharpe and Shawyer 2016, 57). The Canadian government had supported the Halifax Relief Commission after the Halifax Explosion in 1917 destroyed 1,650 houses. It had sponsored a Soldier Settlement scheme after World War I (Legislation [Canada] 1919). More recently, the Dominion Housing Act (Legislation 1935) and the National Housing Act (Legislation 1938) were designed to stimulate the construction of new owner-occupied houses by private-sector builders through the provision of mortgages (Hulchanski 1986, 19–39).

Newfoundland, too, had planned housing schemes for the less fortunate. The Newfoundland Royal Commission, which investigated Newfoundland's financial woes in 1933, included reference to the TPC's tentative scheme in 1931 to remove 1,000 families from central St. John's to new, planned settlements beyond the city limits. This plan was not followed through for lack of funds (Amulree Commission, paragraph 615). The Commission itself had recommended returning unemployed men in St. John's to their outport homes (Amulree Commission, paragraph 616).

The Commission of Government had echoed these recommendations by initiating its land settlement scheme in 1934, which placed poor people from the towns on blocks of agricultural land with the hope that they would take up farming (Handcock 1994). The new Cooperative Division of the Commission of Government had imitated a Nova Scotian cooperative house program as recently as 1938. This was another plan to place families on farm acreages to see whether "the expenditure on able-bodied relief could be co-ordinated with reconstructive effort" (Sharpe and Shawyer 2016, 86–119). Unfortunately, both of these plans were meeting with less than hoped-for success.

Even in the best of circumstances the commissioners might have been reluctant to accept Meaney's proposal because of their disappointing experience with their own reconstruction projects elsewhere in Newfoundland. But external events now made it impossible. Within a month, before there could be any further discussion of the housing situation, Newfoundland was at war and the government had to begin dealing with other pressing matters. It would be almost two years before the housing question came back on the agenda.

5

WAR AND MODERNITY COME TO ST. JOHN'S

> By the end of 1940, even before the influx of the Americans, St. John's had undergone quick and unanticipated change. "We have become a fortress," said the *Evening Telegram*. Not only Canadians, but the Militia, sailors from the Royal Navy and merchant marine, foreign sailors, construction workers from outside the capital, military police, and officials of various stripes coming and going had turned the quiet old city into a noisy, crowded garrison town. (O'Flaherty 2011, 65)

World War II, 1939-45

The events of World War II overwhelmed St. John's Municipal Council. The strategic advantages of Newfoundland — its location, which brought the eastern edge of North America far out into the Atlantic, and its active iron ore mines on Bell Island, familiar to German industrialists — brought the war to its doorstep.

The war came to St. John's in a hurry. On 1 September 1939 the government passed the Act for the Defence of Newfoundland, giving it the power to make war regulations (Legislation 1939a); on 3 September Newfoundland declared war; on 5 September a recruiting office was opened for volunteers to serve with the British Army, Navy, and Air Force, and in October the government created the Newfoundland Militia for Home Defence (Legislation 1939b).

During the next five years, a military landscape was imposed on St. John's (Sharpe and Shawyer 2010, 21–80). Residents lived and worked within a fenced network of "no-go" areas. The Canadian Army camp was established in Lester's Field on Blackmarsh Road, and the Canadians also installed gun batteries at Chain Rock, Hill O' Chips, George Street, Cape Spear, and Calver's Field on Newtown Road. They built a detention camp at Rennie's Mill, and their headquarters in Bannerman Park. The Americans settled at their newly built Fort Pepperrell on the north side of Quidi Vidi Lake with additional camps on Signal Hill and the White Hills. They built a huge dock at the east end of the harbour, below the Battery. The Canadian Air Force built Torbay airport and also barracks on Kenna's Hill. The Canadian Navy established a barracks complex (HMCS Avalon) on McLea's ground north of LeMarchant Road (Buckmaster's Field), and operated the numerous structures on both the north and south sides of the harbour that

Figure 5.1. HMC Dockyard at the harbour's edge and HMCS Avalon Naval Barracks beyond in Buckmaster's Field, St. John's, 1942 (RE 93-2412, Minister of Works and Services).

Figure 5.2. The Light Anti-Aircraft Battery on Hill O' Chips, St. John's (TRPAD VA 147-422).

made up HM Canadian Dockyard. Many other ancillary buildings were scattered throughout town, including recreational facilities and clubs, storage buildings, and shooting ranges at the Sand Pitts near Long Pond and on the South Side hills (Neary 1988, 144–82).

The Municipal Council Copes with the "Friendly Invasion"

The Municipal Council was besieged by all these wartime activities. Water, sewerage, roads, employment, and accommodation were all affected. The Council benefited from the fact that some of the water and sewer infrastructure required by the various military establishments was provided by the Canadian and American military at their own expense, thereby extending the city's serviced area at no immediate cost to the Council. But on the whole it was a difficult time for the city.

The transient nature of military postings makes it impossible to give an exact count of the number of military personnel who occupied St. John's on any given day. However, it is likely that on some days in 1943–44 as many as 11,000 Canadians and 5,500 Americans were added to the city's population of 40,000 (Sharpe 2018). Although the majority of these personnel, especially the Americans, lived in the various military establishments, some, often accompanied by wives and family, lived off-base, putting additional pressure on an already overcrowded situation: "there are many cases on record where in a single house of seven rooms no less than four families are living and sharing the single bathroom." The Tourist Bureau turned itself into a housing bureau and by October 1943 had placed more than 5,000 people in rooms or flats (*Evening Telegram* 1943g).

Significant numbers of people migrated into the city from the outports seeking work on the Canadian and American bases (Sharpe and Shawyer 2010, 72). The pressure on accommodation forced the Newfoundland government to impose rent controls (Fraser, Neary, and Baker, 2010: 128–29). So many people had come to the city, so many houses were being converted into boarding houses and rooming houses, and so many new military hostels and recreation facilities were being built that water and sewer facilities and ash and garbage collections were strained beyond capacity (SJCM 17 Apr. 1942, 131).

There was a sudden rise in the requests for permits for cafés and tea-rooms, a blessing for those whose accommodation did not include access to a kitchen. The unemployment queues vanished; there were jobs for everyone. But prices rose as materials were prioritized for the war effort. Commercial goods competed with military materials for shipping space to Newfoundland. Streets and roads suffered from heavy military equipment moving around town. The Council, faced with the cost of street repairs, complained constantly and bitterly to the military authorities. Municipal

Evening Telegram 21 October 1943, page 3

Families Living in One Room Owing to Lack of Houses

Overcrowding of City May Have Bad Effect On Health of Community

Never before in the long history of St. John's has the housing situation been so acute and it has reached the stage now where families are living in one room which is hardly conducive to the health of the community as a whole.

Last month the Food Controller issued some startling figures relative to the number of ration-book holders living in St. John's and that total was then 81,934, an increase of 30,000 in pre-war St. John's. Ever since then more people have come to the city seeking shelter and a few have left it.

The Newfoundland Tourist Bureau has been trying to cope with the unprecedented situation by acting as a home bureau and since the first servicemen and their families came here have placed over 5,800 in rooms, flats and houses. At present 71 applications are on the Bureau's books awaiting accommodation. But many others who have not applied to the Bureau are also looking for "some place to go."

The Food Controller informs The Telegram that 2300 ration books have been issued to servicemen not housed in barracks and hutments, or in other words boarding or living in houses in St. John's. Most of these men have brought their wives here and thereby helped in putting a premium on houses and rooms, etc.

SLEEPS IN AUTO

The question of finding adequate lodging for everyone is of national importance and should be the concern of the Government, the Municipality and the citizens generally. One man is reported to be sleeping in his automobile while there are many cases on record where in a single house of seven rooms no less than four families are living (each in one room) and sharing the single bathroom.

RENTS EXTREMELY HIGH

If there were adequate inspection of the homes offered to servicemen and civilians many people would not be allowed to rent their rooms. In answer to their advertisements for flats or house-keeping rooms some navy wives, for example, have been offered a bedroom with iron bedstead and straw mattress and one chair, also use of a kitchen and a toilet without bath, all for $45 a month! Then there are other would-be hotel keepers liberally offering a couple of rooms partly furnished for $75 a month.

Figure 5.3. "Families Living in One Room Owing to Lack of Houses" (*Evening Telegram* 21 Oct. 1943).

fire and police personnel were burdened with more responsibility even though the military provided some of their own men for these services. Many dwellings and commercial businesses were expropriated to make way for the activities of war: farms on the north shore of Quidi Vidi Lake gave way to the American base; dozens of commercial enterprises located on Water Street were forced to relocate to make way for naval activity at the harbour; and the fishing community in the Battery was severely compromised by the construction of the American dry dock. All this, and blackouts too (Sharpe and Shawyer 2010, 21–80; Sharpe and Shawyer 2012).

In the midst of this upheaval, St. John's Municipal Council still had to cope with its daily rhythm of running the town and to look to the future by creating some kind of plan for the city (Neary 1994, 179–93; Neary 1988, 183–213).

The War Opens a Window on the World

The invasion of Newfoundland by Canadian and American service personnel had a profound impact on the city's landscape. Equally important was the effect on Newfoundlanders' view of their country. Compared to the places from which many of the military personnel had come, St. John's was a primitive place, and some of the visitors clearly made that observation known. (Neary 1995). In the spring of 1943 the American vice-consul wrote that "practically the entire population is living in substandard housing conditions.... Only a nucleus of merchants, professional persons and civil servants maintain a standard of living comparable to that of an average community in the United States" (Mackenzie 1992, 68–69). Once made aware of the differences in living conditions between Newfoundland and the United States, "The people of Newfoundland could never go back to what they had been" (Neary and O'Flaherty 1983, 153).

The war brought a cultural shift of focus to the country. In 1939 Newfoundland's institutions, educational system, and cultural paradigms were an amalgam of British and Irish traditions. Newfoundlanders were still Eu-

> # 733 City Homes Are Without Sewerage And Water Facilities
>
> *City Engineer Reports 281 Houses Are Unfit For Installations; 14 Streets Lack Water And Sewer Connections*

Figure 5.4. "733 Homes Are Without Sewerage and Water Facilities" (*Evening Telegram* 14 Dec. 1945).

ropeans. The North American servicemen arrived to a small, impoverished, disenchanted country that was "suddenly turned into a classroom in which Newfoundlanders began to learn about the world to the west of them, a world upon which they had traditionally turned their backs." The foreigners, especially the Americans, "inspired a vision of a better, sunnier, happier life" (Jackson 1986, 70).

Governor Walwyn tersely remarked that Newfoundlanders were "dazzled by American dollars, hygiene, and efficiency" (Neary 1994, 182). Ed Roberts, a future member of the provincial cabinet and later the lieutenant-governor, summarized the overall impact of the wartime meeting of Newfoundland and "mainland" cultures:

> The war brought prosperity, a happy condition unknown to Newfoundlanders for twenty years. . . . A rising tide of expectations, of demands for a better life, swept across the country. Most importantly, the war restored self-confidence. A country and a people who had known nothing but adversity, and who had forfeited their self-government as the penalty for bankruptcy, regained their pride and determination. (Roberts 1967, 102)

The newly acquired Newfoundland reverence for the modernity of life on the mainland had a significant influence on the development of Churchill Park. Among a certain portion of the population, there was a strong desire to replace their overcrowded and worn city with one filled with symbols of a new-found confidence and prosperity. They felt a need to prove that Newfoundlanders were just as capable, just as urbane, as anybody else in North America. These convictions provided the confidence to create a new cultural landscape — the North American-style suburb that would become Churchill Park.

The Municipal Council and Town Planning

The discussions with town planners Dalzell and Todd and the work of the TPC had all helped to move the Council forward in the practice of town planning. The One Mile Area had been instituted in the 1921 Act (s. 90) and the city was given "the power to regulate," but no Council had given voice to that power until 1936. At that time, with an eye to the escalating number of occupant-built houses in the unserviced One Mile Area, Carnell's Council laid out regulations "respecting the opening of streets and erection of buildings" (SJCM 6 Aug. 1936, 209-11; Legislation 1937, s. 19[4]). Another item, one from Gosling's Charter, was the advice to create a Municipal Arrears Commission to take control of the collection of arrears of taxes. This was enacted in the amendments to the Municipal Act in 1937 (Legislation 1937, s. 242).

The concept of zoning, introduced in the 1937 Act (s. 19), was also new. This section gave Council the power to make bylaws "to prohibit the use of land or the erection or use of buildings within any defined area." St. John's had long had defined fire zones in which it was not lawful to erect any wooden structures. But the Council had been slow to apply the zoning concept more widely to define different kinds of land use or to protect property values.

Towards the end of the 1930s, the Depression had eased a little, and with the advent of wartime prosperity the number of residential building permits began to rise dramatically. Though residents of the city had never been afraid of airing their complaints to Council about any number of concerns — impassable streets, lack of sanitary collection, clogged catch basins, filthy stables, dangerous chimneys, drainage problems — now, proud new property owners were anxious to secure the value of their property against potentially negative intrusions. As the number of new dwellings began to increase, so did the complaints. For example, several residents of Deanery Avenue successfully protested against a neighbour's application for a poultry house (SJCM 27 Apr. 1939, 429). Residents who had erected $28,000 homes near Glenridge Crescent on Robinson's Hill were dismayed when a local landowner sold small building lots nearby on Portugal Cove Road on which, they claimed, "shacks" were being erected. The landowners attended a Council meeting to complain (SJCM 9 Nov. 1942, 341).

Table 5.1. Building Permits, 1939, 1941, 1943.		
Building Permits Issued	Within City Limits	Within One Mile Area*
1939	42	11
1941	78	16
1943	156	80

*These numbers do not record the hundreds of houses built without building permits. Council made decisions on each of these cases, but they were single decisions, each pertinent to a particular building or site. The Council found it difficult to see past the individual complaints in order to consider the broader concept of zoning an area.
Source: Engineer's Annual Report: Building Permits, Minutes of St. John's City Council, CSJA RG 01-02, Building Application Series 1911–1986.

In 1942, when discussing a dispute on Golf Avenue, the frustrated city solicitor took the opportunity to make some reflections to Council about zoning: "This little matter reminds me to remind the Council again that by neglecting to make use of the zoning powers which it acquired in the 1937 Act (s. 19), it is still in the same helpless position as before: that is, it cannot refuse to grant a permit for the erection of a shop plumb between two dwellings." He went on to say that if "a street has not been zoned as a residential area, the owner of the land there is entitled by law to a building permit *providing the building complies with the building regulations.* The town, especially where there is vacant land, *should be zoned for the class of building to which it is suited* — commercial, manufacturing, residential, etc. It is a big job but it's the only way for the Council to get hold of any effective control over building sites before it's too late" (SJCM 26 May 1942, 160; emphasis added). No action was taken by the Council on this issue.

During the 1930s the St. John's Municipal Council had been trying to regulate standards for the trades by implementing licences for the tradesmen. They drafted codes for plumbing and electrical and wiring, as well as a building code. They had been tracking projects to make sure that all the plans and specifications listed in the building permit were being properly followed during construction. Now, during the war, they took advantage of the presence of American, Canadian, and UK military to consult them about "best practices" in all these matters as they applied their codes.

The Municipal Council Pursues Councillor Meaney's Proposal

A year after Meaney's proposal on housing was sent to the Commission of Government, Councillor James Spratt (*ENL* Spratt) noted that the Commission had not yet responded. After a second year went by without any word from the Commission, Council decided to take action. Perhaps the councillors were emboldened by Archbishop Edward Roche's recent pastoral letter, in which he said:

> The houses in some of the congested sections of the city are small, overcrowded, ill-lighted, ill-ventilated, and generally

> unsuitable for habitation. . . . while it [this situation] is unsolved we are paying a heavy toll in disease, ill health, and misery among our people. (*Daily News* 1941a)

In any event, on 6 March 1941, Council unanimously resolved:

> that we again approach the Government on the subject and request early decisions thereon, that this Council may be enabled to meet its responsibility in the matter of promoting and aiding some scheme for providing decent, cheap and healthful housing for those unable to provide such housing for themselves without financial aid, and contribute to the fullest possible extent towards the elimination of slum areas and the blighted sections now existing in our city. (SJCM 6 Mar. 1941, 340)

Council also decided that the Commission of Government would be asked to consider the matter as quickly as possible (Mahoney 1941). This time the Commission did reply, bluntly rejecting the proposal.

The government's principal rationale in rejecting the Council's resolution was that "what lies at the bottom of the problem of housing in the City is *the existence of a distressingly large number of families living in permanent poverty.*" The commissioners made the same link between income and housing conditions as Mayor Carnell had made several years before, "that the present deplorable condition of many of our citizens and the prevalence of disease and increase of mortality was due not to housing conditions but to malnutrition *and to the fact that family wage-earners are given no opportunity to earn a living*" (SJCM 28 Feb. 1935, 361; emphasis added).

In the UK, some segments of the poorest population were provided for by the government and/or charitable institutions. Although not perfect, their intervention in the housing market was backed by relatively robust financial backing and administered with tight control over the level of income and "suitability" of the residents. In Newfoundland the proportion of the permanently poor was so large and the financial resources of the government so limited that it was impossible to emulate the British example. Gosling, Cook, Dalzell, Todd, Carnell, and Meaney had all recognized this, and it is no surprise that the experienced commissioners did so as well. The permanent poor were trapped in a vicious cycle of intermittent work and low wages, the result of an economy too dependent on the production and export of commodities subject to the vagaries of the world economy. As Public Utilities Commissioner W.W. Woods explained in a memorandum to the city clerk in 1941, the Commission declined to participate in any housing scheme:

> unless it can reasonably be expected to achieve its object without involving the Government or the City in financial commitments beyond their resources. In our view the ultimate object of any scheme which would merit support by the Government and the City should be to provide accommodation to which those occupying the worst houses in the City could be transferred. . . . *It might be possible to build new houses for existing householders who are above the line of extreme poverty, the houses vacated by them being used to replace the houses unfit for further use.* (Woods 1941; emphasis added)

In other words, because new houses would have to be paid for by the people who live in them, they would have to be built for those above the poverty line. The Gosling houses in Quidi Vidi, Anderson's project on Merrymeeting Road, and the railway houses had all been built with this in mind. But what about households that fell below the line?

Commissioners Woods, Penson, and Puddester accepted the idea that if new houses were built for a class of worker that could afford them, the very poor would then be able to take over the accommodations vacated by the occupants of the new houses. This process, referred to as the "move-up principle" by the three commissioners and also by Supreme Court Justice Brian Dunfield, who would soon become the driving force behind the Churchill Park project, formed the basis of housing policy in North America for several decades after it was adopted by housing policy-makers, who called it "filtering" (Ratcliff 1945; Grigsby 1963; Altshuler 1969; Lansing, Clifton, and Morgan 1969). Filtering theory proposed that by adding a new house to the stock, a family would "move up" from their house into the new one, and thus create a vacancy for someone else to move up into the house they had vacated. This would create a "vacancy chain," incorporating houses of successively lower quality. This theory assumed that those who lived in the least expensive and poorest-quality dwellings in town would be willing (and able) to risk "moving up" to "better" accommodation, which might not be of much higher quality than what they were leaving, but at least somewhat better. Their former dwelling could then be demolished. Unfortunately, this idea worked better in theory than in practice. Many vacancy chains were broken before poorer households could benefit, either because the vacancy was taken up by a newly formed family that had not previously occupied a dwelling in the city, or by a household moving in from outside the city. In neither case would an existing household in the town be able to participate in the chain (Sharpe 1978).

Proponents of the theory argued that in the end everybody who participated in the vacancy chain would be better off. Woods accepted the basic concept, but questioned the basic assumption because while "wage earners who could pay rents of $16 to $33 a month might be found to take the new houses which would be built under the scheme ... they would vacate houses commanding in the open market rents far above those which the occupants of the houses to be demolished could afford to pay."

However, for better or worse, the concept of "filtering" now became a principal argument in support of the idea that building houses in a new suburb in the valley north of the town would help to provide better housing for the poor.

Finally, at the same time as the Commission rejected the Meaney proposal, it suggested that Council ask the large employers to gather data on the housing conditions of their employees. The idea was that the information might form the basis for a cooperative plan involving employees, employers, the city, and the government, in order to develop small but useful housing schemes for the lowest-paid workers.

This modest proposal was to have unimagined consequences. It was the key to the development of Churchill Park.

6

"A HUMILIATING CATALOGUE OF FACTS"

> We have here in St. John's probably the most backward town on the east coast of North America. . . . We have no master plan to guide the development of our city and suburbs . . . we have no building code . . . . and I do not suppose there is any city our size in North America where anybody can build anything as he likes and almost wherever he likes without any sort of guidance or control. In other words, we are still, to all intents and purposes, running our city like a fishing village. (Brian Dunfield in *Daily News* 1943e)

In the election of December 1941, Andrew Carnell was returned as mayor along with Councillors James J. Spratt, who was involved in the construction trade and had an interest in unions (*ENL* Spratt), John P. Kelly, store manager, and journalist John T. Meaney (*ENL* Meaney). New members were Oliver Vardy, a former journalist who had been involved in radio broadcasting, editing, and advertising (*ENL* Vardy), Edward Lawrence, a business owner, and Eric Cook, the deputy mayor and son of former Mayor Tasker Cook (*ENL* Cook). These men would initiate a titanic upheaval in the city's housing market.

Tasker Cook had been a consistent opponent of housing reform, at least in part because he was determined not to add to the city's debt. But his son proved to be of a different persuasion. Eric Cook's personal agenda was to find a way to improve the conditions for those living in the dilapidated houses downtown (Parker 1999).

The Commission of Enquiry on Housing and Town Planning

When the members of Council assembled for their regular meeting on 19 February 1942, while the war raged on, Deputy Mayor Cook argued that the post-war housing survey for which the Council had allocated $2,500 should be undertaken immediately. The motion, seconded by Councillor Vardy, received unanimous approval. Council then gave Cook permission to convene a meeting of representatives of the most important groups in the community to discuss the housing problem and to seek possible solutions for it (SJCM 19 Feb. 1942, 55). Cook, Spratt, and Meaney were authorized to create an invitation list including representatives from a wide range of civic interests (*Evening Telegram* 1942a). The list was approved by a unanimous vote of Council on 5 March 1942 (SJCM 5 Mar. 1942, 66).

Those who agreed to serve on what would become the Commission of Enquiry on Housing and Town Planning in St. John's (CEHTP) were: Rev. E.C. Knowles, United Church Conference; Brigadier Joseph Acton, Salvation Army; Eric Jerrett, Church of England; James V. Ryan, Railway Employees Welfare Association; William F. Breen, St. John's Longshoremen's Protective Union; Cyril F. Horwood, St. John's Rotary Club; Dr. Leonard Miller, Child Welfare Association; Francis M. O'Leary, Newfoundland Board of Trade; Gordon F. Higgins, Irish Benevolent Society; and William J. Frampton, Newfoundland Federation of Labour. Allan M. Fraser, professor of economics and history at Memorial University College, was later co-opted to the group (CEHTP 1, 9). Reverend Knowles resigned in March 1943 when he left the country and the United Church nominated architect Thomas A. Lench as his replacement.

The Commission of Government approved the creation of the CEHTP on 17 April 1942 under section 92 of the 1921 Act (Town Planning Commission) on the understanding that the government would not be involved in the operations of the CEHTP, and that its report would belong to the city (Carnell 1942).

The CEHTP had two goals:

(1) to investigate the state of housing in the city so that the Council could develop a plan to build houses for those who were unable to buy a house for themselves;

(2) to consider the general replanning of the city.

Cook continued to drive the enquiry process along. He knew that the Housing Commission would need a strong person to take the lead, someone with a certain gravitas and eloquence, who would be able to persuade the Commission of Government to accept the CEHTP's recommendations, based on the proposed survey of households. He convinced Mayor Carnell to recommend Mr. Justice Brian Dunfield of the Newfoundland Supreme Court as the right man for the job. Cook was named vice-chair.

Introducing Brian Dunfield

Brian Edward Spencer Dunfield was the son of an Anglican minister. He had a degree in Economics from London University, had read law with Sir Edward Morris, and was called to the bar in Newfoundland in 1913. In 1923, after some years in private practice, he joined Hawes and Company Limited (London), a brokerage firm specializing in salt fish for Newfoundland exporters (*ENL* Hawes and Company; Smallwood 1937c). He returned to the practice of law in 1925 and two years later joined the Department of Justice. Dunfield's great interest in urban reform led to his appointment in 1930 to the St. John's Town Planning Commission under the chairmanship of Justice Kent (*ENL* Dunfield).

Dunfield was a man with an "insatiable interest in everything." He was considered to be "very clever and intelligent," and had "one of the finest legal minds Newfoundland ever produced" (Winter 1998). Disliked by some, he was held in high regard by others. Some of his peers characterized him as "tactless" and "liable to blow off steam" (Bartlett 1999; Cook 1982; Clutterbuck 1938), but one of them said that "he speaks without any self-seeking motive and with a wide social concern" (Paton 1938). He was

Figure 6.1. Justice Brian Edward Spenser Dunfield, chairman of the Commission of Enquiry on Housing and Town Planning in St. John's (1942–44); chairman of the St. John's Housing Corporation (1944–49) (Sir Brian Dunfield Papers, Archives and Manuscripts Division, Queen Elizabeth Library, Memorial University of Newfoundland).

known to say that he made his decisions before leaving the bench, and then found the law to support it. Perhaps this was the reason he complained that his judicial duties were insufficient to occupy his afternoons (Winter 1998). Eric Cook offered him the chance to fill that gap.

He seems to have been a person who, when animated by a cause, followed it relentlessly, without giving due consideration for the opinion of others, no matter who they were (Mahoney 2001). His status in St. John's society permitted him to say publicly what many others might have thought privately, and he was never hesitant to speak his mind. One of his favourite audiences was the Rotary Club, which met in the Newfoundland Hotel. Radio station VOCM had its studio in the hotel and broadcast the Rotary meetings. By speaking here, Dunfield was able to address not only some of the most influential men in town, but the rest of the country as well.

On 20 May 1942 Chairman Dunfield presided over the first meeting of the CEHTP (see Appendix 1). In his eloquent opening address he said:

> If, as a body representing the public, we can evolve a sound working scheme for improving the housing situation, a scheme which the Municipal Council and the government can see their way through to adopt and put into operation, we shall render the greatest service to the community it is possible to imagine. (*Evening Telegram* 1942b)

Dunfield's talking points were urban reform in general and housing reform in particular. He was blunt when he described the current situation:

> Nothing has a greater effect upon the health and general social condition than the housing standard. It must be admitted in this respect we fall very short indeed . . . in our town . . . even substantial houses . . . too often present an appearance of dilapidation and disorder, more appropriate to a temporary mining town than to a capital. (*Evening Telegram* 1942b)

Dunfield's imagination soared as he contemplated an experiment that would bring Modernism to the planning of St. John's (Shawyer and Sharpe 2005). He conceived an urban landscape that was very different from the familiar Newfoundland streetscapes dominated by ranges of tall three-storey houses, windowless on the side walls, built flush to the edge of the sidewalk. His goal was to create:

> a class of surroundings which have not yet been seen in St. John's, by emulating the modern Canadian and American suburb where houses are set well apart along streets lined on both sides with a broad strip of lawn which the tenants and owners take pride in keeping trim and neat because children, like cows, ought to be on grass and under trees, not on sidewalks. (*Daily News* 1945b)

It sounded like an image from an American movie.

Dunfield firmly believed that the new Housing Commission would be able to come to grips with the long-standing problem of inner-city housing deterioration. The tool by which this would be effected was "filtering," which, as we have seen, was the leading-edge theory widely embraced by members of the Commission of Government and Frederick Todd, among other housing experts, as the "best practice" of the day. He announced that he planned to build as many as 1,000 houses in order to relieve the "terrific pressure on the City . . . so that the worst of the slum houses would begin to fall vacant and could be demolished" (*Evening Telegram* 1942b). He accepted the fact that the rise in land prices that would result from the clearances would necessitate that the new houses be built outside the town boundary. But he saw the potential advantage of this. Dunfield was a proud, intelligent, and well-educated Newfoundlander who was well aware of the need to restore people's self-esteem after enduring years of the Depression and the withering criticism of their living standards by foreign journalists and politicians, and now, by Canadian and American military personnel. He appears to have taken on the project of changing the urban face of St. John's as a personal crusade. On one occasion he reminded the Rotarians that:

We are the North American community which collapsed and threw its hand in, and that is a disgrace to us all.... Just think how nice it would be if it could go forth to the world in a year or two that down in Newfoundland they were reconstructing their capital in a more thorough and wholesale way than had ever been done anywhere else. Why should we not be leaders? Let us get together and try.... Once building prices become reasonable [i.e., after the war is over], we can give a man a first-rate little house for no more than he is paying for rent today. (*Evening Telegram* 1943d)

The Six Reports of the CEHTP

Between November 1942 and August 1944 the CEHTP issued six interim reports. Dunfield drafted almost all of them himself, although he reported that "all material was read, discussed and amended in Committee, twice in typescript and twice in proof print, with intervals between readings, before being signed by the members" (Dunfield 1944a). But most members of the Commission had very little input to the reports (Cook 1982; Winter 1998). One of the members said that if the Commission had consisted only of Dunfield and 10 Newfoundland dogs, the reports would have been the same (Miller 1981). The reports are a delight to read. Dunfield insisted that all the reports had to be written in "popular form" with "numbered chapters and paragraphs" and in a "more colloquial style than is usual in official reports" to ensure that "it be understood by every citizen, down to the humblest" so that "the people should get more while the expert or official reader need not get less" (CEHTP 3, 9). Dunfield's vigorous public speeches, most of which were reprinted in one or both of the local newspapers, made him the public face of the Housing Commission.

First Report: Describing the Twin Objectives of the CEHTP

The principal object of the Commission was bold: "to recommend a scheme for the rehousing of a proportion and ultimately the whole of the poor and

NEWFOUNDLAND GOVERNMENT

COMMISSION OF ENQUIRY ON HOUSING AND TOWN PLANNING IN ST. JOHN'S

Appointed on May 12th, 1942, under the Public Enquiries Act 1934.

First Interim Report. November, 1942
  City Architect; Building Regulations, etc.

Second Interim Report. February, 1943
  King's Bridge Road Junction.

Third Interim Report. June 3rd, 1943
  General Review of Housing Conditions;
  Outline of Proposals for Remedies.
          (Printed in separate pamphlet of 130 pages)

Fourth Interim Report. October, 1943
  Temporary Regulations to secure width of future streets, etc.

Fifth Interim Report. January, 1944
  Detailed Proposals and Provisional Estimates for Suburban Extension and Housing.

The Evening Telegram
St. John's.

Figure 6.2. The cover of the consolidated edition of CEHTP Reports 1–5, 1942–44.

the low-income classes, and for the replanning of the city" (CEHTP 1, 4). Unfortunately, in the euphoria of the moment, the Commission boasted that it would take on a task it was unable to complete.

There were two possible strategies. One was to clear out the housing areas of the central city and then either rebuild the houses there or convert the area into open space. The other strategy was to redistribute the central-city population to new suburban areas. The sheer scale and ambition of the proposal were astonishing, and promised much more than could possibly be accomplished all at once, particularly for a nation at war.

The report recommended that the city immediately enact its draft building code and hire a city architect who would take over from the medical officer the responsibility of condemning insanitary buildings. It is easy to interpret this first report as a condemnation of the Council's past failures to improve the standard of housing in the city. The Newfoundland government, the Municipal Council, and the residents of St. John's had lived for a long time with the hope of "something being done" about the poor housing in town. But some of the councillors felt uneasy about the nature and scale of the proposed project and argued that a commitment of this scale couldn't be justified under current circumstances. Councillor Meaney was quite taken aback. This proposal was so far beyond his own more modest proposal for 500 houses. The negative reactions of individual councillors foreshadowed the criticism that the Council as a whole would later make of the proposed scheme (SJCM 7 Dec. 1942, 361; 10 Dec. 1942, 363). Even at this early stage of the project the mayor had to use his casting vote twice during the Council's debate to ensure the reluctant passage of the recommendations of the first report.

Second Report: Proposing a New Circumferential Road North of the City

This one-page report addressed a matter of practical urban planning. American and Canadian military officials had agreed to subsidize the widening and improvement of King's Bridge Road. This road was the principal approach to both the American Fort Pepperrell at Quidi Vidi and the Canadian air base at

Torbay, and the heavy traffic was causing serious damage to a road that had not been designed with this in mind. Taking advantage of this improved access to the area north of Empire Avenue that the repairs would make possible, the report proposed the construction of an "outer circumferential road" to cut across the fields and a jumble of country lanes, to create a direct east–west link between Torbay Road and Freshwater Road (CEHTP 2, 11 [page reference to consolidated edition of Reports 1–5]). The new road, which would become Elizabeth Avenue, was intended to be the spine of a new housing area to be built north of Empire Avenue in the Freshwater Valley. The commemorative plaque on the east end of King's Bridge, which crosses Rennie's River, reads: "King's Bridge constructed by the City of St. John's, Newfoundland Government, Canada, United States Army. Contractors McNamara Construction Co Ltd., Toronto, Canada. Designed by J.W. Beretta Engineer Inc., San Antonio, Texas, September, 1943."

Third Report: General Review of Housing Conditions and an Outline of Proposals for Remedies

At 130 pages, this was the longest of the Commission reports. As the title suggests, the report had two parts. The first contained an analysis of the data collected at the government's suggestion the previous year. The questionnaires were distributed throughout the city by four students from Memorial University College. Completed questionnaires were returned by 5,700 families who lived in 4,613 houses, just over 70 per cent of all the houses in the city. Residents were asked where they lived, whether the dwelling was owned or rented, family composition, income, employer, and presence of water, sewer, and bathroom. They were also asked whether they would like to move to "the suburbs," but only a quarter of those in the inner city showed any interest in that suggestion (CSJA RG 08-109; see Appendix 2).

The results of the survey, which classified housing into six categories, present a dramatic picture of the problems faced by the city (see Table 6.1):

Class A (Excellent) and Class B (Good) and Class C (Fair) "enjoy modern conveniences in full." Residents are generally in secure employment: shop and office workers, craftsmen dominate.

Class D "tolerable but poor, ought to be replaced." Some shop and office workers but labourers and longshoremen dominate.

Class E "Bad, should be condemned at an early date." Labourers and longshoremen dominate but there are some craftsmen.

Class F "Very bad, condemned or should be condemned immediately." Labourers and longshoremen.

Table 6.1. Housing Conditions, St. John's, 1943						
Class	No. of Houses	Water and Sewer*	Owners	Tenants	Occupants	Persons/ Bedroom
A	260	260	214	57	1,392	n/a
B	736	736	561	239	4,199	n/a
C	1,867	1,866	1,277	968	2,329	1.92
D	1,000	928	569	723	7,392	2.16
E	525	230	278	446	4,057	2.32
F	225	48	49	332	2,130	2.63
Total	4,613	4,068	2,948	2,765	21,499	

*Number of houses with a piped water supply and sewer connection.
Source: Adapted from CEHTP 3.

Among the findings of this report were the following:

- In total there were 900 houses (19 per cent) without sewer connections.
- Classes A, B, and C had an average of 6.6 persons per house.
- Class F had an average of 9.4 persons per house. Only one house in class F had a bath and only 21 per cent had water and sewer connections.
- Just over 60 per cent of the houses in classes C through F had no bath although "housing without a bathroom is not civilized housing" (CEHTP 3, 22).
- Many of the class F houses were overcrowded. The overall average was 1.621 persons per room and 2.63 per bedroom. These were compared with the London City Council's (United Kingdom) maximum permitted density of 1.25 persons per room (CEHTP 3: 12).
- The 1921 St. John's Municipal Act (s. 355) stipulated that a house should have a living room of not less than 132 square feet, one bedroom not less than 128 square feet, and no other room less than 70 square feet. The charitable Peabody Trust in London describes one of its housing projects, built in Bethnal Green in 1910, as having a living room of 156 square feet and bedrooms of 117 square feet (www.peabody.org.uk; Wagg and McHugh 2017).
- From classes A to F, the proportion of owner-residents decreased and the proportion of tenants increased. Of the houses in classes A, B, C combined, 68.3 per cent were owned by residents of those houses. In class F, only 21.7 per cent houses were owned.
- Almost all the houses in the inner city were in classes D, E, and F. To put it simply, in that part of town, there were too many tenanted houses lived in by too many occupants with too few sanitary conveniences.

Figure 6.3. 1–3 Joy Place, 5 May 1947. A year later the house was scheduled for demolition but a family was still living there, awaiting rehousing (CSJA 11-01-103).

Figure 6.4. Wickford Street, looking east towards St. Andrew's Church, 1950s (CSJA 11-02-016)

Figure 6.5. Number 38 Lime Street, a "cellar" house, awaiting demolition, 1950s (CSJA 11-02-052).

The third report included "A Social Worker's Picture" with examples of some of the worst situations (CEHTP 3, 30):

> A family of eleven were evicted from their home, a three-room flat without sanitation. They were given shelter by a

relative in a four-roomed bungalow, also without sanitation. The combined families numbered sixteen. The children of the evicted family sickened with enteritis and two of them died.

A family lived in a basement. The back of the house was rotten and snow was piled on the bedroom floor. The large double bed was removed to the kitchen. The family of six, including a three months infant, slept in this bed.

A young couple had one child. Although healthy from birth and a strong child, it contracted enteritis [gastrointestinal disease] and died. An infant, shortly afterwards was attacked by a rat while sleeping in its cot and had to be taken to hospital for treatment.

The "Housing and Health" section highlighted the dire consequences of insufficient sunlight, poor ventilation, dampness and cold, impure or inadequate water supply, and absence of sanitary facilities. Another section was graphically described as "The Slaughter of the Innocents." It noted that the five-year average infant mortality in Newfoundland was 96 per 1,000 live births compared to 65 in Canada and 59 in the UK. The five-year average mortality from tuberculosis, that great killer so familiar in Newfoundland, was 145.6 per 100,000 in Newfoundland compared to 61 in Canada and 70 in the UK.

The Public's Reaction to the Report: "A Humiliating Catalogue of Facts"

The third interim report was generally well received. The governor commended Dunfield for "doing a splendid job with your committee" (Walwyn 1943). Public opinion was also supportive. The bleak statistics gathered from the questionnaires seem to have brought the despair of those living in the "dilapidated houses" downtown into sharp focus for residents who were unaware of the misery in their midst. The report was described as "a humiliating catalogue of facts" by one local newspaper, which added, "we must accept the indictment that we have tolerated in our midst conditions that are a disgrace to our personal and civic pride and to our human instincts" (*Daily News* 1943a).

But Dunfield was adamant that the facts be known. He needed the public's awareness and acceptance of the terrible living conditions in the town in order for them to understand the need for reform. He realized that the report was "too long for rapid study by those unaccustomed to such things" but was astute enough to know that the success of his proposed solution to the inner-city housing crisis required carefully nurtured public support. He believed that if every household had a copy of the report, and time to study it, it would serve as a "primer on civic affairs and a valuable stimulus to thought" (Dunfield 1943b). He convinced the Council to print 5,000 copies of the report and had them delivered to every household in town by the Boy Scouts.

Meanwhile, the City Assessment Rolls included an ever-increasing number of houses, sometimes entire streets, labelled as "Not Fit For Habitation."

7
"A BOLD SCHEME FOR DOUBLING THE LIVING SPACE OF THE TOWN"

The second part of the third interim report hijacked Meaney's modest proposal to build 500 houses within the city limits. The proposed project was breathtaking in its scope:

> What we have put before the public in this report is a bold scheme for, in effect, *doubling the living space of the town* . . . by making a *new planned garden suburb* in . . . *the valley north of the town.* . . . The elements of the situation are that most of the houses in the older parts of the town need twice the land they have, that a large part of the population needs twice the room-space it has now, and that a great part of our houses are of a very low grade. Let us as a community look a generation ahead now, make a bold, united effort and lay our plans for more space and better houses once and for all. (CEHTP 3, 112; emphasis added)

This report introduced the term "garden suburb" to the local vocabulary but didn't define what it meant. Ebenezer Howard's utopian vision of industrial cities ringed by a green belt of preserved countryside containing a constellation of garden cities was never implemented anywhere, for political and financial reasons. But even stripped of its utopian foundation, the idea of residential developments combining careful land-use planning and innovative landscape design to foster a strong sense of community was widely adopted.

126   CORNER WINDOWS AND CUL-DE-SACS

Figure 7.1. "To double the living space of the town": a view north across Bannerman Park and Circular Road towards the northern valley (LAC, REA 260-4).

Such developments were completely unrelated to Howard's original idea, but most people were unaware of that. Most people have always got Howard wrong. Lacking an understanding of his principal message, they confuse garden suburbs, which were small-scale developments of single-family houses surrounded by gardens and built on the outskirts of cities, with garden cities, which were supposed to offer a full range of services and employment opportunities (Hall 1988, 87). Garden suburbs were the antithesis of Howard's plan, indicative of the kind of urban sprawl he was trying to prevent. However, privately developed garden suburbs arose spontaneously in various parts of England where planners considered them to be a much superior alternative to the high-density, multi-family dwellings that characterized French and German cities (Abercrombie 1910, 88). Despite the conflation of two quite different ideas, garden suburbs became virtually synonymous with modern residential planning practice in the early twentieth century, and they proliferated all around the world (Freestone 2015, 371). A recent survey describes more than 900 of them (Stern, Fishman, and Tilove 2013). None of them make any pretense of furthering Howard's goal of creating a new way of urban life. They are just a way of organizing suburban space. But they have provided many aesthetically pleasing, habitable, and successful communities (Connor 2015, 519). Churchill Park was designed to be one of them. Given Dunfield's virtual monopoly over the writing of the CEHTP report, his having lived in England for some years while he attended university, and his knowledge of English planning practice, it is probably safe to assume that he brought the idea to Newfoundland. In doing so he may have used the term inappropriately. In theory a garden village was spatially independent of the city but linked to it, initially, by streetcars and incorporated a small cluster of shops (Sutton 2021). So it can be argued that the Churchill Park plan comprised three villages and therefore wasn't a true suburb. But Dunfield referred to it as a garden suburb and we have continued to do so.

The CEHTP calculated that it would take 1,000 houses to replace both the condemned and condemnable houses identified in the survey and that they should be built outside the city boundary by a new organization in a carefully planned manner over a 20-year period (CEHTP 3, 44).

But how was this to be accomplished? How, and where, was the necessary land to be found? Dunfield agreed with Thomas Adams and Arthur Dalzell that the post-World War I housing crisis in Canada was largely the result of suburban land speculation and that "excessive prices for land are the first and worse obstacle to good housing" (CEHTP 3, 95). "For every additional dollar the small home-builder has to pay out for land, he has a dollar less to spend on the house." In a statement based on Fabian socialist philosophy, which advocated that any unearned increment should be part

Figure 7.2. "A garden suburb in the valley north of the town," aerial 1941 (Newfoundland and Labrador Air Photo and Map Library, Department of the Environment).

of social rather than private capital (Lewis and Shrimpton 1984, 226), Dunfield wrote that "we have to set off the interests of a limited number of landowners, their old-fashioned right to gather in, because of their lucky position, unearned increment from the community, against the interests of the poorer classes, their health and their comfort, and that of their children" (CEHTP 3, 88). The report proposed that this goal would be achieved by expropriating all the land required for the project.

The area north of the city boundary at Empire Avenue was already experiencing unplanned and unregulated suburban development by the time it was chosen as the location for the new development. There were about 300 different blocks of property in the area. Several of the bigger blocks belonged to large dairy farmers: "Bloomfield Farm Dairy" (James Halliday) and "Westerland" (*ENL* Macpherson), both on Newtown Road, and "Rose's

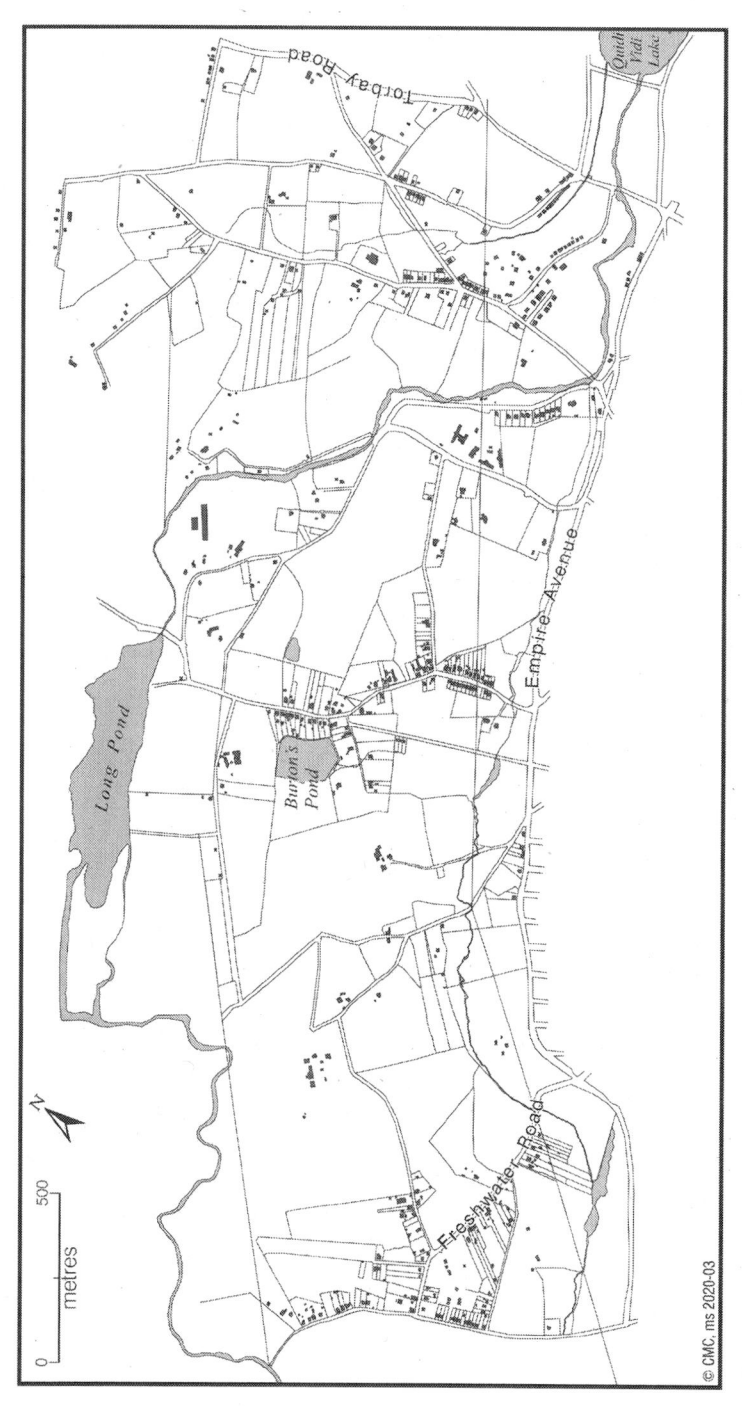

Figure 7.3. Settlement in the northern valley before expropriation. Base map 1945 courtesy of the government of Newfoundland (Charles Conway).

Dairy Farm" on Mahon's (now Gooseberry) Lane. The Church of England Boys' Orphanage ran a large farm north of Burton's Pond. Other large blocks belonged to large estates, investment companies, and the Catholic Church, the Church of England, and the Congregational Church. Much of that land was rented out as pasturage.

There were also many small rural properties of two or three acres and about 150 small surveyed building lots, most of them an acre or less in size. Half of them had houses built on them. These lots, almost without exception, were located on the main roads leading out from town. The majority were owner-occupied. The rest were leased from the institutional landowners. A few other houses were scattered along the lanes and pathways among the open fields. The plan was to expropriate only enough of the field or garden portion of the lots to permit the widening of an existing road or to create a new residential street. Existing houses would not be disturbed (*Daily News* 1944a).

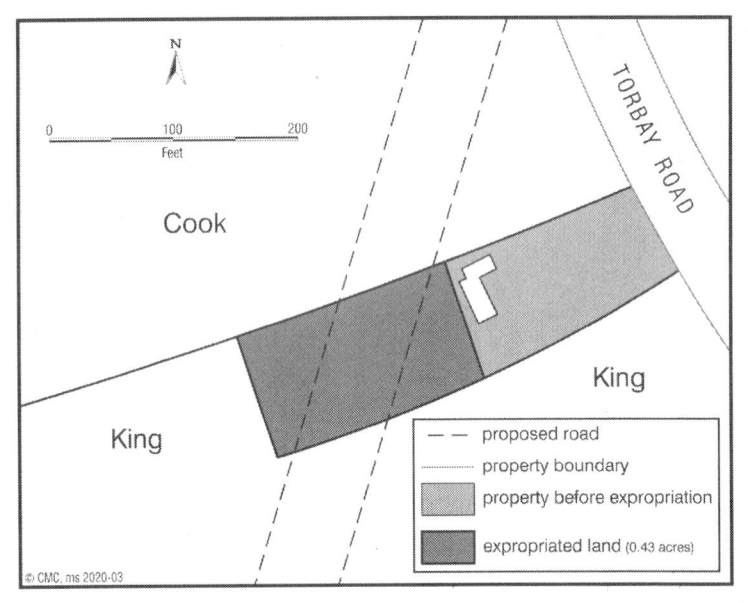

Figure 7.4. Expropriation of part of the Rendell property to make way for Elizabeth Street (Newfoundland and Labrador Registry of Deeds V184-102 1944; Charles Conway).

Figure 7.5. Urban houses in the northern valley: (top) 4 Allandale Road; (middle) 20–22 Allandale Road; (bottom) 144 Empire Avenue (A.J. Shawyer).

Properties: Expropriation, Compensation, and Cost of Acquisition

The expropriation of land was controversial. The question of how to determine the appropriate level of compensation was even more difficult. To acquire the land as economically as possible, the CEHTP proposed the use of a compensation scheme then being discussed in the UK, but not legislated until 1947 (Cherry 1988, 116). The scheme was outlined in the report of the English Expert Committee on Compensation and Betterment, established in 1941 and chaired by Baron Uthwatt of Lathbury. The Uthwatt Committee was mandated to devise a scheme that would compensate owners of land for any depreciation of the value of their land as a consequence of a planning decision. The principal recommendation was that the price paid by a public authority for the compulsory acquisition of land should be limited to the existing use value of the land, not some estimate of its value under some indeterminate future development (Cullingworth 1976, 133). Dunfield learned about this report from Paul Meschino, the architect of the St. John's Housing Corporation, who had heard about the report, but hadn't read it, while he was a student at the University of Toronto (Meschino 1999).

Dunfield and Eric Cook went to Canada to seek advice from the Sun Life Assurance Company on how best to estimate the existing value of the land to be expropriated. The company considered that the cost of land should not be worth more than 10 per cent of the value of the structure on it (CEHTP 5, 21; Dunfield 1944c). Working from this figure, and considering current land prices in St. John's, compensation for the "frontage" land on an existing road was set at a maximum of $20 per linear foot, with an average of $8. The surveyors calculated that there was sufficient frontage in the proposed housing area to accommodate 1,292 50-foot-wide building lots. If all the land were acquired and developed at once, the total compensation to owners would be more than a half-million dollars.

Because the scheme was intended to take 30 years to complete, only a few lots would be developed each year. Therefore, the value of frontage lands had to be discounted to reflect the current value of the anticipated future price. Applying a 4 per cent discount rate over 30 years reduced the current total value of frontage lands to a precisely calculated $297,883. This amount was to be divided proportionately among the landowners. In defence of the scheme the report suggested that the amount received would be "far more than the actual present value of any moneys they are ever going to receive from buyers actually proposing to build, as opposed to speculative buyers" (CEHTP 3, 91; 5, 23).

To arrive at the current value of the "back lots" and land in agricultural use, the Commission adopted the system being used by Mr. Justice W.A. Higgins, chairman of the wartime Board of Arbitration. He had devised a scheme to evaluate the compensation claims for land expropriated for American bases in St. John's. Higgins set the compensation for productive land at $400 per acre, pasture land at $250, uncleared land at $100, and marshland at $50 (*DNB* William John Higgins; Sharpe and Shawyer 2010, 44–46).

Higgins also gave additional amounts for "disturbance of business" (Sharpe and Shawyer 2012, 44). The CEHTP decided not to recognize "disturbance" in the proposed housing area. Instead, it offered a lease-back to farmers to allow them to continue farming until such time as their land was needed for the construction of houses. This was a bitter blow to farmers like the Hallidays of Bloomfield Farm Dairy. The planned route of Elizabeth Avenue cut across the middle of their farm, making day-to-day operations impossible (*Daily News* 1944b, 1944d; *Evening Telegram* 1944c). Years later, reflecting back on the 1944 expropriation of his grandfather's 66-acre farm, Robert Halliday said: "the scheme that was developed for the compensation of the land was probably not bad, but there was a total lack of consideration for the confiscation and expropriation of businesses. That is where he [Dunfield] showed [his] arrogance and a complete lack of respect for the people he was driving off the land" (quoted in Murray 2002, 252). Halliday's property was reduced to 2.9 acres (Brown 1998, Map 18).

The report predicted that the final total cost of acquiring land for the proposed new development would be $673,689. This included about 720 acres of land immediately north of the city limits at Empire Avenue in what would soon be referred to as the "Housing Area," and an additional 158 acres in the "Kenmount Annex" between Kenmount and Thorburn Roads. The report argued that even if this detached area of land along Kenmount Road wouldn't be needed for another 20 years, it would be a valuable asset for the city, easily integrated into existing developments with only an additional mile of (proposed) streetcar track (CEHTP 5, 25). There is no evidence that anybody disputed this figure, and the "guaranteed" acquisition price may have been one of the reasons the government approved the scheme. As it turned out, this predicted cost was more or less accurate. Approximately 200 expropriation awards were made to landowners in the Housing Area (*Evening Telegram* 1945a–f). The final tally for 782 acres of expropriated land was $786,580.46 (*Evening Telegram* 1947b).

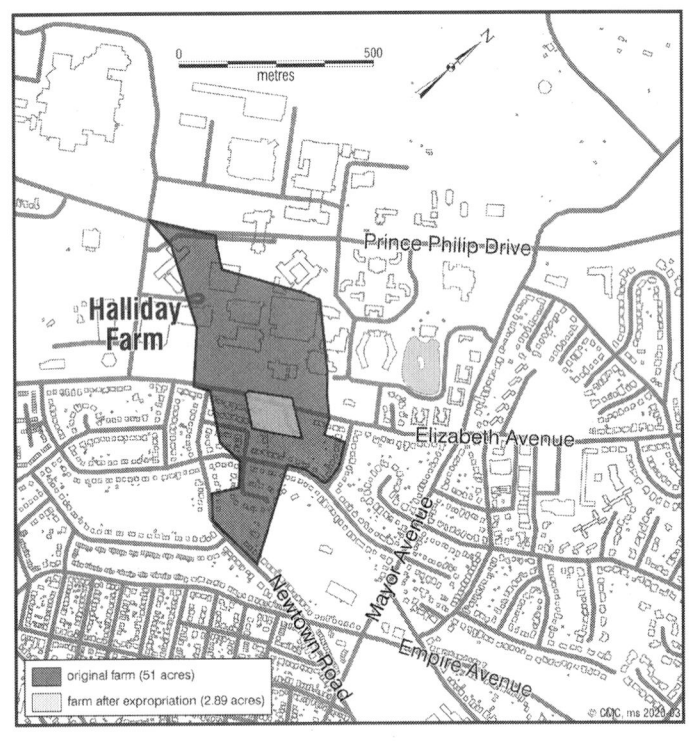

Figure 7.6. Expropriation of the Halliday farm, 1944. Note that most of the main campus of Memorial University of Newfoundland is located between Elizabeth Avenue and Prince Philip Drive, on land expropriated from the Halliday farm (map by Chris Brown and Charles Conway).

Figure 7.7. Bloomfield Farm Dairy advertisement (All Newfoundland Directory 1936).

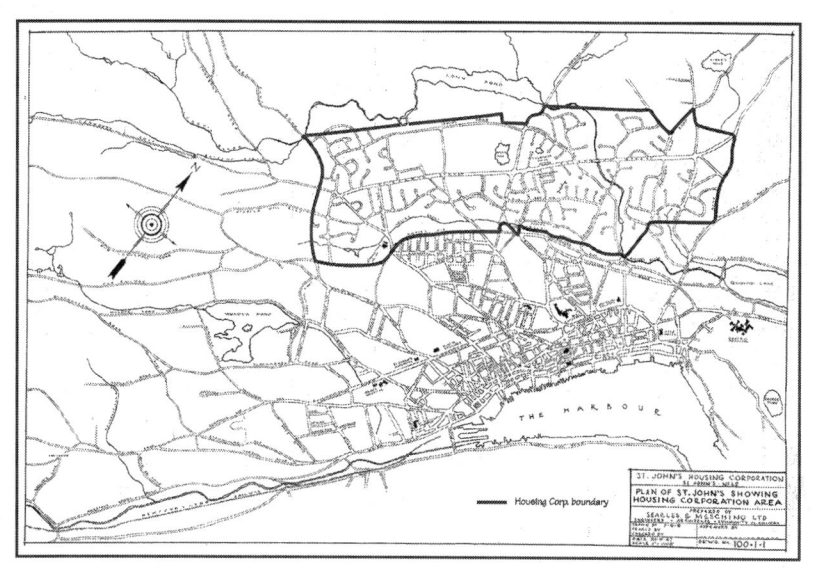

Figure 7.8. The Housing Area defined (1947).

What Kind of Houses? How Will They Be Financed?

In addressing the Canadian Club in 1910 Henry Vivian, the highly regarded English town planner, extolled the virtues of the single-family house:

> [we require] the individuality of a home.... No [people] can really lead the nations of the world, or even long survive, if the great masses of its people are housed in tenements with a staircase for a playground and the window ledge for a garden. (Vivian 1910, 403)

The members of the CEHTP agreed with this sentiment and assumed that most people would want a detached house:

> The house in a range is an undesirable survival of the past. A brief examination of the town will disclose that new build-

> ings for very many years past have consisted almost entirely of detached, or very occasionally semi-detached houses.... The trend in public desire is unmistakable. Today even a man of small means wants a house he can walk around, with a bit of garden and a place for the garage he hopes to have some day. (CEHTP 3, 41)

This vision had widespread public appeal. A local columnist had already claimed that "a pretty little cottage with a small garden" would inspire a sense of pride in the owner (*Daily News* 1942). New houses built on the streets north of LeMarchant Road, such as Pennywell and Golf, had already demonstrated the gradual adoption of modern design. They were generally detached and set back from the sidewalk, although still maintaining the tall two-storey structure on a narrow lot.

The third CEHTP report devoted an entire chapter to a discussion of housing finance. It was argued that since private enterprise could not, or would not, meet the need for low-income housing, governments must either provide it or facilitate its provision. The report cited the schemes in Canada and the United States where funds were advanced by private lenders under a guarantee from government (CEHTP 3, 51–60; Sharpe and Shawyer 2016, 30–33, 121–30). Dunfield argued that such a scheme would have advantages:

> If our government should do what is being done today in every progressive country in the world, and that is put public credit behind housing so that the low-income home-seeker may get a house on loan of 80 or even 90 per cent of the value at the lowest possible rate of interest, payable off over at least 25 years bimonthly instalments, as is done in Canada, Australia and the United States, we can give a man a first-rate little house for no more than he is paying for rent today. (*Evening Telegram* 1943d)

But this could not be the preferred solution to the housing problem in St. John's because Newfoundland had no financial institutions that loaned out large sums on the security of real estate. Even if some Canadian life insurance companies, or other lending bodies, were willing to take mortgage on houses in the new suburb, their need for profit would make it difficult, if not impossible, to provide housing at prices local households could afford. So the proposition was that the houses be financed on the rental-purchase system. This would ensure that an unsatisfactory tenant could be handed the portion of money paid to date (which included interest, taxes, maintenance fees, and principal) that eventually would have gone towards house purchase and ownership, and the house could be reclaimed and resold. This system would provide complete protection of the money invested because title to the property would be held by the lender until payment was complete. Such a proposal required the creation of an independent housing corporation, in this case, the non-profit St. John's Housing Corporation (SJHC) (CEHTP 5, 66–74).

The St. John's Housing Corporation

The assumption was that a public corporation would be the best means of providing housing for the "poorest classes." Furthermore, if it were run by a board made up of representatives from labour, government, and business, it would be divorced from local politics. Money would be raised by the sale of debentures, to a total amount fixed by statute, and offered at the lowest possible rate of interest. Such a corporation would be able to adopt a "go-slow" approach. It could first experiment by building eight to ten houses so that designs and costs could be worked out. Such an approach could not be adopted by a private, for-profit body.

The report made it clear that houses built by the proposed corporation would have to be purchased by those who could afford to pay for them. For those who couldn't, "sub-economic" rental houses would be needed, and the proposed corporation would not be able to take on the cost of providing permanent subsidies to build and maintain them. As several members of the Commission of Government had already pointed out, they would have to be provided by charitable organizations (CEHTP 3, 67–68). Here was the first hint of what some considered a betrayal of the poor, who were supposed to be the beneficiaries of the project.

This report reflects Dunfield's considerable knowledge of contemporary town planning as well as his appreciation of the need to keep the public informed of the work of his Commission. He did so through repetition of the basic ideas in speeches and newspaper reports, although he sometimes got carried away by his enthusiasm. On occasion he made public comments that conflicted with each other, and the lack of caution and consistency created significant problems for the newly formed St. John's Housing Corporation. For example, the report noted that building materials were expensive because of wartime shortages so a large-scale building project could not be undertaken immediately. It recommended that no more than 10 houses be built immediately so design ideas and construction techniques could be tested, costs confirmed, and public interest generated (CEHTP 3, 73). This was a sensible position. However, a few months later, Dunfield told the Council that he was "anxious to proceed at once in disregard of the high cost of building" (SJCM 5 Oct. 1943, 236).

The Public's Reaction to the Proposal

The third interim report described a future residential landscape that would be completely different from anything seen in St. John's. The new houses built north of LeMarchant Road tended to be detached, and some had a piece of ground big enough to accommodate a car. But the neighbourhoods were traditionally convenient with corner shops and small commercial enterprises. In Dunfield's plan, commercial activity would be strictly confined to the main street (Elizabeth Avenue) and separate from the residential streets.

Public opinion was divided. Some members of the public were excited and the local press reported enthusiastically: "Since our indifference and narrow mindedness have been squarely put before us during the past two years by outsiders who make us blush, perhaps we shall now see a Garden City of homes" (*Evening Telegram* 1943e). The *Daily News* (1943d) noted that "this is the first concrete and apparently sound proposal to be put forward for the total re-planning of St. John's" and further stated that the Commission's proposal "presents a feasible solution to long-standing problems, a courageous and constructive, bold and imaginative plan" (*Daily News* 1943e).

But others in town were less enthusiastic about the proposed development. The St. John's Trades and Labour Council was disappointed that the project was going to be built "in house" by a proposed corporation and not draw from the tradesmen in the town. Furthermore, Dunfield told them that he wanted "quality control" of the construction and "strict engineering management," implying that he would not get that from the local tradesmen (CEHTP 5, 33).

In addition, the Municipal Council was unhappy that some of the major recommendations of the report were completely at odds with those of Councillor Meaney's 1939 proposal. He stressed that any new housing should be within the city limits where water and sewer services already existed. He argued that there was no need to create a new house-building organization because the city's tradesmen possessed all the necessary skills and experience. Finally, he recommended that neither level of government should undertake to build the houses themselves. In brief, the Council was of two minds about the report and invited Dunfield to attend a Council meeting to discuss it. A vote on the motion to adopt the report was tied. Once again Mayor Carnell used his deciding vote to approve the motion. Whether it would be successful or not, it was the only proposal in town to offer to build the new housing that the city desperately needed.

In the summer of 1943, while Council was discussing the third report, Councillor Meaney died, so he never got to see the concrete results of his impassioned plea for a solution to the city's housing problems. His seat was filled by Allan M. Fraser, professor of economics and history at Memorial University College. Councillor Lawrence also died that summer, and he was replaced by Harry G.R. Mews, manager of the St. John's office of the North American Life Insurance Company.

The Fourth and Fifth Interim Reports

To ensure that the traffic congestion that plagued the city was not transferred to the new suburb, streets in the new suburb were to be wider than those in the old city. The brief fourth report recommended the drafting of a proper master plan and an accompanying set of zoning regulations.

The fifth report, on the other hand, fleshed out the details of the project proposed in the third report. The area north of Empire Avenue was now beginning to be referred to as "The Housing." Skeptics were now calling the project "Dunfield's Folly" because it was believed by some that the area was so far away from the centre of the city that nobody would ever want to move there.

A project of this scale required significant engineering expertise and the CEHTP had to look beyond its own members to secure it. By a cruel twist of fate they were successful because of Dunfield's connection with a national tragedy. The deadliest structural fire in Newfoundland (or what is now Canadian) history occurred on 12 December 1942 when 99 people died in the Knights of Columbus Hall on Military Road. Eighty of the victims were Newfoundland, Canadian, and American servicemen. Dunfield was selected to chair the Commission of Enquiry into the causes of the fire. The Canadian and American commanding officers requested that a military officer be permitted to attend the meetings of the Commission. Dunfield agreed, and chose Lt. Colonel J.W. Beretta of the U.S. Corps of Engineers as the American representative. When Dunfield learned that Beretta ran an engineering company back home in San Antonio, Texas, he asked him if he knew anyone who could act as a consulting engineer for the CEHTP. Beretta suggested his company's vice-president, A.E. (Ed)

Searles, who was then at loose ends due to the scarcity of civilian work. In August 1943 Searles agreed to a two-month contract, which turned into an eight-year career with the SJHC, during which he bought one of the new houses on Dartmouth Place in 1949 (Dunfield 1943c; *Evening Telegram* 1943c).

One of the first major issues Searles had to address was sewerage, knowing that the system he designed would have a significant impact on the layout of the new suburb. In addition to the farms and building lots in the northern valley beyond Empire Avenue, there were two large orphanages and the recently built RCAF barracks complex on New Cove Road. All depended on cesspits or septic tanks for the disposal of sewage and on wells for their source of drinking water. Unfortunately, the city's main sewer, which ran along Empire Avenue, was at an elevation higher than the floor of the northern valley, where the houses would be built. The only place where gravity drainage could bring sewage out of the valley was near the Church of England cemetery beside Quidi Vidi Lake, at the extreme east end of the ridge separating the valley from the city. From there it would have to get to the harbour. The most efficient, but expensive, solution was to dig a tunnel from the lake to the harbour near Temperance Street. Fortunately, the city engineer knew that in the late nineteenth century, Harvey and Company had begun to dig a tunnel from the harbour towards the lake to bring water to a harbourside factory (CEHTP 3, 77–79). The idea was abandoned after 585 feet of tunnel had been cut, but the old tunnel was still there, and accessible through the basement of a house on Temperance Street. After examining

Figure 7.9. A.E. Searles, engineer for the SJHC (1943–51). Photo taken in 1967 (F.P. Meschino).

it, Searles calculated that it could easily be extended to the lake by means of a new tunnel.

Searles's plan for the new suburb (Searles 1944) incorporated several modern features drawn from the plan for Radburn, New Jersey, a development to which Dunfield referred in some of his speeches (C.S. Stein 1957; Schaffer 1982). Radburn was not a perfect example of garden suburban planning. The designers had planned to orient family life towards large parks and green spaces but their plans were thwarted by practical considerations. The reality for most women was that they spent much of their time in the kitchen, which looked out over the street. Since children played in the street, as they are wont to do, maternal supervision made the streets the focal point of the community. This was not what the designers had anticipated (Connor 2015, 520). Nevertheless, the Radburn plan was influential in the planning profession because it incorporated Clarence Perry's idea that a town should consist of an agglomeration of neighbourhoods, each just large enough to require one elementary school (Perry 1929). Searles adopted this idea and proposed that the St. John's development would contain three "villages," connected by a new circumferential road that became Elizabeth Avenue. The villages would be separated from each other, and from the city, by green belts. Several other characteristics of "modern" town planning were also incorporated. Each village was divided into "superblocks" delineated by major roads and perforated by smaller streets, cul-de-sacs, and pedestrian walkways linking the residential streets to areas of open parkland.

Don Mills, on what was then the northern outskirts of Toronto, has pride of place in the Canadian suburban literature. It has been described as the hallmark of Canadian suburbia, representing "the epitome of modernist garden city principles: separation of uses; low-density development; a hierarchy of streets; shopping concentrated in retail malls and strips; loops, crescents, and cul-de-sacs; buffers of green space or high-density housing to protect single-detached housing; and extensive open space systems" (Grant 2000, 449). Churchill Park can be described in precisely the same way, except for the lack of high-density housing. The first house was built in Churchill Park in 1944, nine years before the first house in Don Mills.

The convenience and safety of pedestrians was of paramount importance in the plan Dunfield described as "strictly modern whereby traffic will be routed by a limited number of main streets, giving access for vehicles externally, while residences will be sited on short or dead-end streets . . . with banjo turnarounds" (*Daily News* 1945j). "The contrast with the older town is very striking. Instead of every street corner being a point of traffic danger, there are only three or four main traffic intersections in the whole area" (Dunfield 1950a, 94). The proposed three villages were centred on the circumferential road that became known as Elizabeth Avenue. Village "A" lay between Torbay and New Cove Roads, near Mount Cashel; Village "B" between Mayor Avenue and Rennie's Mill Road south of the Church of England Orphanage (Arts and Culture Centre today); and Village "C" between Freshwater Road and Horwood's Road, centred on Lamb's Lane. Each village was to be connected to the existing city by a new tramline, and each would have as its focal point a small green and a shopping centre. A fourth Village "D" was targeted for possible later development.

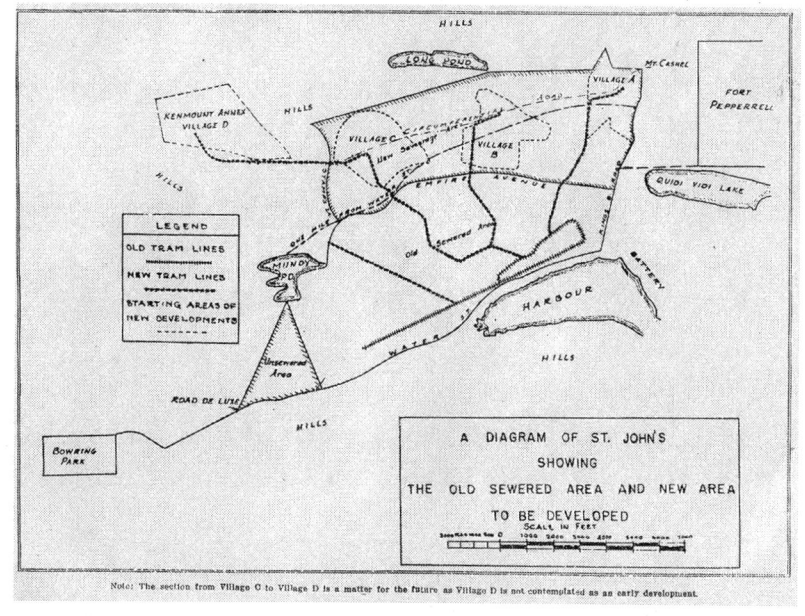

Figure 7.10. The Concept Plan 1943.

The lot sizes were generous, minimally 50 x 115 feet or 5,750 square feet in area. The residential streets were carefully laid out so as not to require the demolition of any existing houses or the rerouting of existing streets and lanes, including Mahon's Road (Gooseberry Lane), Clark Avenue (which became a section of Elizabeth Avenue), and Lamb's Lane. For a short time in the spring of 1944 there were rumours that whole blocks of houses, especially near Robinson's Hill and on Glenridge Crescent, would be demolished. Dunfield put the rumours to rest by assuring reporters that Searles had managed to lay out the streets of the entire development "without necessitating the disturbance of any existing houses except one or two small ones in the section near Lamb's Lane, which it may be necessary to move back a little from the edge of the proposed street" (*Daily News* 1944a).

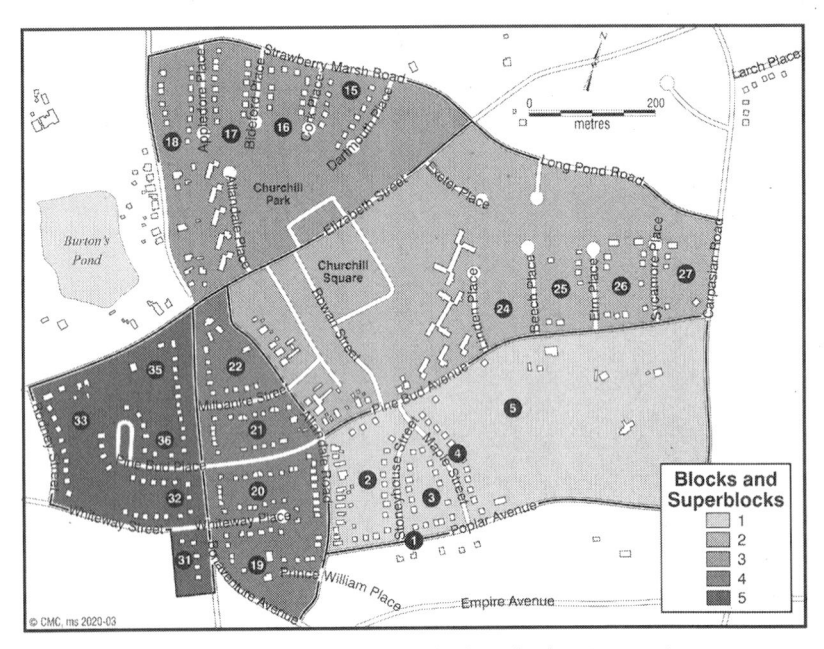

Figure 7.11. Map of Blocks and Superblocks (Charles Conway).

Thousands of trees were to be planted along the streets because "no suburb could be considered modern without them" (CEHTP 5, 24). The plan called for 1,200 houses. This would yield a gross residential density between 4.5 and 5 houses per acre, considerably less than the 17 dwelling units per acre that characterized the downtown core (CEHTP 5, 40–41).

Additional Recommendations

The report included the estimated costs for servicing the expropriated land and building 1,200 houses. There were two components to the estimated costs of the project: "unrecoverable," such as the cost for the sewer, main streets, and trees and landscaping; and "recoverable," for the cost of land, local sewers, and water mains. The estimated cost to the city of St. John's was $1,261,800 and to the Commission of Government, $827,100. But there were large unknowns in these estimates: the rising costs of materials during and after the war, for construction of the houses and for infrastructure. It was glibly predicted that the total return on the investment, including taxes and interest payments by the tenants, would be approximately $3.5 million over the proposed 30-year development period (CEHTP 5, 25–28).

A final and surprising recommendation was that building should begin immediately. Six months earlier, the original idea of building had been to build only a few "good, small" houses to test design ideas and confirm cost, the latter reckoned at $2,500 per house. Now the CEHTP threw this cautionary plan to the winds and proposed a first instalment of 100 houses, smaller ones costing $4,375 and those of a "better type" costing $6,125 (CEHTP 5, 32). This enthusiastic but ill-informed decision was to come back to haunt the CEHTP as the scheme progressed and the program fell on hard times.

One month later, a committee of the Commission of Government met with the St. John's Municipal Council and the CEHTP on 12 February 1944 to discuss the five reports. The meeting was chaired by H.A. Winter, commissioner for home affairs and education. It was a momentous occasion. Winter opened the proceedings by remarking "that legendary figures, the future historian, should be justified in recording this date and meeting as the starting point of a genuine revolution in the conditions of our city." He heaped praise on Dunfield and the other members of the

CEHTP for their excellent work, "the energy with which its members set about it; the thoroughness of the survey . . . which they have made; and the comprehensive grasp of the whole situation manifested by the five reports which they have submitted." In an uncharacteristically honest moment he also made note of something that has perhaps been too long ignored — how extraordinary it was that the meeting even took place. "For the Commission to have persuaded two such ordinary intractable bodies as the Commission of Government and the St. John's Municipal Council into acceptance in principle of its recommendation with all their large and far-reaching achievements, is in itself no mean achievement" (*Daily News* 1944g).

Sixth Report: The Commission Resigns

The sixth and final report of the CEHTP, dated 5 August 1944, noted "with great satisfaction" that all the principal recommendations of the Commission had now been adopted by both the government and the Municipal Council. It recommended that the Town Planning Commission (TPC), disbanded in 1934 after a short life, be re-established on a permanent basis. Their work now complete, the members of the Commission for the Enquiry into Housing and Town Planning offered their resignation to the governor (CEHTP 6, 3).

The government accepted the resignation of the members and their final recommendation. A permanent Town Planning Commission (TPC) was appointed on 24 October 1944, the day before work began on the new northern suburb. The TPC had four members: Col. Sir Leonard Outerbridge, St. John's businessman; Gerald S. Doyle, O.B.E., K.S.G., druggist; Dr. H.L. Pottle, director of child welfare; and Brian Dunfield, who was named chairman and remained so until 1951.

The TPC immediately contracted Professor John Bland, director of the McGill University School of Architecture, to visit St. John's to provide advice on the new city plan and to examine the plans for the new northern suburb. The map he attached to his 1946 report was the first land-use map of the city, and the first map to show the outline of the proposed Housing Area (Bland 1946a).

From Dream to Reality: Filtering Out the Poor

Publication of the CEHTP's household survey in June 1943 exposed the enormity of the housing problem, which was much more serious than anyone had imagined. In January 1944 the fifth report estimated that at least 2,400 new houses would be needed before the worst parts of the slum could be pulled down (CEHTP 5, 34). By this time it was obvious that the bold promises of 1942 couldn't possibly be met and that public expectations were going to have to be tempered.

Without apology the fifth report said that the proposed Housing Corporation would not be able to build houses for the poor. There would not be free houses for anybody. The scheme "will merely seek to build a great many houses because there are not enough and as there come to be enough, after pulling down the worst, people will shuffle and deal for themselves all the houses, new and old, according to their own means and fancy, finding their own level." The report extolled the virtues of filtering, whereby "everybody can, so to speak, move up one step" (CEHTP 5, 36).

Dunfield warned the Rotary Club of "a lot of loose talk about slum clearance. That is the ultimate object, but it cannot be the immediate object.... We shall have to do some slum clearance if and when we can, but in the meantime we first have to provide for those who can pay their way" (*Daily News* 1945b).

By now the basic need of the city for more houses was so well understood that nobody argued that the housing scheme should be abandoned. Dunfield may truly have believed that building a new garden suburb on the outskirts of the city would improve housing conditions in the inner city. But most of the members of the CEHTP, and of the St. John's Housing Corporation that was created to manage the project, were more pragmatic.

They didn't believe that there was any realistic prospect of that happening (Winter 1998). Nor did Paul Meschino, the Corporation's architect. Recognizing that conditions in the downtown were "unbelievably bad," he was never convinced that there was a relationship between the Corporation's new houses and slum clearance: "In clearing slums you don't build on 50 foot lots. You build 60 units to the acre. And you don't build slum clearance units miles away from where people work. But that's what they said they were doing and I did what I was told to do" (Meschino 2000).

8

DEALING WITH THE OPPOSITION

The Commission of Government approved the recommendations of the Housing Commission on 21 January 1944. The Municipal Council did so as well, on 5 February. With these approvals in hand Governor Walwyn immediately sent a despatch to the Dominions Office in London informing them that the inquiry into housing conditions in St. John's "has now reached a stage indicating that practical steps of much importance and magnitude will, subject to your approval, have to be taken in the near future." He described the proposals as a "bold scheme [which] offers the only real hope of solving the problem." He did warn about "the possibility of organized objection by interested parties at a later stage when legislative action is taken to provide the necessary powers." However, he stressed that the Commission of Government shared the view of the Housing Commission that immediate action was necessary "while public interest is aroused," and that unless an early start is made a golden opportunity will be lost (Walwyn 1944b).

Everything was now in place, including the financing. All that was required was the approval from Viscount Cranborne, the secretary of state for dominion affairs. The project would be financed by the proceeds of bonds issued by the St. John's Housing Corporation and guaranteed by the government, supplemented by a financial contribution from the Municipal Council. The Council's contribution to the project was made possible by an unexpected windfall. Mayor Carnell and Councillors Vardy and Cook had finally convinced the government that the Council was being forced to spend money it did not have on a problem it had not caused: the repairs of the serious deterioration of the streets by the incessant traffic of heavily laden military trucks travelling between the harbour and the Canadian military camp at Buckmaster's Field and the American base at Fort Pepperrell. In March 1944, the commissioner for finance, with permission from the dominions secretary, was allowed to waive the city's outstanding debt of $1 million (Cranborne 1944a). This debt, which had haunted the city virtually from its beginning, was now gone, and this so improved the city's financial situation that it was able to raise a $3 million loan and give $1.2 million of it to the new St. John's Housing Corporation (SJHC) to support its operations.

The enabling legislation was drafted in March by a committee composed of the commissioners of justice and defence, home affairs and education, Brian Dunfield, and Eric Cook (Walsh 1944b). The St. John's Housing Corporation Act created the St. John's Housing Corporation (hereafter SJHC) to oversee the construction of the project (Legislation 1944a). The St. John's Housing Corporation (Lands) Act empowered the Corporation to expropriate the land required for the new suburb (H.A. Winter 1944b; Legislation 1944b).

It seems astonishing that such a huge project was undertaken when the nation was still at war and so many questions remained unanswered. Would there be enough workers available to do the work? Would the landowners accept the compensations calculated for the expropriation of their lands? Would sufficient building materials be available? And what about elevated wartime prices?

Although the commissioners were well aware of the need for housing for those who lived in the inner city, they also saw that the project made a good deal of sense for the future of the entire city. Houses were being built along Empire Avenue, which followed the line of the old railway track, but it remained a rough track not yet made into a street. The circumferential road would provide a much-needed new route across the top of the city, relieving the strain on Empire Avenue and the few other cross-town streets. Furthermore, the new trunk sewer would open up a large tract of land for development and hopefully would have the effect of lowering the cost of development land within the existing city.

There was an important political consideration as well. It now looked as if a successful conclusion to the war was possible in the near future, and there were already rumours about the post-war reintroduction of an elected government for Newfoundland. The Commission's time on the island would soon be coming to a close. The commissioners may have thought that a successful housing scheme would not only provide a much-needed fillip to the post-war expansion of St. John's, but would be appreciated as an important part of their Newfoundland legacy.

Every successful public endeavour requires a champion, and Brian Dunfield passionately filled that role. He brought "a charismatic force to the politics and the planning" (Mellin 2011, 38). He supervised the laying out of the whole northern valley with meticulous care and attention to every detail, an astonishing achievement that showed his grasp and understanding of the art of town planning. He came to "love every pebble" in the area (Bartlett 1999) and overrode every complaint against the scheme. He convinced himself — but not quite everyone else — that building houses for the middle class, in the immediate term, was as good a goal as building houses for the poor.

Selling the Project to the Dominions Office in London

Governor Walwyn knew that the new suburb would be a benefit to the city in the long term. He also knew that the Dominions Office of His Majesty's government in London controlled the budget of the Commission of Government and that wartime exigencies required that expenditures on non-essential items be minimized, and it would be difficult to convince the dominions secretary of the merits of the scheme (Walwyn 1944i). But he was prepared to try. However, he first he had to win a battle on the home front.

Figure 8.1. Governor Vice-Admiral Sir Humphrey T. Walwyn (1936–46) (*Book of Newfoundland 1967*, vol. 3, 217).

When the two draft housing bills were published in April 1944, several of the landowners in the Housing Area reacted violently against both the expropriation of their property and the method proposed for compensation. Sir William Horwood, the chief justice of Newfoundland, was first off the mark. He complained that not only would the SJHC have the authority to expropriate agricultural land with a system of compensation he believed unfair, but that the land now privately occupied would be passed into the possession of other persons who would own houses built on that land and therefore it would not be used for public purposes (Horwood 1944). Prominent lawyer R.J. Furlong protested that the Uthwatt scheme of compensation was "entirely revolutionary in this country" and, furthermore, that "the scheme ignores, or even impedes, the basic purpose of the Housing Commission, which was to tackle the slum evil." He also objected to the fact that the power of expropriation would be delegated to a quasi-public corporation (SJHC). And he filed an objection on behalf of the Archbishop of St. John's that expropriated church properties would, at the end of the proposed lease of 99 years, come into the possession of the SJHC (Furlong 1944a, 1944b; *Evening Telegram* 1944c).

This wasn't the only opposition. A group of 51 landowners submitted a lengthy brief that incorporated references to several British commissions of enquiry on housing and town planning. The group argued that the combined effect of the two proposed bills would violate the established principles governing property rights. The principal objections were the use of expropriation for acquiring the land, the destruction of productive farmland, the absolute control that the SJHC would exercise over the entire area, and the impropriety of a Supreme Court justice (Dunfield) chairing

The Housing Legislation

MEMORANDUM ON DRAFT BILLS SUBMITTED BY MR. R. S. FURLONG

Editor Evening Telegram.

Dear Sir,—I was recently given an opportunity by the City Council to address certain representations to them on the subject of the proposed legislation for the setting up of the Housing Corporation and the acquisition of land in the suburbs of St. John's.

Subsequently I prepared a more formal memorandum on the legislation which I have sent to the Government of Newfoundland. It has been indicated to me that a considerable section of the public is displaying interest in this legislation and with this in mind I append hereto a copy of the memorandum with the hope that it may prove sufficiently interesting for you to accord it the hospitality of your columns.

Yours faithfully,
R. S. FURLONG.

Figure 8.2. "The Housing Legislation," letter from R.S. Furlong (*Evening Telegram* 8 May 1944).

the Corporation (Lewis 1944; *Daily News* 1944b). Furthermore, the method of assessment for lands to be expropriated was considered "vicious and contrary to justice." The group intimated that, if necessary, it was prepared to "pursue the matter to the British House of Commons" (*Evening Telegram* 1944b) and perhaps even to the King.

The most prominent member of this group was Harold Macpherson, chairman of the Royal Stores, an anchor commercial establishment on Water Street, and the owner of "Westerland," a thriving and highly respected agricultural estate that lay within the proposed Housing Area. Assuming that his lands were to be taken immediately, he sent letters of protest to the Commission of Government in May, and to the Dominions Office, with copies to a number of prominent politicians, in September (Macpherson 1944). Macpherson specifically accused Dunfield of arbitrarily taking more land than was needed, unnecessarily interfering with important agricultural areas, and robbing the landowners of their constitutional right to have their claim for lands expropriated settled by arbitration, as was the normal practice. According to Macpherson, Dunfield expressed surprise that any part of Westerland was included in the area to be expropriated. Macpherson blamed this on Searles, saying "it is evident that the boundaries of the area were defined by an American Engineer [Searles] seeking a highly paid job as such but without other interest in Newfoundland's economic affairs" (Macpherson 1944).

The governor was concerned that objections from such a prominent member of the community might indeed lead to questions being asked in the British Parliament, and that this could jeopardize the project. He asked Dunfield to assure Macpherson that his land would not be encroached upon for many years (Walwyn 1944a). Whether Dunfield offered this assurance is unknown, but by the fall Walwyn was able to report to London that the opposition from the landowners was beginning to die down (Walwyn 1944h). To Sir Peter Clutterbuck, the assistant under-secretary for dominion affairs, he wrote that "Macpherson, Dunfield and Emerson (commissioner of justice and defence) have gone off to Branch [a town south of St. John's] for the weekend, so the position is not very strained" (Walwyn

1944i). Clutterbuck, who later became high commissioner to Canada (1946–52), replied, "We have heard nothing further about the proposed petition to the King, so perhaps that has been dropped, and this awkward corner has been safely turned" (Clutterbuck 1945). And so it turned out.

When the compensation awards were made the next year Macpherson received almost $64,000, the largest award made by the Board of Assessors — 10 per cent of the total amount of compensation — and nothing more was heard of his objections (*Evening Telegram* 1945a–e).

However, this was in the future, and the dominions secretary was sufficiently alarmed by the landowners' protests that he asked the governor to delay the third reading of the two bills necessary for the project to advance until the complaints had been investigated (Cranborne 1944b). Walwyn's reply was uncharacteristically blunt. He wrote: "the Commission are seriously disturbed by implications of your telegram because delay involved will be very harmful, if not fatal, to the scheme and because reference to Uthwatt Report and expenditure question indicates misunderstanding of true nature of proposals and conditions obtaining in city and housing area" (Walwyn 1944d).

Walwyn vigorously defended the Uthwatt expropriation method to the Dominions Office even though he personally disagreed with it. He called it "a form of socialism which I don't like," and "tending toward communism." He defended it because he was convinced that the new suburb would be of long-term benefit to the city (Walwyn 1944i). He argued:

> it is imperative that the English critics should appreciate that price of land in and near St. John's has been for many years fantastically high, amounting to from one-fifth to one-third the value of houses built thereon. . . . It is of the essence of present scheme that Housing Area be acquired in one block on [using] an average foot basis for frontage lands and a fixed base for agricultural lands. (Walwyn 1944d)

The governor believed that most of the objections came from the landowners and "a ring of lawyers in St. John's who are at the back of this agitation and would like to keep up the high housing costs" (Walwyn 1944i). But he also knew that the Municipal Council was opposed to the extraordinary broad powers granted to the SJHC and that some of the principal critics argued that the appointment of its members by the government would usurp the authority of "the last vestige of an elected assembly in Newfoundland" (Furlong, 1944a).

In spite of the expressed opposition of some of the landowners, Walwyn knew there was widespread support for the scheme among those who hoped to benefit. The Carpenters' Protective Association of Newfoundland, the St. John's Trades and Labour Council, and the Newfoundland Protective Association of Shop and Office Employees publicly supported the two bills and lobbied for them to be enacted as quickly as possible. In his despatches to London, Walwyn impressed upon the Dominions Office that the general public was in favour of the housing scheme:

> Publication of Bills has evoked strong support from . . . labourers, shop assistants, clerks and the like. We have reason to believe they are also warmly approved by the bulk of citizens who give consent mainly by silence. . . . There would be widespread dissatisfaction if scheme were abandoned. . . . Conditions in St. John's in respect of cleanliness, sanitation, overcrowding and layout are deplorable. If nothing is done now, the Housing Area in question will in time become little better than a slum area as is evidenced by such building as has taken place there during the last ten years. The effect of abandoning or possibly even of postponing scheme would be disastrous not only to St. John's but to many parts of the country which look to it for a lead, and regard scheme as first major step in reconstruction. Similar favourable condition and spirit are unlikely to recur for many years. Contrariwise prompt and energetic action by us, and a plan determined to tackle this great evil, will have a most salutary effect. (Walwyn 1944d)

In the face of the governor's animated defence of the scheme, and with his assurance that there was a broad base of support for the proposal, the dominions secretary in London capitulated on 29 June 1944. "If the Commission of Government are satisfied as to the fairness of figures and as to their ability to meet any criticism which may be directed against them, I should not wish to question their views.... In all other respects I approve of the arrangements" (Cranborne 1944e).

A Sharp Reminder

While the merits of the two housing bills were being debated in the homes of the privileged, life in the city continued as before. One particular incident provided a poignant reminder of the consequences of poverty and poor housing in and around the city. In June 1944, the citizens of St. John's were riveted by accounts of the death of Mary Ellen Hutchings. This 10-year-old girl died in a squalid shack on Blackhead Road from a combination of starvation, exposure, and gangrene resulting from earlier frostbite. The house lay outside the city limits but inside the One Mile Area over which the city had jurisdiction. It was only a short distance from the offices of the newly instituted Child Welfare Division of the Department of Health and Welfare. Letters to the editors of both the daily newspapers in St. John's excoriated city councillors and officials for neglecting their basic duty to provide care (*Evening Telegram* 1944d, 1944e; *Daily News* 1944f).

Mary Ellen's death renewed public concern about the proliferation of "shacktowns" in the outer areas of the city and the persistence of so many badly degraded houses in the central city. It did not, however, lead to immediate action. Dunfield took the opportunity to firmly reiterate that the new Housing Corporation would not provide a short-term solution to the problem of crowded and dilapidated housing:

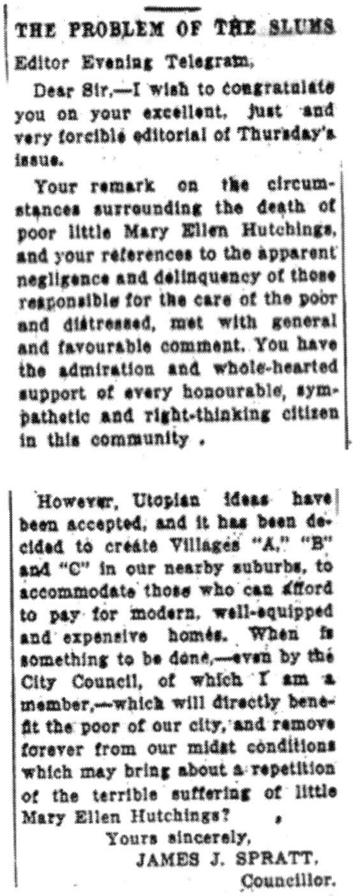

> **THE PROBLEM OF THE SLUMS**
>
> Editor Evening Telegram,
>
> Dear Sir,—I wish to congratulate you on your excellent, just and very forcible editorial of Thursday's issue.
>
> Your remark on the circumstances surrounding the death of poor little Mary Ellen Hutchings, and your references to the apparent negligence and delinquency of those responsible for the care of the poor and distressed, met with general and favourable comment. You have the admiration and whole-hearted support of every honourable, sympathetic and right-thinking citizen in this community.
>
> However, Utopian ideas have been accepted, and it has been decided to create Villages "A," "B" and "C" in our nearby suburbs, to accommodate those who can afford to pay for modern, well-equipped and expensive homes. When is something to be done,—even by the City Council, of which I am a member,—which will directly benefit the poor of our city, and remove forever from our midst conditions which may bring about a repetition of the terrible suffering of little Mary Ellen Hutchings?
>
> Yours sincerely,
> JAMES J. SPRATT,
> Councillor.

Figure 8.3. A letter from Municipal Councillor James J. Spratt (*Evening Telegram* 8 June 1944).

> We have spent generations putting together a town that is 60 percent substandard and it is quite useless to hope or expect that this situation can be cured quickly or cheaply.... Therefore it is as well to face the fact that no immediate relief can be hoped for by the very poor except by the general raising of the standard of accommodation over a long period of years. (Dunfield 1944e)

The Leasehold Question

The St. John's Housing Authority Act stipulated that the Corporation could lease, but not sell, any of the expropriated land (Legislation 1944c, 516[1]). The term of the lease was initially set at 99 years but was extended to 999 years before the legislation was approved. This gave the SJHC the authority to hold and manage the lots on behalf of the city for a millennium. The idea didn't appear out of the blue. It appeared in a single sentence in the fifth report of the CEHTP, but no one seems to have paid any attention to it at the time (CEHTP 1944a, 39). However, vigorous objections were raised when the bill was debated. The Municipal Council was "strongly of the opinion that . . . leasehold tenures are undesirable. The ultimate aim should be unfettered freehold ownership" (Mahoney 1944). And it was clear by this time that the private houses built up along the newer streets that had been developed north of LeMarchant Road, and to the west of Leslie Street, were a mixture of traditional leasehold and increasing incidence of freehold (CSJA, RG 01-12, Assessment Rolls, 1935). Dunfield, on the other hand, argued "there should not be any freeholds in a city" (Dunfield 1944d).

It seems astonishing that the CEHTP would propose leasehold tenure on a housing project aimed at alleviating problems created by the traditional leasehold structure a century before. But there was a logical explanation for the insistence that land in the new housing area should be held on leasehold tenure.

The city had the authority to control building within one mile of the municipal boundary, but it had not adopted a zoning bylaw at the time the Corporation began its work. To prevent the new suburb from becoming another shacktown, the SJHC Board adopted a lease that imposed much more detailed obligations on the tenants than a normal zoning bylaw would have done. The buyers were committed to a 30-year rent-to-purchase agreement and therefore were "owners," but they were to be subject to a lease requiring that the properties be maintained "to the satisfaction of the Corporation." The explanation for this was the worry that first-time property owners might not have the knowledge or commitment to maintain their property to an acceptable standard:

> Unless the Corporation has a free hand in enforcing tidiness and cleanliness of surroundings until the public has got into the necessary habit, our new suburb will look little better than the old city — which is incredibly dirty and untidy. Our people are astonishingly careless of the appearance of their grounds and that observation does not apply to the poor alone. . . . If land were held on long lease at a peppercorn rent [symbolic rent, one dollar per year], the Corporation would, at any rate, by putting in suitable covenants, be in the position that it could give, in the last resort, a hopeless tenant back his money and tell him to go and live somewhere else. It is essential that the kind of citizen who keeps the rusting corpse of a motor car in front of his house should be left out of any decent neighbourhood, or it will not remain decent. (Dunfield 1944d, 3)

The SJHC lease required that tenants paint their house every four years with two coats of oil paint; to build a fence to the rear of the property line, but not in front of it; not to plant trees or shrubs in front of the property line; to keep any flower beds in the front yard within three feet of the property line, and to ensure the beds are kept tidy and "in character with the neighbourhood"; to hang laundry only in the back yard; not to park cars or leave rubbish of any kind on the front lawn area; and to keep the lawn "cut and tidied during the summer and autumn in accordance with the character of the neighbourhood" (see Appendix 3).

The SJHC considered the occupants of the houses to be tenants because they had agreed to acquire ownership on the "rental purchase" system. Monthly payments had been calculated as sufficient to recoup the cost of construction, utilities, insurance, and taxes during the first 30 years. A $5 per month "maintenance rent" would be deposited into an account from which money to repair the house could be withdrawn, if the Board approved the request. For the remaining 969 years of the lease an annual peppercorn rent of $1 would be paid, either by the original tenant or a subsequent occupier.

As it turned out, the concerns about inadequate maintenance were unfounded. All the tenants maintained their property to the satisfaction of the Corporation, none of the original tenants defaulted on their monthly payments, and in time the peppercorn rent was unofficially forgiven (although it was always accepted if offered) (Ryan, 2014).

9

SHOVELS IN THE GROUND

The SJHC held its first board meeting on 20 July 1944, two days after the Commission of Government approved the two requisite bills (H.A. Winter 1944a). The men appointed to steer the SJHC through its daunting undertaking were Brian Dunfield, chairman, and five members carried over from the earlier CEHTP: Lewis H.M. Ayre, William F. Breen, William J. Frampton, Gordon F. Higgins, and F.J. O'Leary. Three new members were appointed: Charles Peet, president of the Newfoundland Protective Association of Shop and Office Employees, and Chesley A. Pippy and Gordon A. Winter, merchants (Walsh 1944c). As personal circumstances changed, Breen was replaced by William George Sullivan, M.B.E., president of the LSPU, and Frampton was replaced by F.A.F. Lush, secretary of the Federation of Labour. Surprisingly, Eric Cook was not appointed to the original Board. However, when Sullivan resigned, the Board requested that Cook be named to replace him as he was "the originator of our entire movement" (Organ 1947).

The Trunk Sewer

Work began immediately. The first thing to do was proceed with the preliminary work already begun by Ed Searles, the consulting engineer who had joined the project in August 1943. Convinced by Searles's argument that sewerage was the first priority, the Board authorized him to begin work at once on the trunk sewer and the tunnel between Quidi Vidi Lake and the harbour (*Evening Telegram* 1944a). Excavation for the sewer began at the beginning of November 1944, with technical assistance provided by the manager of the Bell Island iron mines (*Evening Telegram*, 1944j). Because the tunnel lay outside the Housing Area, a new section 110 (1) had to be added to the City of St. John's Act giving the Corporation permission to excavate within the city (Legislation 1945b). Miners from St. Lawrence were hired to dig the 1,300-foot-long tunnel. They began working from both ends and broke through the last bit of rock a year later, on 9 November 1945. Two days later, on Remembrance Day, Dunfield and several members of the Board of the SJHC walked through the tunnel from the lakeside to Temperance Street and back again (*Daily News* 1945f).

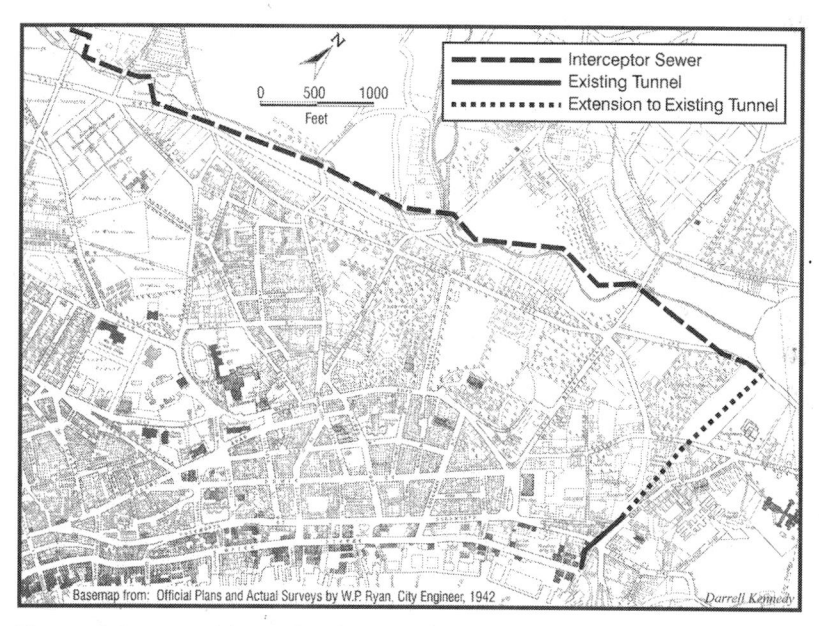

Figure 9.1. Map of the collector sewer through the northern valley and the tunnel to the harbour (Darrell Kennedy).

The drainage infrastructure for the housing project was plagued with problems. Storm drains, initially omitted in order to cut costs, eventually had to be retrofitted at great expense. Water mains in the cul-de-sacs were dead-ended, causing stagnant water to pool there and contaminate the supply to neighbouring houses. Poor-quality materials, the only kind available during the post-war shortages, led to inevitable problems. The original 4-inch cast-iron water mains were too small and subject to corrosion so they had to be replaced. The individual water service lines were of poor-quality lead, and they had to be replaced. Windsor Lake, source of the area's water, was considerably higher than the housing area and the inlet pressure at most houses was about 140 pounds per square inch, far above the norm of 50 psi. Pressure reduction valves had to be retrofitted to all the houses in 1950 to prevent damage to plumbing fixtures and water heaters. Curbs and gutters, made up of short sections of precast concrete rather than a continuous pour, deteriorated quickly (Martin 1950). However, despite these problems, the northern valley was serviced and made ready for the construction of the houses.

At the Board's fourth meeting in August 1944, Searles showed the Board his plans for a factory to produce concrete sewer pipe and building blocks. This idea came out of the blue, never having been mentioned in any of the CEHTP reports. But it was approved, and Searles immediately went to the US to see if he could find the necessary equipment. He did, and work on the plant was underway by December. It was located on the west side of Freshwater Road, just north of Empire Avenue on the site now occupied by the Canada Revenue Agency tax centre. The first blocks were produced on 27 July 1945 and the first pipe the next day. When the plant was in full operation it produced pipe ranging in size from 6 to 30 inches, and blocks at the rate of two per minute. Further expansion of the Corporation's ability to produce its own building material came in February 1945 when the Board decided to expropriate Fagan's barn on Lamb's Lane and convert it to a sash and door plant. Production was preplanned and carefully controlled. Every door and window was identified by type and house number. The facility also produced precut framing lumber so that carpenters wouldn't have to saw it on-site.

The local trade unions were almost completely shut out of the project. All the work on the project, and in its factories, was performed by the Corporation's own employees. The Corporation was able to find enough men to do its work, but, not surprisingly, relationships with the city's labour organizations were poor. However, the project provided much-needed employment. At the peak of its operations the SJHC employed 655 men and provided a weekly payroll of $24,000. By the end of 1950 it had paid out $2,320,000 in wages (St. John's Housing Corporation 1951, 17).

Figure 9.2. The block and pipe plant, Freshwater Road. The site is now occupied by the CRA Taxation Centre (F.P. Meschino).

Figure 9.3. Concrete pipes stacked outside the plant (F.P. Meschino).

Figure 9.4. Concrete blocks stacked outside the plant (F.P. Meschino).

Figure 9.5. The sash and door plant, Lamb's Lane (NLHC).

Turning the Sod

At 2:30 in the afternoon of 25 October 1944 a small group of commissioners, members of the Municipal Council, the Housing Commission, and a small crowd of onlookers gathered in a roped-off enclosure beside Klondike Farm on Torbay Road to witness the formal commencement of construction at the point where the new westward-running circumferential road would begin (*Daily News* 1944c). Deputy Mayor Eric Cook performed the honours, using a new shovel that had been bought specially for the event. It was fitting that Cook was the man of the hour because he was the one who had originally proposed that Council undertake some sort of a plan for "the betterment of the town" more than two years previously (SJMC 1942).

Figure 9.6. Turning the sod for the garden suburb: Eric Cook, left, and Brian Dunfield (*Daily News* 25 Oct. 1944).

Dunfield made another memorable speech:

> We are gathered here today to take the first step in a programme which we all believe may bring marvellous changes to our city in the future. For many years we have suffered from congestion and from slums, from expensive building land and from shortage of sewered areas. . . . This is not a programme to be carried out in a year, nor in five years . . . . It may take a generation to realize the effects of this scheme in the fullest measure . . . . I hope that you and I at least, Mr. Deputy Mayor, if we have twenty years of life left for us may be able to stand here in 1964 and look westward along a beautiful tree-lined area flanked on all sides by streets and squares and attractive houses occupied by 25 percent of our population, and with the pressure upon our older city progressively relieved and the way clear for steady improvement. We may see a day when the children of the next generation will everywhere be comfortably housed and playing upon lawns and in parks, and where slum hovels and playgrounds in the gutter are a thing of the past. (*Evening Telegram* 1944h)

With the formalities out of the way, Deputy Mayor Cook climbed up on a bulldozer belonging to the McNamara Construction Company so that he could see the commencement of work on Elizabeth Avenue at first hand (*Daily News* 1944c).

The absence of the Mayor Andrew Carnell from the ceremony was indicative of the tensions that already existed between the Municipal Council and the SJHC. A few days prior to the ceremony the mayor had given Dunfield a verbal commitment that he would perform the ceremony. However, Dunfield's formal invitation included a request that the Council agree to name the circumferential road Elizabeth Street "in honour of the present, and probable future queen." (Dunfield, of course,

Figure 9.7. The Elizabeth Avenue bridge over Rennie's River under construction, 1944 (NLHC).

is referring to both the Queen Mother, wife of George VI, and the future and still reigning Elizabeth II.) Claiming that the SJHC had usurped the right of the Council to name the city's new streets, and that "because there was a petition before Parliament about the matter" (presumably the expropriation process), the mayor informed the Corporation on the morning of the ceremony that he would not attend (Minutes of the SJHC, 27 Oct. 1944).

The Housing: Owner-Occupied and Detached

Shelter is a basic human need as well as an important cultural expression (McCann 1996, 133; J.B. Jackson 1985, 3). The house, whether rented or owned, is the most common element in the taken-for-granted landscape. During the first two decades of the twentieth century, the Canadian populace had turned away from renting to indulge a desire for home ownership. There were discussions at the time about home ownership being a way to promote thrift, and giving freedom of choice of living space, or even securing stability in marriage (Harris 2012). Home ownership was an indicator of economic well-being and social mobility. Home ownership came to define the middle class.

Home ownership in the outports was traditional in Newfoundland where houses were usually built by the owner, his friends, and his family. This contributed to the high level of home ownership in Newfoundland as a whole — 85 per cent in the 1945 census. This compared to 41 per cent in Canada. But in St. John's, with its long history of landlords and leases and houses built in ranges, only 60 per cent of the dwellings were owner-occupied and only 53 per cent of those were detached.

Paul Meschino Joins the Team

We have seen how A.E. Searles, by chance, came to be employed by the CEHTP and then by the SJHC. The same is true of architect Paul Meschino, who was sent to St. John's because the British Admiralty decided to build a new naval escort base in the city in 1941. He eventually became the Corporation's architect. Francesco Paolo (Paul) Meschino was born in a small village south of Rome in 1912, a year before his family moved to Toronto. He graduated from the architecture program at the University of Toronto in the spring of 1939, having studied the principles of Modernism, landscape architecture, and town planning. The planning lectures were taught by Humphrey Carver, who was then working in the

Figure 9.8. Paul Meschino (1912–2007), architect for the garden suburb, 1945–53 (F.P. Meschino).

School of Social Work with Albert Rose but who would go on to an illustrious though largely unrecognized career at Central Mortgage and Housing Corporation. At his graduation Meschino was awarded the Toronto Architectural Guild Gold Medal and the Darling and Pearson Prize for Exceptional Architectural Design. He spent the summer working with Carver on preliminary designs for the Regent Park social housing project before opening his own architectural practice in September 1939. Wartime shortages of clients and materials soon forced him to close his practice.

In 1941 the Canadian government created Wartime Housing Limited (WHL) and Doug Kertland, a Toronto architect, asked Meschino to join it (Meschino 2002). By 1943, Canadian wartime industries employed 848,000 workers. Whole communities were created by WHL adjacent to military bases and munitions factories. Meschino received valuable experience working on the designs of small, economical houses.

Then, in the spring of 1943, the British Admiralty began a major expansion of the convoy escort base in St. John's. The director of the Wartime Bureau of Technical Personnel asked Meschino if he would be willing to leave WHL to work with the Works and Buildings Division of the Royal Canadian Navy (RCN). Meschino had no idea how or why they picked him, but he agreed. He was called on a Monday night early in May and told to be in Ottawa by Wednesday. He asked for a couple of days to sort out the projects he was working on, got to Ottawa on Friday, and was in St. John's by Sunday (Meschino 2002). Once in St. John's, he began work on three projects: a large barracks complex on the Southside Hills, the controlled minefield station at the mouth of the harbour, and the ship repair facility at Bay Bulls (Meschino 2000). He had to provide all his own tools and supplies, including thumb tacks and set squares.

That fall, Meschino's intrepid 23-year-old fiancée Phyllis, accompanied by her parents and his widowed mother, drove his car to North Sydney, Nova Scotia. The fuel for the five-day trip was scrounged from every family member and friend. Along with the car, she then boarded the ferry to Port aux Basques and crossed the Cabot Strait only a year after the sinking of the ferry S.S. *Caribou* by *U-690*, abandoning her travelling companions in

North Sydney because they didn't have permission to leave Canada and enter what was then a foreign country. In fact, that she was allowed to travel on to Newfoundland was unusual: wives of Canadian service personnel were permitted to join their husbands in Newfoundland, but Phyllis was only a fiancée and Paul wasn't a naval officer. At Port aux Basques she put the car on the train and set off for St. John's, where she arrived on a Saturday. She and Paul were married the next Monday at Gower Street United Church (Martha Meschino, 2021). Then they had to find accommodation in the city's overcrowded housing market. As a married man Paul couldn't continue to live in barracks at HMCS Avalon on Buckmaster's Circle, where in his opinion the most important perk was access to the showers! They found a single room on the second floor of a three-storey downtown house. The house was already occupied by a husband and wife, their six children, a son-in-law, and a maid. The 12 people shared the one bathroom and the warmth from one radiator in the hallway. Paul and Phyllis had no kitchen so they ate supper, and usually lunch as well, at Stirling's Restaurant at 354 Water Street. Mrs. Stirling always sat the "CFAs" (i.e., the "Come From Aways") at a separate table. It was here that Ed Searles and Paul Meschino first met.

Having been favourably impressed by Searles's work, Dunfield decided to engage the J.W. Beretta Company as the consulting engineers for the housing project. The contract was signed in August 1944. By then, Meschino's work for the RCN was beginning to wind down, and on 22 April 1944 Searles asked Meschino to consider coming to work with him. By early September Meschino and Beretta had agreed on a satisfactory contract. The problem was that Meschino was still employed by the RCN and obtaining a release was a complicated business. Dunfield, Searles, and one of the commissioners went to the office of Canadian High Commissioner Paul Burchell in Newfoundland on 25 August to argue for his release. Burchell appealed to Arthur MacNamara, the Canadian deputy minister of labour, and to the Department of External Affairs. Then MacNamara had to request clearance from the Wartime Bureau of Technical Personnel and the Naval Office in St. John's. In the end, everybody agreed, but said that the release couldn't be effective until the middle of December. In the meantime, Meschino had to apply to the Labour Exit Permit Department and the Mobilization Board for permission to continue working outside of Canada (Meschino 2000). While he was waiting for the necessary authorizations, Meschino worked for the Corporation on nights, weekends, and holidays from early October 1944 until early January 1945, when he was finally able to join the Beretta organization. His mandate was to do the land planning, lay out the streets (with the exception of Elizabeth Avenue, which had already been planned), and design the houses. Searles and Meschino remained with the Beretta organization until October 1947, when they resigned, formed their own company, and took over the engineering contract for the project.

Meschino Brings House Styles from "Away" to Newfoundland

Meschino's houses were built on the cusp of Newfoundland's embrace of Modernism. During his time with the Corporation he found himself sandwiched between conservative traditionalism, which characterized the country, and the desire of Joey Smallwood, the first premier of the new province, to promote progress and modernity. Optimism reigned in post-Confederation Newfoundland. In the 1950s and 1960s, an era characterized by what now seems a naive belief in the potential benefits of progress, architects working in the province enthusiastically embraced Modernism (Mellin 2011, 7).

Modernism was intended to break with the past and introduce new forms of expression in all forms of literature and art, including architecture (Waldron 2005). Meschino was a man to do this. He had been trained in the modernist tradition and his first house commission was a clear reflection of the modern idiom of Frank Lloyd Wright and Richard Neutra: a flat-roofed bungalow in the Armour Heights subdivision of North York that featured the corner windows that would become one of the trademark architectural features of the houses he built in Churchill Park.

Figure 9.9. Meschino's first house commission, Armour Heights, Toronto, 1939) (F.P. Meschino).

Figure 9.10. A "Cape Cod" house in Churchill Park: 15 Appledore Place (C.A. Sharpe).

The most common house type in North America during and immediately after the war was the so-called "Cape Cod," which has been characterized as the "quintessential Canadian house" (McKellar 1993). This house type was used exclusively by Canadian Wartime Housing Limited (WHL) and its successor, the Veterans' Housing Limited (VHL). The type was widely featured in post-war mail-order catalogues of house blueprints (Massey and Maxwell 1999) and in CMHC house design catalogues (Latremouille 1986, 87; Teodorescu 2012). In the United States the best-known examples are the 17,447 identical "Capes" built from 1947 onward in Levittown, New York (Kelly 1993; Kushner 2009). But "modern" was an impossible style for small urban homes (Gowans 1992, 285). If one was given the mandate to design an inexpensive, two- or three-bedroom home, where economy was more important than pretension, the inevitable result would probably be a house very like the ubiquitous Cape Cod.

A "Cape" was typically one and a half storeys with a large, fairly low-pitched gable roof, sometimes with dormers. It had barely perceptible eaves and gable overhangs. There were sash windows and usually a centrally located chimney (Noble 1984, 223; Gowans 1992, 52; Ennals and Holdsworth 1998, 75; Baker 1994, 7). They were commonly clad in unpainted wooden shingles or clapboard, and figured prominently in images celebrating "the American Dream" (Schoenauer 2000, 416).

Between 1944 and 1947 Meschino designed 244 houses for the SJHC. Forty-five per cent of them were the Cape Cod type: 15 per cent bungalows and 30 per cent one and a half storeys. He also produced 30 other house designs, which included semi-detached bungalows and two-storey houses, one pair of four-unit terraces, and detached two-storey houses (Appendices 4 and 5).

Meschino did not consciously set out to build Cape Cod houses and didn't think he had, although other architects disagree (Mellin 2011, 156). He remembered being told that he had "to design inexpensive houses intended for poverty-stricken war veterans who did not yet have a job" (Meschino 2000). Accordingly, he incorporated a lot of design features in

Type 3.11 The classic Churchill Park 'Cape Cod' with 3 bedrooms and basement.

Type 3.15 Two storey with 3 bedrooms and basement.

Type 4.103 Two storey with 4 bedrooms and basement.

Type 3.111 Single storey with 3 bedrooms and basement.

Type 12.101 Four family row with 3 bedrooms and basement. 114-120 Bonaventure Ave.

Type 11.103 Two storey with 3 bedrooms and basement.

Figure 9.11. Examples of Paul Meschino's house designs (NLHC).

his houses that were specifically geared to SJHC's needs and budget restraints. He also introduced modern designs and interior features that were not familiar to householders in St. John's but emulated contemporary Canadian houses. Mayor Carnell criticized the houses as being so small there wasn't room enough to swing a cat (Bartlett 1999), but in a city that had suffered for so long from a chronic shortage of decent housing, the houses were a revelation. Meschino, however, described his small, unpretentious barebones houses as so "minimal" that he would never have been able to sell them in Toronto. But he and Phyllis remembered living quite comfortably in one of houses on Bideford Place (Phyllis Meschino 2000).

Meschino worried that even experienced carpenters would need guidance in building houses that were not typical of St. John's. He made very detailed drawings of everything in the houses, including kitchen cabinets, trashcan holders, and bookshelves, and even indicated precisely where soap dishes and toilet paper holders should be placed in the bathrooms. Unfortunately, very few local carpenters — as few as one in 25 — could read blueprints. The president of Memorial University College came to the rescue and agreed to offer training in blueprint reading, free of charge (*Daily News* 1945d).

There is a stylistic uniformity to the houses because the leases gave the SJHC the authority to control even the colour of the paint. To avoid visual monotony, Meschino carefully designed a variety of house types, sizes, and colours on each street. He specified on the construction schedule the colours to be used on each house for siding, trim, and windows. Meschino preferred quiet colours, especially creams and greys, and mixed them himself at the Corporation's paint plant on Freshwater Road.

Meschino took care to situate every house to its best advantage on its site with reference to orientation and grade, as Frank Lloyd Wright recommended. His blueprints showed the elevation of all four sides of every house type and indicated the ground level. He used garden, stair, and porch walls to create layers between the street and the house on sloping lots. Integrated garages were built where sloped sites provided the opportunity. Many of these features, all of them characteristic of "modern" architecture, can still be seen in the heart of Churchill Park today, on Maple and Stoneyhouse Streets and Pine Bud Avenue.

Figure 9.12. A one-and-a-half-storey house with garage on a steeply sloping site: 7 Cork Place (F.P. Meschino).

Inside Meschino's Houses: A New Style of Living

The Churchill Park houses may not have been "modern" in the architectural sense, but they incorporated many modern features. They all had full basements, built-in kitchen cabinets, bathrooms, and central heating. While such features were already familiar elsewhere in Atlantic Canada, they were exciting innovations in St. John's. The rooms were modest to small in size. There was a small eating area rather than a full dining room. The main floor rooms were open-plan, connected by archways instead of corridors and doors, thus bringing the corridor space into the rooms. This plan, which saved money by reducing the number of doors, was appreciated by the men on the SJHC Board, but not by many of the housewives, who would have preferred a more traditional plan with separate rooms. The corner windows, which Meschino had used in the design of his first house in Toronto, became a signature feature of the Corporation's houses, and allow the rooms to be flooded with natural light.

Figure 9.13. Corner windows in the living room at 2 Beech Place (C.A. Sharpe).

Another characteristic feature was the "patent side ventilator" used by Richard Neutra in some of his California and Mexican houses (Mellin 2011, 76). The introduction of "picture windows" by the Libbey-Owens-Ford Glass Company in the 1930s, whereby large, unobstructed expanses of glass framed views of the outdoors, required a new type of ventilation (Wright 2008, 127). Neutra used horizontal louvres to permit passive cross-ventilation (Drexler and Hines 1982), placing them under the soffits (Tippey 2016). In his Corporation houses Meschino placed them on one or both sides of the windows, but in two of the houses he built as private commissions he used horizontal louvres under the windows. A flyscreen was fitted to the back of the louvre, which was closed off by a pair of narrow wooden shutters held in place by a short rotating wooden bar. They were intended to "reduce draughts, conserve heat, exclude flies and reduce expense." Dunfield said the Board thought they would do all that, but "at any rate we propose to see how housewives like them" (*Daily News* 1945d). Continuing doubts led to a lengthy defensive explanation by Dunfield:

The double sashes are fixed although the inner one can be taken down for cleaning, and thus there is no draught whatever around the window. The ventilation consists of a louvre at the side, or at both sides. As seen by the public so far these sashes have been installed with only a single glass and with the louvres wide open and we are not surprised that some people thought they would be rather breezy. We have in mind the carpenter whom we asked what he thought of them. He, having seen them only with the open louvre, replied politely that he thought they would be lovely in the summer. However, as installed, there will be behind the louvre a wire fly screen; behind the fly screen a special four-piece shutter, tight against draughts and adjustable in several different positions so that the occupier can have anything from a little to a lot of ventilation at will. The ventilation shutter will be concealed behind the curtains. This design is becoming popular in Canada and the United States and has been proved satisfactory there. It does not cost more than an ordinary window and we are putting in a limited number only to see how the public like them. (*Evening Telegram* 1945e)

The public didn't like them. As predicted, they were "breezy," impossible to seal properly, and the cause of great discomfort during the winter.

Inside Meschino's Houses: Retaining Newfoundland Tradition

There were only two issues over which Meschino and the Board of the SJHC disagreed: central heating and fitted kitchen cupboards. Meschino considered them necessities. Several members of the Board disagreed. Their view was that a fireplace, in combination with the kitchen range, would provide adequate heat. They also assumed that a kitchen with a

Figure 9.14. Louvres, exterior view: 2 Beech Place (C.A. Sharpe).
Figure 9.15. Interior view of closed louvres: 2 Beech Place (C.A. Sharpe).
Figure 9.16. Louvres on a corner window: 4 Appledore Place (C.A. Sharpe).

stand-alone sink and virtually no cupboards would suffice. However, Meschino won this argument. In August 1945 the Board agreed to the installation of kitchen cabinets and "some sort" of central heating. They permitted the installation of "gravity hot air" furnaces, some oil-fired and some coal-burning, in the basement. None of the Corporation houses was equipped with a forced-air heating system in the beginning. Tenants who wanted to convert them to a forced air system had to buy and install a motor and fan themselves. In return, Meschino had to put in fireplaces, although he considered them unnecessary when there was central heating. But the Board insisted that a house without a fireplace would be difficult to sell to

182   CORNER WINDOWS AND CUL-DE-SACS

Newfoundlanders. The debates, and the outcomes, are a reflection of the controversial transition from traditional to modern in Newfoundland.

Meschino placed the fireplace in the centre of the house primarily for reasons of economy, although this was another of Frank Lloyd Wright's favourite design ideas. Centrally located fireplaces do not take up any more floor space than those located on an outside wall, do not interfere with windows, and do not reduce usable wall space. This location permits a better arrangement of furniture. In the Corporation's houses, the chimney

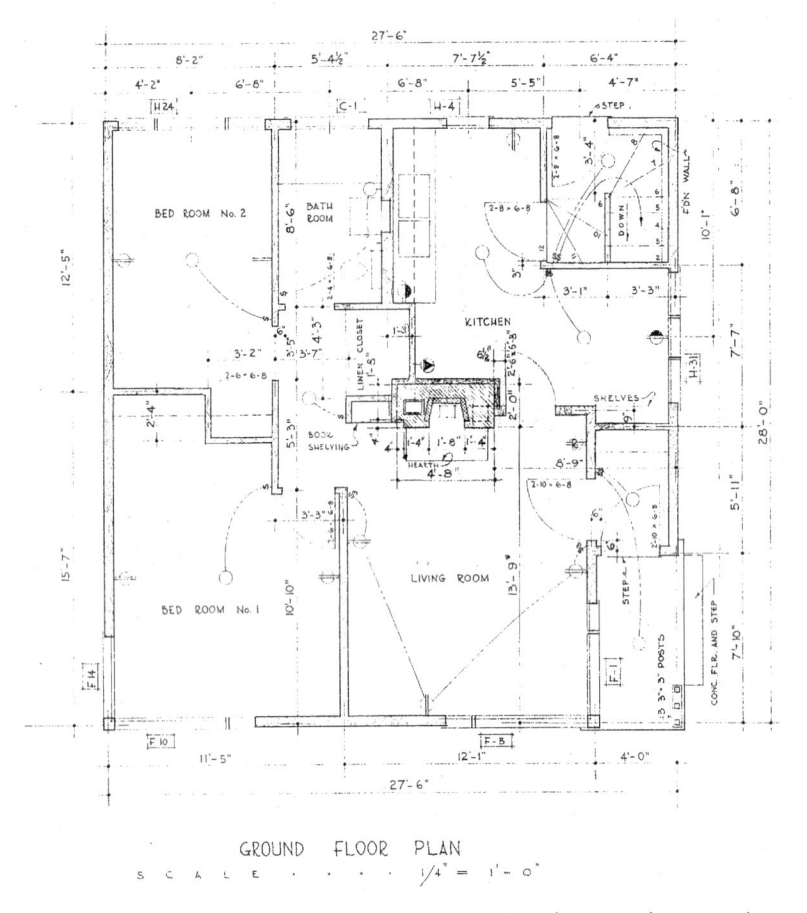

Figure 9.17. Ground floor plan, house type 2.1 (single-storey house with two bedrooms and basement (NLHC).

Figure 9.18. Centrally located fireplace, 4 Appledore Place (C.A. Sharpe).

had three flues: one from the fireplace, one from the furnace, and one from the kitchen range, which was heated by either oil or solid fuel.

Meschino's formal contract with the SJHC ended on 1 November 1952 because, given the now-restricted mandate of the Corporation, there was insufficient work to warrant his continued employment. But during his time with the Corporation he attended 208 (87 per cent) of 239 Board meetings. He remained in St. John's for another two years, providing architectural advice to the Corporation and designing houses under private contracts.

Meschino was one of the eight founding members of the Newfoundland Association of Architects in 1949 (Mellin 2011, 260). Prominent Newfoundland architects who were contemporaries of Meschino held him in high regard and believed that his talents were wasted in St. John's, where people could not afford the kind of house he was capable of designing (Campbell 1999; Noseworthy 1999). After leaving the SJHC he accepted a private commission from Mr. and Mrs. Joseph Goldstone, owners of the

London, New York and Paris department store on Water Street, to build a house on one of the most dramatic residential lots in the city. Mrs. Goldstone originally wanted a classic Colonial style house, but Meschino convinced her to try something completely different. The result is a stunning, Frank Lloyd Wright-inspired house on Rostellan Avenue. It overlooks Rennie's River, and the sound of rushing water and views of the river are essential visual and auditory features of the house. The horizontal terraces and cantilevered roofs oppose the vertical elements of the bedroom wing and chimney. The house was the first in St. John's to feature an open plan interior on the main level. The house was the featured Home of the Week in the *Toronto Telegram* on 5 December 1953 and had an important influence on housing design in Newfoundland (Mellin 2011, 253). Meschino considered it to be as avant-garde as anything he could have designed in Toronto (Meschino 2000). It is the kind of house that he would build in Toronto for the rest of his career, including his own house in the Windfields Farm development in Don Valley Village. St. John's

Figure 9.19. The west front of the Goldstone house; note the horizontal and vertical ventilation louvres (C.A. Sharpe).

architect Robert Mellin made some sympathetic additions to the Goldstone house and was awarded the Newfoundland Historic Trust's 2003 Southcott Award for outstanding achievement in heritage restoration. It is the first modern building in Newfoundland to be so honoured (Mellin 2011, xii).

Meschino returned to Toronto in January 1953. He enjoyed a successful career there and later in Naples, Florida, where he worked until his retirement in 1978. In the summer of 2000, thanks to the generous financial support of the Smallwood Centre of Memorial University, the authors were able to bring Paul and Phyllis Meschino to St. John's for a week-long visit. They were able to see what had become of his work in the half-century since they had left and to revisit their old neighbourhood, where three of their children had spent their early years. They were both amazed, and gratified, to discover how significant "The Housing" had been in the history of the city. Paul died in 2007 at the age of 95 and Phyllis died in 2016, at the age of 96.

Figure 9.20. Paul and Phyllis Meschino and architect Robert Mellin examining plans in the Department of Geography, Memorial University of Newfoundland. June 2000 (A.J. Shawyer).

Figure 9.21. Paul and Phyllis Meschino beside the Churchill Park display in Churchill Square, 9 June 2000 (A.J. Shawyer).

10

MR. DUNFIELD'S FOLLY?

> It is unfortunate that the cost of these houses ... is so high ... as to restrict a young couple with a growing family from making an investment ... these new houses are beyond the means of the ordinary wage earner. (*Evening Telegram* 1946b)

1945: The Rising Cost of Construction

Meschino presented his plan for the layout of Village "B" to the Board on 11 May 1945, and his first house plans on 25 May. The Board was shocked by the projected cost of the houses, which was far higher than the estimates made in the third and fifth reports of the CEHTP (CEHTP 3, 60; CEHTP 5, 32; Cook 1982).

In 1935 only 25 per cent of owner-occupied dwellings in the country were valued at $3,000 or more, but in 1945 this had risen to 69 per cent (Lewis and Shrimpton 1984, 235). Even so, it appeared that the cost of housing in the new suburb was going to be well above the average. Meschino estimated that a one-and-a-half or two-storey four-bedroom house and lot would cost about $7,000. This no doubt reflected the inflationary effect of the war, which had increased the cost of living in Newfoundland by more than two-thirds between 1938 and 1946.

Nothing could be done about the high cost of building materials. This was an inevitable result of pervasive post-war shortages. The minutes of the SJHC reflect a constant preoccupation with the question of how to

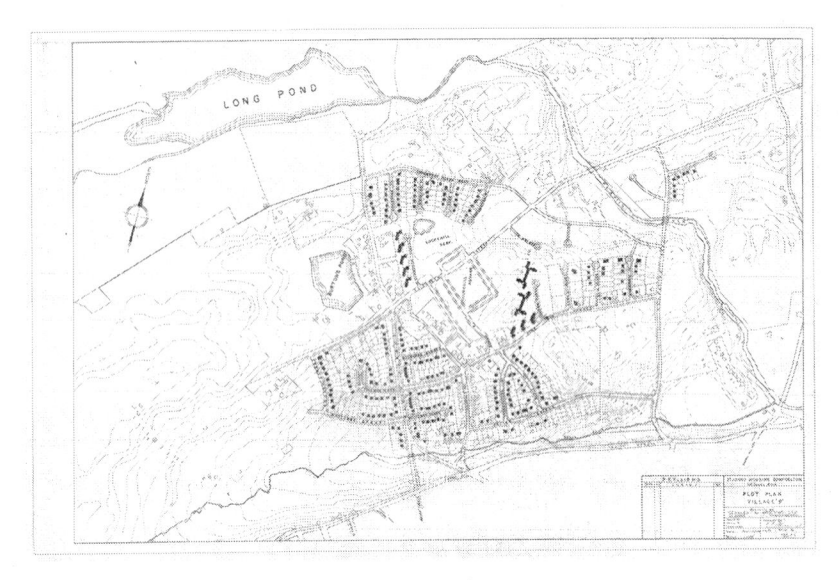

Figure 10.1. Plot plan Village "B," 5 March 1946 (NLHC).

reduce costs in the face of prices over which the Corporation had no control because, during the war, industrial production was diverted from civilian to military use. In Newfoundland the post-war situation was worsened by the continued existence of Canadian and American export quotas and it was unlikely that quotas would be increased any time soon. The Canadian Wartime Prices and Trade Board kept 80 per cent of all industrial output for its own use and for exports to Britain. It released 10 per cent for domestic consumption and 10 per cent for export to all foreign markets, which included Newfoundland. In spite of entreaties made to Canadian officials by the SJHC Board and other Newfoundland representatives, the country's share of the quota was not increased.

Gypsum wallboard was in such short supply in Canada that even pre-approved orders could not be filled. The arrival of one shipment at the beginning of 1947 alleviated one of the causes of slow progress, but there were many others. The demand for Johns Manville asbestos siding led to an embargo from the mainland and the cancellation of existing orders. It was almost impossible to get door hinges, electrical components, plumbing fixtures, and rockwool insulation — the list went on (*Evening Telegram* 1947d). And then there was the unexpected: a shipment of cast-iron soil pipe sufficient for 125 houses was lost when the SS *Moyra* ran aground near Quebec City in June 1945 and was abandoned by its owners.

Another problem was the difficulty in finding construction equipment. Only used machinery was available and it, too, was in short supply. The SJHC managed to buy two power shovels and a backhoe from the Admiralty but dealing with the complex paper trail to release them took most of the summer. The Corporation bought used trucks from the US Army but there were no replacement tires. None of these shortages of materials or equipment was solely responsible for the cost overruns, but the cumulative effect on the Corporation's construction activities was significant, and, eventually, would become fatal.

The SJHC Board discussed many possible ways to reduce the construction cost. The foundation could be made of concrete blocks rather than poured concrete, and the concrete basement floor could be eliminated; only a single layer of flooring could be installed upstairs; all interior painting could be left to the tenant; asphalt shingles could be replaced by torch-on roofing; storm windows could be left off; wallboard could be used instead of plaster in the bathroom and the walls in the rest of the house covered with ten-test, a wax-impregnated wood fibreboard with a very rough finish that is difficult to paint. Making all these modifications would have shaved about 20 per cent off the original estimate, but the result would have been a much less desirable house. In the end, the Board decided to stick with the original plans for the moment, except for the use of ten-test when wallboard wasn't available. This would turn out to be a very unpopular decision. In the end, because "circumstances often intrude upon intentions" (Goddard 1988, 100), the earnest and well-intentioned efforts of the Corporation to control the costs were unsuccessful. The result was unfortunate but predictable. By the end of 1945 the Board was aware that the funds available would be sufficient to complete only one of the three planned villages.

Construction Begins: "Citizens Enthused Over New Houses"

Work began on the first three houses, numbers 4, 6, and 8 Maple Street, on 27 July (*Evening Telegram* 1945d). The year's building plan called for 100 houses and all had been started by the end of the year (*Evening Telegram* 1945e; see Appendix 6). The scale of the project, with its new streets and new-style houses rising on former farmland at the edge of town, drew great public interest.

On 8 October Governor Walwyn, accompanied by his private secretary, Lt. Harold Goodrich, and Dunfield, came to inspect the work (*Evening Telegram* 1945g). The tour began with an inspection of the Temperance Street end of the sewer tunnel. The group then examined the trench for the trunk sewer, the proposed site of the eastern village centre, the bridge carrying Elizabeth Street over Rennie's River, the houses being built on Pine Bud Avenue, the layout of the northern part of Village "B," the woodworking plant on Lamb's Lane, and the proposed site of the western village centre. They finished up at the pipe and block plant, which also housed the Corporation's offices. Here the governor spent a long time discussing house plans with Paul Meschino and was "very much impressed by the

Figure 10.2. Maple Street under construction (NLHC).

work in the drafting room." In light of the criticism already circulating about them, it is interesting that press reports of this meeting note that "a very attractive feature of all the houses is the new type shutters built on either side of each window which enables the regulating of ventilation" and

Figure 10.3. Stoneyhouse Street under construction (NLHC).

Figure 10.4. Bideford Place under construction (NLHC).

Figure 10.5. Left to right: Dunfield, Lt. Goodrich, Governor Walwyn, and Paul Meschino in the SJHC drafting office (*Daily News* 8 Oct. 1945).

Citizens Enthused Over New Houses

Hundreds of citizens visited the new houses under construction on Village A, off Allandale Road, on Sunday. They came away enthusiastic over the dwellings which have been designed by Paul Meschino, and several of which are now practically completed.

The interest in the new building area by the public seems rising steadily, with Sunday setting an all high for visitors to the site.

Figure 10.6. "Citizens Enthused Over New Houses" (*Daily News* 9 Oct. 1945). Note that this was, in fact, Village "B," not Village "A."

repeat the unsubstantiated comment that "this type of window is being used extensively throughout Canada and the United States" (*Evening Telegram* 1945g; *Daily News* 1945e).

The next day the Housing Area was opened to the public. The press report noted that there appeared to be increasing interest in the project, and many of the visitors were very enthusiastic about Meschino's nearly completed houses. Unfortunately the houses were going to be very expensive. The Municipal Council was alarmed by the fact that the cost would put them beyond the reach not only of the poor but also of most wage earners. Undaunted, the SJHC Board decided to build 200 more houses in 1946 without seriously addressing the problem of cost.

Unexpected Demands: The "Widows' Mansions" and the "Soldier Emergency"

The Corporation's house building did not occur in a vacuum. The problem of the dilapidated houses and distressed families in the inner city remained unresolved. The Council had contributed $1,200,000 to the SJHC project in the hope that it would go some way towards relieving the situation in the inner city. Clearly, this was not going to be the case.

The Council went back to the government with their well-worn argument that the rehousing of persons vacated from unfit housing in the inner city was the responsibility of the government, not the Council, and also expressed a growing antipathy towards the SJHC. Mayor Carnell took up Councillor Meaney's arguments that there were areas within the city limits that could easily be provided with water and sewer services and developed for housing. Trunk services had now been extended north across LeMarchant Road along the major streets — Casey, Prince of Wales, Campbell, all of which had seen many houses built in recent years. Councillor Vardy, who would later become chairman of the SJHC, strongly expressed his disappointment at the failure of the Corporation to solve the problem of providing housing for the destitute. The commissioner of public health and welfare, Sir John Puddester, showed some empathy and suggested that the SJHC could build apartments for the very poor.

In 1945 the government and the Council put together a plan to build 100 dwellings for "indigent" persons, defined as widows with children living in extreme poverty (SJCM 11 Jan. 1945, 6; 5 Apr. 1945, 73; 27 Oct. 1945, 271). The government committed $250,000 and Mayor Carnell offered to provide a serviced site within the city boundary for the development. He suggested the Ebsary farm area near Mundy Pond, where Vickers and Vimy Avenues are today. This area was within walking distance of schools, churches, and shops. The city would pay to expropriate and service the land. The plan would begin with 155 houses and aim for 300 in the next few years. The Dominions Office in London supported this initiative for distressed persons, but did not approve of the cost, suggesting that building in flat blocks would be less expensive than building individual houses (Cranborne 1945b).

Dunfield wanted no part of this project. In the first place he didn't like subsidized housing. He also knew that the Corporation would face opposition from local tradesmen in the city if he brought his Corporation workmen inside the city limits to construct the houses. And he argued that the Corporation already had enough on its plate, given the plan to build 200 more houses in 1946. "There is no use landing ourselves in a disappointment by trying to do too much" (Dunfield 1945b).

Dunfield got his wish. The Ebsary project, commonly referred to as the Widows' Mansions, was a joint project by the city and the government. It evolved into eight blocks providing 68 new, fully serviced apartments. Each apartment had three bedrooms, a kitchen, living room, and a full bathroom. Each had a storage space in the basement, hardwood floors, and an oil heater in the hallway. Government assistance allowed the apartments to be rent-free for widows and their families and other distressed persons. Families moved into what was the first public housing project in Newfoundland in early 1948 (*Evening Telegram* 1948a). It was a small start, but an important beginning to the solution of the housing crisis in the inner city.

While the Ebsary discussions were going on, a new and urgent need was brought to the SJHC's attention. Captain Lewis Brookes, liaison officer with the Newfoundland Regiment, was invited to attend a meeting of the SJHC to discuss the problem of housing returning soldiers, an issue already being debated in the local press. One editorial writer lamented that "there is neither cottages, bungalows or apartments" for returning veterans (*Daily News* 1945a). Brookes predicted that 500 veterans would be returning home soon, many with wives and families, and possibly at least 150 of them would

Figure 10.7. Ebsary estate on Cashin Avenue southeast of Mundy Pond, 1949 (Newfoundland Department of Natural Resources, NFL-SP-6-133).

Figure 10.8. Ebsary estate, Widows' Mansions, 1947 (CSJA 11-01-104).

Figure 10.9. Widows' Mansions, Ebsary estate, 1952–53 (CSJA 01-46-013).

be seeking to remain in St. John's. He worried that the soldiers' British wives "would be used to living in surroundings of a higher standard" than what they would find in Newfoundland, and he hoped that the SJHC would be able to help, although the new houses would be too expensive for most of the veterans to take on as rental-purchase (Dunfield 1945a).

The Board suggested that the SJHC could perhaps build blocks of flats to offer the veterans on a purely rental basis, until they moved on to the next chapter of their lives. Dunfield agreed with Brookes that this was a serious issue because if the veterans found that, to get a roof over their heads, they had to double up with somebody "in a miserable house without a bathroom and in a miserable street, they will suffer grievous shock and disillusionment, as we saw so often after the last war" (Dunfield 1945a). "The Soldier Emergency" required immediate action and if the government would provide a loan of $350,000 to $400,000 the Corporation promised to build 100 rental apartments "and treat married returned soldiers as having a preferential claim upon them as tenants, so long as the situation requires it." The government agreed with this plan and approved a loan of $450,000 "to cover the probable cost of 100 small houses or flats in the Housing Area preference for which will be given to returned ex-servicemen" (Walsh 1945b).

This agreement to build apartments for which returning veterans were to be given first right of refusal absolved Dunfield and the SJHC from any responsibility to participate in the Ebsary scheme. However, the SJHC was now committed to building blocks of flats, something it had not originally planned to do. This became a heavy responsibility in addition to the commitment to build 100 houses in 1945 and 200 houses the next year.

Meschino drew up plans for eight buildings, each containing five three-bedroom "economy" flats. They would be located on Pine Bud Avenue and Allandale Place, built of concrete blocks up to the window line with asbestos shingles on a wood frame above. He estimated they would cost $4,500 per unit to build. Two larger buildings, each containing 26 flats, were built on Linden Place, bringing the total number of flats to 92. Modern architectural practice required the accommodation of automobiles wherever possible (Mellin 2011, 9). The integrated garages in the Pine Bud and Allandale apartment buildings (converted to apartments some years ago) reflected this concern, as do the vehicular entrance canopy and underpass in the Linden Court buildings.

The flats received rave reviews in the local press. They are "completely equipped with every convenience. Each flat is self-contained and each has a living room with the well-liked and attractive long corner windows. . . . Never before in Newfoundland has the stress been placed so much on apartments, but it is believed the public will respond readily to the innovation" (*Daily News* 1945g). They were described as "perhaps the finest monument to the careful planning of the Housing Corporation" (*Evening Telegram* 1946b).

Figure 10.10. Building 90, Allandale Place (F.P. Meschino).

Figure 10.11. Pine Bud apartment building: five units and garages (F.P. Meschino).

Figure 10.12. Linden Court apartment entrance (F.P. Meschino).

Unfortunately, the construction cost of each of the 92 flats was just over $7,000, almost a third more than the original estimate. This put the monthly rent in the vicinity of $50, compared to the city average for an apartment of about $26. Even so, Dunfield wanted to build more of them because he believed there was an appetite for them, that they would mix well with the houses, and that they would be a good long-term investment. The government said "No" (Quinton 1947b).

1946: The Changing Landscape

The combination of Searles's survey work in the northern valley, Meschino's street layout, and Dunfield's determination to design a radically new development is clearly shown in Figure 10.13. Together, these three men, perhaps by accident as much as intent, achieved the essence of the garden suburb ideal that was extolled by Howard, Vivian, and Adams, and brought to St. John's by Dalzell and Todd. Village "B," which was intended to be the template for the other two proposed villages, stood in stark contrast to the crowded living conditions of the inner city. It was characterized by a separation between the main traffic streets (Elizabeth, Bonaventure, Mayor) and the narrower residential streets, with commercial activity separated from residential areas. The generous residential lots gave each household their own private space. There was lots of public open space, too. Meschino planned what he called a "direct" cul-de sac that opened onto the public parkland. He eschewed the more typical "U-type" cul-de-sac, which required a pathway, too often not properly maintained, between residential properties (Meschino 2000).

The original plan was based on the idea that three separate villages would be built but Village "B" is the only one that was completed. Figure 10.13 shows the outline of Churchill Square, awaiting development: the Soldier Emergency apartments on Pine Bud Avenue, Linden Court beside the Square and on Allandale Place, west of the open space on the north side of Elizabeth Avenue. Regular rows of small houses line the short new streets. Pre-Churchill Park houses, their mature vegetation in a darker shade, line Allandale Road, from the Belvedere cemetery in the bottom right corner of the image north past the new Elizabeth Avenue and Burton's Pond. Although the plan to expropriate all the land in the Housing Area was controversial, the pre-Churchill Park landscape was left mostly undisturbed. All the existing roads and houses were left in place and the new roads and houses were added to the new landscape around them.

It is easy to imagine Dunfield's pride and satisfaction when he opened his newspaper on 5 June 1946 and saw the full-page advertisement announcing that after years of planning, the first 30 completed houses were now ready for sale. They consisted of six bungalows, 17 storey-and-a-half houses, and seven two-storey houses (Figure 10.14). They ranged in size from 800 to 850 square feet. The full-page advertisement emphasized a number of features that were avant-garde at the time: a full bathroom with hot and cold water, a built-in medicine cabinet, three inches of insulation in the attic, full basement, a furnace on a concrete pad, a double kitchen sink, built-in kitchen cupboards, and asphalt roof shingles (see Appendix 7). In November the new governor, Gordon Macdonald, inspected the new houses and created a memorable "photo op" of a woman showing off her new kitchen.

Figure 10.13. Vertical aerial photograph of Churchill Park Village "B," 1948 (NFL-SP 6-133, Government of Newfoundland and Labrador).

Critics complained that the rooms were small. Dunfield agreed they were, but argued that this was more than compensated for by the quality of the houses. "Anybody who wants more space can have it, but he must pay for it. We are trying to keep costs down" (*Daily News*, 1945h).

Who Could Afford to Buy the Corporation's Houses? The SJHC Tries to Economize

By the time they went on the market, the average price of a Corporation house, including land, was more than $11,000, very much out of line with

Figure 10.14. Maple Street streetscape showing a variety of house types and standard features such as the distinctive corner windows, ventilator louvre beside the windows, concrete block foundations, and square window with diagonal mullions in the vestibule. Some also have a built-in garage (Newfoundland and Labrador Housing Corporation).

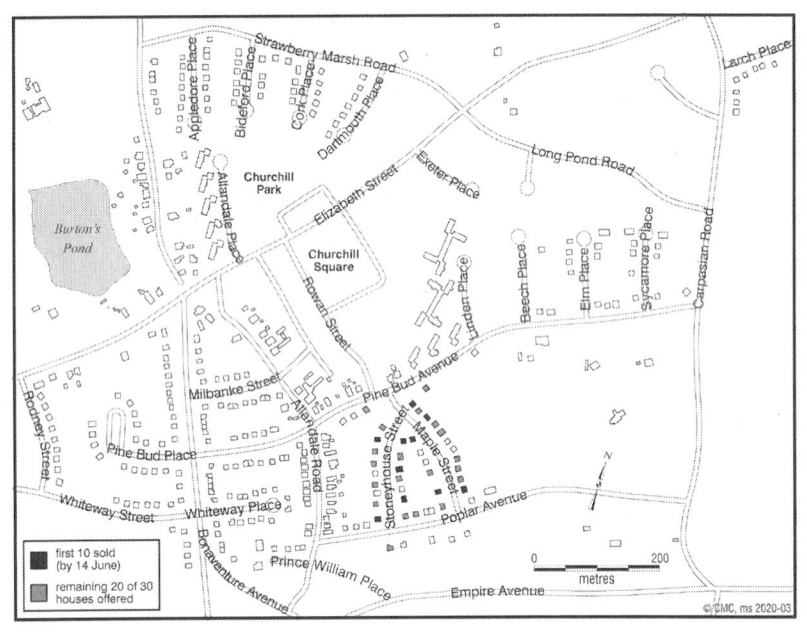

Figure 10.15. The first 30 houses were built on Maple and Stoneyhouse Streets. They were offered for sale on 5 June 1946, and the first 10 houses were sold by 14 June (Map by Charles Conway).

Figure 10.16. Visiting a Churchill Park kitchen, 7 November 1946; left to right: Dunfield, Governor Macdonald, a proud housewife, Kenneth Macdonald (private secretary and son of the governor), and an unidentified man (NLHC).

the going prices in town (*Daily News* 1946a, 1946d, 1946e; *Evening Telegram* 1946e). In 1945 the average price of an owner-occupied single detached house in St John's was $4,710. Only about 10 per cent of the houses had values in excess of $8,000 (Dominion Bureau of Statistics 1949). Stories in the local press acknowledged that house prices everywhere were high, even in the United States where the government subsidized the construction of veterans' houses (*Daily News* 1946d, 1946e; *Evening Telegram* 1946e). However, the basic criticism of the Corporation's houses was "not that they could have been built for much, if any, less, but rather that they are too expensive to be owned by the average salaried person in need of better housing" (*Evening Telegram* 1946g).

This story even reached the mainland press. According to the caption on a photograph of Cork and Dartmouth Streets that appeared in a Montreal newspaper: "Housing project on the city's outskirts is first organized answer to the slum problem. Here a model development can bear comparison with anything on the North American continent. Only flaw is the high cost of the project" (Johnstone 1946, 5). In the immediate post-war period, the project was bold, big, and astonishing in its audacity. It is unlikely that anyone in St. John's had ever seen more than two or three houses put up by a builder at the same time. But here was a huge field full of them! A formerly rural landscape was transformed within the space of a few years in a process that could not have been more different than the slow and gradual accretion of individual shacks and houses at the edge of town.

Figure 10.17. Stoneyhouse Street looking north (*Montreal Standard* 23 Nov. 1946).

John Bland, director of the School of Architecture at McGill University, agreed that the houses were "admittedly not lower income housing" but acknowledged that the high cost was due to the North American shortage of building materials and the Corporation's need to import almost all materials from Canada, with the attendant export restrictions and import duties. He praised the project for its boldness, and noted that opening up a new housing area as large as the old city was no small undertaking and that the project met a vital need (Bland 1946b, 302).

In 1946 the SJHC Board began to reconsider some of the unpalatable suggestions for reducing costs that it had discussed but not implemented in 1945, before the first 30 houses went on the market. The Board decided that the price of the second group of houses, including land, must not exceed $7,000 each. To achieve this, the houses would have a concrete block, rather than a poured concrete foundation, no concrete basement floor or front steps, straight-edged rather than diagonal tongue-and-groove cladding, ten-test walls, and softwood floors. There would be no insulation beyond that afforded by the fibreboard that, according to some members, would have "some insulating value." Dunfield argued it would only cost $62.50 to put some insulation in the attic, and doing this would make the houses much more comfortable. If this was done as a matter of course he thought that potential customers should be offered the opportunity of having insulation installed during construction, with the cost added to the purchase price. This idea didn't fare well. A majority of the Board members argued that this would attract people in the "upper salary brackets," violating the original intention of providing minimum houses. The Corporation wouldn't install furnaces or ductwork, so new tenants would have to make do with a hall heater or a ductless or floor furnace (Sharpe and Shawyer 2016, 271). The Board was convinced that these measures would reduce the cost by about $2,500, lowering the monthly payment by about 15 per cent (*Daily News* 1946j; *Evening Telegram* 1946l).

One of the concessions was to use Homasote as the exterior cladding. This was a cellulose-based fibreboard made of recycled paper and an adhesive, compressed under high pressure and high temperature. It contained no adhesives, but was held together by the surface tension between the fibres and a 2 per cent wax binder. Beginning in 1915 it was used to line the interior of railway cars and as tops for automobiles. Then in the 1920s it began to be advertised as "an improvement over wood ... for every possible use – inside or out" (*Evening Telegram* 1928). It was used as wall sheeting until the 1970s and is still used as a sound- and shock-deadening material in theatres and gymnasia. It was cheap, and available when other sheeting materials were not, but it was not suitable for exterior use, at

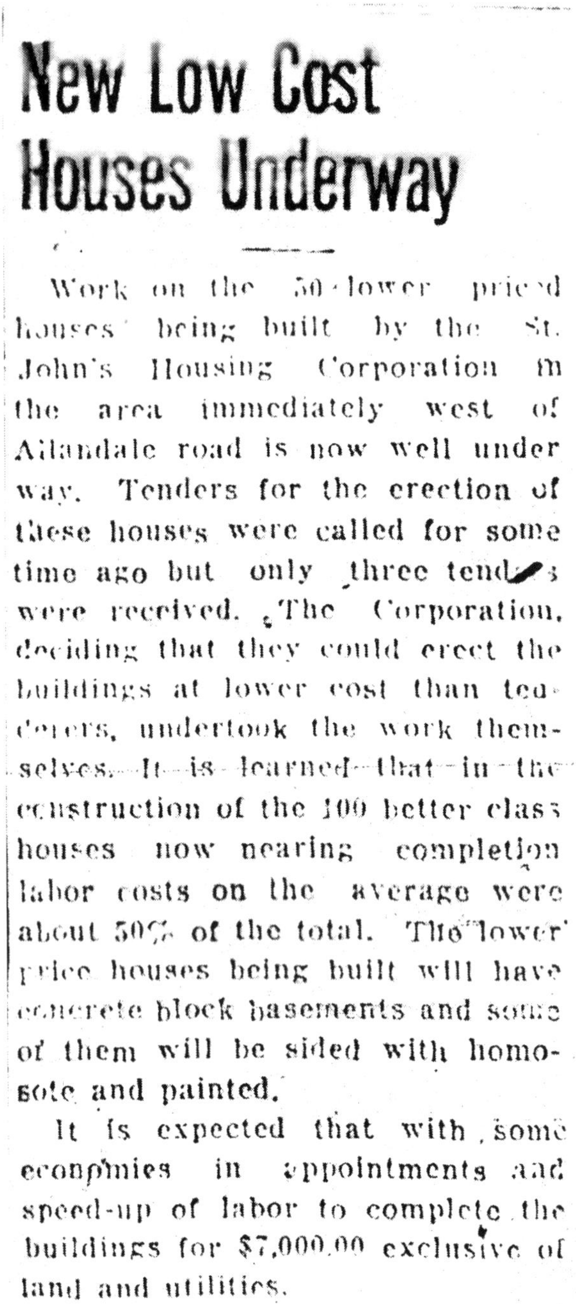

New Low Cost Houses Underway

Work on the 50 lower priced houses being built by the St. John's Housing Corporation in the area immediately west of Allandale road is now well under way. Tenders for the erection of these houses were called for some time ago but only three tenders were received. The Corporation, deciding that they could erect the buildings at lower cost than tenderers, undertook the work themselves. It is learned that in the construction of the 100 better class houses now nearing completion labor costs on the average were about 50% of the total. The lower price houses being built will have concrete block basements and some of them will be sided with homosote and painted.

It is expected that with some economies in appointments and speed-up of labor to complete the buildings for $7,000.00 exclusive of land and utilities.

Figure 10.18. "New Low Cost Houses Underway" (*Evening Telegram* 12 Sept. 1946).

> **ST. JOHN'S HOUSING CORPORATION**
>
> # NEW and CHEAPER HOUSES
>
> We beg to draw the attention of purchasers to our new houses in Block IV, between Allandale Road and Mayor Avenue.
>
> These houses are mostly a trifle larger than those of our first programme, somewhat cheaper in finish and equipment, but first-rate houses in every respect, and will come out substantially lower in price than those of last year.
>
> They are now available for purchase, finished or unfinished.

Figure 10.19. "New and Cheaper Houses" (*Daily News* 11 Feb. 1946).

least not in St. John's. However, in an attempt to reduce costs, the Corporation made the disastrous decision to clad at least 25 houses with it. Two years later they all had to be re-sided with other materials at the Corporation's cost. Because the houses had been sold on a 30-year rental-purchase agreementthe occupiers were considered to be tenants so the Corporation, as landlord, was responsible for the repairs. The cost of re-cladding the houses ranged from $400 to $700 each, exceeding the amount of the original saving.

Hoping they would be less expensive, the Board decided that a third of the houses in the second (1946) cohort should be semi-detached and that some four-unit terraces should be built as an experiment. It turned out that the per-unit cost was reduced only minimally, and the houses in the four-unit groups proved almost impossible to sell. Only two of the four-unit terraces were built. They are located on the east side of Bonaventure Avenue, north and south of Milbanke Street (Appendix 9).

Another strategy, adopted less than two months after the first houses were put on the market, was to sell unfinished houses at reduced prices. The purchaser could then choose a variety of (cheaper) options: wallboard instead of plaster, provide his own stove or heater, omit linoleum in kitchen and bathroom, dispense with hardwood flooring, do without built-in kitchen cabinets, etc. This would be a saving of $1,000 or more and yet the house would be well built with insulation and double-sash windows (*Evening Telegram* 1946b).

The Corporation also tried to sell serviced lots, in all three villages, to private developers (*Evening Telegram* 1946f). To entice customers, much was made of the fact that the Housing Area was "zoned" and thus protected against the deterioration of value that might be caused by the intrusion of "undesirable uses and buildings" (see Appendix 8). Zoning was a practice new to St. John's. The lots sold for $950 each and were taken up by commercial building firms, private individuals, and, in time, by a number of cooperative housing groups (Sharpe and Shawyer 2016).

Unfortunately, these attempts at economy were unsuccessful. Within a month of the first houses being released for sale, the SJHC Board met with representatives of both governments "to consider the position arising out of the high cost of the houses so far constructed and the consequent difficulty in finding purchasers for them." The outcome was that "all parties found themselves agreed" that the 1946 program of 100 cheaper houses would be reduced to 50. The houses would be concentrated near Mayor Avenue in the central Village "B" and were to be "of as many different experimental types as possible in the effort to construct a house of adequate quality within the reach of the lower income classes" (*Daily News* 1946b; *Evening Telegram* 1946g). However, it was agreed that whatever economy measures were effected, basements would not be omitted and cheap roofing would not used. After only one year of operation, the Corporation's original plan to build 200 houses in 1946 had been swept away.

Was the entire SJHC project in jeopardy? Both the public and newspaper editors were worried, using words like "disappointing" and "disconcerting" to describe the high cost of the Corporation's housing and expressing concern that the entire project might be abandoned. Dunfield had no intention of allowing that to happen and tried to turn adversity into opportunity. He promised that Village "B" would be completed by the end of the year: existing streets finished, curbs and gutters installed, the park planted with trees and shrubs, the bus road from Allandale Road to the Square ready for use, and the Square itself laid out. "People will see what the place will really look like, and how attractive and convenient it is going to be. . . . the houses the best value for money in town, houses of Canadian or American standard, and above the standard we usually build here" (*Evening Telegram* 1946j). Writing to Governor Macdonald several months later he was even more emphatic. Referring to his earlier travels on the mainland, he said "I have been there. We are giving a better house for money today than the biggest speculative building in the eastern USA — Leavitt [sic] Brothers on Long Island, New York. I have seen them, and others have agreed with me who have seen them" (Dunfield 1947a).

It seems strange that the CEHTP could have erred so badly in making the original cost estimates, and then that the SJHC Board accepted the flawed estimates without question. The Board should have had a more realistic idea of costs. In 1944 architect William J. Ryan provided the CEHTP a plan and cost estimate for a small home: $5,792.65 for a house with a concrete foundation and basement floor, but no furnace, only "chimneys and a grate" (Ryan 1944). Several members of both the CEHTP and the

SJHC knew a lot about construction. James V. Ryan was president of the Railway Employees Welfare Association (REWA), which had built 124 houses for employees on Topsail and Craigmillar Roads; Francis M. O'Leary was the manager of his family's building supply company; William J. Frampton was vice-president of the Newfoundland Federation of Labour; Charles Peet was president of the Newfoundland Protective Association of Shop and Office Employees; and Chesley A. Pippy owned the Newfoundland Tractor Company, which sold heavy equipment. These members of the Corporation board should have been able to evaluate the cost estimates critically, but apparently none of them protested that the estimates in the CEHTP reports had been too low. In his defence, Dunfield argued that neither the government nor the Council, the members of the SJHC Board, or any citizen had questioned the original CEHTP cost estimates (Dunfield 1947f). Dunfield, however, was a patrician lawyer rather than a tradesman. He was concerned almost entirely with the big picture rather than day-to-day practicalities, and either relied on others for advice that was never offered, or, if it was, ignored it.

During 1946 the conversations between the government and the Corporation continued to be unfailingly polite but increasingly stern. In light of that, Dunfield must have appreciated the press report that commented: "as the housing area takes form it is impressing itself on all visitors as a magnificent example of what a modern city should be like" (*Daily News* 1946h).

The SJHC Begins to Lose Control of the Project

By the beginning of October, 70 houses had been sold, in spite of the costs, the majority to white-collar professionals. But in an ill-fated attempt to increase sales the SJHC Board made a crucial error. The minimum down payment was supposed to be $1,000. Some of the applicants did not have that much in hand but the Board let them purchase anyway, on the strength of a promise to pay later. This, of course, did not always happen and the issue became a bone of contention when Dunfield was called to testify before the Finance Committee of the National Convention to Discuss the Future of Newfoundland (Finance Committee 1946a). The role of the Convention was to discuss the political future of Newfoundland, which had been under Commission of Government since 1934. We now know that on 22 July 1948 Newfoundlanders would vote, by a narrow margin, to join the Canadian Confederation, but this was by no means certain two years earlier.

Dunfield faced hostile questions from the Committee. Many of the members expected Newfoundland to return to responsible government and they were worried about the costs that a new national government would face. The long-term cost of continued operation of the SJHC was considerable. It had already requested and received additional funding well in excess of the original estimates, and the Committee was not pleased about this. To make matters worse, Dunfield once again had to defend the failure of the Corporation to make any difference to the lives of those who lived in the inner city (Finance Committee 1946a, 40). Dunfield turned to filtering to try to placate his critics:

> Unless the government is able to find, say, $15 million, which is out of reach, and they would have to kiss most of that money goodbye, we cannot clear the slums directly. There, we say, let us apply the Canadian or American system, seek out the man, going as low down the scale as we can, who, if he gets a long-term mortgage at low interest rates, can at least afford the house he wants. He will move out and everybody else will move one place up. That seems the best method suitable to our conditions, and the only method the financial situation will enable us to apply. (Finance Committee 1946b)

The Finance Committee was not convinced and it agreed with the government that there should be no new construction until all the houses presently under construction were completed, at which time the situation would be reviewed. And this was only the second year of the project's life.

Dunfield, emboldened by the public's enthusiasm for the new houses, ignored the decision made in July that only 50 houses would be built in 1947. He planned several dozen apartments and 160 houses and asked for an additional loan of $2,000,000. He defended the high costs in a personal (rather than an official) letter to Finance Commissioner Ira Wild. In the letter, addressed to "My dear Ira," he made the astonishing comment that "I find a temptation on the part of my Board, and Treasury may be under the same temptation, to take too businesslike a view of this housing enterprise." In his view the project was a "more academic" exercise than a practical concern for the process of implementation (Dunfield 1946c).

Perhaps Dunfield thought the government would not dare to refuse the loan, considering the desperate need for houses. But the SJHC was already carrying a combined debt of almost $3.4 million from the government and the city. R.L.M. James, who had succeeded Ira Wild as commissioner of finance on 12 September 1946, issued a sharp rebuke, noting that the poor had apparently been left out of the plans for the new development:

> Sooner or later, the Government will have to put its hand in its pocket and produce a lot of money for the demolition and reconstruction of slum property. I should like to see us reserve our resources . . . for this stage, *leaving the present campaign for re-housing the middle classes to private enterprise.* (James 1946; emphasis added)

This was a turning point. The government had lost its faith either in the housing project or in Dunfield, or both. The new government attitude threatened the whole SJHC project. In November 1946, Commissioner of Home Affairs and Education Walsh sent a memorandum to his Commission colleagues that essentially sounded the death knell for the SJHC's role as a builder of houses. Walsh underscored the fact that the cost of the Corporation's houses far exceeded the estimates made in the fifth report of the CEHTP:

> I think it is only fair to say that few, if any, [of the Corporation's houses] have been disposed of to the middle class and poorer workmen in whose interests the scheme was originally adopted . . . [and] while it is desirable to have a garden suburb for St. John's, it seems to me that the conditions described by the Housing Commission in the Third Report are not likely to be remedied for many years by building houses at the cost of which they are being built by the Corporation. . . . The cheaper houses will cost between $7,000 and $8,000 and are really out of the reach of the middle class workmen.

He concluded:

> I recommend that great caution should be exercised in the further financing of this project by the Government. It seems to me that for the year 1947–48 the Corporation should proceed to install roads, sewage and other services in the whole area, and complete the apartments and houses already under construction. When the area has been properly laid out, one should expect to find that private builders will wish to acquire land for erection of houses at their own cost. *It is immaterial from the Government's point of view whether houses are built by the Corporation or privately if building is in accordance with plans approved by the Corporation.* (Walsh 1946b; emphasis added)

If the SJHC built no more houses, it would not sink further into debt. The alternative new idea was that the Housing Area could be fully serviced, its building lots made available for sale, and the area filled with new houses (to the standard set by the SJHC) by the emerging post-war commercial real estate market. Walsh's sentiment showed that the intent of Councillor Meaney's proposal, the CEHTP reports, and the SJHC — that all ideas and projects would depend on government and/or Council funding — could be swept aside. The future of housing development in St. John's would be turned over to the new-style "developers" who were now purchasing a dozen or more lots at a time on a new street and all the building permits for them. Commercial modernity had come to the St. John's housing market.

The outcome of the government's review of the request for further financial support was a decision that no such financial support would be given to the Corporation until the houses and flats then under construction were completed. Then there would be sufficient information to undertake a complete review of the existing position and a decision on future policy would be made at that time (Walsh 1946d).

The Housing Area Gets a Name

The area north of the old city boundary along Empire Avenue had been referred to as the "northern valley" by the CEHTP and by the SJHC as the "Housing Area." Colloquially, people referred to it as "The Housing." When the post office began to plan for mail delivery in the new suburb the Board decided that the area should have a formal name and on 1 November 1946 made the unanimous decision that Village "B" should be called "Churchill Park." In December 1947 the boundary of the city of St. John's was extended to incorporate the Churchill Park housing area (Quinton 1947c).

The 1947 map of the Housing Area (Figure 7.8) identifies the open space north of the Village "B" commercial centre as "Churchill Park," but the name had not been applied to the entire village. During their research the authors have used the name to describe the entire expropriated area, but many residents to whom we have spoken dispute such a large-scale application of the name. Local realtors agree with them. In advertisements, realtors restrict the name Churchill Park to the area including all that part of Village "A" from Portugal Cove Road west to Carpasian Road, and Village "B" from there west to Bonaventure Avenue, excluding the Corporation's houses on Whiteway and Rodney Streets. They do not include Village "C," in which none of the houses were built by the Corporation.

1947: The Axe Falls on the SJHC

As the new year dawned, the Corporation again ignored the government's stated position that no new houses could be built until all those already under construction had been sold. Rather, it decided to build more houses of a single type, intermediate between the very expensive 1945 type and the cheaper 1946 version. Insulation, storm windows, and complete kitchens were to be restored. Dunfield was adamant about the latter. Replacing most of the cabinets with shelves and eliminating one of the sinks would save about $150, but he argued this was false economy. He argued that the kitchen, as originally designed, was immensely appealing to the women who saw it, and was an important sales feature. The Board accepted this argument but agreed that a furnace and any required heating ducts would have to be provided by the tenants (Dunfield 1947b).

Despite its earlier decision the government agreed to advance a further loan of $1,250,000 to build 100 "low-cost" houses, but with stringent conditions. The construction of more apartments was forbidden. The Corporation was to complete all the unfinished houses and apartments and to develop 200 sites to be made available to private contractors. A free grant of $125,000 was given to complete the road system. Ninety-two houses were started during the year, bringing the total number to 243 (see Appendix 9).

Meanwhile, the 1945 and 1946 houses were selling steadily, although not without problems. The first 30 houses that went in 1945 had been sold, bravely but foolishly, before the final costs were known. By the end of the year, facing opposition from the buyers who argued that the final price was greatly in excess of what they had been led to believe it would be, the Board decided to sell a group of 20 houses at less than cost, and as a result the Corporation incurred a loss of $35,000. The same mistake was made with the apartments. The rent was set on the basis of an estimated construction cost that had now risen to $9,000. In the end the real cost came to $13,000 per unit (SJHC 1951, 14). The gap between cost and revenue was a public relations disaster for the Corporation.

The Municipal Council was by now very strident in its criticism of the Corporation. Mayor Carnell was not pleased that the infrastructure in the Housing Area — water lines, sewers, roads — was far better than in the city. He felt the money given to the Housing Corporation by the city would have been better spent within the city boundaries and that "if the Corporation had built more houses instead of asphalt roads, more would have been done to alleviate the housing situation" (*Evening Telegram* 1947c). He had cause to be angry. For years the Municipal Council had been unable to secure adequate government financing for even the most basic city infrastructure. It continued to be distracted by the fact that houses condemned as unfit for habitation could not be demolished because there was no adequate alternative accommodation for their occupants. The following report of the city engineer to Council was typical of the continuing downtown situation:

> There are two wooden buildings situated on the south side of New Gower Street. . . . 181 is owned and occupied by the owner. 183–185 is owned by the Bridges Estate. At the present time there are eight people occupying 183–185 without the owner's permission, as they moved into the building after it had been boarded up by the owners.
> Both these buildings are in a very dilapidated condition. . . . In both buildings the windows and the doors at the rear are broken and the clapboard has been stripped off . . . the stairs are practically useless, and their chimneys in their present condition constitute a serious fire hazard.
> As both these units are depreciated well beyond 50% I would recommend [to Council] that the owners be served with demolition orders. (SJCM 21 Aug. 1946, 226)

Council agreed to demolish both buildings.

The government argued that it had already contributed substantial amounts to the new suburban project and to the Widows' Mansions. They had no more money for tackling the slum situation. The Council replied that it had spent $1.2 million on the housing project and $8,000 on purchasing and servicing the Ebsary land for the Widows' Mansions. But their most extreme vitriol was aimed at the Housing Corporation. The mayor said that the city had been "sold out" when it gave $1.2 million to the Corporation. They had understood, from the CEHTP's reports, that their money would be spent "removing the unsightly hovels in which people are living in the central city" (Mahoney 1947).

Councillor Harry Mews, who would become mayor after Confederation, accused the Corporation of misleading the citizens of St. John's: "Now we find that we are getting something that will stand as a monument to the Chairman of the Housing Corporation, prominent businessmen, and state officials. We gave them our money and now we have no money to clean out the slums." He accused the government of spending like a drunken sailor on the housing and then having the nerve to ask the Council to give more. "Whatever is behind this, it is not the welfare of the ordinary man" (*Evening Telegram* 1947a).

The Council was correct that the SJHC had absolutely no effect on relieving the housing problem for families who lived in condemned buildings downtown. The Municipal Council suggested that the Corporation be given a special grant to extend its work to include remedial measures in slum clearance. If this was not possible, the Council suggested it might relinquish its investment in the SJHC and spend its money directly on the slum problem itself (Pottle 1947a).

Dunfield knew that the effect of the SJHC on the shortage of decent housing in the inner city would be limited. To new Commissioner of Home Affairs and Education H.W. Quinton, who had replaced A.J. Walsh on 1 January 1947, he wrote: "I fear that new modern accommodation for the lower working classes is as far out of reach as it has always been, failing a subsidy to carry the difference. We can help only by making it possible for them to move up into better second-class accommodation. And that is the same everywhere" (Dunfield 1947c). To Commissioner of Public Health and Welfare H.L. Pottle, he said: "we thought of building cheap workmen's and veterans' quarters. We cannot, without subsidy. No one can. So we built what we could, and it turns out to be coveted middle-class housing because of our low standards here. So what? . . . Estate development, to expand the town, is a good thing in itself. Nothing else will solve the congestion problem" (Dunfield 1947f).

The government was not convinced. On 19 December 1947, the government ordered that the operations of the Corporation were to be curtailed to the greatest possible extent. The government would consider at a later date whether provision would be made in the budget estimates for 1948–49 for the completion of the houses under construction.

The halcyon days of Mr. Dunfield and his St. John's Housing Corporation were over.

11

CANADA ENTERS THE DISCUSSION

> Dear Mr. Smallwood: I heard over VOCM today that you intend doing something in regards to the slum conditions of this town. Please remember that James Street and vicinity are not the only place in town in which people are living in squalor. I have a wife and three small children 1, 2, and 4 years old. . . . When it rains, the children play at boating in [on] the kitchen [floor]. (Letter to the Premier, 1949, J.R. Smallwood Collection 075 MUN 1:43:003)

1948: Phasing Out the SJHC

As 1948 dawned, 141 houses remained unfinished and 14 of the 50 houses completed in 1946 had not yet been sold (Appendix 7). The Corporation needed cash flow to finish them. The SJHC real estate account, which held the down payments and rental-purchase payments, was being used to support operations even though that money was supposed to be repaid to the government. Not only was the Corporation's financial future uncertain, but so too was its political future.

The Commission of Government knew that on 1 April 1949 it would be replaced by an elected provincial government and the commissioners of finance and home affairs were not inclined to approve more large loans to the Corporation. They knew that the new provincial government was going to face a budget deficit and didn't want to make it worse. They did agree to loan an additional $400,000 for the Corporation, but with the condition that $200,000 be returned immediately to the real estate account; the remainder was to be "devoted exclusively to the completion of as many as possible of the houses now under construction, and not to road work, tree planting, the extension of water or sewer systems or any other purpose." There would be no new building (Pottle 1948).

The Corporation refused to accept these conditions and stopped all work on 18 May 1948. The contract with Searles and Meschino was terminated on 5 July, although Meschino was kept on as supervising architect.

News of the shutdown did not come as a surprise. Rumours had been circulating for some time that the Corporation was in trouble. "Only time will tell whether or not the Housing Corporation plans were too grandiose for the community, or if the increased cost of labour and material contributed to no small degree to the suspension of the scheme" (*Evening Telegram* 1948e).

The public could watch the deterioration of unfinished houses and see the lack of landscaping around the completed houses. There was public anger at the irregular and unfair handling of down payments. And the trade unions were unhappy. The Longshoremen's Protective Union, the Labourers' and General Workers' Protective Union, and the Building Craft Association, representing bricklayers and masons, electricians, plumbers and steamfitters, tin and sheet metal workers, had sent a set of critical resolutions to the government (Earle et al. 1947). And complaints filtered through to the government from former employees of the Corporation who not only said that the houses were too expensive, but alleged that they were "unsuitable for various structural reasons" (*Evening Telegram* 1948b).

At this point a new player entered the game.

The Central Mortgage and Housing Corporation

As Newfoundland prepared to join Canada, David Mansur, the president of the Central Mortgage and Housing Corporation (CMHC), asked the Newfoundland government to provide all the details of the SJHC's history and activities. While admitting its failures, that it had been unable to build low-cost houses for the inner-city poor and had relied on "filtering" to solve the downtown housing crisis, the government argued that much good had come from the project:

> The general basis of the operation was that the number of houses in St. John's was insufficient and must be added to; and that the space occupied by the town was insufficient and must be added to.... The Corporation installed sewerage, heretofore non-existent, supplemented the main road system and extended the water system, which was very scanty. As in the case of other organizations in recent years, it was found impossible to erect houses and apartments of somewhat better standards, relying on the movement of population to make matters easier for the lower paid working classes. The general deficiency of dwellings was estimated by the Commission of Enquiry of 1942–44 to be about 1,500. The Corporation and private enterprise over the past four years have made good about half this deficiency in about equal proportions. The Corporation has been selling most of its houses on a deferred payment plan up to 30 years, but has rented a few houses and has rented 92 apartments. About two-thirds of the Corporation's units, including all the flats, are finished. About one-third of the houses are unfinished, though all are well advanced towards completion. (Carew 1948)

The government's response confirmed the SJHC estimate that $400,000 would be needed to complete the remaining unfinished units and to install the last of the utilities. However, "the Corporation is at the moment somewhat held up, as the Government has not found itself able so far this year to lend it this balance" (Carew 1948). Mansur wanted to finish

Figure 11.1. David Mansur, C.B.E., president of the CMHC (1946–54) (Bacher 1993).

the houses and find tenants for them. He estimated that the unfinished houses would depreciate over the winter by about $100,000 and that it was "deplorable" that there was no money to finish them (Organ 1948). But there was not, and in December the Corporation decided that the 18 houses in Block 21, bounded by Pine Bud Avenue, Milbanke Street, Bonaventure Avenue, and Allandale Road, would have to be boarded up.

The apartment program was also in disarray. The Board had known for some time that the rents were too low to cover the operating costs of the apartments but waited for a year after the first tenants moved in before taking appropriate action. In January 1948 tenants were notified that when their current leases expired the rents would increase by $10 a month. Five ex-serviceman tenants appealed to the Rent Control Board, which not only cancelled the increases on their apartments, but all other apartments as well.

The Corporation was losing $34.53 per month on each of the 92 apartments. One reason was that the heating costs far exceeded the original estimates. The solution was to lock all the thermostats at 72 degrees. When two tenants of the Pine Bud apartments refused to allow the Corporation's men in to do the work, the thermostats were adjusted externally.

The original intention for building the apartments, and the basis on which the government had provided an additional loan for their construction, was that veterans would be given first preference. However, there were only a few applications from veterans. None applied in 1947 or 1948.

And in the following several years, only half the applicants were veterans. The others were professional men, some of whom were prominent members of the St. John's business community (Tessier 1951). But by the beginning of 1949 all the apartments were occupied.

In regard to houses, 140 had been sold and 93 were incomplete. The Board offered to sell the houses at reduced prices but there was little interest.

1949: Brian Dunfield Leaves the SJHC

The Commission of Government, which would cease to exist at midnight on 31 March 1949, did not include any money for the Corporation in the budget for 1949–50, although Dunfield continued to plead for an additional allocation. The commissioners were not receptive. Their final review of the SJHC accounts revealed that 67 purchasers had paid less than the required down payment for their houses and in 26 cases had paid nothing at all. Dunfield's argument for this situation was compassionate but not helpful: "The Board . . . has always been driven back to the normal business view that the character and position (as regards stability of employment) of the person seeking credit was more important than the mere fact of his having some loose cash" (Dunfield 1947b).

The Commission's frustration with Dunfield was solved by Confederation. Section 35 of the (Canadian) Judges Act (1946) stipulated that judges devote themselves exclusively to their judicial duties. Dunfield could not continue as a judge and at the same time continue as chairman of the SJHC. He was furious, but he decided to stay on the bench and resigned from the SJHC on 26 March 1949 (Dunfield 1949). His retirement was honoured at a dinner and reception on 31 March 1949, the last day of Newfoundland's existence as an independent Dominion. The invitation was illustrated with images of two Corporation houses, drawn by Paul Meschino (see Appendix 10). Commissioner for Home Affairs and Education Pottle graciously acknowledged Dunfield's departure:

> The Commission of Government have accepted with great regret your resignation as Chairman of the St. John's Housing Corporation. I wish to convey to you, on their behalf as well as my own, an expression of sincere appreciation and thanks for the very valuable public service rendered in this capacity since July, 1944. The duties and responsibilities devolving upon you were such that could only be borne by a person possessed of dynamic energy, wide vision and capable leadership, and, moreover, one willing to sacrifice the greater portion of his leisure time to such a public-spirited undertaking. The results which have attended the work of yourself and your colleagues are already a cause for pride and gratification. May I add my personal compliment and best wishes on the honour of Knighthood recently conferred upon you by His Majesty the King. (Pottle 1949)

Brian Dunfield relinquished the chairmanship of the SJHC just prior to the date of Confederation but maintained his passionate interest in town planning. He had been a member of the Town Planning Commission of St. John's in 1944 and served as chairman from 1945 to 1951. He became the national president of the Community Planning Association of Canada from 1953 to 1956 and was named chairman of the Corner Brook Development Corporation in 1965, a position he held until his death in 1968.

1950: Loose Ends, and a Tangle of Financial Troubles

After Dunfield's departure, the SJHC soldiered on and adapted to life in the newest province of Canada. Gordon Winter, an original member of the SJHC Board and a future lieutenant-governor of the province, became the new chairman but otherwise the composition of the Board remained unchanged. Winter and his colleagues were faced with outstanding debts,

Figure 11.2. The original SJHC Board, photographed at Dunfield's retirement dinner, 1949. Left to right, front row: Lewis Ayre, Gordon Winter, Brian Dunfield, Chesley Pippy; back row: Charles Peet, Gerald S. Doyle, O.B.E., Eric Cook, F.A.F. Lush, Grant R. Jack (city engineer) (F.P. Meschino).

unpaid interest charges, and an inventory of 93 unsold houses that were deteriorating because of dampness and mould. Reluctantly, the government provided an additional $238,438 to finish the houses on the condition that every possible "non-essential" element would be eliminated. These houses would have no upper kitchen cabinets, no storm windows or interior painting, and only linoleum covering over the subfloors (Forsey 1949). This was a sad denouement for the "first rate little house" that Dunfield had promised to the "low-income home seeker" in 1943 (*Evening Telegram* 1943d).

In October 1950 the provincial Rent Control Board ruled that all the Corporation's apartments should be excluded from the provisions of the 1943 Rent Restrictions Act (Tessier 1951). The Corporation then served a

Figure 11.3. Gordon A. Winter (1912–2003) (*Newfoundland Who's Who 1952*, 98).

two-month notice to quit on all 92 tenants with the proviso that they could renew the lease at a substantially increased rent: by 46 per cent, to $110 for a three-bedroom unit. Veterans were exempt from the general increase. Their rent was limited to a maximum of 20 per cent of their monthly income, although this took no account of what the actual dollar increase would be. The public response to what many saw as an arrogant and unjustifiable action by the Corporation was the formation of the 200-member Churchill Park Citizens' Association, which included Eric Cook's law partner, Rupert Bartlett, and Alan Fraser of the Economics Department of Memorial University. The Association asked for a two-month delay in the imposition of the increased rents, to permit a review of the financial situation that the Corporation cited as the necessity for the increase in rents (Fraser 1951). The Association's challenge was unsuccessful and the affair left a widespread legacy of bitterness, not only among the tenants but also among those in the city who had never believed that the SJHC would have any significant effect on housing conditions.

By July 1950 the inventory of unsold houses was reduced to 40 and only five remained by the end of the year. The first chapter in the life of the SJHC ended on 31 December 1950 when the Board resigned, having been informed that the provincial government had decided to appoint a full slate of new members.

1951–81: A New Mandate and a New Philosophy for the SJHC

The chairman of the new Board was Oliver Vardy (MHA, St. John's West), who lived in a Corporation house on the northwest corner of Elizabeth and Bonaventure Avenue. The Board was composed of seven members of the House of Assembly, St. John's Mayor Harry G. Mews, and the city engineer. Of the new Board members, only two had experienced the turbulent years of the original SJHC. Vardy had been a member of the Municipal Council from 1941 to 1949 and clinical psychologist Herbert Pottle, PhD, had served as commissioner of public health and welfare for almost two years prior to Confederation.

The new Board drastically revised its mode of operation. The original Board met every Friday, often until midnight. The new Board met on Friday afternoon at 2:30 and adjourned at 5:00. Dunfield's Board held 226 meetings during its five years. The new Board met 298 times over 31 years. During the last decade of its life it averaged only five meetings a year.

The original Board had done its best to deal sympathetically with complaints from occupants about problems with furnaces and wall covering. The new Board abandoned the paternalistic attitude of the original Board and adopted a much less charitable approach. Tenant complaints were now routinely dismissed on the grounds that the SJHC had used the best materials available at the time of the construction and tenants would henceforth have to take their complaints directly to the appropriate manufacturer's agent.

Figure 11.4. Oliver Vardy (1906–80) (*Newfoundland Who's Who 1952*, 95).

The SJHC now had a very restricted mandate. It would no longer construct houses. The focus was now to be on the subdivision of the undeveloped acres of the land originally expropriated by the SJHC and their sale to private house builders and building contractors. However, Dunfield maintained an influence over some important aspects of the Corporation's activity. He successfully argued that the 800 acres acquired by the SJHC in 1944 should be kept as leasehold to the Crown (Dunfield 1950b). His view prevailed until 1986 when the lots still under 999-year leasehold were converted to freehold by an Order-in-Council. The leases on the lots sold to CMHC in 1952 have never been converted en masse, but many of them have since been sold to new owners and converted to freehold as a condition of the sale.

During the last 30 years of its life, the Corporation developed and serviced more than 2,000 new lots north and west of the original Housing Area. Between 1951 and 1981 the SJHC expanded the city's footprint by acquiring an additional 70 acres of land in the Thorburn Road/Oxen Pond Road area and developing about 300 lots there. It also transferred more than 150 acres to CMHC, which then developed 520 building lots, making a notable inroad against the city's historic housing shortage.

The SJHC had offered lots for sale to private builders as early as 1946 and now had the opportunity of working with the Central Mortgage and Housing Corporation, which was looking for land on which to build houses for veterans, as it was doing elsewhere in Canada. The city and the government cooperated in providing services to lots purchased from the SJHC in what became Tunis Court off New Cove Road. Fifty prefabricated houses imported from Montreal were erected and offered to veterans (Joe Ryan 2003).

In 1966, when the US Army closed Fort Pepperrell, on the north side of Quidi Vidi Lake, the Corporation acquired 200 apartment units from them and the area was renamed Pleasantville. The SJHC renovated the apartments for civilian occupancy.

In 1981 the 37-year-old SJHC was merged with the Newfoundland and Labrador Housing Corporation (NLHC). By that time it had built 333 houses; built or acquired and renovated 623 apartments; developed 2,200 acres of serviced land; and sold 4,100 building lots to private house builders, families, cooperatives, CMHC, and development companies. Much of this development occurred well beyond the original footprint of the expropriated

Housing Area. These numbers record a remarkable achievement made possible by the original determination and passion of the CEHTP and the first Board of the SJHC. In 1978 SJHC Chairman F.J. O'Leary boasted that the SJHC was responsible for acquiring and servicing almost a quarter of the area inside the city boundary (Vardy 1967; O'Leary, 1978).

The Residents of the Inner City Are Finally Rehoused

> THE DAILY NEWS, ST. JOHN'S, NEWFOUNDLAND
>
> # Nfld. Slum Clearance Agreement Signed In Ottawa And St. John's
>
> *Federal Government to Provide 75% of Cost of Program; Provincial Government to Pay Balance*
>
> Newfoundland's scheme for slum clearance and provision of low-income housing in St. John's was given the green light on Friday when officials of the provincial and federal governments signed an agreement putting actual construction machinery into motion.

Figure 11.5. "Slum Clearance Agreement Signed" (*Daily News* 14 June 1950).

Over the half-century prior to Confederation efforts to deal with the desperate housing situation in the inner city had been made by many well-intended citizens in St. John's — Dr. Brehm, Mayor Gibbs, Mayor

Gosling, Hon. John Anderson, the Rotary Club, Councillors John Meaney and Eric Cook, Mayor Carnell, and Commissioner Puddester (the Ebsary project), the CEHTP, and the SJHC. These various efforts were to no avail. Neither the Newfoundland government nor the Municipal Council had the resources necessary to fund a large-scale and ongoing war against the housing crisis. All of these efforts had relied on minimal funding from the tight budgets of the government or the Municipal Council.

Success in making inroads against the housing crisis did not come until the SJHC began to sell lots to the commercial housing market that evolved after World War II. And, after Confederation, the CMHC facilitated the long-awaited solution for those who lived in the worst houses in the city and who had never "filtered up" to houses vacated by those who migrated to Churchill Park or anywhere else. In 1952 a household survey by City Planner Stanley Pickett revealed than many of these inner-city families, on long-term leases, paid very little rent and some none at all, declaring that they had never been asked to pay rent. Some respondents had never heard of a landlord for the property they occupied because many of the properties had long since been abandoned, even condemned (CSJA RG 08-06). Over the years, many dilapidated houses had been condemned, bought out by the authorities, and razed.

The CMHC, working in financial partnership with the new Newfoundland provincial government, made it possible to fulfill one of the original intentions of the CEHTP. The dilapidated houses in the inner city were finally demolished and new homes built to accommodate those with low incomes. Section 35 of the 1949 National Housing Act introduced a federal-provincial cost-sharing agreement — 75 per cent federal and 25 per cent provincial — for the construction of low-cost homes. This, in combination with Newfoundland's 1955 Slum Clearance Act and the availability of the SJHC's serviced land in Churchill Park, made it possible to accommodate some families from the inner city in a number of new housing projects.

Premier Smallwood was first in line when the new cost-sharing housing program was announced. "Westmount," F.P. 1/1950, the first project in Canada funded under the new program, surrounded the "Widows' Mansions" with 140 new units. In the Churchill Park area, F.P. 3/1951 provided 152 housing units on Empire Avenue, Anderson Avenue, Freshwater Road, Graves Street, Little Street, and Hoyles Avenue. F.P. 4/1954 provided 36 units on streets north of Empire Avenue: Wallace Place, Whiteway Street, and Newtown Road. The 46 units of F.P. 5/1954 on Livingstone and Goodview Streets were the only ones built in the inner city. The 146 units of "The Courts" on Anderson Avenue were built under F.P. 6/1955 in the original Housing Area. HMCS Avalon, the wartime RCN base in Buckmaster's Field, provided space for 310 units built under F.P. 8/1965.

These projects represented a significant beginning to the process of clearing the dilapidated housing in the inner city. But it wasn't nearly enough to satisfy Stanley Pickett. When he left his position as city planner in 1956 he decried the fact that fewer and fewer of the tenants selected for the projects were being chosen from the lists of those living in condemned houses in the central city. The 140 units of the Westmount project led directly to the demolition of 98 houses, most of them in the central area. But the 152 units of F.P. 3 led to only 24 demolitions, of which only three or four were in the central area because "the St. John's Housing Authority was anxious to secure good tenants and was more influenced by potential ability to pay than by the needs of slum clearance" (Pickett 1956). Housing officials thought that the "ideal" type of family for detached houses was the nuclear family. Thus the philosophy underlying the urban renewal and slum clearance programs required the selection of "appropriate" families as tenants in the new social housing projects. The single-parent mother-led families who lived in the inner city did not meet this criterion and were not selected (Knott and Phyne 2018).

The city offered compensation to inner-city landowners in order to acquire their properties. If it wasn't accepted, expropriation occurred. By 1968, the last of the worn-out, dilapidated dwellings, a few possibly dating back to the 1840s, were gone. The new F.P. housing blocks accommodated hundreds of families with modern plumbing and "tight roofs and snug walls" — the basics Gosling had tried to provide in his housing rehabilitation program 30 years before. The contribution of the federal–provincial housing

June 23, 1964

Mr.
Barter's Hill,
St. John's.

Dear Mr

    The City Council intends acquiring the balance of the area between New Gower Street and Queen's Road on the south, and Livingstone Street and Central Street on the north. The acquisition of lands in that area began more than twenty years ago as it contained some of the oldest housing in the City.

    City officials have made studies of the housing in this district and in recent weeks have made offers to purchase the balance of the properties for the purpose of facilitating clearance and redevelopment.

    As yet there has been no agreement with regard to your property although an offer to purchase has been made. The Council desires to acquire your dwelling without prolonged arbitration proceedings if that is possible. I am therefore instructed by the Council to offer you any one of the following properties in substitution for your home –

        51 Brazil Square
        9 Bannerman Street
        54 Flower Hill
        48 Flower Hill
        36 Livingstone Street

    These properties are now in the market and either is available for purchase for you by the Council with your approval. It is considered that these dwellings are at least reasonably comparable and equivalent to your present home.

    A reply is requested before June 30. It may not be possible to obtain either of these dwellings for you after that date.

                Yours very truly,

                City Clerk.

Figure 11.6. Expropriation letter, Barter's Hill 1964 (CSJA RG 01-16).

projects was complemented by the city's purchase of a number of downtown houses, which were adapted to accommodate displaced inner-city families (Phyne 2014; Phyne and Knott 2016; CSJA RG 09-04).

However, as Frederick Todd had warned when visiting St. John's in 1930, removal of the old tenements would increase the value of the land such that the cleared sites would not be rebuilt with parks and housing. And so it was. The newly cleared land provided space for the new City Hall,

Figure 11.7. Clearance on James Street, late 1940s (CSJA 11-02-040).

Figure 11.8. Clearance on Wickford Street, 1950s (CSJA 11-02-021).

Cabot Place, the Delta Hotel, and Mile One Stadium. Sebastian Court, 29 townhouses belonging to St John's Non-Profit Housing, was tucked into the space east of City Hall where James Street had been and takes its name from another one of the vanished downtown streets.

12

CHURCHILL PARK: A DARING EXPERIMENT

Churchill Park has an important but generally unrecognized place in the history of Canadian planning. It doesn't appear in the celebration of garden suburbs or in the literature describing the slum clearance and urban renewal projects of the 1960s. But it deserves to be included in the history of both of these urban social phenomena in Canada.

Only two Canadian urban developments are internationally recognized as garden suburbs. The Town of Mount Royal, planned by Frederick Todd, was built in 1911 for the Canadian Northern Railway. The Cité-jardin du Tricentenaire, built between 1941 and 1947 in Montreal, was a project of l'Union économique de l'habitation. Don Mills, built by the industrialist E.P. Taylor north of Toronto, starting in 1951, was intended as a full-service new town in the garden city tradition (International Garden Cities Institute 2018). The development of Churchill Park was contemporary with two of these projects.

The CEHTP was a group of civic-minded individuals who sought to find a way to alleviate the lack of affordable housing in St. John's. They undertook extensive research predicated on two goals: "to recommend a scheme for the rehousing of a proportion and ultimately the whole of the poor and the low-income classes" and "for the replanning of the city" (CEHTP 1, 3). Their six reports laid out precisely how this could be achieved.

St. John's Housing Corporation (SJHC) was in charge of the actual building of Churchill Park. This organization, legitimized by the government of the day and the St. John's Municipal Council, with the approval of organized labour, had been born out of the extensive research undertaken by the CEHTP.

The Two Mandates of the CEHTP

The SJHC was an unusual organization. It was neither a Crown corporation nor a private organization, nor was it a department of government. It was put together to achieve two goals as laid out by the CEHTP: to build houses, sorely needed in St. John's, and to use the opportunity to embark on the larger plan of initiating proper urban planning for the town.

To build the houses, it had first to acquire land. All the land within walking distance of the city was privately held and for their purposes the SJHC had to expropriate land from several hundred landowners. To compensate these owners, the SJHC used an innovative method described in a British report but which the British government itself had refrained from adopting because it was thought to be too radical. Against traditional practice, the compensation was based on the present value of the land, not a potential value dependent on future development.

Another unique characteristic of the development was that this huge project was undertaken during the period when democratic government in the colony of Newfoundland had been suspended and it was ruled instead by Commission — three members appointed from Newfoundland and three members appointed from Britain — and the governor. Permissions — for the use of the compensation method, for contributions towards financing the project — had to be approved by the Dominions Office in London. And there was a war on. This was a burden on the project as supply chains were interrupted and the price of construction materials skyrocketed.

Something else played a role in the story. Ameliorating the appalling lack of accommodation in St. John's, especially the overcrowded area back of New Gower Street, had stymied the government and the Municipal Council for years. But when the war brought more than 10,000 troops to town to defend the North Atlantic (they lived mostly in barracks but many in the town), they were everywhere about, remarking on how dirty and backward was the town. This was not complimentary to the local residents and embarrassing for Newfoundlanders, especially when these remarks were mixed with glowing descriptions of life on the mainland, remarks verified by American movies. With this experience, people in St. John's were excited to accept the CEHTP plan that promised modern houses with modern conveniences — 1,000 new houses were mentioned. And developing 800 acres, increasing the size of the town by one-third — that was unimaginable. It was comparable in magnitude to stories of the Great Fire of 1892, when much of the town had burned to the ground (but not those weary tenements near New Gower). Such a large project also offered jobs. It was bigger than any other project recently built in town: Gosling's row of houses on Quidi Vidi Road and Anderson's houses on Merrymeeting, both in the early 1920s, and even REWA's 124 houses on Topsail and Craigmillar in the late 1930s.

But the reality came to be different. During the first five years of its existence (1945–49), despite wartime exigencies, the SJHC built 233 houses and 92 apartments and sold 250 building lots to private developers. This was a major achievement and added substantially to the number of new houses in town. The new houses were small. "I made them as low cost as I could make them and still make them a house" (Meschino, 2000). However, they boasted every convenience — bathrooms, basements, built-in kitchens, controlled heating. But the price of these modest houses was beyond even a tradesman's income, let alone the poor, and they were eagerly purchased by the professional class. And "filtering" of the poor into houses of a higher standard was forgotten. There was no impact on the huddle of worn-out, overcrowded houses near New Gower Street.

The SJHC carried on after Confederation in 1949 and continued to administer land and building lots available for purchase by individuals and the new commercial developers. At the time of its merger with the Newfoundland and Labrador Housing Corporation (NLHC) in 1981, the Corporation could boast having built 333 houses, built or renovated 623 apartments, developed 2,200 acres of serviced land ready for development, and sold 4,100 building lots. It cannot be denied that it had contributed substantially to the housing inventory of St. John's. But the problems of the inner-city slum remained.

The second mandate of the CEHTP was to "re-plan the city" (CEHTP 1, 6), to make possible the future orderly development of St. John's. Todd had told the Rotary Club 15 years before that "Town planning is first of all a practical thing and may be defined as the scientific and orderly disposition of land and buildings with a view to obviating congestion and securing the economic and social efficiency, health and well-being of the community." Recognizing that planning was still a largely unknown activity, subject to irrational criticism, Todd reassured his audience that "the adoption of a comprehensive city plan need frighten no one. It means only the exercise of such prudence and foresight as is necessary to insure the success of any undertaking which deals with future events" (Todd 1930, 1).

The Municipal Council was bitterly disappointed that the SJHC had not demolished or replaced the downtown slum, or had not created alternative housing for the poor elsewhere in the city. However, the Council benefited in other ways from the work of the CEHTP. The decision by Dunfield to ensure that the six reports of the CEHTP were easily readable and widely available, and then to distribute a copy of the third report to every household in town, was a master stroke. It was, as Dunfield had hoped, "a primer on civic affairs and a valuable stimulus to thought" (Dunfield 1943b). It was an educational device for householders, professionals, tradesmen, the government, and City Hall.

"The Housing" was different from the latest rows of new and modern terraced houses built on Quidi Vidi, Merrymeeting, and Topsail and Craigmillar, praised as they were. "The Housing" gave the Council a first glimpse of what a modern city landscape could be: planned in orderly fashion for commercial and residential use, and for traffic, with recreational space and houses fully serviced and detached, each with a garden. Recall Dunfield's admonition that "nothing has a greater effect upon the health and the general social condition of the people, especially of the young, than the housing standard" (*Evening Telegram* 1942b). Compared to the tenements back of New Gower Street, this was healthy living. There were other lessons for the Council, too. In imitation of what they observed in the construction of the houses in the northern valley, they were encouraged to move ahead in their professionalization of the building trades by licensing tradesmen and drawing up a building code (1946), creating the office of a building inspector (1944), securing a zoning plan (1946), and hiring their first town planner (1950). All these new initiatives represented a radical departure from past practice in the city when the city engineer was responsible for screening all applications for building permits, inspecting construction techniques, and planning the city's streets and sewer infrastructure. We now expect that suburban expansion will be regulated by "status quo" professional planning practice. There was no such expectation in St. John's in the 1940s, so "The Housing" was the first example of modern planning practice in Newfoundland.

The Three Villages

Of the three villages proposed in Searles's concept plan, only Village "B" was developed as planned. It incorporates all the features that make it a model garden suburb. The streets are graduated: main streets for through-traffic and lesser streets for the quiet residential areas. Commercial activity is strictly confined to Elizabeth Avenue and yet serves all three villages, each of which is anchored to it. Detached houses are sited with gardens. Green space is set aside to provide parks and sports areas. Footpaths link the streets and the open spaces. Hundreds of trees, many imported from England (*Daily News* 1946k), were planted to provide a gentle contrast to the robust native conifers. Such a design for suburban growth may be commonplace today, but it was an exciting innovation for the city in 1945.

When World War II broke out, the area north of Empire Avenue was still "the country." But in spite of the naysayers, commercial activity came very quickly to the new suburb. Supermarkets, providing one-stop shopping with generous parking lots for easy access, were new to St. John's. As another sign that "the modern" was making inroads in the local landscape, the Ayre family was one of the first major businesses to augment their traditional Water Street location with three new supermarkets, one located in each of the three village centres. They were bought by the Weston family in 1963 and converted to Dominion Stores. All had closed by the end of the 1990s. The one in Village "A" became a Lawton's pharmacy (2013); the one in Churchill Square became a "Save Easy" (2007–12) that was replaced by a combined retail and apartment complex in 2021; and the one in Village "C" (Summerville) was enlarged and converted into a retail/residential condominium complex.

Figure 12.1. The Ayre's Supermarket in Village "C" on Elizabeth Avenue at Paton Street (*Evening Telegram* photo).

Allandale Nurseries was an early business in Churchill Square (Village "B"). A single flat-roofed building at the northwest corner of the Square, designed by Meschino, now a restaurant, began its life as Elizabeth Drugs. In 1951 Alex Hann built a butcher shop on the west side of the Square, a service station opened behind the drug store in 1954, and in 1963 the Ayre family built the Giant Mart department store on the south side of the Square. The park on the north side of Elizabeth Avenue, across from the Square, was dedicated in 1954. That same year, the city approved plans for a large commercial/residential building containing 60 apartments along the entire east side of the Square (see Appendix 11). On 28 February 1956 the *Daily News* printed an artist's sketch of the building under the banner headline "Housing Corporation's new $1 million apartments." George Cummings, a prominent modernist architect, designed the building with an underpass for access to the "Soldier Emergency" flats on Linden Place and Pine Bud Avenue. Construction of Cummings's building was stalled for almost two years because of a vigorous debate between Dunfield, who was chairman of the TPC, and the Municipal Council about the best way to develop the Square.

Figure 12.2. Churchill Square apartments under construction c. 1955; note the men installing the Arcade Stores sign (NLHC).

A second apartment complex was erected on Elizabeth Avenue in 1966 on a site that had always been reserved for an apartment building (Smallwood 1956). The Corporation promised that Elizabeth Towers would be an "ultra-modern" seven-storey building with 86 "prestige" apartments for "mature couples." This was such a new and important development for the whole city that there were printed invitations for the opening ceremony. The first tenants moved in three years later.

242 CORNER WINDOWS AND CUL-DE-SACS

> ELIZABETH TOWERS LIMITED
>
> requests the pleasure of your company
>
> at the Turning of the First Sod
>
> at the Site of Elizabeth Towers New Highrise Apartment Building
>
> on Elizabeth Avenue between Downing Street and Portugal Cove Road
>
> by
>
> The Honourable Joseph R. Smallwood, D.C.L., LL.D., D.Litt., M.H.A.
>
> Premier of Newfoundland
>
> at 3:00 p.m., on Friday, May 20th, 1966.

Figure 12.3. Invitation to the opening of Elizabeth Towers, 20 May 1966 (NLHC).

Figure 12.4. The sod-turning ceremony for Elizabeth Towers, 20 May 1966: Premier J.R. Smallwood (left) and Oliver L. Vardy, chairman of the SJHC (F.P. Meschino).

Figure 12.5. Elizabeth Towers (A.J. Shawyer).

Life in Churchill Park

The purest expression of Dunfield's garden suburb is Village "B," focused on Churchill Square. In this village, the SJHC built 242 houses in a classic garden suburb landscape of controlled streets and open space. And it was attractive. One respondent told us that when he was married in 1947 he could have bought a downtown house for about $5,000 but instead he bought a house on Bideford Place for $14,740, having been enticed by the attractiveness of the neighbourhood and the modern design of the house (Penney 2001).

Paul and Phyllis Meschino lived in a Type 3.13 house on Bideford Place during their time in St. John's (Appendix 4). They and their children have fond memories of the house, which was small but served the needs of their growing family. A bigger kitchen with more cabinets, larger bedrooms, and a shower in the bathroom would have been desirable. But adding these features would have increased the cost, and it would have been impossible to include them (Meschino 2000).

Dora Russell wrote "The Women's Pages" in the *Evening Telegram* at the time that Churchill Park was under construction. In the spring of 1947

244   CORNER WINDOWS AND CUL-DE-SACS

Figure 12.6. Oblique aerial photograph from 1947 of Village "B," looking south and showing Appledore, Bideford, and Cork Place, the five apartment buildings on Allandale Place, part of Linden Court, and the site of Churchill Square. The "wishbone" of Maple and Stoneyhouse Streets is just above (south of) Churchill Square, and the houses in Blocks 4 and 5 farther to the right (west). The Anglican Girls' Orphanage (established 1918) is in the lower left corner of the photograph and Burton's Pond is on the right-hand side (F.P. Meschino).

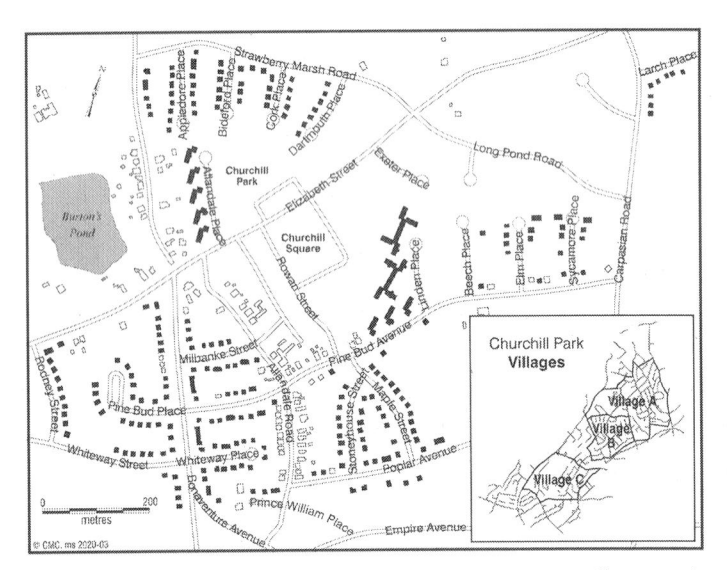

Figure 12.7. Map of SJHC houses and apartments (Darrell Kennedy and Charles Conway).

Figure 12.8. Dartmouth Place in the 1950s; A.E. Searles's house, later owned by Eric Cook's law partner Rupert Bartlett, is on the left side of the image (F.P. Meschino).

Figure 12.9. Tom, Carol, and Barbara Freeman beside their house at 6 Beech Place (House #217 on the left side of the image) in the 1950s (F.P. Meschino).

Figure 12.10. 13 Bideford Place in winter with the Church of England Girl's Orphanage in the background (Nathan Penney).

she surveyed a cross-section of residents and provided the following summary of their responses.

> In the St. John's Housing Corporation area in Churchill Park, the majority of the finished houses are now occupied and landscaped. This section is beginning to take on a very attractive appearance, a fulfillment of the prediction that this would be a "garden suburb" of St. John's.
>
> The majority of householders are well-satisfied despite the high cost of their houses. The average house costs $11,500 plus the land which runs to about $1,000. Typically, a householder pays down $1,000 and agrees to pay $65–$70 monthly for 30 years. These payments include insurance, a maintenance fund for repairs, and city taxes. Some house-

holders find that they are paying less than their previous exorbitant rents in town.

There is both praise and complaints about the features of these modern houses. The central heating system is welcome. It is efficient and cheap. The ventilation louvres are a nuisance because they are not properly fitted. The housewives say that the open plan of kitchen, dinette and living room make for easier family living, and more convenient cleaning, and that the air conditioning system rids the house of kitchen odours quickly. However, inferior quality wallboards make painting difficult and inferior quality floorboards are not easy to maintain. Basements are roomy and many residents plan to turn them into laundries, playroom, or extra bedrooms.

The area is still under construction. Dust and rubble and mud are everywhere. There are as yet few streetlights and no postal delivery. Probably more than a few housewives would not have moved to Churchill Park had there been houses available elsewhere. But on the whole, the housewives are pleased with their situation. The chief drawing card was, in the first instance, the easy financial arrangements, but now they like their home for its comfort and convenience. They all have a garden, and some have a garage. And, of course, they had equity in a house. It may be said that from the angle of the residents, this venture has proved satisfactory.

The housing Corporation project has undoubtedly relieved the housing shortage in some measure. Yet, despite this new supply, there is still a shortage. (Miller 2015)

The Board of the SJHC, and those members of the CEHTP, and Dunfield, of course, must have been delighted with this newspaper article. The fortunate families who had chosen to buy a house in Churchill Park affirmed the value and the lifestyle of the garden suburb.

The immediate post-war period was characterized by the belief that one could always achieve better living through technology. This was thought to be particularly important for women as they struggled to handle their multiple roles as house managers, domestic engineers, and keepers of the family health. There was, of course, no question that those roles legitimately belonged to women. As condescending and patronizing as this now sounds, it was an accurate reflection of a widespread contemporary viewpoint. Many Canadian women and men, frustrated by years of shared accommodation with parents or in-laws, perhaps in a house lacking modern conveniences, understandably viewed new houses like those offered in Churchill Park as a dream come true.

These first-time residents of Churchill Park were undemanding when it came to the features of their house, which was likely the first one they had ever owned (Royal Architectural Institute of Canada 1960, 197). The women of Churchill Park were no different in this regard from women in England (Attfield 1989) or Canada (Strong-Boag 1991). They were largely unconcerned about the critics' view of suburbia and its houses. For them, the conveniences, safety, and creature comforts of the Churchill Park houses were greater than anything they had previously experienced. No analysis of a post-war suburb can ignore this.

Churchill Park has held its value through to today (see Appendix 12). The first occupants of the houses were families with professional incomes, who not only maintained their properties but as early as 1949 began to expand the footprint of their houses with extra bedrooms, sunrooms, expanded kitchens, and also garages (Sharpe and Shawyer 2005, 125–33). The area has also benefited from the development of an adjacent, stable, institutional landscape in the 1950s and 1960s: Memorial University, Confederation Building, the College of the North Atlantic, the Arts and Culture Centre, the Provincial Library. In 1966, Premier Smallwood announced the creation of the C.A. Pippy Park, the intent of which was to provide all these provincial buildings with a "park-like setting" so that it would be a "landscaped showpiece for the great symbols of the province" (Shawyer 2005, 123). It is not surprising that local real estate advertisements today, more than 50 years later, refer to the area from Allandale Road to Portugal Cove Road as being "the most sought after residential area in St John's" (Appendix 1).

Brian Dunfield and His Passion for "The Housing"

Dunfield's daughter, Dorothy, recalled that every morning when her father walked her to school along New Gower Street, he lamented the wretched landscape through which they passed. He was appalled that people lived under such conditions. When "The Housing" was under construction, he would often head off to his work at court early, at about 8:00 a.m., so that he could drive through the housing area to see its progress. And he sometimes took his family on a tour of the site (Dorothy Dunfield 1999).

Carrie Toope began to work as a housemaid for the Dunfield family in 1940 when she was 16, and she was there when Dunfield began to draft the six reports of the CEHTP. She characterized him as an impeccably dressed gentleman who loved gardening and was always courteous and kind. Carrie told us that Dunfield said he "wanted people to be able to rent-to-buy so they would have something of their own in the end." He set her wage with this goal in mind. Carrie never did live in such a house but she knew what they looked like. Cardboard models of Meschino's house designs were arrayed on the mantel in Dunfield's living room (Toope 2012).

In 1944 the Municipal Council, the Commission of Government, and organized labour all supported the housing solution as it had been proposed, defined, and described in the reports of the CEHTP. However, in what might be described as a classic example of the public policy error of "premature disclosure," no alternative plan was ever discussed. This was likely because of Dunfield's personal commitment to this once-in-a-lifetime opportunity to create such a plan. And he did so with dedicated energy and overwhelming enthusiasm. Churchill Park was his project, for better or worse. The project was supported by the public, not because of its specific, innovative details, meticulously described, but because it broadly promised a solution to the housing problem. It was an exciting vision of modernity.

But Churchill Park was a failure as a social experiment. Its original goal of providing housing for those with lower income was never met. What it provided was middle-class suburban housing, which was not what St. John's needed most urgently. While it was described as a residential development "as fine as anywhere in cities of comparable size in Canada or the United States," it was also criticized because "the much heralded Housing Corporation, originally designed as an ancillary to a city-wide drive to clean up the slums, became the mecca of citizens in search of homes, and not in the least bit associated with the residents of the condemned area" (*Evening Telegram* 1950).

The creation of the new suburb became an end in itself. It did not satisfy the expectations of any of those who had given it their support, nor indeed, even the members of the Corporation. With reference to the goal of the provision of housing for the poor:

> The main incentive which fired the enthusiasm of the members of the Corporation was the hope and expectation that [it] would be able to construct houses suitable for the lower salaried working men at prices which would be within the reach of their financial resources. It is one of the great disappointments that this objective was not fully achieved. (SJHC 1951, 9)

With reference to the goal of introducing modern town planning to St. John's, there was more success, as we have described. However, the bold words and brave recommendations in the six reports had to be supported by a lot of effort by the SJHC:

> There had been very little growth in the city for many years and what new houses had been erected were built in a patch-quilt fashion with no organized programme of zoning

or preparation for future expansion. As a result, the Corporation was faced with a major selling job to convince the citizenry in general that what they were doing was for the ultimate good of the community as a whole. (Vardy 1967, 393)

Dunfield had raised great expectations and they had come to nought — at least in the provision of housing for anyone less than the professional class. But whether you could afford to live in Churchill Park or not, its creation went a long way towards ameliorating the public shame of "the humiliating catalogue of facts" described in the CEHTP's third report. Everyone could take pride in the fact that St. John's could now boast of a neighbourhood of modern streets and houses comparable to any in Canada and the US. Dunfield's vision had brought Modernism to the city. The only unwarranted claim was the persistent argument that by means of "filtering up," the project would provide a long-term solution to the *whole* housing question (Lewis and Shrimpton 1982, 237).

Paul Meschino, with his cutting-edge training in architecture and town planning, accidentally fell into the position of architect for the SJHC. Looking back at this early episode in his long career, he told us that "regardless of Dunfield's drive to solve the slum clearance problem, he in fact jump-started the St. John's economy and opened up the northern valley to development. What he did was of monumental historic significance" (Meschino 2000).

The southern border of the Housing Area, which was taken into the city in 1945, ran along Empire Avenue. Although the Housing Area was only a mile from the downtown, critics referred to it as "Dunfield's Folly" because, they said, the northern valley was so far away it was "in the country": people would not want to live so far from town, nor would businesses go there. And public transportation would not be provided (Riggs 1997, xxii).

Mayor Carnell described the Housing Area as "The New Jerusalem" (Revelation 3:12 and 21:12). Ebenezer Howard (1898) had used a few lines from William Blake's poem, "Jerusalem" (1804), at the beginning of his book, *Tomorrow: A Peaceful Path to Real Reform* (1898), which became the inspiration for the Garden City movement. A modern interpretation is that the term generally refers to a new beginning. But it can be used in an ironic or derogatory way (Hawkin, Rollman, and DeRoche 1999). Carnell used the term derisively because "he hated Dunfield and everything he stood for" (Bartlett 1999). The mayor resented the fact that so much of the city's money had been spent outside the city limits to build a suburb that could never be Utopia for the residents of the inner city.

Both descriptions — "Dunfield's Folly" and "New Jerusalem" — became embedded in references to Churchill Park by contemporaries and then by historians of the city's development (Miller 1981; Winter 1999; Vardy 1967, 393; Baker 1983a, 31; Denhez 1994. 100; Penney 2001). Years later, in a television address, Dunfield confessed that the housing project had been popularly referred to by both of these unflattering epithets (Dunfield 1965).

Churchill Park, the core of the SJHC's accomplishments, has generally lived up to the expectations of Dunfield and his colleagues. It might not have been the "New Jerusalem" for those who lived on Lion's Square, Dammerill's Lane, and Notre Dame and Wickford Streets, but it was not "Mr. Dunfield's Folly" either.

APPENDIX 1

The Re-Planning of St. John's

Address of Hon. Mr. Justice Dunfield, Chairman, at the First Meeting of the Commission of Enquiry into Housing Conditions in St. John's, 21 May 1942

INTRODUCTORY

Gentlemen. This being our first meeting as a constituted body I should like to open by welcoming the members who have undertaken to play their part in the big task we have before us. Besides being, if I may be permitted to say so, a competent and well-selected assembly of citizens, you have the advantage that each of you is the chosen representative of a constituency in the form of a church or society or organization of considerable numbers; and I am your nominee as chairman, and thus I think it may almost be said that we are a selected body representing the citizens of St. John's. This is only as it should be: for there is no more important question in our town at present than that of housing and if as a body representing the people we can evolve a sound working scheme for improving the housing situation, a scheme which the Municipal Council and the government can see their way to adopt and put into operation, we shall render the greatest service to the community it is possible to imagine.

I avail of this opportunity to thank you for the complement which you have done in selecting me to be your chairman; a compliment which I shall do my best to deserve by giving the closest possible attention to the work of this Commission.

Town planning is an inseparable part of the housing problem, and in this connection it is an interesting coincidence that I, who now occupy the place of my respected predecessor the late Mr. Justice Kent, Chairman of the late Town Planning Committee, should have the privilege of taking over the work which he commenced, and to which he gave so much valuable effort, with a view to incorporating it into our present operations.

IMPORTANCE OF PROBLEM

It is hardly necessary for me to point out to you or to the public the importance of the problem of housing, associated as it is as I have already said, with the problem of town planning. Nothing has a greater effect upon the health and general social condition of the people, especially of the young, than the housing standard. It must be admitted that in this respect we fall very short indeed. We have substantial slum or semi-slum area. This perhaps is not our fault; it is the result of historical conditions and possibly of missed opportunities after the fire of 1892, as well as the depression in recent years which for the time being rendered a large part of the population unable to keep its housing up to standard. But it is not merely the slum areas which disfigure our town. The houses occupied by the middle class of fair income are in many cases not at all what they should be, in quality, or in surroundings. Even the areas occupied by people of means exhibit in the main the architectural ideas of thirty to fifty years ago, accompanied by an unsystematic lay-out.

I noted the other day in an American book on house design a picture of a house which had been reconstructed. There was also a picture of it in its original state, in which it was described as a typical house of a 'blight' area. Unfortunately it was also typical of three quarters of the houses in this city. The first page of another book was occupied by pictures of two small houses of the same size, one designed as it ought to be, the other, for comparison, as it ought not to be. Unfortunately the one presented as an awful example of bad design was typical of the majority of small houses being put up on the outskirts of St. John's today. Then too, in our town, even where the house is substantial and adequate, the surroundings, the fences, the front garden and the back yard too often present an appearance of dilapidation and disorder more appropriate to a temporary mining town than to a Capital. A Frenchman who lived among us for some years wrote a book about us, in French. It is years since I read it, but I seem to recollect that he said something to this effect, that he had never seen a country where the people were so completely utilitarian and had such a complete disregard for the aesthetic side of life. What he said was true, and we have little excuse for it; for the improvement of appearance is not so much a matter demanding expenditure as a matter demanding a little energy and forethought.

There may be some who suppose that a housing policy consists merely in expropriating slum areas, pulling down the houses and building something new in another place; but that is a debated method and the matter has many more aspects than that. Housing is a matter partly of finance, partly of house design, partly of town planning, partly of social and economic study, partly of education; and a long-term housing scheme should contemplate the improvement of the housing standards of all classes, and the ultimate transformation of the town to which it relates.

This is not a poor little town; for its size it is probably a rich little town, even if the riches are not too well distributed; but it does not make the most of its opportunities, as everyone who has travelled abroad and seen foreign towns must realize. We have sections such as, for example, Water Street from the War Memorial to the Post Office, the residential streets from the Hotel by way of Circular Road to Rawlins' Cross, considerable portions of LeMarchant Road, and so forth, which are quite creditable; but everybody knows that there are other parts of the town from which, if you were taking a foreign visitor round, you would try to steer him away, because you would be ashamed of them. We have here a great field for study and a great opportunity for improvement.

A PROPITIOUS TIME FOR OPERATIONS

It seems to me that the Council has done very well indeed to choose this particular time for initiating an Enquiry into local housing: and in this connection I should not forget to mention the name of Deputy Mayor Cook, for I think it is no secret that the initiative is his. The name of Cook is well regarded in St. John's and if this enquiry results as well as we may hope it will, the Cook family will have done one more service to their native town.

I think the time is very propitious for these reasons. First it is probable that no financing can be undertaken until the conclusion of the war, which means that we have one or two years at least to give to an exhaustive study of the situation. Secondly, our people are experiencing a boom in employment which we may reasonably expect to continue in some measure until the end of the war. If present conditions continue for another year or two it may surprise us to find how many of the working class are able to pay for, or at least make a good down payment upon, a new house. Even if left alone they will spend some money on their homes at any rate in cases where they are owners. If any plan devised by us can provide them with greatly improved houses and surroundings for their money, we shall have enabled them to avail of an opportunity which may not recur for a long time. It may be that we cannot hope for continued prosperity after the war: but if the working classes are put in a position to spend their money to the greatest advantage on new houses . . . there is no doubt that a well-organized scheme can give them better value for their money than they can obtain for themselves, [and] then they will at any rate have a much better start towards what may lie ahead. Thirdly, the labour market may need some stimulus after the war, and substantial building schemes would provide employment. Fourthly, there may be opportunities of picking up a good deal of expensive material, for example plumbing fittings, at a very cheap rate when the many temporary structures belonging to the war effort come to be dismantled: and there may be war buildings available as temporary housing to accommodate those, if any, whose homes are pulled down for replacement.

Then, finally, we have received, notably at the hands of our American friends, some valuable lessons lately in rapid mass construction. The organizations and methods which have built places like Fort Pepperrell and which put up the new U.S.O. building in sixty days, have much to teach us, and perhaps to do for us, if our deliberations result in any scheme for new construction.

BRANCHES OF THE SUBJECT

The subject of housing has many branches. As I have already said, it is not at all a question of finding some vacant land, putting up a few houses on some hit and miss design, and seeing whether you can let them. It is not merely a case of finding a slum area, expropriating it, tearing it down and putting up new houses on it. That may or may not be the best method of approach. It is not even confined to the provision of housing for those on the lowest income levels, although that is the principal part of it. You have first to consider whether your town is properly laid out; whether central sections of it are too congested, and what is happening on the outskirts. St. John's is steadily developing new sub-standard areas in certain places. It has been said by a writer on the subject that the first step in slum clearance is to prevent a town from making new slums. You have to consider the possibilities of the various areas; and then you have to suggest to the Municipal council the establishment of building zones. This is not a new point and I have been glad to learn from the papers that the Council have already been giving it some thought. You cannot, for example, expect wealthy citizens to put up $15,000 houses if in a few years they are going to find $2,000 or $2,500 houses put up beside them, for this will depreciate the value of their property. You cannot expect lower-income citizens to put up $2,500 houses if in a few years they are going to find felt-covered shacks put up beside them. You are not going to find any wise citizen prepared to build a good house in a place where tomorrow he may find a factory on one side and a laundry on the other.

ZONING PROVISIONS

Under a zoning system buildings of certain types and classes only may be built in certain areas. This involves the establishment of standards of design and construction within which citizens intending to build in those areas may exercise their choice. It involves also the establishment of standards as to the number of houses per acre which may be permitted in the different zones and the distance apart at which they must stand in order to provide access for sunshine and open views from the windows. Quite lately I have seen a new small house built outside the town with nice views from all sides; and then within a year or two I have seen another one jammed up within six feet of it, so that it now has neither southerly view nor sun in the morning. That is the result of unchecked land speculation. The arrangement and spacing of houses is involved also with the cost of the necessary connecting streets, sewers and water system. Again, if the population of congested areas must be spread out, as is usually necessary, and if new building is to be done on the outskirts of the town, the question of the transportation system arises since a man must not be out of reach of his work.

EDUCATIONAL ASPECT

Then, finally, there is the educational aspect of individual house construction. It is a commonplace that a good house need not cost more than a bad house, and may cost less, because brains have been built into it. There are many houses in this town, both among those built years ago and among those still going up, where you can see a large percentage of the cost is wasted on useless accessories for want of a good design. Take for example the houses of about thirty years ago. You will find verandahs abounding. I have one myself. (I must say I bought my house [and] I had nothing to do with the design). They are frequently on the wrong side. They are generally unused by anybody but the dog. They hinder the access of light to the rooms, they are quite unnecessary as shelter in our climate and they represent the expenditure of money which with good designing might have added a couple of rooms to the house and left it better-looking. Look about you as you go round the town and see how much money has been wasted in this way. That is the sort of thing which cannot be afforded in modern housing schemes, where every brick and plank has got to produce full value in housing space. Modern designs carefully avoid waste of this kind. But judging by current building, modern house designing is practically unknown in St. John's. Few seem to employ an architect. There is an immense amount to be learnt, especially from the United States, on the handsome and economical designing of individual houses, especially the small or medium house. Information on designing ought to be placed by official agencies at the disposal of every citizen, and this is what I speak of as the educational aspect of housing. There is also the need for education on the subject of keeping the surroundings of the house in good shape.

NECESSITY FOR STUDY

But of course the central problem and the central difficulty of all housing schemes is the devising and financing of decent modern housing at cheaper rates for the lowest-income third or quarter of the population. This is not an enterprise to be tackled without exhaustive study. Fortunately the subject is not new. Housing schemes, assisted and otherwise, of one kind or another, are numerous all over the world. The largest and best of them arose in Europe during the ten or fifteen years following the last war. During that period, in an area inhabited by about 130 million people, or about the same population as that of the United States, some four and a half million of houses were put up with public assistance of one kind or another, whether by way of cheap finance or otherwise, and nearly sixteen percent of the population was housed in such houses. There have been a few such schemes in North America also, but our continent, with its individualistic tendency has gone in mainly for, and made very great progress in, the design of the individual house. For organized large-scale housing schemes we have to look mainly to Europe. Germany in the period between the wars, built some two and a half million houses. Great Britain about half as many, and other countries very considerable numbers. The best schemes probably for our study and emulation are those in the Scandinavian countries, Norway, Sweden, Denmark and Finland, where social conditions, building methods and climates are not unlike our own. There is for us not much to be learnt (except in so far as they are examples of finance), from the schemes of Paris, Vienna or Berlin: they are beyond our means: but we can gather much from the successes and mistakes of Stockholm, Oslo and Helsinki. There is a wide literature on the subject and it is possible to obtain many excellent books describing, with plans and illustrations, the different methods which have been attempted in design, layout, construction and finance. It is from the study of what others have done in the past that we can best plan what we may do in the future.

COMPLICATIONS OF THE SUBJECT

As an example of the kind of problem which is met with in connection with housing I may refer again to that of slum clearance.

Some municipalities and governments in other countries have gone about this by the direct process of expropriating slum property, pulling it down and rebuilding on the site. The argument in favour of this is that you get an immediate clearance of the bad areas of a town, which are very often in places where they have a serious influence on the town's appearance and general social features. The main objection to this method is that unless landowners are ruthlessly expropriated, land costs too much. The housing erected on it has, therefore, to be skimped, and even so ends by costing too much. There is therefore difficulty in getting the people who occupied the land before back into the same area: and, in any case, it is almost always necessary to reduce the density of the population in a sub-standard area, so that they cannot all get back. They tend to crowd into the sub-standard areas and so make matters worse. I note that English legislation has gone to considerable lengths in striking down the values artificially given to slum property by the relatively high density of population, and the high rate of rentals in relation to the capital values of the houses. The practice advocated in many countries is to develop housing settlements on the outskirts where land is relatively cheap or even vacant. This avoids the necessity of attempting to shift the existing population out and back, and brings about a sort of automatic improvement of congested areas, in that, as population drains from them, municipalities are in a position to raise their standard of requirements and to carry out condemnations, and thus thin out and improve the slum. On the other hand, when building is done in outside localities, the consideration of transportation between the housing and the areas where work is carried on has an obvious bearing on the cost.

Then, again, it is necessary to find means or measures whereby housing which is intended to be in the main cheap housing shall be prevented from passing into the speculative market: because, being carefully designed and well laid out, it is normally better than old housing, and will tend to be in sharp demand if its location is at all satisfactory: and so rents will rise and the object be defeated.

Then, again, there is the controversy as between the individual house, well-spaced out, and the housing block or tenement containing a large number of families, with a certain measure of common services. Some cities have specialized in one method or the other. Others have combined them. Probably each serves its own special purpose.

As I have already said, our best examples of principle and method are to be found in Europe, whereas our best examples of design and material for the small house, such as is suitable to this country, are to be found in America.

I mention these few points, which are the result only of a very brief consideration of the subject, to indicate the complications to be met and the impossibility of coming to any conclusion as to the best method without close and extended study. One thing, however, is, I think, certain, and that is that by careful and thorough design and large-scale organization it is possible to provide the people with better value in housing than they can obtain for themselves.

THE BENEFITS OF THE HOUSING PROGRAMME

A housing programme inevitably implies some degree of public aid towards the housing of the lowest-income-quarter of the population. Apart from the humane considerations involved in assisting those who cannot wholly look out for themselves, including the class who cannot afford to buy anything at all but only to pay a low rent, a community cannot but benefit from the elimination of slums and the provision of healthy housing. It benefits in the reduction of crime and juvenile delinquency, in the improvement of health conditions, and in the raising of educational and cultural standards. We often wonder why so many people, and especially children, spent so much of their time about the streets by day and by night. The answer is in a good many cases that if we had the class of housing that they have to put up with we also should find the streets pleasanter and more interesting than at home.

Working-class housing is in some sense a public utility, like railways, telephones and the rest. Liberal writers and labor movements tend nowadays to assert that just as every citizen is entitled to look to his government for paved streets, tramways, street lighting, police protection, telegraphs, telephones and the like, so he is entitled to look for a reasonably minimum of housing accommodation of decent standard and in reasonably clean and attractive surroundings. Dirty, slummy neighbourhoods spell bad social organization. Looked at in this light, housing is a thing to be organized and engineered with the best available skill, and of course proportioned as far as possible to the prospective revenue; but yet, on account of its indirect benefits to the community, it ought to be treated as a necessity, even if, in the case of the lowest-income classes, it cannot quite pay its way. You may have read in your papers on the Thursday before Easter a pronouncement of the new Archbishop of Canterbury, Dr. William Temple, who is a very liberal thinker and writer on social subjects. He mentions six things which a Christian community is, he says, entitled to claim from its government; and in the forefront, as his No. 1, he put this: "Every child should find itself a member of a family housed with decency and dignity, so that it may grow up unspoiled by underfeeding or overcrowding, by dirty and drab surrounds, or monotony of environment."

CONCLUSION

Having thus glanced very hastily at the subject I now venture to suggest for your consideration our best line of action. It is a suggestion only, for our course, our line of action, will be determined, not by the Chairman, but by the general consensus of opinion upon this Commission of Enquiry.

I think, first, that each and every one of us must familiarize himself with the town. We all have our own haunts and beats, so to speak, outside of which we seldom stray; and I venture to suggest that there are streets and regions in this town where some of us have never been and to which we could not, unassisted, find our way. I think we have all to get into our heads a complete picture of every street and locality, and with the assistance of the City Engineer, to learn to know those streets and localities in relation to the sewerages and water layout.

Then I think that we shall have to conduct a very thorough survey covering every house in town and to classify those houses in some convenient way. For example, we might class them as Excellent; Good; Fair and not needing interference; Tolerable but poor and better replaced; Bad, and ought soon to be condemned; Very bad: already condemned or ought to be condemned immediately; and having thus classified the houses I think that we should get them laid out in different colours on a large plan so that we can see at a glance where and how extensive our bad areas are.

Then, further, I suggest that we may have to carry out a survey of the population. As to every house in classes (d), (e) and (f) I think we shall need to know how many people live in it, how many rooms there are, who is owner or tenant, and what is his occupation, and if a tenant, what rent he pays: and we may have to ask him whether he wants a house of his own; what he could pay for it, or what he could pay as a deposit towards it; or what annual rent he would expect to be able to pay after the War period for the purpose of buying a house on the hire-purchasing system, that is to say, buying, as it were, out of the rent.

There again, we shall have to make allowance for the temporary prosperity which is putting money into people's pockets, and for the possible or probable slump or condition of unemployment which may arise after the War; and all these matters we shall have to consider in conjunction with an investigation as to what sum small houses or large tenements can be built for, and what is the best and cheapest system of building. When we have done all this we should know with fair precision (a) what we want to get rid of; (b) what we need to provide; (c) what the people can, for their part, finance; and (d) what can be obtained for them: and on the basis of these facts we shall be able to consider our plan.

The City Council has very kindly provided a small vote to finance our operations, and we may hope that their staff will be able to give us a good deal of information and assistance.

At any rate it is certain that we cannot venture upon a problem of this kind without first obtaining full and accurate data — in other words, forming as correct and as complete a picture of our town as we can put together.

Then, while with the assistance of such staff as we may have, we are collecting this information and classifying it, I think that we ourselves should study housing problems abroad as set forth in the extensive literature on the subject and endeavor to provide ourselves with a really good background of information.

We have, as I have said, in all probability plenty of time to do this; and a further reason for taking our time is that not until the end of the War, when we can see the general and financial conditions then prevailing, shall we be able to formulate a scheme adapted to those conditions as we find them. But if we have collected the necessary data and made ourselves thoroughly familiar both with them and with the questions of principle involved, we should then be in a position to formulate recommendations fairly rapidly.

This then, gentlemen, is a hasty and preliminary view of our housing problem as I personally see it. I am not now attempting to lay down a programme nor to dictate what we ought to do, first, because it is a matter for the Commission of Enquiry as a body and not for me alone and, secondly, because at this state I pretend to know but little about it. As Chairman I am a sort of referee. At present I am merely suggesting a few rules of play and throwing the puck on to the ice; and I may say it is a very large puck and very slippery ice. It is now for you, the team, to chase it about, and I hope that by the time the bell rings at the conclusion of the War, we may be in a position to score a goal.

APPENDIX 2

Commission of Enquiry on Housing and Town Planning Questionnaire, July 1942

Part I

1. Name (head of family)
2. Address
3. Does family occupy whole house or part only?
4. Number in household living on the premises:
    (a) Adults (persons over 15 years)
    (b) Children under 5 years
    (c) Children 5 to 15 years
    (d) Lodgers
    (e) Other persons
5. Number of rooms occupied:
    (a) Bedrooms
    (b) Kitchen
    (c) Other rooms
    (d) Bathroom with W.C.
    (e) W.C.
6. Has the house:
    (a) Running cold water?
    (b) Running hot water?
    (c) Kitchen sink?

(d) Bath or shower?
(e) Fitted toilet basin?
(f) Water closet?
(g) Sewerage connection?
(h) Heating system?
- i) Steam
- ii) Hot water
- iii) Hot air
- iv) Hall stove

Note: If more than one of any of these, add a figure after your answer. If shared with another family, say "Use Of" instead of 'Yes'. If plumbing out of order, say so.

7. Is the structure or framework of the house sound?
8. Is the outside of the house sound and weatherproof?
9. How old is the house (if you know)?
10. Are you
    (a) Owner of house and land? or
    (b) House owner paying ground rent? or
    (c) Tenant of house?
11. If you pay ground rent, how much do you pay, to whom and how often?
    Amount
    Landlord
    How often?
12. How many feet of frontage have you?
13. If you are tenant only of house, what house rent do you pay, to whom and how often?
    Amount $
    Landlord
    How often
14. Do you do repairs or does the landlord?

Part II

QUESTIONS AS TO YOUR POSITION REGARDING A NEW HOUSE
Note: Evidence under this head is confidential and solely for the use of the Commission in estimating the need for new houses and the financial position of the public. No details or any person's answers will be made public in any way.

15. What is your occupation?
16. What is your age?
17. Who is your employer, if any?
18. How long have you been with him?
19. Do you desire to own a house of your own if you do not own one now?
20. If you own your house now, do you desire a new or better one?
21. Would you prefer to have it in town? Or in the suburbs with a little ground round it?
22. If you do not desire to own, would you rather:
    (a) Rent a separate house, or
    (b) Rent private apartments in a larger building?
23. If you could get more space for your rental money in an apartment building than in a separate house, would you choose:
    (a) The house, or
    (b) The apartment building?
24. How many rooms (besides bathroom, W.C., etc.) do you feel that you need for reasonable comfort?
25. If a house-building scheme were planned and financed, how much cash (if any) would you probably put up towards the price of a house, in say two years from now, if present conditions continue?
26. Whether you expect to be able to put up any cash or not, how much per month could you find, beginning say two years from now, towards buying a house in the rental plan? (that is, you pay so much a month and occupy the house, and the payments pay off the cost of the house in ten or twenty years, or such time as may be arranged?)

Note: Think over questions 25 and 26. On a building scheme you might either:

> Buy your house by rental payments
> Pay part in cash and the balance by rental payments, or even
> Pay full cost in cash if the scheme could build for you better and more cheaply than you could get house built yourself.

27. Can you do building work, either with or without expert help?
28. Would you be interested in any scheme under which the cost of a house was reduced by your doing part or all of the building work yourself?
29. What is the family income now?

    Note: Answer to this question only if you wish, but if you do, it will help us.

30. What was the family income before the war and the commencement of work on military bases?

    Note: We ask this question because payments under a building scheme will no doubt extend over a period after the war when there will not be as much work as at present.

31. After the war construction period is over, will you still probably be able to pay (a) the cash sum and/or (b) the monthly rental you spoke of in answer to questions 25 and 26?

    (a) Cash
    (b) Monthly rent

32. How long have you lived in St. John's?
33. Do you intend to make St. John's your permanent place of residence?

APPENDIX 3

A Standard St. John's Housing Corporation Lease (House No. 31, 12 Maple Street)

This lease made at St. John's in the Island of Newfoundland between the St. John's Housing Corporation, a statutory corporation created by the St. John's Housing Corporation Act 1944 (hereinafter called 'the Landlord' which expression where the context so admits shall include the reversioner for the time being immediately expectant on the term hereby granted) . . . of the one part and [name of tenant] of St. John's aforesaid Agent (hereinafter called 'the Tenant' which expression where the context so admits shall include such tenant's successors in title) of the other part

Witnesseth as follows:

1. In consideration of the sum of $1,000 on the execution of this Lease paid by 'the Tenant' to the 'landlord' . . . and of the rent and covenants on the part of the 'the Tenant' hereinafter reserved and contained 'the Landlord' hereby demises to 'the Tenant' all that piece or parcel of land situate on the East side of Maple Street in the Housing Area as defined in the St. John's Housing Corporation (Lands) Act 1944 and bounded as follows that is to say on the West by the Eastern boundary of Maple Street aforesaid by which it measures in a slightly curved line Fifty-one (51') more or less on the East by other land of the Landlord by which it measures Fifty feet (50') more or less on the North by other land of the Landlord leased to Clarence

A. Knight by which it measures One hundred and fifty-one feet (151') more or less and on the south by other land of the Landlord leased to Thomas J. Fitzpatrick by which it measure One hundred and Fifty-seven feet (157') more or less the same being lot 23 in Block 4 of Village "B" super Block 1 of the house and block layout of the Landlord.

TOGETHER WITH the messuage or dwelling house erected thereon by 'the Landlord' at the Landlord's expense and known as No. 70 (Street Number 12 Maple Street) and also such of the furniture, chattels, and effects in or about the said dwelling house as are specified in the Schedule hereto annexed EXCEPT and reserved unto the Landlord or any person, body, or corporation authorised by it the right of constructing, placing, laying, inspecting, repairing, maintaining, and renewing any water and/or sewer pipes or mains in and under any part of the land hereby demised and for that purpose the right to enter upon (with or without vehicles, machinery, or equipment), dig, break, excavate, and trench any part of the land hereby demised and upon such entry the Landlord shall acquire an easement for such water and/or sewer pipes or mains under, across, or through the said land AND the right of constructing, placing, laying, inspecting, repairing, maintaining, and renewing any wires, cables, or other equipment for the supply of electricity or telephonic communication across, over, or under any part of the said land and for that purpose the right to enter upon (with or without vehicles, machinery, or equipment), dig, break, excavate, trench, and/or erect poles or other equipment upon any part of the said land and upon such entry the Landlord shall acquire an easement for such wires, cables, and poles under, across, or through the said land AND the right of planting, protecting, and maintaining trees, shrubs, hedges, grass, or other vegetation upon any part of the said land and for that purpose and for the purpose of renewing any such planting the right to enter upon, dig, break, excavate, and trench any part of the said land AND it is hereby expressly declared and agreed that neither the Landlord nor any person, body, or corporation authorised as aforesaid shall at any time be under any obligation to pay compensation to The Tenant for any of the said easements or in respect of any damage caused by the said works to fences, gardens, or trees AND the Tenant hereby agrees not to impair access along the line of any easement by permitting any erections to go thereon or otherwise and where the line of the said easement is along the rear of the said land to erect only easily movable sections of fencing TO HOLD the said messuage premises and furniture, chattels, and effects (hereby called 'the said demised premises') to the Tenant from the 1st day of November, 1946 for the term of nine hundred and ninety-nine (999) years YIELDING and paying therefor unto the Landlord during the first thirty years of the said term the rents following namely:

(a) the yearly rent of seven hundred and twenty six dollars and twelve cents ($726.12) payable in equal monthly payments of sixty dollars and fifty-one cents ($60.51) on the first day of each month in advance the first of such payments to be made on the 1st day of November, 1946

(b) a yearly insurance rent equal in amount to the sum which the Landlord shall pay in that year in respect of insurance of the said demised premises pursuant to its covenant hereinafter contained payable in equal monthly payments on the first day of each month in advance the first of such payments to be made on the 1st day of November 1946

(c) A yearly tax rent equal in amount to the sum which the Landlord shall pay in that year in respect of taxes, rates, duties, and assessments whether municipal, parliamentary, governmental, or otherwise now charged or hereafter to be charged upon the said demised premises or upon the Landlord on account thereof payable in equal monthly payment on the first day of each month in advance the first of such payments to be made on the 1st day of November 1946

(d) A yearly maintenance rent of sixty dollars payable in equal monthly payments of five dollars on the first day of each month in advance, the first of such payments to be made on the 1st day of November, 1946 to be applied by the Landlord towards maintenance and repair of the said demised premises it being understood that any part of the said maintenance rent not so applied will be refunded to the Tenant as and when the annual rent payable hereunder shall become the sum of One Dollar AND it is hereby expressly declared and agreed that the payment of such maintenance rent shall not in any way operate to release the Tenant from his obligation to maintain and repair the said demised premises or from any covenant on his part hereinafter contained AND the new yearly rent of One Dollar during the reside of the term payable in advance on or before the first day of August in each and every year.

2. The Tenant for himself, his executors, administrators, and assigns covenants with the Landlord and its successors in title and assigns as follows:

(1) To pay the yearly and other rents hereinbefore reserved at the times and in the manner at and in which the same are hereinbefore reserved and made payable without any deduction

(2) As and when the rent hereinbefore reserved shall become the yearly sum of One Dollar to pay all taxes, rates, duties, and assessments whatsoever whether municipal, parliamentary, governmental, or otherwise now charged or hereafter to be charged upon the said demised premises or upon the Landlord on account thereof

(3) To pay a reasonable proportion of the expense of repairing and maintaining all party walls, fences, or hedges used or to be used in common by the occupier of the said demised premises and the occupiers of any adjoining or neighbouring premises and such proportion in the case of dispute or difference shall be determined by the Landlord's engineer or agent for the time being whose decision shall be final and binding upon all parties

(4) To repair well and substantially and keep in repair the said demised premises and every part thereof together with the fences and all other buildings and erections which at any time during the said term may be upon any part of the said demised premises

(5) In the event of the said demised premises or any part thereof being destroyed or damaged by fire and the insurance money under any policy of insurance effected thereon by the Landlord being by reason of any act of default of the Tenant wholly or partially irrecoverable forthwith in every such case to rebuild and reinstate at his own expense the said demised

premises to the satisfaction of the Landlord's engineer or agent being allowed towards his expenses of so doing upon such rebuilding and reinstatement being completed the amount (if any) actually received in respect of such destruction or damage under any such insurance as aforesaid

(6) To take due and proper care of the demised furniture, chattels, and effects and keep them clean, in good repair, and preserved from injury and from deterioration otherwise than by reasonable use and wear thereof, and damage by accidental fire and so far as possible forthwith to replace with articles of the same sort and equal value such as may be lost, broken, or destroyed or to compensate the Landlord in damages for any omission to replace as aforesaid and to repair and make good such articles as may be damaged (except as aforesaid) and not to permit any article to be removed from the demised premises otherwise than for necessary repairs without the consent of the landlord.

(7) To paint, grain varnish, and colour all the external wood and iron work and parts usually painted, grained varnished, and coloured of the said dwelling-house, and all other buildings and erection which at any time during the said term may be upon the said demised premises once in every fourth year of the said term with two coats of paint mixed in oil and other suitable materials in a workmanlike manner and to paint in like manner and grain varnish and colour all the inside parts of the said demised premises usually painted and grained, varnished, and coloured once in every seventh year of the said term.

(8) At the end or sooner determination of the said term peaceably to surrender up to the landlord the said demised premises well and substantially repaired, painted, and decorated in accordance with the covenant hereinbefore contained.

(9) To permit the landlord or its agent or engineer with or without workmen and others twice or oftener in every year during the said term at reasonable times in the daytime to enter upon the said demised premises and every part thereof to view the state and condition of the same and of all defects, decays, and wants of reparation there found to give notice in writing by

leaving the same at or on the said demised premises to or for the tenant to repair all such defects, decays, and wants of reparation.

(10) Within three months next after every such notice and to make good all such defects, decays, and want of reparations at the cost of the tenant.

(11) Not at any time during the said term without the previous consent in writing of the landlord to erect or put up any building or erection or make any alteration of addition to any erection or building whatsoever in or upon the said demised premises or any part thereof.

(12) Not without the consent in writing of the lessor first obtained to permit the said demised premises or any part thereof to be used for the keeping of horses, cattle, cows, calves, sheep, lambs, pigs, hens, chicken poultry, ducks, geese, turkeys or other livestock, nor to permit any building to be erected for or converted to use as a stable.

(13) Not without the consent in writing of the landlord first obtained to permit the said demised premises or any part thereof to be used for any trade or business whatsoever but to keep and use the same as a private dwelling house PROVIDED THAT a professional man may maintain an office or surgery for his own use in the house where he resides without breach of this covenant AND not to permit anything to be set up or used or done upon any part of the said demised premises which may be noxious, noisy, or offensive or be any disturbance or annoyance to the tenants or occupiers of premises adjoining or near thereto.

(14) That the said demised premises or any part thereof shall not be used for any illegal or immoral purpose and that nothing shall be done upon them which may be to the annoyance of disturbance of the landlord or its tenants or the occupiers of any adjoining or neighbouring premises or whereby any insurance for the time being affected on the said demised premises or any part thereof may be rendered void or voidable or in anywise affected.

(15) Not except by way of mortgage to assign, underlet, or part with the possession of the said demised premises or any part thereof without the consent in writing of the landlord first obtained such consent however not

to be unreasonably withheld in the case of an assignment to a respectable and responsible person.

(16) Within six (6) months from the date hereof to fence off in a proper manner to the satisfaction of the lessor's engineer or agent those parts of the said demised premises extending from the front building line to the rear of the property.

(17) Not to place any trees, hedges, shrubs, fences, erections, or structures of any kind without the approval of the lessor's engineer or agent on that part of the said demised premises which lies between the front building line and the street line (hereinafter described as "the front lawn area").

(18) Not to park any vehicle or place or leave objects, debris or rubbish of any kind on "the said front lawn area" and to keep the said area reasonably cut and tidied during the summer and autumn in accordance with the character of the neighbourhood.

(19) Not to make any flower beds in "the said front lawn area" extending more than three feet in front of the building line and if flower beds be made to keep them reasonably tidy and in character with the neighbourhood.

(20) Not to hang out clothes or wash save in the area to the rear of the dwelling-house.

(21) Not to erect radio poles or masts without the prior approval of the landlord's engineer as to their character and position.

(22) Not to damage or remove or permit to be damaged or removed without the consent of the lessor's engineer or agent any tree now growing upon the said demised premises or any tree, shrub, hedge, grass, or other vegetation provided and placed upon the said premises by the lessor but on the contrary to preserve and encourage the same.

(23) Not to put garbage or ashes in extemporised containers but to use at all times a standard covered can.

3. PROVIDED ALWAYS that if the rents hereby reserved or any part thereof shall be unpaid for twenty-one (21) days after becoming payable (whether formally demanded or not) or if default shall be made in the performance or observance of any of the covenants, conditions, or agreements on the

part of the Tenant herein contained then and in any such case it shall be lawful for the Landlord or any person or persons duly authorized by it in that behalf into and upon the said demised premises or any part thereof in the name of the whole to reenter and the same to have again, repossess, and enjoy as in its first and former estate anything herein contained to the contrary notwithstanding and thereupon the term hereby granted shall cease without prejudice to any right of action or remedy of the Landlord in respect of any antecedent breach of any of the covenants by the Tenant hereinbefore contained

4. The Landlord hereby covenants with the Tenant as follows:
(1) to insure and (unless the insurance so effected shall become void through or by reason of the fault of the Tenant) to keep insured until such time as the rent hereinbefore reserved shall become the yearly sum of One dollar out of the insurance rental payable hereunder by the Tenant the said demised premises from loss or damage by fire to the full value thereof and to cause all monies receive by virtue of any such insurance to be applied as far as the same shall extend in rebuilding and reinstating the said demised premises
(2) That the Tenant paying the rents hereinbefore reserved and performing and observing the covenants, conditions, and agreements on the part of the Tenant hereinbefore contained shall and may peaceably and quietly hold and enjoy the said demised premises for the term hereby granted without any interruptions from or by the Landlord or any person lawfully claiming through under or in trust for him
(5) The Tenant acknowledges that he has fully inspected and examined the said dwelling-house and agrees to accept it 'as is'

IN WITNESS WHEREOF the St. John's Housing Corporation has caused these presents to be executed in accordance with its regulation this 8th day of April A.D. 1947 and the said Bernard Vincent Andrews has hereunto subscribed and set his hand and seal this 5th day of April A.D. 1947.

The seal of the St. John's Housing Corporation was affixed hereto in the presence of

Gordon Winter
Eric Cook

The seal of the St. John's Housing Corporation was duly affixed to this deed and the same was delivered in the presence of R.J. Organ

SIGNED SEALED AND DELIVERED BY THE SAID Bernard Vincent Andrews in the presence of Paul G. Tessier, St. John's, Solicitor.

THE SCHEDULE ABOVE REFERRED TO:
One oil-burning furnace and fittings.

APPENDIX 4

Paul Meschino's House Designs and Inventory of SJHC Houses (showing the number of houses built for each)

House Designs

Plan #	Description
2.1/2	single storey with basement (3)
2.3/4	single storey with basement and garage (4)
3.1/2	1½ storey with 3 bedrooms and basement (3)
3.7/8	1½ storey with garage and basement (6)
3.9/10	1½ storey with 3 bedrooms, basement, and garage (10)
3.11/12	1½ storey with 3 bedrooms and basement (10)
3.13/14	single storey with 3 bedrooms, basement, and garage (13)
3.15/16	2 storey with basement (10)
3.17/18	2 storey with basement (2)
3.19	2 storey with basement (2)
3.21	single storey without basement (0)
3.101/102	1½ storey with 3 bedrooms and basement (10)
3.103/104	2 storey with 3 bedrooms and basement (18)
3.105/106	2 storey with 3 bedrooms and basement (18)
3.107/108	single storey without basement (2)
3.109/110	2 storey with 3 bedrooms and basement (12)
3.111/112	single storey with basement (6)
3.113	single storey with basement (3)

3.115	1½ storey with 3 bedrooms and garage (1)
3.201	single storey masonry with basement (1)
4.1	1½ storey with 4 bedrooms and basement (2)
4.5/6	1½ storey with basement and garage (12)
4.7/8	1½ storey with basement (8)
4.9/10	2 storey with basement (10)
4.101/102	1½ storey with 4 bedrooms and basement (12)
4.103/104	2 storey frame with 4 bedrooms and basement (18)
4.105	single storey frame with basement (5)
4.107/108	2 storey with basement (6)
4.201/202	1½ masonry with basement (4)
11.1	single storey semi-detached with basement (2)
11.3	single storey semi-detached with basement and garage (2)
11.5	2 storey semi-detached with basement (1)
11.101/103	2 storey semi-detached with basement (7)
12.101	4 family row with basement (2)
15.3	Buildings 90-95 Allandale Court Apartments (5)
15.4	Buildings 83-85 Pine Bud Apartments (3)
15.5	Building 110 Linden Court Apartments (1)
15.6	Building 111 Linden Court Apartments (1)

Appendix 4 (cont.)
Inventory of Houses

\multicolumn{6}{c	}{St. John's Housing Corporation Houses}
Civic Address	House Number	Design Type	Civic Address	House Number	Design Type
Allandale Road			Bonaventure Avenue		
29	125	3.103	99	167	3.11
82	51	4.1	101	166	3.106
84	52	36	102	128	4.101
86	53	3.12	103	165	4.103
88	54a	11.1	105	164	3.109
92	55	4.7	106	136a	11.103
Appledore Place			107	161	3.11
1	95	3.15	108	129	4.104
3	69	4.9	109	160	3.101
4	44	4.8	110	130	3.105
5	68	4.6	111	155	3.101
6	30	3.12	112	131	3.106
7	56	3.1	113	154	4.101
8	37	3.11	114	138d	12.101
9	50	4.6	116	138c	12.101
10	45	4.1	118	138b	12.101
11	49	3.13	120	138a	12.101
12	31	3.12	121	181	3.101
13	48	3.11	122	139d	12.101
14	32a	11.1	123	182	4.201
15	47	3.12	124	139c	12.101
16	32b	11.1	125	183	3.101
Beech Place			126	139b	12.101
2	228	4.108	127	184	3.201
6	217	4.108	128	139a	12.101

Bideford Place			129	185	4.101
3	100	3.1	130	134	3.105
5	96	3.13	131	216	4.105
6	36	3.12	132	145	3.105
7	46	4.6	134	151	4.105
8	43	4.8	136	152	3.102
9	97	2.3	138	153	4.105
10	37	3.11	140	150	3.111
11	35	3.1	Carpasian Road		
15	34	3.13	68	1008	4.107
Chestnut Place			70	1007	3.11
1	215	4.201	72	1006	4.104
Cork Place			Maple Street		
2a	58	3.16	1	21	4.7
5	102	2.3	2	12	3.14
6	59	4.1	4	28	3.2
7	41	3.1	5	8	2.2
8	60	3.16	6	27	3.1
9	42	4.6	7	4	3.2
10	61	4.8	8	26	4.1
11	40	3.13	9	3	4.1
Dartmouth Place			10	22	4.8
1	104	3.13	11	2	3.8
3	98	2.3	12	70	3.15
5	62	3.9	14	20	4.1
7	63	4.5	16	11	3.9
9	64	3.13	18	77	3.14
11	65	3.1	20	10	3.9
15	66	4.6	22	76	4.5

Elizabeth Avenue			Milbanke Street		
210	193	3.112	1	124a	11.101
217	194	3.112	2	149	3.102
219	195	4.105	3	124b	11.101
Elm Place			4	148	4.102
5	214	3.105	5	123	3.104
7	213	3.103	6	147	4.101
8	189	3.111	7	122	3.103
9	212	3.104	8	146	3.101
10	192	3.113	9	121a	11.101
11	211	3.106	11	121b	11.101
12	210	4.105	13	120	3.104
Larch Place			Poplar Avenue		
8	1001	4.108	34	78a	11.3
10	1002	3.106	36	78b	11.3
12	1003	3.103	38	88	4.5
14	1004	3.104	41	87	3.17
16	1005	3.105	42	9	2.2
Pine Bud Avenue			43	86	3.18
4	187	3.109	44	79a	11.3
10	186	4.104	45	89a	11.5
37	23	4.9	46	79b	11.3
45	25	4.1	47	89b	11.5
51	105	4.102	48	7	3.1
52	171	3.14	50	6	3.9
53	106a	11.101	53	18	3.7
54	170	3.115	54	24	4.6
55	106b	11.101	55	17	3.8
56	169	4.5	58	82	4.9
57	107	3.103	60	81	3.25

58	168	3.105	Prince William Place		
59	108	3.104	2	144b	11.103
61	109a	11.101	4	144a	11.103
63	109b	11.101	6	143	3.101
64	133	4.103	8	142	4.202
65	112	3.103	Rodney Street		
67	113	3.106	2	203	3.109
69	132	4.103	4	202	4.104
Pine Bud Place			6	201	3.106
1	159	4.101	8	200	3.101
2	156	4.102	10	199	4.202
3	158	3.109	12	198	3.113
4	157	3.11	14	197	3.111
5	177	3.105	16	196	3.113
6	227	4.104	Sycamore Place		
7	178	3.103	2	205	3.109
8	226	4.108	3	188	3.103
9	179	3.104	7	191	3.13
10	225	3.106	8	206	3.106
11	180	3.106	9	190	3.112
12	224	4.104	10	207	3.101
14	223	3.109	11	209	4.105
15	218	3.105	12	208	4.105
16	222	3.14	Whiteway Street		
17	219	4.103	1	163	4.104
19	220	3.103	2	162	4.103
21	221	4.6	4	172	3.106

Stoneyhouse Street			6	173	4.103
1	71	4.7	8	174	3.109
2	13	3.14	10	175	3.11
3	16	3.11	12	176	4.104
4	80	2.4	22	204	4.5
5	72	3.15	Whiteway Place		
6	14	3.12	1	119	3.103
7	73	4.9	2	118	3.103
8	19	4.1	3	135	3.103
9	74	3.15	4	117	4.102
10	5	3.14	5	126	4.101
11	15	3.11	6	116	4.101
12	1	3.7	7	140	3.107
15	75	3.15	8	115	4.103
17	29	4.7	9	141	3.108
Strawberry Marsh Road			10	137b	11.103
105	103	3.19	11	127	4.102
107	39	2.2	12	137a	11.103
109	38	3.8	14	114	4.104
111	101	3.19			
115	33	3.7			

APPENDIX 5

Selected House Plans

ST. JOHN'S HOUSING CORPORATION
ST. JOHN'S, NFLD.

FLOOR PLANS
OF SINGLE STORY SEMI-DETACHED
HOUSE WITH BASEMENT & GARAGE.

PREPARED BY
J. W. BERETTA ENGINEERS, INC.
SAN ANTONIO, TEXAS :-: ST. JOHN'S, NFLD.

DRAWN BY W·W·H	APPROVED BY
TRACED BY	
CHECKED BY	
DATE 29,10,45,	JOB NO.	DRAWING NO 11·3·1
SCALE 1/4"= 1'-0"		

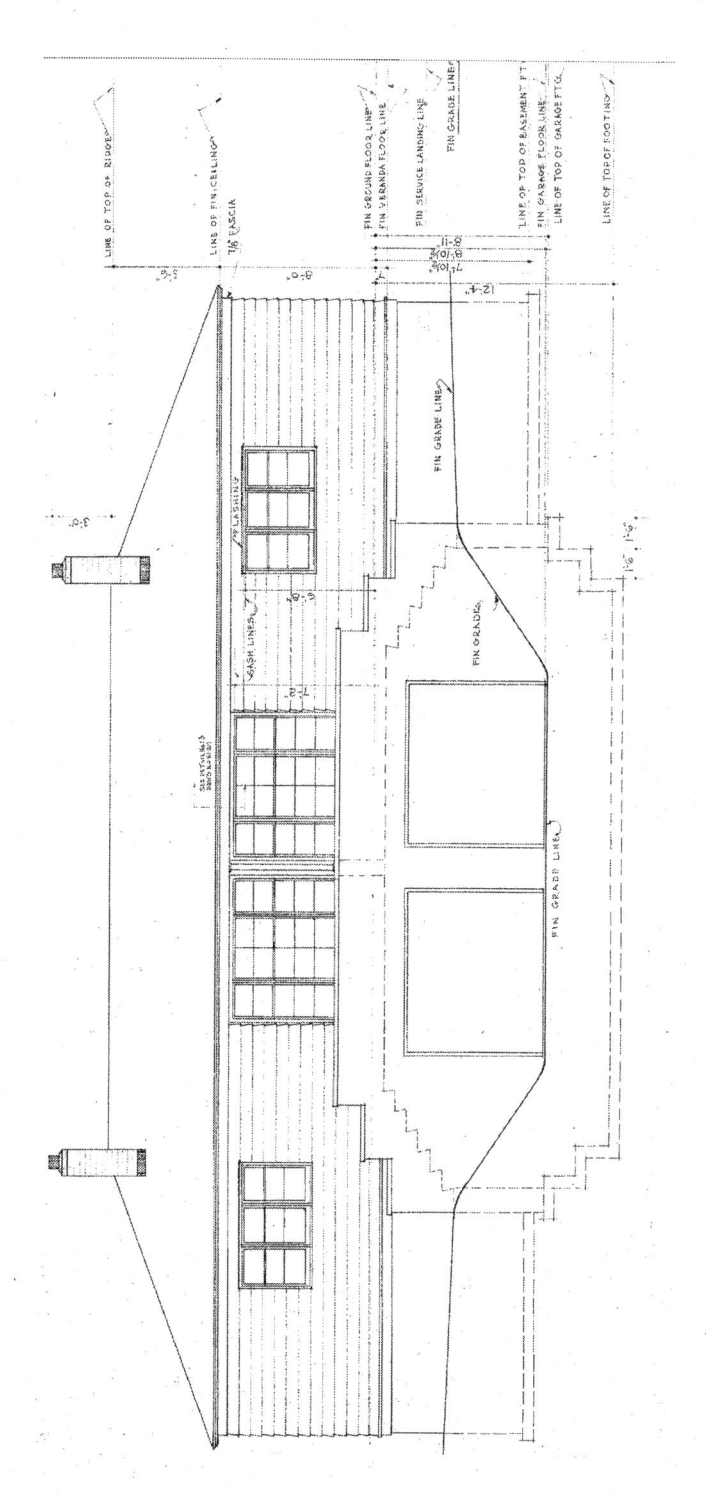

288   CORNER WINDOWS AND CUL-DE-SACS

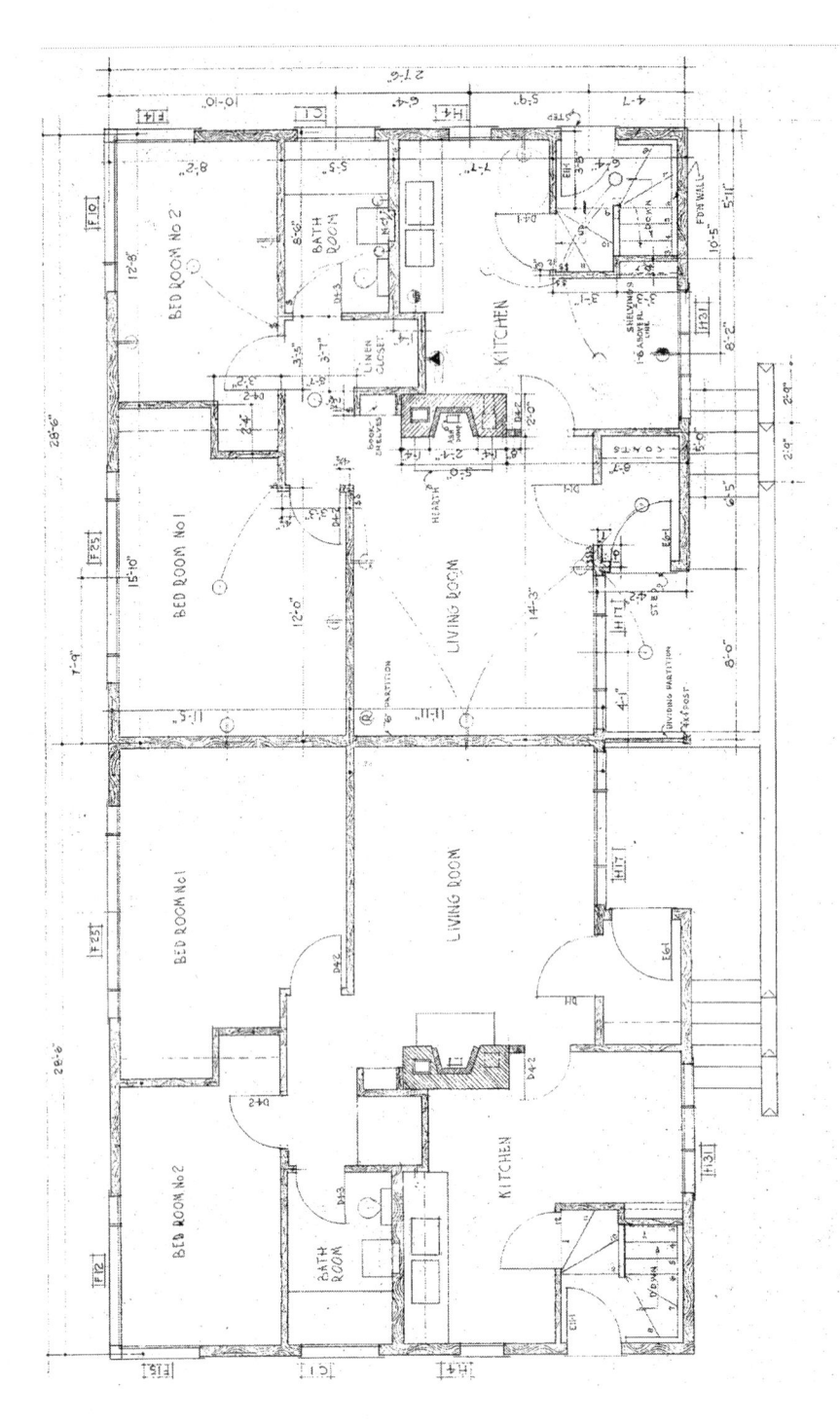

· GROUND FLOOR PLAN ·

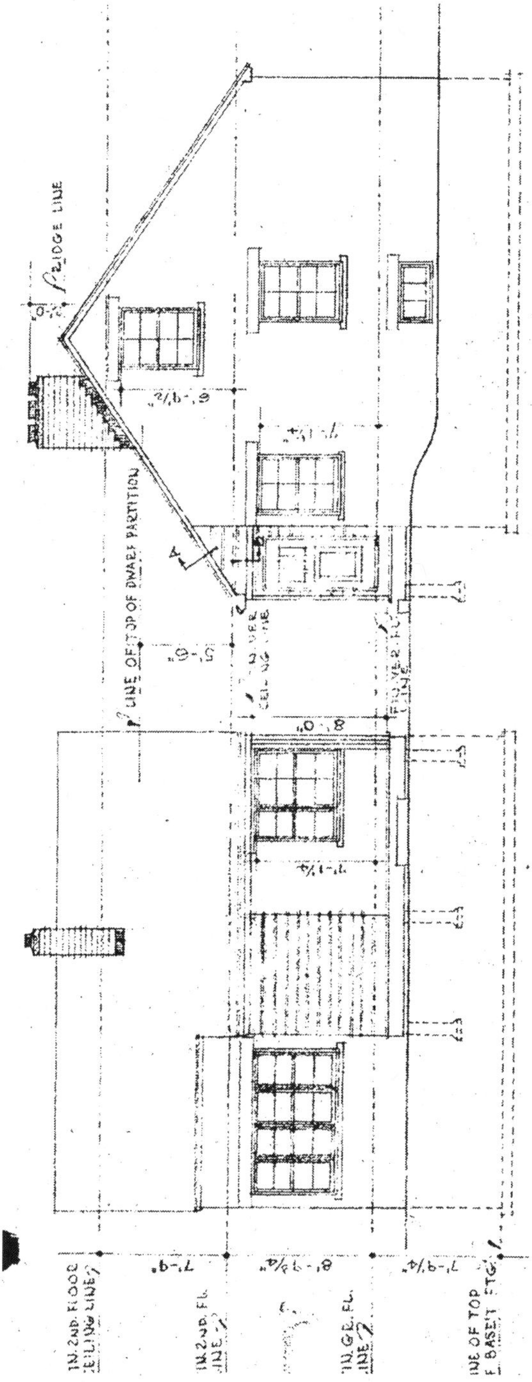

EAST ELEVATION
SOUTH ELEVATION
LINE OF TOP OF DWARF PARTITION

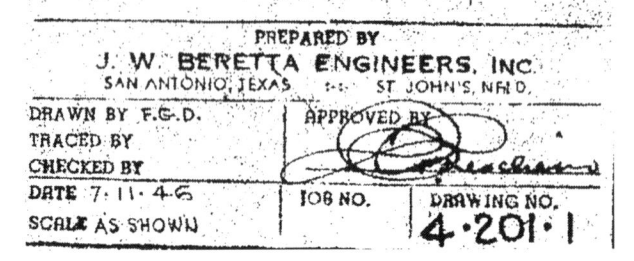

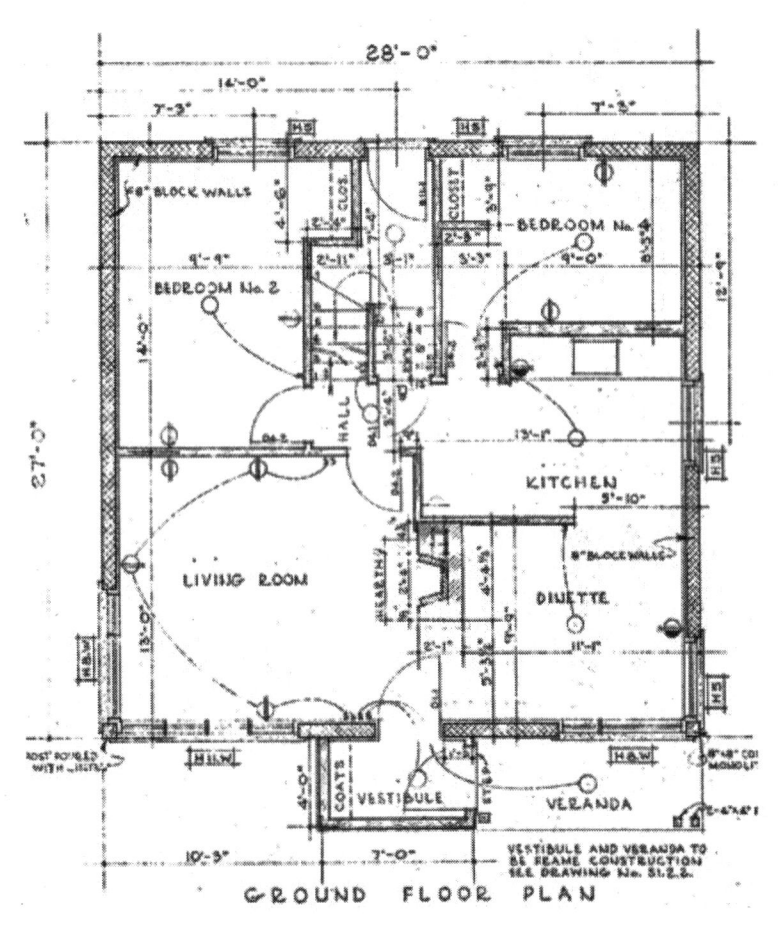

ST. JOHN'S HOUSING CORPORATIO[N]
ST. JOHN'S, NFLD.

FLOOR PLANS & ELEVATIONS
OF
1½ STORY MASONRY HOUSE WITH BASEMENT

PREPARED BY
J. W. BERETTA ENGINEERS, INC.
SAN ANTONIO, TEXAS — ST JOHN'S, NFLD.

DRAWN BY F.G.D.	APPROVED BY	
TRACED BY		
CHECKED BY		
DATE 7·11·46	JOB NO.	DRAWING NO. 4·201·1
SCALE AS SHOWN		

GROUND FLOOR PLAN

VESTIBULE AND VERANDA TO BE FRAME CONSTRUCTION SEE DRAWING No. S1.2.2.

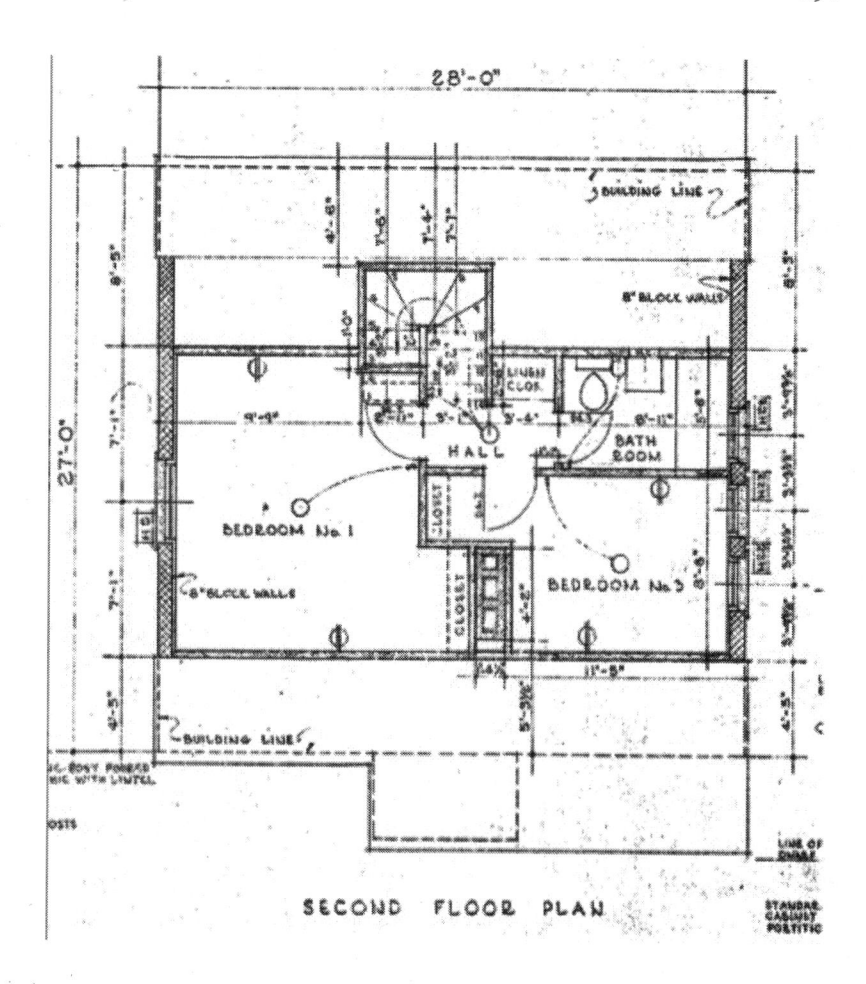

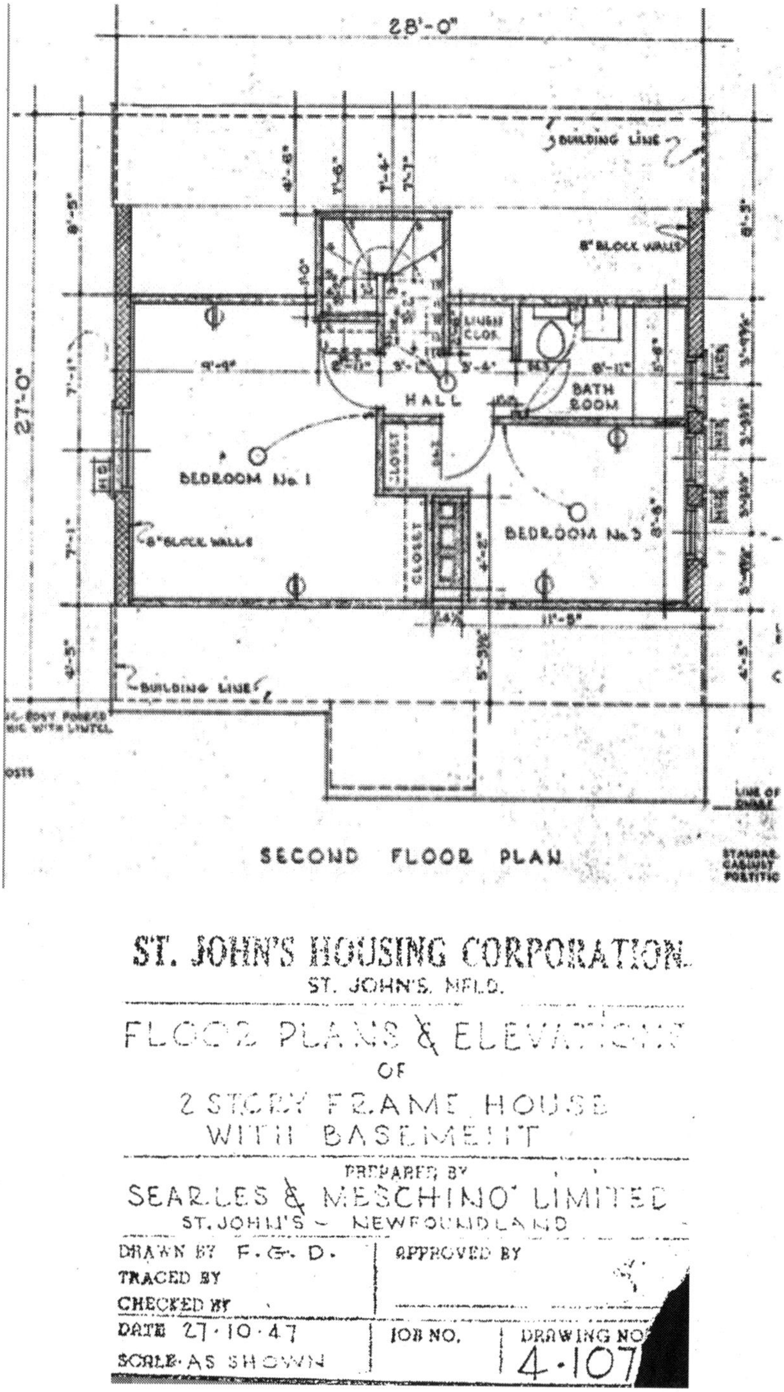

SECOND FLOOR PLAN

ST. JOHN'S HOUSING CORPORATION
ST. JOHN'S, NFLD.

FLOOR PLANS & ELEVATIONS
OF
2 STORY FRAME HOUSE
WITH BASEMENT

PREPARED BY
SEARLES & MESCHINO LIMITED
ST. JOHN'S — NEWFOUNDLAND

DRAWN BY F.G.D.
TRACED BY
CHECKED BY
APPROVED BY
DATE 27·10·47
SCALE AS SHOWN
JOB NO.
DRAWING NO. 4·107

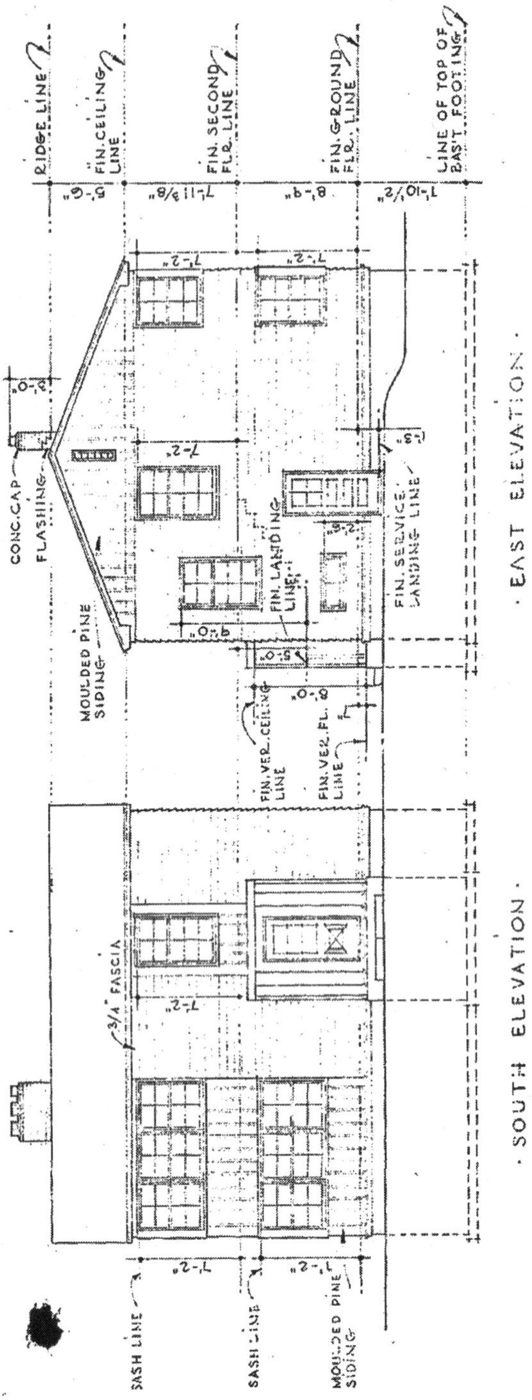
RIDGE LINE
FIN. CEILING LINE
FIN. SECOND FLR. LINE
FIN. GROUND FLR. LINE
LINE OF TOP OF BAST. FOOTING
CONC. CAP
FLASHING
MOULDED PINE SIDING
FIN. LANDING LINE
FIN. SERVICE LANDING LINE
FIN. VER. CEILING LINE
FIN. VER. FL. LINE
3/4" FASCIA
SASH LINE
SASH LINE
MOULDED PINE SIDING
· EAST ELEVATION ·
· SOUTH ELEVATION ·

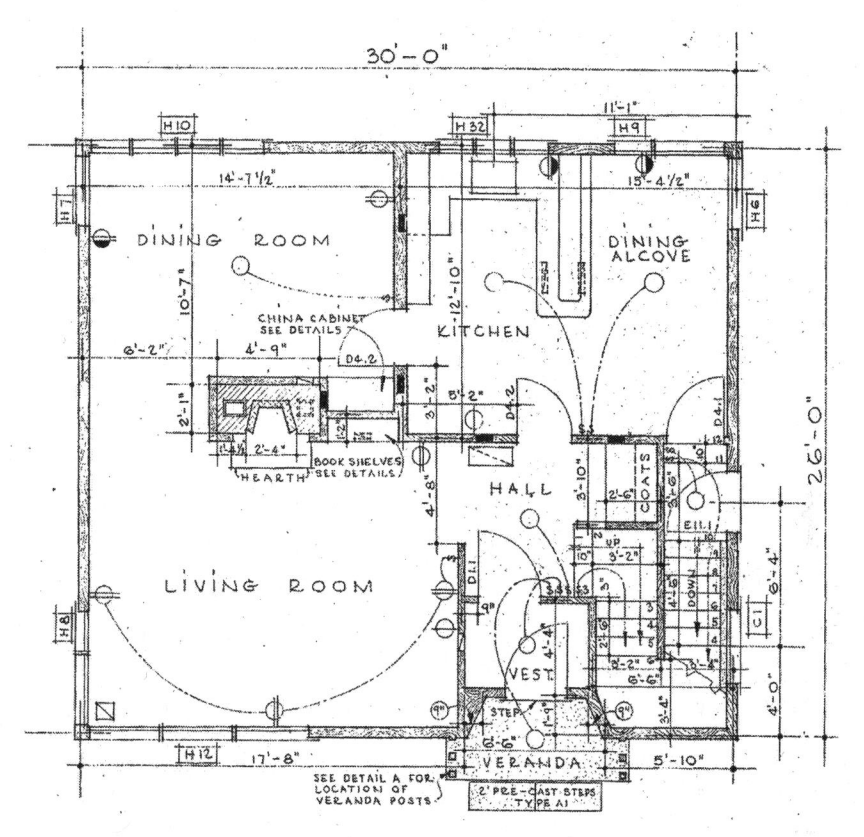

· GROUND FLOOR PLAN ·

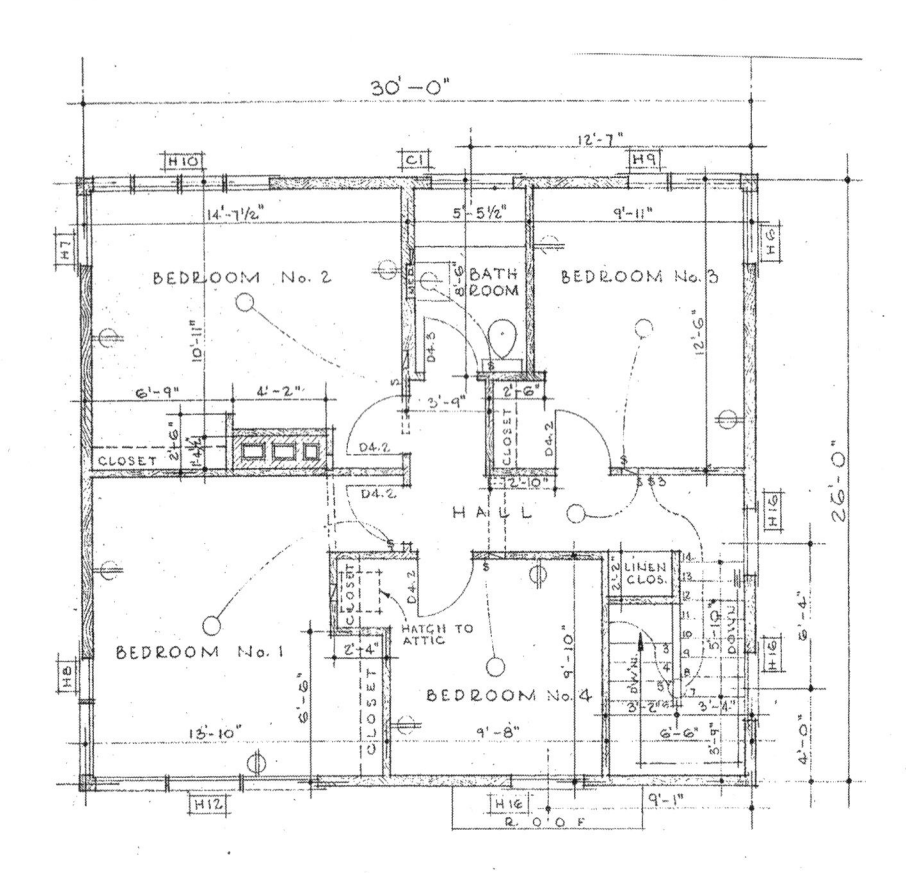

294 CORNER WINDOWS AND CUL-DE-SACS

· SECOND FLOOR PLAN ·

APPENDIX 6

Newspaper Report, Sept 1945

Fifty-One Houses in Course of Construction: Review of Operations of Housing Corporation. Program Includes Apartments

With the summer over and the autumn ahead of us the time seems to have come for a short report to the public on the progress of our affairs, says the St. John's Housing Corporation.

1. GENERAL PROGRESS

We feel that our general progress is a little behind schedule in spite of a hard struggle on our part, but this cannot be helped. There is much difficulty in these days in getting either materials or machinery. We are not like builders of war construction, with unlimited funds and government priorities; we have to scramble for our materials and our machinery like any other builder. However, matters are gradually getting ironed out. Our organization is building up and the operation is beginning to gather speed.

2. BUILDING PROGRESS

At the moment we have 51 houses in various stages, from a roof and clapboarded shell to a hole in the ground. Our programme is still to have from 100 to 125 houses closed in by the time the snow comes. Some should be ready at that time, provided we can overcome certain supply difficulties; others can be finished internally in the cold weather. This will have the additional advantage that we shall be able to give employment to the best of our men for most or all the winter, thus holding our organization together. A loyal, industrious and well-selected working force is the first essential to cheap housing.

3. OUR NEW INDUSTRY

The factory on Freshwater Road is now approximately completed and is actually turning out good concrete sewer pipe and good concrete blocks. We still have to add to our block machinery, as we hope to use this material extensively next year. A concrete block foundation is about $300 cheaper than a poured foundation, and if properly waterproofed will be equally satisfactory except in wet ground where poured foundation will have to be used. On foundations only we hope to pay for our factory in the course of time. Concrete pipe is just as good as vitrified or pottery pipe if properly made, and if it were only at the same price we should make it as everything in it is local except the cement and it gives local labour; but over and above that it should be considerably cheaper than vitrified pipe. We hope also to do some building in concrete block next year. Our principal difficulty in this connection is the scarcity of bricklayers and masons and we expect to have to train men in this work if we are to do any considerable amount of it next year. We see a very considerable future for concrete block building in this city. If blocks can be produced cheaply enough, whether by ourselves or by commercial producers, it means that the city will gradually get away from the heavy expense of painting and external repairs which is the principal burden on the owners of wooden houses. We expect also to make ready-mixed concrete for pouring when required. We shall need a good deal of sewer pipe before our programme is completed, and any extra will be available for general public purposes.

4. THE SEWER TUNNEL

This is proceeding steadily also, with parties of miners under Mr. Bernard Brennan drilling and blasting from both ends. At the south end we have recently struck a vein of quartzite rock and this is slowing us up a bit. However, we hope that within a few weeks the two working parties will join hands. After that the lower part of the tunnel has to be lined with cement and it will then be ready for its duty of conducting to the sea sewerage from three square miles of the northern suburbs, both in our area and out of it. We are beginning to make some 24-inch and some 30-inch concrete pipe for the large mains and have just been able to buy from the Canadian authorities a "back hoe" (power shovel working in reverse) which will be used to dig the large trenches. These machines are very hard to get at present and we have been fortunate in getting this one. As soon as it has been overhauled we hope to start putting the sewer connections under King's Bridge and Rennie's Bridge.

As a Canadian paper said recently, to carry a tunnel through two thousand feet of rocky hill in order to sewer three square miles of country is quite a spectacular operation for a small city. Unfortunately, however, it is underground so it does not make much show.

5. MACHINERY

We are gradually obtaining sufficient machinery to carry out the necessary road and sewer work in the development of the area during the next few years.

6. LAND

Our engineers, Messrs. J.S. Beretta Engineers, Inc., and their architect Mr. Paul Meschino, B.A.Sc., Member Royal Architectural Institute of Canada, have done a very nice job in laying out our central village; and this has the entire approval of Prof. Bland, who has spent the past two months here to advise the Town Planning Commission and whose report will soon be published. We are not sure whether the impression prevails in some quarters that we are keeping all land for our own building. This is not so, and we shall be more than glad to see private builders take sites from us in our village or, indeed, anywhere in our area where the water and sewerage are soon to come. We hope to have water and sewerage connection throughout the central village this autumn. Unfortunately we are not yet in a position to say precisely what sites will cost. When we get the whole of the awards from the arbitrators for land we shall be able to figure out the average cost to us per acre and per site. As regards water, sewerage, sidewalks, road and other amenities we can estimate on the cost of these, but cannot tell exactly how they will work out until the work is per site for these facilities. In the meantime, however, we are putting, for safety, a provisional outside price on lots (which will be complete with all facilities) to enable us to set a lower price. We shall make a return in cash to any purchaser on this provision arrangement, so as to bring his land down to the same price we have to charge purchasers generally. We have already sold three lots on this provisional arrangement. Anyone interested should enquire at our office.

7. TYPE OF HOUSE

Houses will be of all types. It happens that a batch of houses with sloping roofs have been built first and that these include a number of small two-bedroom types. There will, however, be houses with a squared-up second storey and houses with three and four bedrooms so as to suit all tastes and needs. All houses are being provided with heavy rock-wool insulation and double sashes. As we see it, no one can afford in these days to be without insulation and double sashes. With these installations the cost of keeping the house warm in winter should be brought down from a half to two thirds below the cost of heating an uninsulated house with single sashes and at present prices of fuel there should be enough saving in heating to pay for the insulation and double sashes in five to seven years and leave the tenant with the annual saving for the rest of the life of the house. If the additional cost is spread by instalments over 15 to 25 years the tenant will begin to realize the saving at once, as the difference in the monthly instalment will be trivial.

8. SPECIAL WINDOWS

Some interest seems to have been aroused by the special side ventilation which we are trying out in a few of our houses. The double sashes are fixed (although the inner one can be taken down for cleaning) and thus there is no draught whatever around the window. The ventilation consists of a louvre at the side or at both sides. As seen by the public so far these sashes have been installed with only a single glass and with the louvres wide open and we are not surprised that some people have thought that they would be rather breezy. We have in mind the carpenter whom we asked what he thought of them. He, having seen them only with the open louvre, replied politely that he thought they would be lovely in the summer! However, as installed there will be behind the louvre a wire fly screen; behind the fly screen a special four-piece shutter, tight against draughts and adjustable in several different positions, so that the occupied can have everything from a little to a lot of ventilation at will. A ventilation shutter will be concealed behind the curtains. This design is becoming popular in Canada and the United States, and has been proven satisfactory there. It does not cost more than an ordinary window, and in large sizes less. We are putting in a limited number only, to see how the public like them.

9. "THE MAGIC HOUSE"

We have under discussion a scheme for helping the poorer man which we hope we may be able to try out next year. We are building some houses of the smallest possible size and cost, but there is a "minimum" figure below which a soundly built house with basement and bathroom cannot be built with paid labour and present cost of materials, and those who cannot pay that price will have to continue to do with second-hand houses unless someone pays a part of the cost for them. We are discussing therefore the Swedish "Magic House" idea which was mentioned in the third Report of the Commission of Enquiry on Housing and Town Planning. Under this scheme the Corporation would advance material stage by stage and provide plans and technical advice so that a man could build a house for himself with the assistance of his family and friends, and pay off his debt over a number of years at a low interest. In view of the general handiness of our people we feel that this scheme has a future. Some further announcement will be made about it later.

10. APARTMENT BUILDINGS

We feel that we must have some rental accommodation, especially in view of the fact that we have now so many married ex-soldiers looking for a place to live. We had hoped at one time to build some three-storey blocks of small economical apartments in concrete block, but cannot do it this year as we have not yet enough block or enough masons. With a view to saving time we are discussing therefore the idea of putting up a number of small blocks in wooden construction, each containing four to six small, three-bedroom or two-bedroom flats, and as this type of construction is entirely in line with our house building we shall be able to get ahead with it faster. We have every hope of having one hundred apartments closed in before the winter. They will then become available from time to time during the winter as we can get them varnished inside and equipped. They will be as economical as is compatible with sound construction and will be centrally heated, and we believe they will be found attractive.

11. TOWN LAYOUT

Our village B will have as its centre a small town square about 500 x 300 feet with a street round it and a public garden in the middle. This square, which will be the civic focus of the community, will in the course of time, we hope, be enclosed with buildings of the commercial and apartment type, including a range of shops either built by the owners or built by ourselves and rented. We have not come to grips with this problem yet. A site on this square will also be reserved in the hope that at some future day the moving picture interests may feel like establishing a cinema there.

12. GENERAL SURROUNDINGS

The village will contain considerable park areas for the general benefit of the inhabitants, which will be landscaped and planted with trees in due course. We hope to make it a very attractive place to live. Our tenants, and private purchasers of sites, will also have the advantage that the value of their property will be protected, because not only will we in conjunction with the City, pass zoning regulations, but we will also protect the situation ourselves by refusing to make available sites for any purpose which would tend to depreciate the neighbourhood and diminish the value of property. In other words, shops, laundries, garages and other non-residential establishments will be kept strictly to the areas appointed for them and away from the residences.

13. POLICY RE HOUSES

We are not going to put a price or a completion date on any of our buildings until we have reached the point where we can be sure of the final cost of the buildings and the cost of land and where intending tenants can see exactly what they are going to get for their money. We proposed above all things to avoid the situation where a house which is supposed to be of a certain price turns out to cost more. When we are ready to offer inspection and take applications, notice will be given to the newspapers and everyone will have the same chance of applying.

14. GENERAL

We are working hard on this project. The Board meets every Friday night for two or three hours, and committees on works and supplies meeting on intervening days. We are endeavouring with the aid of our expert assistants to apply all the best and latest ideas and build up an efficient organization with a view to giving the public the best possible value for their money on the best possible terms, and will leave no stone unturned to this end.

Source: *Evening Telegram* 7 Sept. 1945, 7.

APPENDIX 7

Text of Full-page Newspaper Advertisement

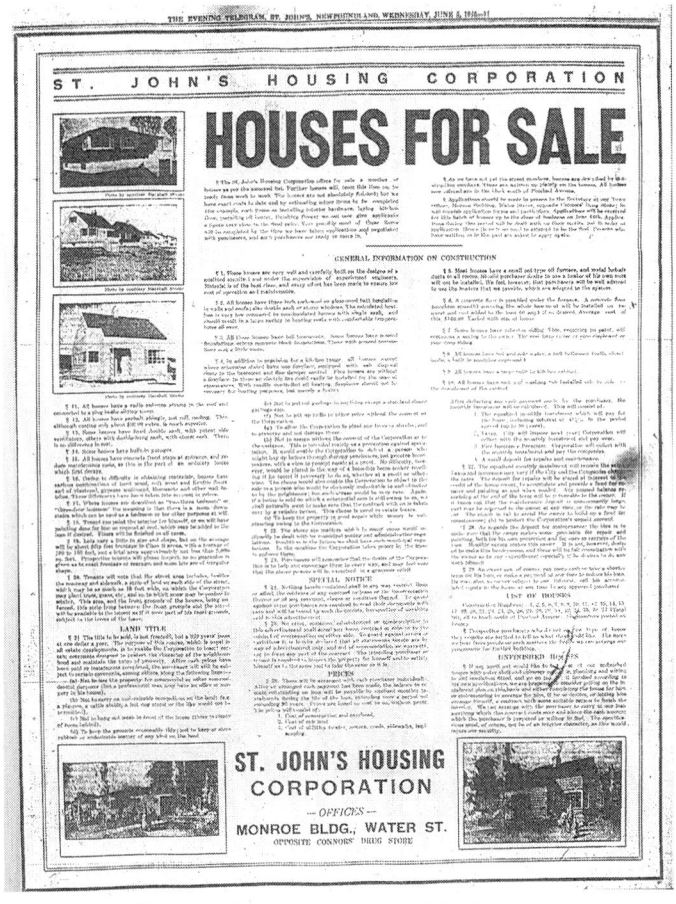

"Houses for Sale" (*Evening Telegram*, 5 June 1946).

ST. JOHN'S HOUSING CORPORATION

HOUSES FOR SALE

The St. John's Housing Corporation offers for sale a number of houses as per the annexed list. Further houses will, from this time on, be ready from week to week. The houses are not absolutely finished; but we have exact costs to date and by estimating minor items to be complete (for example, such items as installing interior hardware, laying kitchen floor, installing oil heater, finishing floors) we can now give applicants a figure very close to the final price. Very possibly most of these items will be completed by the time we have taken applications and negotiated with purchasers, and such purchasers are ready to move in.

As we have not yet the street numbers, houses are described by a construction number. These are written up plainly on the houses. All houses now offered are in the block south of Pinebud Avenue.

Applications should be made in person to the Secretary at our Town Office, Monroe Building, Water Street, opposite Connors' Drug Store; he will furnish applications forms and particulars. Applications will be received for this batch of houses up to the close of business on June 14th. Applications during this period will be dealt with on their merits, and in order of application. Hence there is no need to attempt to be the first. Persons who have written in the past are asked to apply again.

GENERAL INFORMATION ON CONSTRUCTION

1. These houses are very well and carefully built on the designs of a qualified architect and under the supervision of experienced engineers. Material is of the best class, and every effort has been made to ensure low cost of operation and maintenance.

2. All houses have three-inch rock-wool or glass-wool batt insulation in walls and roofs; also double sash or storm windows. The calculated heat-loss is very low compared to non-insulated houses with single sash, and

should result in a large saving in heating costs with comfortable temperatures all over.

3. All these houses have full basements. Some houses have poured foundations, others concrete block foundation. Those with poured foundations cost a little more.

4. In addition to provision for a kitchen range all houses, except where otherwise stated have one fireplace, equipped with ash disposal chute to the basement and flue damper control. Five houses are without a fireplace. In these an electric fire could easily be installed for the sake of appearances. With readily controlled oil heating, fireplaces should not be necessary for heating purposes, but merely a luxury.

5. Most houses have a small pot-type oil furnace, and metal hot-air ducts to all rooms. Should purchaser desire to use a heater of his own ours will not be installed. We feel, however, that purchasers will be well advised to use the heaters that we provide, which are adapted to the system.

6. A concrete floor is provided under the furnace. A concrete floor (machine smooth) covering the whole basement will be installed on request and cost added to the loan (if any) if so desired. Average cost of this, $140. Varied with size of house.

7. Some houses have asbestos siding. This requiring no paint, will represent a saving to the owner. The rest have cedar or pine clapboard or pine drop-siding.

8. All houses have hot and cold water, a full bathroom (bath, closet, basin, a built-in medicine cupboard).

9. All houses have a large built-in kitchen cabinet.

10. All houses have sink and washing tub installed side by side in the drainboard of the cabinet.

11. All houses have a radio antenna strung in the roof and connected to a plug in the sitting room.

12. All houses have asphalt shingle, not roll, roofing. This, although costing only about $30 extra, is much superior.

13. Some houses have fixed double sash, with patent side ventilators, others with double-hung sash, with storm sash. There is no difference in cost.

14. Some houses have built-in garages.

15. All houses have concrete front steps at entrance, and reduce maintenance costs, as this is the part of an ordinary house which first decays.

16. Owing to difficulty in obtaining materials, houses have various combinations of hardwood, softwood and Kentile floors, and of plastered, gypsum wallboard, Homasote and other wall finishes. These differences have been taken into account in price.

17. Where houses are described as "two-three bedrooms" of "three-four Bedrooms" the meaning is that there is a room downstairs which can be used as a bedroom or for other purposes at will.

18. Tenant can paint the interior for himself, or well have painting done for him on request at cost, which may be added to the loan if desired. Floors will be finished in all cases.

19. Lots vary a little in size and shape, but on the average will be about fifty foot frontage in Class B area, with a rearage of 100 to 150 feet, and a total area approximately not less than 5,000 sq. feet. Prospective tenants will please inspect, as no guarantee is given as to exact frontage or rearage, and some lots are of irregular shape.

20. Tenants will note that the street area includes, besides the roadway and sidewalk, a strip of land on each side of the street, which may be as much as 15 feet wide on which the Corporation may plant trees, grass, etc., and on to which snow may be pushed in winter. This area, and the front grounds of the houses, being unfenced, this strip lying between the front grounds and the street will be available to the tenant as if it were part of his front grounds, subject to the terms of the lease.

LAND TITLE

21. The title to be sold is not freehold, but a 999 year's lease at one dollar a year. The purpose of this course, which is usual in all estate developments, is to enable the Corporation to insert certain covenants designed to protect the character of the neighbourhood and maintain the value of property. After cash prices have been paid or instalments completed, the purchaser will still be subject to certain covenants, among others, along the following lines:

(a) not to use the property for commercial or other non-residential purposes (but a professional man may have an office or surgery in his house);

(b) not to carry on undesirable occupations on the land: (e.g. a pig-pen, a cattle stable, a hot dog stand or the like would not be permitted);

(c) not to hang out wash in front of the house (there is plenty of room behind);

(d) to keep the grounds reasonably tidy; not to keep or store rubbish or undesirable matter of any kind on the land;

(e) not to put out garbage in anything except a standard closed garbage can;

(f) not to put up radio or other poles without the consent of the Corporation;

(g) to allow the Corporation to plant any trees or shrubs; and to preserve and not damage these;

(h) not to assign without the consent of the Corporation as to the assignee. This is intended mainly as a precaution against speculation. It would enable the Corporation to defeat a person who might buy up houses through dummy purchasers, not genuine homemakers, with a view to prompt resale at a profit. No difficulty, however, would be placed in the way of a bona-fide home-maker reselling if he found it necessary to do so, whether at a profit or otherwise. The clause would also enable the Corporation to object to the sale to a person who would be obviously undesirable to and objected to by the neighbours; but such a case would be very rare. Again, if a house is sold on which a substantial sum is still owing to us, we shall naturally want to make sure that the contract with us is taken over by a reliable person. This clause is usual in estate leases.

22. The above are matters which in many cases would ordinarily be dealt with by municipal zoning and administrative regulations. Doubtless in the future we shall have such municipal regulations. In the meantime the Corporation takes power by the lease to enforce them.

23. Purchasers will remember that the desire of the Corporation is to help and encourage them in every way, and may feel sure that the above powers will be exercised in a generous fashion.

SPECIAL NOTICE

24. Nothing herein contained shall in any way restrict, limit or affect the contents of any contract of lease or the interpretation thereof or of any covenant, clause or condition thereof. To guard against error purchasers are required to read their documents with care and will be bound by such documents, irrespective of anything said in this advertisement.

25. No error, omissions, misstatement or indescription in this advertisement shall annul any lease, contract of sale or be the subject of compensation on either side. To guard against error or variations it is hereby declared that all statements herein are by way of advertisement only, and not of representation or warranty, not to form any part of the contract. The intending purchaser or tenant is required to inspect the property for himself and to satisfy himself as to the same and to take the same as it is.

PRICES

26. These will be arranged with each purchaser individually. After an arranged cash payment has been made, the balance to remain outstanding on loan will be payable by equalized monthly instalments during the life of the loan, extending over a period not exceeding 30 years. Prices are based on cost to us, without profit. The prices will consist of:

    1. Cost of construction and overhead,

    2. Cost of raw land,

    3. Cost of utilities (water, sewers, roads, sidewalks, landscaping)

After deducting any cash payment made by the purchaser, the monthly instalment will be calculated. This will consist of:

    1. The equalized monthly instalment which will pay for the house, including interest at 4½ percent in the period agreed (up to 30 years)

    2. Taxes. City will impose next year; Corporation will collect with the monthly instalment and pay over.

3. Fire Insurance Premium. Corporation will collect with the monthly instalment and pay the companies.

4. A small deposit for repairs and maintenance.

27. The equalized monthly instalment will remain the same. Taxes and Insurance may vary if the City and the Companies change the rates. The deposit for repairs will be placed at interest to the credit of the house-owner to accumulate and provide a fund for repairs and painting as and when needed. Any unused balance remaining at the end of the term will be returnable to the owner. If it turns out that the maintenance deposit is unnecessarily large, part may be returned to the owner at any time, or the rate may be cut. The object is (a) to assist the owner to build up a fund for maintenance; (b) to protect the Corporation's unpaid account.

28. As regards the deposit for maintenance: the idea is to make sure that the owner makes some provision for repair and painting, both for his own protection and for ours as carriers of the loan. Monthly saving makes this easier. It is not, however, designed to make this burdensome, and there will be full consultation with the owner as to any expenditure; especially if he desires to do any work himself.

29. An owner can, of course, pay more cash or take a shorter term for his loan, or make a payment at any time to reduce his loan. He may also, as owner subject to our interest, sell his accumulated equity in the house at any time to any approved purchaser.

LIST OF HOUSES

Construction Numbers: 1, 2, 5, 6, 7, 8, 9, 10, 11, 12, 13, 14, 15, 17, 19, 20, 21, 23, 24, 25, 26, 27, 28, 29, 71, 72, 74, 75, 76, 77 (total 30) all in the block south of Pinebud Avenue. All numbers posted on houses.

Prospective purchasers who do not see the type of house they require are invited to tell us what they would like. The more we hear from people on such matters the better we can arrange our programme for further building.

UNFINISHED HOUSES

If any applicant would like to take over one of our unfinished houses with outer shell and chimney, cupboards, plumbing and wiring in and insulation fitted, and go on to have it finished according to his own specification, we are prepared to consider selling on the instalment plan on this basis and either complete the house for him or endeavouring to arrange for him, if he so desires, or letting him arrange himself, a contract with some suitable person to finish the interior. We can arrange with the purchaser to carry in our loan everything which this contract costs over and above the cash amount which the purchaser is prepared or willing to find. The specifications must, of course, not be of an inferior character, as this would injure our security.

Source: *Evening Telegram* 5 June 1946.

APPENDIX 8

SJHC Classified Advertisements, 1946

St. John's Housing Corporation

Class A Building Sites

The St. John's Housing Corporation, proceeding on the principle that every house built, of whatever class, is a house added to the City's stock, and that the new suburb is for the benefit of all classes, is setting aside a Class A Zone or area.

This area is to be strictly reserved for residential purposes, and land will be let only for residences of good class, to be built and financed by their owners. We indicate tentatively as the minimum for this area a house of good design measuring about 15,000 cubic feet (excluding basement) or about 20% larger than the largest houses we are now building. Sites will be laid out to suit applicants, and for houses of this class sites larger than our standard 50-foot lot are desirable.

Sewers, water and streets will be put in and tree-planting done in due course.

This area, strictly controlled and tastefully developed will, it is hoped, become in course of time the most attractive modern residential locality near the City. Persons contemplating the erection of high class accommodation are recommended to apply to our offices.

Source: *Daily News* 11 Feb. 1946.

St. John's Housing Corporation

Land for Private Builders

During the present season of 1946 we expect to be in a position to have sites freely available for private builders, in the East, Central and West Villages.

Up to the present, owing to shortage of equipment, we have had all that we could do to put in utilities for our own buildings, but this year we aim at developing with sewers, water and streets, more land than we need for our own use.

The cost of a site of about 5,570 square feet complete with utilities is expected to work out at about $950, viz., raw land $250; complete utilities about $12.50 per front foot, including road, sewers, water, probably sidewalk, landscaping. This area being zoned, controlled and protected against all misuse, as well as scientifically planned, house values there in the future should be steadier than in other areas. Zoning and control prevents depreciation of values by the entry of undesirable uses and buildings. Under the Canadian and American Housing Acts the inspector enquires whether the area is properly zoned before they will approve a building loan.

We sell only to people bona fide intending to build, including professional builders. The procedure is that we give on a small deposit an option for two years. If purchaser does not build within that period, the land reverts to us. If he does build, he then completes the payment and sets his titles. Instalment terms will be accepted on land.

For further information, apply to R.J. Organ, Secretary, Monroe Building, Water Street (opposite Connor's Drug Store).

Source: *Evening Telegram* 22 June 1946.

APPENDIX 9

Location of the SJHC Houses

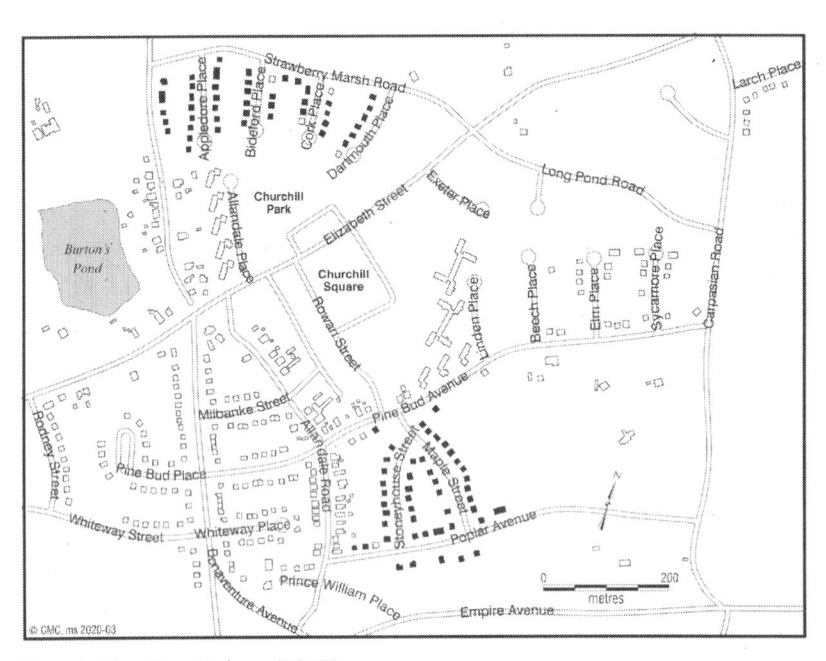

Map 1: The First Cohort (1945)

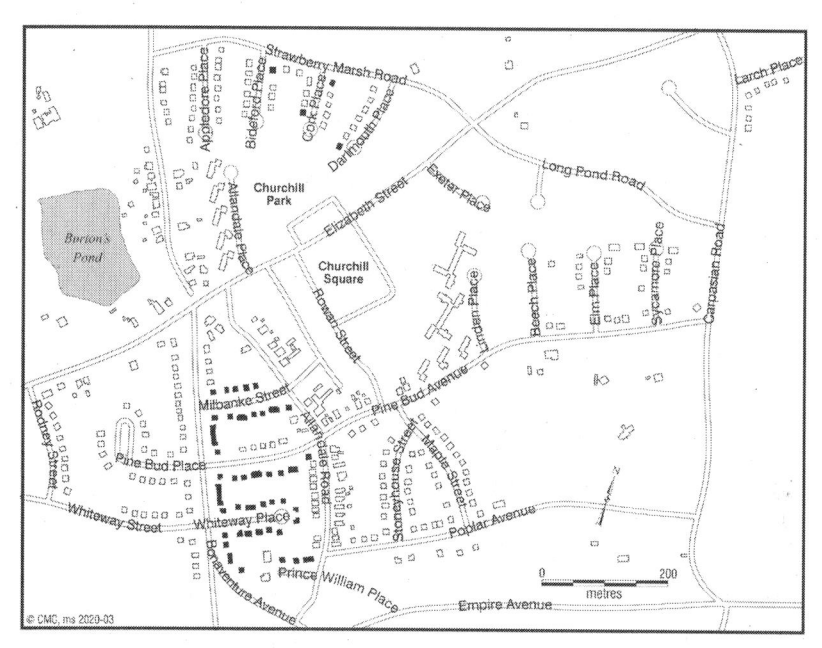

Map 2: The Second Cohort (1946)

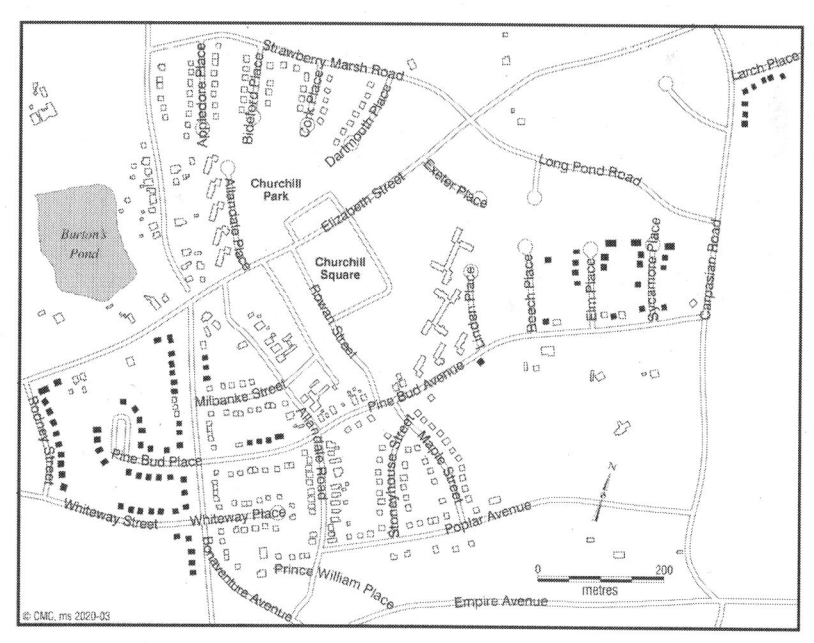

Map 3: The Third Cohort (1947)

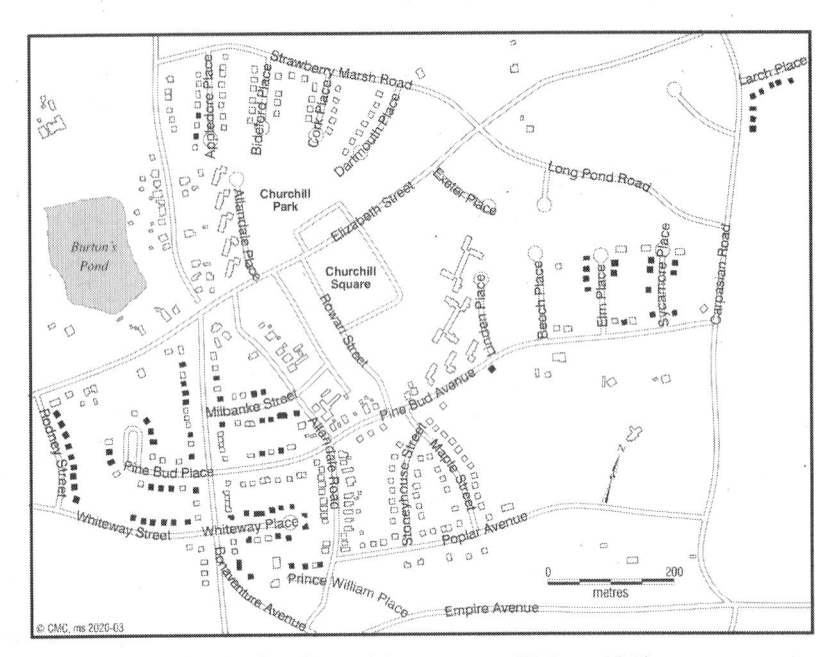

Map 4: The Unfinished and Unsold Houses on 25 June 1949

APPENDIX 10

Invitation to the Dinner in Honour of the Retirement of Brian Dunfield as Chairman of the St. John's Housing Corporation, 31 March 1949

Invitation to Dunfield retirement (reverse). Artwork by Paul Meschino.

Invitation to Dunfield retirement (front). Artwork by Paul Meschino.

APPENDIX 11

Press Release on Churchill Square Apartments, March 1956

In response to a request from the SJHC for approval of the construction of a new apartment building to be erected in Churchill Park, I am glad to say that the Government have given their approval for the project and have authorized and instructed the SJHC to award the necessary contracts immediately so that construction can proceed without delay.

This new and very large apartment building, which will be the largest in Newfoundland, containing sixty apartment units, will be a three-story structure, with 15,000 square feet of commercial space on the ground floor. It is to be located on the east side of CS and will serve to enhance the Churchill Park area and complete the development programme originally contemplated. The centre square itself is to remain as an open space and it is the Government's wish and desire that it shall be developed into a proper park square as soon as the large park area now being developed on the north side of Elizabeth Avenue is completed.

The addition of sixty modern apartment units in this area will serve to ease, somewhat, the great shortage of rental housing accommodation which exists in St. John's today. At the same time, the provision of 15,000 square feet of commercial space on the street level of the new building will make available the necessary ancillary services required for a rapidly developing residential area, and will also tend to keep apartment rentals at a lower level than would otherwise be possible. This commercial area will provide office space for doctors, dentists, lawyers and professional men of all types, as well as certain commercial operations. Already enquiries have been received from parties interested in locating in the new building.

It is estimated that the total project will cost in the vicinity of one million dollars and it is hoped to have it completed and ready for occupancy by late fall or early winter of this year.

The Government are glad to provide the funds for this really worthwhile project and to give it every support and encouragement. We consider it to be a step forward in the development of St. John's and have instructed those responsible to expedite the program with all possible dispatch.

APPENDIX 12

Selected Statistics for Churchill Park, the City of St. John's, and the St. John's CMA, 2016

Churchill Park was different from the rest of the city when it was built in the late 1940s, and it remains so today. Census Tract 13, bounded by the Parkway, Bonaventure Avenue, Rennie's River, and Kelly's Brook, contains 198 of the 242 houses and all 92 of the apartment units built by the Housing Corporation. The data from the 2016 Census of Canada for this tract were used to illustrate the basic characteristics of the heart of Churchill Park. In this table some of Churchill Park's basic characteristics are compared with those of the city of St. John's and the St. John's Census Metropolitan Area. The statistics reveal that Churchill Park differs dramatically from the other two areas on all basic measures of socio-economic status. Because of the developmental history of the area, the houses are older, most likely to be owner-occupied, single-detached dwellings, and far more expensive than those elsewhere. Census families with children are more common, and there are fewer lone-parent families. Unsurprisingly, both average and median household incomes are dramatically higher in Churchill Park, with low percentages of transfer payments, and individuals with university educations, especially post-graduate degrees, are far more common than elsewhere.

	Churchill Park	City of St. John's	St. John's CMA
Population	1,742	108,680	205,955
% change 2011–16	–2.8	2.5	4.6
% pop. 0–14	11.5	13.9	15.8
% pop. 15–64	65.2	69.6	69.4
% pop. 65+	23.3	16.5	14.8
% pop. 85+	3.2	1.9	1.5
Average age	45.5	41.2	40.3
Median age	48.4	40.5	40.3
Dwelling Units			
Number	765	47,625	85,015
% single-detached	62.1	42.7	54.6
% semi-detached	3.3	6.2	4.7
% row	1.3	10.7	7.2
% apt. <5 storeys	19.6	13.0	7.9
% apt. >5 storeys	13.1	25.8	24.6
% apt. or flat in duplex	0	1.1	0.1
Mean value owner-occupied houses	583,681	349,753	348,519
Median value owner-occupied houses	449,520	309,631	319,478
Dwellings built before 1960	70.9	23.1	16.0
Dwellings built 1961–80	15.5	31.2	27.9
Dwellings built 1981–2000	5.2	23.3	27.5
Dwellings built 2001–16	8.4	22.3	28.7
% owners	72.3	61.3	70.0
% renters	27.7	38.6	30.0
Census Families			
Number	500	29,955	59,860

% couple families	88.0	80.3	83.0
% with children	40.0	37.6	42.3
Lone-parent	12.0	19.7	17.0
Income			
Median household income	98,816	69,455	79,750
Mean household income	204,038	97,257	102,635
% market income	94.4	89.2	89.8
% transfer payments	5.6	10.8	10.2
Education (ages 25–64)			
% with bachelor's degree	29.6	21.4	18.8
% with master's degree	26.5	9.4	7.2
% with earned doctorate	8.2	1.8	1.2

BIBLIOGRAPHY

Abercrombie, P. 1910. "Modern Town Planning in England: A Comparative Review of 'Garden City' Schemes in England." *Town Planning Review* 1: 18–34.

Adams, T. 1916. "Housing Conditions in Canada." *Conservation of Life* 2: 10.

———. 1917. "The Use of Land for Building Purposes." *Conservation of Life* 3: 29–32.

———. 1918a. "Government Housing during the War." *Conservation of Life* 4: 25–33.

———. 1918b. "The Housing Problem and Production." *Conservation of Life* 4: 49–57.

Alexander, David. 1976. "Newfoundland's Traditional Economy and Development to 1934." *Acadiensis* 5, no. 2: 65–78.

Algie, Susan, and James Ashby, eds. 2005. *Conserving the Modern in Canada: Buildings, Ensembles and Sites 1945–2005*. Winnipeg: Winnipeg Architectural Foundation.

Altshuler, A. 1969. "The Potential of Trickle-down." *The Public Interest* 15: 46–56.

Amulree, Lord (William W. Mackenzie). 1933. *The Newfoundland Royal Commission*.

Asselin, V. 1998. "Frederick G. Todd et ses contemporaines." *Histories of Landscape Architecture in Canada*. www.apa.umontreal.ca/gadrat/formcont/seminaire98/conference/Asselin/Asselin.html.

Attfield, J. 1999. "Bringing Modernity Home: Open Plan in the British Domestic Interior." In *At Home: An Anthropology of Domestic Space*, edited by E. Cieraad. Syracuse, NY: Syracuse University Press.

Attfield, J. 1989. "Inside Pram Town: A Case Study of Harlow House Interiors, 1951–1961." In *A View from the Interior: Feminism, Women and Design*, edited by J. Attfield and P. Kirkham. London: Womens' Press.

Bacher, J. 1993. *Keeping to the Marketplace: The Evolution of Canadian Housing Policy.* Montreal and Kingston: McGill-Queen's University Press.

Baker, Melvin. 1976. "The Politics of Municipal Reform in St. John's, Newfoundland, 1888–1892." *Urban History Review* 2: 12–29.

———. 1981. "William Gilbert Gosling and the Establishment of Commission Government in St. John's, Newfoundland, 1914." *Urban History Review* 9, no. 3: 35–51.

———. 1982a. "William Gosling and the Establishment of the Child Welfare Association." *Newfoundland Quarterly* 77, no. 2 (Winter): 31–32.

———. 1982b. "Municipal Politics and Public Housing in St. John's, 1911–1921." *Workingmen's St. John's: Aspects of Social History in the Early 1900s*, edited by Harry Cuff, Melvin Baker, and Bill Gillespie, 29–43. St. John's: Harry Cuff Publications.

———. 1982c. "The Politics of Assessment: The Water Question in St. John's, 1844–1864." *Acadiensis* 12, no. 1: 59–72.

———. 1982d. "The Politics of Poverty: Providing Public Poor Relief in Nineteenth Century St. John's, Newfoundland." *Newfoundland Quarterly* 78, nos. 1 and 2 (Spring and Summer): 20–23.

———. 1983a. "In Search of the 'New Jerusalem': Slum Clearance in St. John's, 1921–1944." *Newfoundland Quarterly* 79, no. 2 (Fall): 23–32, 35.

———. 1983b. "The Great St. John's Fire of 1846." *Newfoundland Quarterly* 79, no. 1 (Summer): 31–34.

———. 1983c. "Disease and Public Health Measures in St. John's, 1832–1855." *Newfoundland Quarterly* 78 (Spring): 26–29.

———. 1984a. "The Appointment of a Permanent Medical Health Officer for St. John's, 1905." *Newfoundland Quarterly* 79, no. 3 (Winter): 23–25.

———. 1984b. "The St. John's Fire of July 8, 1892: The Politics of Rebuilding, 1892–1893." *Newfoundland Quarterly* 79, no. 3 (Winter): 25–30.

———. 1984c. "St. John's Municipal Politics, 1902–1914." *Newfoundland Quarterly* 80, no. 2 (Fall): 23–30.

———. 1984d. "Charles Joseph Howlett." *Encyclopedia of Newfoundland and Labrador*: 1092.

———. 1985a. "Prominent Figures from Our Recent Past: John Anderson." *Newfoundland Quarterly* 81, no. 2 (Fall): 42.

———. 1985b. "The Influence of Absentee Landlordism on the Development of Municipal Government in 19th Century St. John's." *Newfoundland Quarterly* 81, no. 2 (Fall): 19–26.

———. 1985c. "William Gosling and the Charter: St. John's Municipal Politics, 1914–1921." *Newfoundland Quarterly* 81, no. 1 (Summer): 21–28.

———. 1985d. "Andrew Green Carnell." *Newfoundland Quarterly* 80, no. 3 (Winter): 17.

———. 1986a. "Municipal Democracy on Trial in St. John's, 1888–1898." *Newfoundland Quarterly* 82, no. 2 (Fall): 21–28.

———. 1986b. "Absentee Landlordism and Municipal Government in Nineteenth Century St. John's." *Urban History Review* 15, no. 2: 165–71.

———. 1987. "Prominent Figures from Our Recent Past: William James Ellis." *Newfoundland Quarterly* 83, no. 1 (Summer): 35.

———. 1994. "The Interplay of Private and Public Enterprise in the Production of Electricity on the Island of Newfoundland, 1883–1966." In *Twentieth-Century Newfoundland: Explorations*, edited by J.K. Hiller and P. Neary, 273–96. St. John's: Breakwater Books.

———, J.M. Pitt, and R.W. Pitt. 1990. *The Illustrated History of Newfoundland Light and Power*. St. John's: Creative Publishers.

——— and Janice Pitt. 1984. "A History of Health Services in Newfoundland and Labrador to 1982." *Encyclopedia of Newfoundland*: 864–75.

Barter, Jonas C. 1930. "Valuation of land and buildings and rebuilding of territory as laid down by Mr. Todd and shown on plans as submitted by him and generally known as Todd's slum area and submitted to City Council 1930." GN2/5, Box 92, File 550.

Bartlett, R.W., Q.C. 1999. Interview by C.A. Sharpe, 24 June.

Bauman, John F. 2000. "The Eternal War on Slums." In *From Tenements to the Taylor Homes: In Search of an Urban Housing Policy in 20th Century America*, edited by John F. Bauman, Roger Biles, and Kristin Szylvian, 1–18. University Park, PA: Pennsylvania State University Press.

Birchall, J. 1995. "Co-Partnership Housing and the Garden City Movement." *Planning Perspectives* 10: 329–58.

Bishop Stirling, Terry. 2020. "To Keep the Well Babies Well: The Child Welfare Association, 1921–1934." *Newfoundland Quarterly* 112, no. 4: 42–50.

Blake, William. 1810. "Preface" to *Milton: A Poem in Two Books*. London: William Blake.

Bland, John. 1946a. *Report on the City of St. John's Newfoundland Made for the Commission on Town Planning*. St. John's: City of St. John's.

———. 1946b. "St. John's, Newfoundland." *Journal of the Royal Architectural Institute of Canada* 23, no. 11 (Nov.): 302–05.

———. 1998. Letter to C.A. Sharpe, 5 Mar.

Bloomfield, G. 1985. "Ubiquitous Town Planning Missionary. The Careers of Horace Seymour 1882–1940." *Environments* 17: 29–42.

Blue, M.T. 1950. Letter to James J. Spratt, Minister of Provincial Affairs, 17 Aug.

Bonnycastle, Sir Richard. 1842. *Richard Bonnycastle in Newfoundland, Vol. 2*. London.

Bridle, Paul. 1948. Memorandum from Paul Bridle, Secretary in the Office of the High Commissioner for Canada, to W.J. Carew, Secretary for Home Affairs, 22 Nov., PRC 14, Box 15-5-3-3, File K, Vol. V.

Brown, Christopher. 1998. "Halliday Place: The Exploration of a Derelict Landscape." BA (Honours) diss., Memorial University of Newfoundland.

Calahan, R. 1914. Letter from city clerk awarding Calahan the tender to install sewerage in five houses, with costs between $51.75 and $81.50. City of St. John's Archives, RG 01-01, Box 191, Miscellaneous 1913–14.

Campbell, Angus. 1999. Interview by C.A. Sharpe, 12 Aug.

Canadian-British Consultants Limited. 1978. *The Battery Neighbourhood Improvement Program Conceptual Plan*. St. John's: Canadian-British Consultants Ltd.

Canadian-British Engineering Consultants. 1966. *City of St. John's, Newfoundland, Mundy Pond Urban Renewal Scheme*. Halifax: Canadian-British Engineering Consultants.

Cannadine, David. 1980. "Urban Development in England and America in the 19th Century: Some Comparisons and Contrasts." *Economic History Review* 33: 309–25.

Cardoulis, J.N. 1990. *A Friendly Invasion: The American Military in Newfoundland 1940–1990*. St. John's: Breakwater Books.

Carew, William J. 1948. Letter from the Secretary of the Commission of Government to Paul Bridle, 26 Nov., PRC 14, Box 15-5-3-3, File K, Vol. V.

Carnell, A. 1942. Letter to W.W. Winter, 11 Apr. Attached to HAE 16-'42. GN 38 S3-1-1, file 3.

Cherry, G.E. 1988. *Cities and Plans: The Shaping of Urban Britain in the Nineteenth and Twentieth Centuries.* London: Edward Arnold.

Choko, M.H. 1989. "De la cité idèal à la maison de banlieue familiale: l'experience de Cité-jardin tricentenaire, Montréal." *Plan Canada* 29: 38–50.

Clemens, Ralph. 1999. Interview by A.J. Shawyer and C.A. Sharpe, 20 Apr.

Clutterbuck, Sir Peter Alexander, G.C.M.G., M.C. 1938. Handwritten memo regarding Brian Dunfield, K.C. DO35/729/N31/25, 8 Dec. Quoted in Neary (1988, 80).

———. 1945. Letter to Governor Walwyn, 8 Feb., GN 1/3/A 1943, Box 253.

Coady, M.M. 1939. *Masters of Their Own Destiny: The Story of the Antigonish Movement of Adult Education through Economic Cooperation.* New York: Harper and Brothers.

CEHTP 1. 1942. Commission of Enquiry on Housing and Town Planning in St. John's. *First Interim Report: City Architect, Building Regulations, etc.* (Nov.).

CEHTP 2. 1943. Commission of Enquiry on Housing and Town Planning in St. John's. *Second Interim Report: King's Bridge Road Junction.* (Feb.)

CEHTP 3. 1943. Commission of Enquiry on Housing and Town Planning in St. John's. *Third Interim Report: General Review of Housing Conditions and Outline of Proposals for Remedies.* (3 June).

CEHTP 4. 1943. Commission of Enquiry on Housing and Town Planning in St. John's. *Fourth Interim Report: Temporary Regulations to Secure Width of Future Streets, etc.* (Oct.).

CEHTP 5. 1944. Commission of Enquiry on Housing and Town Planning in St. John's. *Fifth Interim Report: Detailed Proposals and Provisional Estimates for Suburban Extensions and Housing.* (Jan.)

CEHTP 6. 1944. Commission of Enquiry on Housing and Town Planning in St. John's. *Sixth Interim Report.* (28 July). PRC14, Box 15-5-3-3, Vol. 1, File: Reports).

Commission of Government. 1944a. Minutes 62-'44, 21 Jan., GN 38, S1-1-3.

———. 1944b. Minutes 264-'44, 31 Mar., approval of HAE 21-'44.

———. 1948. Notes of a meeting between the C of G and the St. John's Municipal Council, 2 Mar., GN 2/5, Box 92, File 550.5.

Community Resources Services. 1977. *Battery Neighbourhood Improvement Program, St. John's, Newfoundland.* St. John's: Community Resource Services.

Connor, Michan. 2015. Review of Stern et al., *Paradise Planned: The Garden Suburb and the Modern City. Journal of Planning Education and Research* 35: 519–21.

Cook, E. 1982. Interview by Mark Shrimpton, 3 Sept.

Cox, Gary. 2008. "Compulsory Acquisition in UK Public Housing Estate Renewal: Legal, Planning and Project Delivery Perspectives." In *Compulsory Property Acquisition for Urban Densification*, edited by Glen Searle. London: Routledge.

Cranborne, Rt. Hon. Viscount. 1944a. Despatch 23 to Governor Walwyn, in response to Telegram #306 of 13 Dec. 1943, 7 Feb., GN 1/3/A, File 288.

———. 1944b. Despatch 282 to Governor Walwyn, 15 May, GN 1/3/A, File 288.

———. 1944c. Despatch 328 to Governor Walwyn, 1 June, GN 1/3/A, File 288.

———. 1944d. Despatch 263 to Governor Walwyn, 20 June, GN 1/3/A, File 288.

———. 1944e. Despatch 372 to Governor Walwyn, 29 June, GN 1/3/A, File 288.

———. 1945a. Telegram 130 to Governor Walwyn, 20 Mar., GN 38 S5-2-1, Box 1, File 9.

———. 1945b. Telegram 82 to Governor Walwyn, 26 Mar., PRC 14 15-5-3-3 File 5.

Crosbie, B. 1986. "Between a Rock and a Hard Place: Newfoundland from 1920–1933, a Survey." In *Newfoundland History 1986: Proceedings of the First Newfoundland Historical Society Conference*, compiled by S. Ryan. St. John's: Newfoundland Historical Society.

Crosbie, John C. 1956. "Local Government in Newfoundland." *Canadian Journal of Economics and Political Science* 22, no. 3: 332–46.

CSJA (City of St John's Archives). 1900. Map H080.

———. 1918. Map H 132.

———. 1920. RG 01-13, Box 2, Miscellaneous Engineering Report Book, West St. John's (1920).

———. 1942. RG 08-10, Commission of Enquiry on Housing and Town Planning in St. John's. Questionnaire, July.

———. RG 01-12, Assessment Division Property Files Series.

———. RG 01-13, Box 2, Miscellaneous Series: Engineering Book West St. John's.

———. RG 01-16, Central Area Redevelopment Arbitration Series.

———. RG 08-06, Housing Survey Series 1950–55.

———. RG 09-04. Miscellaneous Real Estate 1953–82.

Cuff, Robert H., Melvin P. Baker, and Robert D.W. Pitt. 1990. *Dictionary of Newfoundland and Labrador Biography*. St. John's: Harry Cuff Publications.

Cullingworth, J.B. 1976. *Town and Country Planning in Britain*. London: George Allen and Unwin.

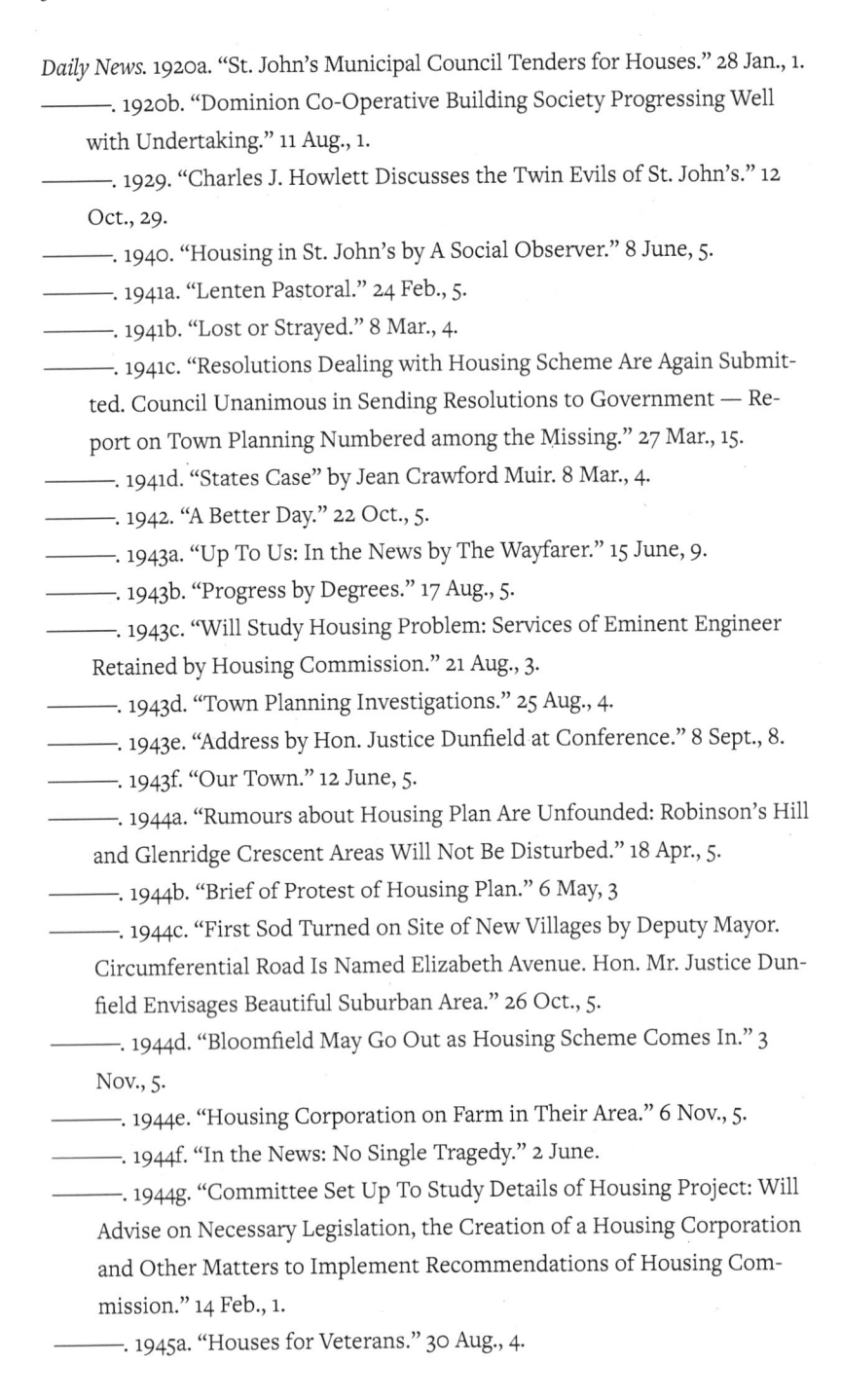

Daily News. 1920a. "St. John's Municipal Council Tenders for Houses." 28 Jan., 1.

———. 1920b. "Dominion Co-Operative Building Society Progressing Well with Undertaking." 11 Aug., 1.

———. 1929. "Charles J. Howlett Discusses the Twin Evils of St. John's." 12 Oct., 29.

———. 1940. "Housing in St. John's by A Social Observer." 8 June, 5.

———. 1941a. "Lenten Pastoral." 24 Feb., 5.

———. 1941b. "Lost or Strayed." 8 Mar., 4.

———. 1941c. "Resolutions Dealing with Housing Scheme Are Again Submitted. Council Unanimous in Sending Resolutions to Government — Report on Town Planning Numbered among the Missing." 27 Mar., 15.

———. 1941d. "States Case" by Jean Crawford Muir. 8 Mar., 4.

———. 1942. "A Better Day." 22 Oct., 5.

———. 1943a. "Up To Us: In the News by The Wayfarer." 15 June, 9.

———. 1943b. "Progress by Degrees." 17 Aug., 5.

———. 1943c. "Will Study Housing Problem: Services of Eminent Engineer Retained by Housing Commission." 21 Aug., 3.

———. 1943d. "Town Planning Investigations." 25 Aug., 4.

———. 1943e. "Address by Hon. Justice Dunfield at Conference." 8 Sept., 8.

———. 1943f. "Our Town." 12 June, 5.

———. 1944a. "Rumours about Housing Plan Are Unfounded: Robinson's Hill and Glenridge Crescent Areas Will Not Be Disturbed." 18 Apr., 5.

———. 1944b. "Brief of Protest of Housing Plan." 6 May, 3

———. 1944c. "First Sod Turned on Site of New Villages by Deputy Mayor. Circumferential Road Is Named Elizabeth Avenue. Hon. Mr. Justice Dunfield Envisages Beautiful Suburban Area." 26 Oct., 5.

———. 1944d. "Bloomfield May Go Out as Housing Scheme Comes In." 3 Nov., 5.

———. 1944e. "Housing Corporation on Farm in Their Area." 6 Nov., 5.

———. 1944f. "In the News: No Single Tragedy." 2 June.

———. 1944g. "Committee Set Up To Study Details of Housing Project: Will Advise on Necessary Legislation, the Creation of a Housing Corporation and Other Matters to Implement Recommendations of Housing Commission." 14 Feb., 1.

———. 1945a. "Houses for Veterans." 30 Aug., 4.

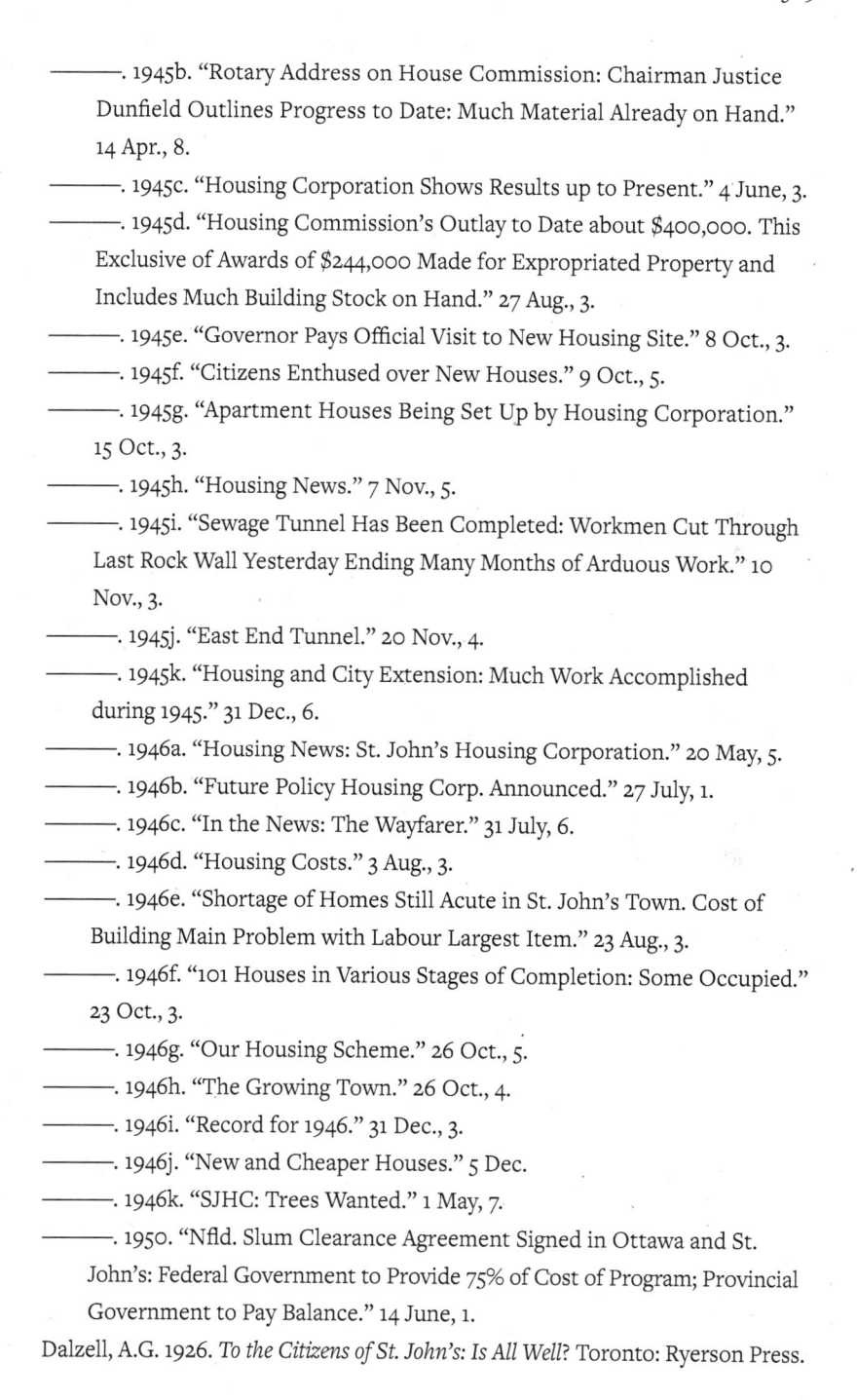

———. 1945b. "Rotary Address on House Commission: Chairman Justice Dunfield Outlines Progress to Date: Much Material Already on Hand." 14 Apr., 8.

———. 1945c. "Housing Corporation Shows Results up to Present." 4 June, 3.

———. 1945d. "Housing Commission's Outlay to Date about $400,000. This Exclusive of Awards of $244,000 Made for Expropriated Property and Includes Much Building Stock on Hand." 27 Aug., 3.

———. 1945e. "Governor Pays Official Visit to New Housing Site." 8 Oct., 3.

———. 1945f. "Citizens Enthused over New Houses." 9 Oct., 5.

———. 1945g. "Apartment Houses Being Set Up by Housing Corporation." 15 Oct., 3.

———. 1945h. "Housing News." 7 Nov., 5.

———. 1945i. "Sewage Tunnel Has Been Completed: Workmen Cut Through Last Rock Wall Yesterday Ending Many Months of Arduous Work." 10 Nov., 3.

———. 1945j. "East End Tunnel." 20 Nov., 4.

———. 1945k. "Housing and City Extension: Much Work Accomplished during 1945." 31 Dec., 6.

———. 1946a. "Housing News: St. John's Housing Corporation." 20 May, 5.

———. 1946b. "Future Policy Housing Corp. Announced." 27 July, 1.

———. 1946c. "In the News: The Wayfarer." 31 July, 6.

———. 1946d. "Housing Costs." 3 Aug., 3.

———. 1946e. "Shortage of Homes Still Acute in St. John's Town. Cost of Building Main Problem with Labour Largest Item." 23 Aug., 3.

———. 1946f. "101 Houses in Various Stages of Completion: Some Occupied." 23 Oct., 3.

———. 1946g. "Our Housing Scheme." 26 Oct., 5.

———. 1946h. "The Growing Town." 26 Oct., 4.

———. 1946i. "Record for 1946." 31 Dec., 3.

———. 1946j. "New and Cheaper Houses." 5 Dec.

———. 1946k. "SJHC: Trees Wanted." 1 May, 7.

———. 1950. "Nfld. Slum Clearance Agreement Signed in Ottawa and St. John's: Federal Government to Provide 75% of Cost of Program; Provincial Government to Pay Balance." 14 June, 1.

Dalzell, A.G. 1926. *To the Citizens of St. John's: Is All Well?* Toronto: Ryerson Press.

Delaney, J. 1991. "The Garden Suburb of Lindenlea, Ottawa: A Model Project for the First Federal Housing Policy, 1918–1924." *Urban History Review* 19: 151–65.

Denhez, M. 1994. *The Canadian Home from Cave to Electronic Cocoon*. Toronto: Dundurn Press.

Dennis, M., and S. Fish. 1972. *Programs in Search of a Policy: Low Income Housing in Canada*. Toronto: Hakkert.

Dennis, R. 1998. "Apartment Housing in Canadian Cities, 1900–1940." *Urban History Review* 26: 17–31.

Dictionary of Canadian Biography (DCB).
    Harvey, Sir John. Vol. 8 (1851–1860).
    LeMarchant, Sir John Gaspard. Vol. 8 (1871–1880).
    MacBraire, James. Vol. 6 (1821–1835).
    Sifton, Clifford. Vol. 15 (1921–1930).

Dictionary of Newfoundland Bibliography.
    William John Higgins: 155.

Dixon, Tim. 2009. "Urban Land and Property Ownership Patterns in the UK: Trends and Forces for Change." *Land Use Policy* 26, Supplement 1: S43–S53.

Dockerill, Bertie. 2016. "Liverpool Corporation and the Origins of Municipal Social Housing, 1842–1890." *Transactions of the Historic Society of Lancashire and Cheshire* 165: 39–56.

Dominion Bureau of Statistics. 1949. *11th Census of Newfoundland 1945*. 5 May.

Drexler, Arthur, and Thomas S. Hines. 1982. *The Architecture of Richard Neutra: From International Style to California Modern*. New York: Museum of Modern Art.

Duley, Margot I. 2014. "Armine Nutting Gosling: A Full and Useful Life." In *Creating This Place: Women, Family and Class in St. John's 1900–1950*, edited by Linda Cullum and Marilyn Porter, 113–45. Montreal and Kingston: McGill-Queen's University Press.

Dunfield, B.E.S. 1943a. "Discussion Regarding Slum Clearance," undated typescript, GN 38 S5-2-1, Box 1.

———. 1943b. Letter to W.J. Carew, 5 June, GN 13/1/B, Box 111, File 68, HAE 31-'43.

———. 1943c. Memorandum to Commissioner of Finance (Ira Wild), 6 Oct., PRC 14, Box 15-5-3-3, File: SJHC 1942–45.

———. 1944a. Confidential notes on Hon. H. Macpherson's letters to Mr. C.W. St. J. Chadwick and others re land expropriation, dated September 11th, 1944 (undated), GN 38, S5-2-1, File 2.

———. 1944b. Memorandum of information available to me at the moment re. the value of land, 10 Apr., attached to HAE 2.(c)-'44, GN 1/3/a.

———. 1944c. Memo on land values in the northern suburb. Application of the 10% rule, 10 Apr., GN 38 S5-2-1, Box 1, File 9.

———. 1944d. Notes for the Government on the Municipal Council's letter of 12 May 1944, 12 May, PRC 14 15-5-3-3 and GN 38 S5-2-1, Box 1, File 9.

———. 1944e. Notes on memorandum addressed by Mr. R.S. Furlong to the Government and the Council re the Draft Housing Bills, n.d., GN 38 S5-2-1, Box 1, File 9.

———. 1944f. Memorandum suggesting effort to improve the condition of 'shack' dwelling-houses before the coming winter (1944–45), 28 Nov., GN 38 S5-2-1, Box 1, File 8.

———. 1945a. Memorandum to Sir John Puddester, Commissioner for Public Health and Welfare, 10 Feb., PRC 14 Box 15-5-3-3, File: Flats-SJHC.

———. 1945b. Memorandum to Sir Albert Joseph Walsh, Commissioner for Home Affairs and Education, 21 Apr., PRC 14 15-5-3-3, File: Homes for Poor and Indigent People.

———. 1945c. Memorandum to Ira Wild, 27 Nov., GN 38 S5-1-4, File 1.

———. 1946a. "Foreword" to John Bland, *Report on the City of St. John's Newfoundland made for the Commission on Town Planning.*

———. 1946b. Letter to A.J. Walsh, Commission for Home Affairs and Education, 5 Oct., PRC 14, Box 15-5-3-3, File: SJHC General.

———. 1946c. Letter to Ira Wild, Commissioner for Finance, 23 Sept., PRC 14, Box 15-5-3-3, File: SJHC General.

———. 1947a. Letter to Governor Macdonald, 28 Nov., PRC 14, Box 15-5-3-3, File: SJHC General.

———. 1947b. Letter to H.W. Quinton, Commissioner for Home Affairs and Education, 15 Jan., PRC 14, Box 15-5-3-3, File K.

———. 1947c. Letter to H.W. Quinton, Commissioner for Home Affairs and Education, 18 Jan., PRC 14, Box 15-5-3-3, File K.

———. 1947d. Letter to H.W Quinton, Commissioner for Home Affairs and Education, 5 May, PRC 14, Box 15-5-3-3, File K.

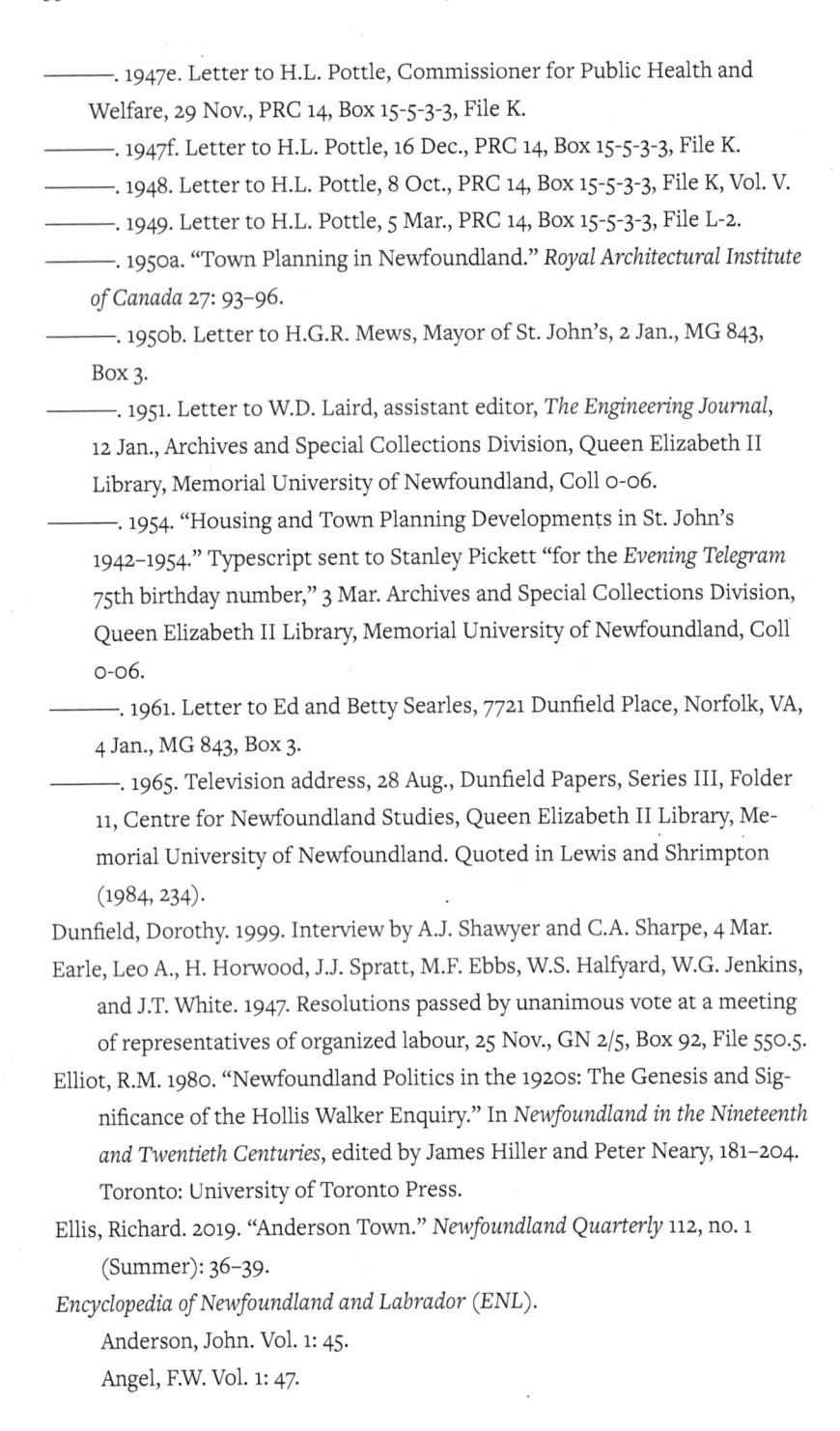

———. 1947e. Letter to H.L. Pottle, Commissioner for Public Health and Welfare, 29 Nov., PRC 14, Box 15-5-3-3, File K.

———. 1947f. Letter to H.L. Pottle, 16 Dec., PRC 14, Box 15-5-3-3, File K.

———. 1948. Letter to H.L. Pottle, 8 Oct., PRC 14, Box 15-5-3-3, File K, Vol. V.

———. 1949. Letter to H.L. Pottle, 5 Mar., PRC 14, Box 15-5-3-3, File L-2.

———. 1950a. "Town Planning in Newfoundland." *Royal Architectural Institute of Canada* 27: 93–96.

———. 1950b. Letter to H.G.R. Mews, Mayor of St. John's, 2 Jan., MG 843, Box 3.

———. 1951. Letter to W.D. Laird, assistant editor, *The Engineering Journal*, 12 Jan., Archives and Special Collections Division, Queen Elizabeth II Library, Memorial University of Newfoundland, Coll 0-06.

———. 1954. "Housing and Town Planning Developments in St. John's 1942–1954." Typescript sent to Stanley Pickett "for the *Evening Telegram* 75th birthday number," 3 Mar. Archives and Special Collections Division, Queen Elizabeth II Library, Memorial University of Newfoundland, Coll 0-06.

———. 1961. Letter to Ed and Betty Searles, 7721 Dunfield Place, Norfolk, VA, 4 Jan., MG 843, Box 3.

———. 1965. Television address, 28 Aug., Dunfield Papers, Series III, Folder 11, Centre for Newfoundland Studies, Queen Elizabeth II Library, Memorial University of Newfoundland. Quoted in Lewis and Shrimpton (1984, 234).

Dunfield, Dorothy. 1999. Interview by A.J. Shawyer and C.A. Sharpe, 4 Mar.

Earle, Leo A., H. Horwood, J.J. Spratt, M.F. Ebbs, W.S. Halfyard, W.G. Jenkins, and J.T. White. 1947. Resolutions passed by unanimous vote at a meeting of representatives of organized labour, 25 Nov., GN 2/5, Box 92, File 550.5.

Elliot, R.M. 1980. "Newfoundland Politics in the 1920s: The Genesis and Significance of the Hollis Walker Enquiry." In *Newfoundland in the Nineteenth and Twentieth Centuries*, edited by James Hiller and Peter Neary, 181–204. Toronto: University of Toronto Press.

Ellis, Richard. 2019. "Anderson Town." *Newfoundland Quarterly* 112, no. 1 (Summer): 36–39.

Encyclopedia of Newfoundland and Labrador (ENL).

Anderson, John. Vol. 1: 45.

Angel, F.W. Vol. 1: 47.

Bonnycastle, Sir Richard Henry. Vol. 1: 227.

Brehm, Dr. Robert. Vol. 1: 249.

Carnell, Andrew G. Vol. 1: 354.

Child Welfare. Vol. 1: 412.

Cook, Eric. Vol. 1: 515.

Cook, Sir Tasker. Vol. 1: 516.

Dunfield, Sir Brian. Vol. 1: 655.

Ellis, William J. Vol. 1: 772.

Gibbs, Michael P. Vol. 2: 520.

Gorvin, John Henry. Vol. 2: 570–71.

Gosling, William Gilbert. Vol. 1: 571.

Government. Vol. 2: 648–51.

Harvey Group of Companies. Vol. 2: 847–48.

Harvey, Sir John. Vol. 2: 848–49.

Hawes and Company. Vol. 2: 853–54.

Health. Vol. 2: 864–89.

Hope-Simpson, John. Vol. 2: 1030.

Hospitals. Vol. 2: 1941–77.

Howlett, Charles. Vol. 2: 1092.

I.O.D.E. Vol. 3: 66.

Kent, Mr. Justice James Mary. Vol. 3: 167.

LeMarchant, Sir John Gaspard. Vol. 3: 278.

MacBraire, James. Vol. 3: 397.

Macpherson, Harold. Vol. 3: 425.

McGrath, James. Vol. 3: 409.

McGregor, Sir William. Vol. 3: 411.

Meaney, John Thomas. Vol. 3: 489.

Mews, Henry George Reginald. Vol. 3: 528–29.

Outerbridge, Leonard Cecil. Vol. 4: 191–92.

Penson, John Hubert. Vol. 4: 251.

Puddester, John Charles. Vol. 4: 471.

Railways. Vol. 4: 512–16.

Rope making. Vol. 4: 632–34.

St. John's. Vol. 5: 31.

Southcott, Mary Meager. Vol. 5: 239–40.

Spratt, John J. Vol. 5: 279.

Tuberculosis. Vol. 2: 430–34.

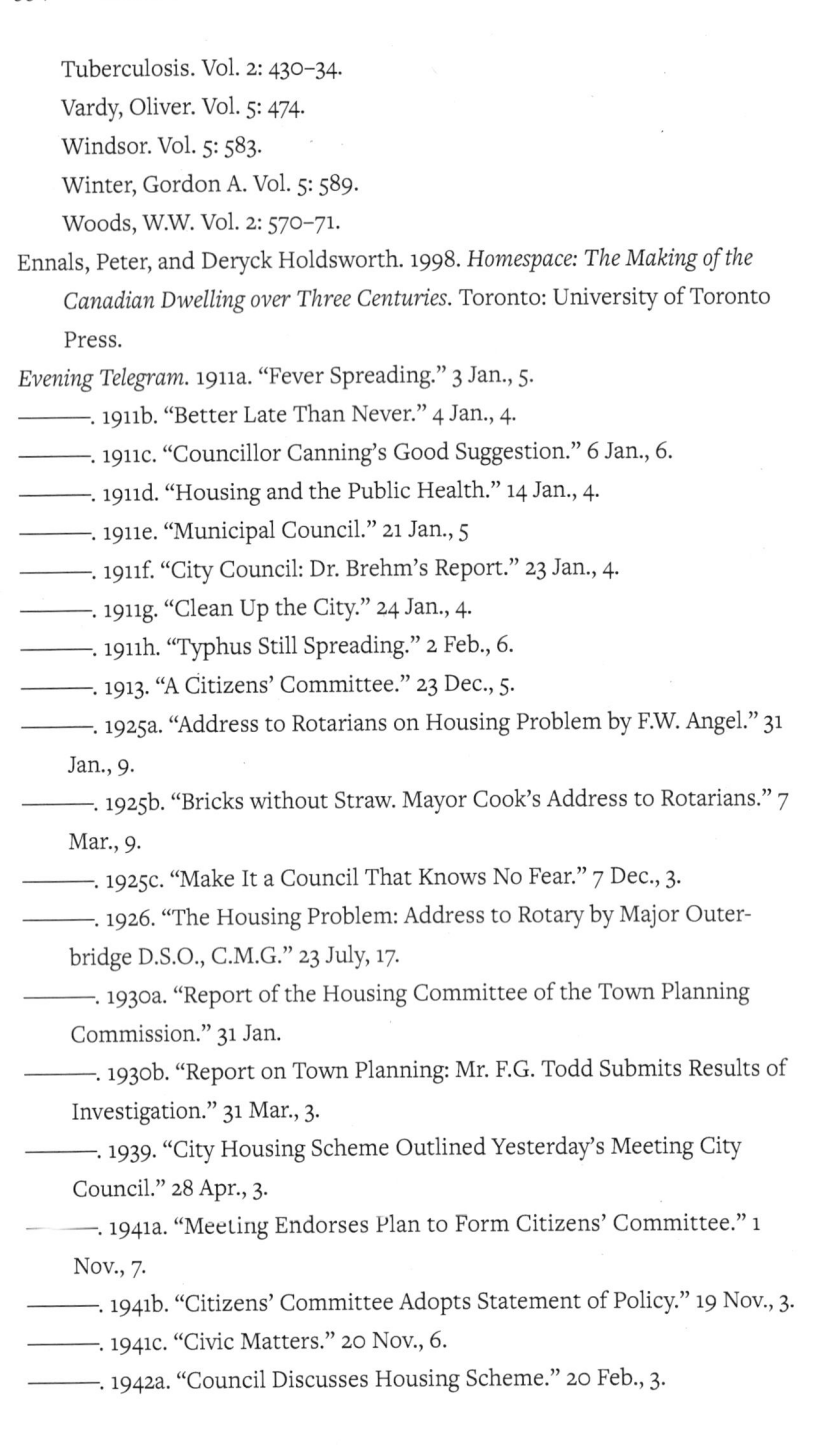

Vardy, Oliver. Vol. 5: 474.

Windsor. Vol. 5: 583.

Winter, Gordon A. Vol. 5: 589.

Woods, W.W. Vol. 2: 570–71.

Ennals, Peter, and Deryck Holdsworth. 1998. *Homespace: The Making of the Canadian Dwelling over Three Centuries*. Toronto: University of Toronto Press.

Evening Telegram. 1911a. "Fever Spreading." 3 Jan., 5.

———. 1911b. "Better Late Than Never." 4 Jan., 4.

———. 1911c. "Councillor Canning's Good Suggestion." 6 Jan., 6.

———. 1911d. "Housing and the Public Health." 14 Jan., 4.

———. 1911e. "Municipal Council." 21 Jan., 5

———. 1911f. "City Council: Dr. Brehm's Report." 23 Jan., 4.

———. 1911g. "Clean Up the City." 24 Jan., 4.

———. 1911h. "Typhus Still Spreading." 2 Feb., 6.

———. 1913. "A Citizens' Committee." 23 Dec., 5.

———. 1925a. "Address to Rotarians on Housing Problem by F.W. Angel." 31 Jan., 9.

———. 1925b. "Bricks without Straw. Mayor Cook's Address to Rotarians." 7 Mar., 9.

———. 1925c. "Make It a Council That Knows No Fear." 7 Dec., 3.

———. 1926. "The Housing Problem: Address to Rotary by Major Outerbridge D.S.O., C.M.G." 23 July, 17.

———. 1930a. "Report of the Housing Committee of the Town Planning Commission." 31 Jan.

———. 1930b. "Report on Town Planning: Mr. F.G. Todd Submits Results of Investigation." 31 Mar., 3.

———. 1939. "City Housing Scheme Outlined Yesterday's Meeting City Council." 28 Apr., 3.

———. 1941a. "Meeting Endorses Plan to Form Citizens' Committee." 1 Nov., 7.

———. 1941b. "Citizens' Committee Adopts Statement of Policy." 19 Nov., 3.

———. 1941c. "Civic Matters." 20 Nov., 6.

———. 1942a. "Council Discusses Housing Scheme." 20 Feb., 3.

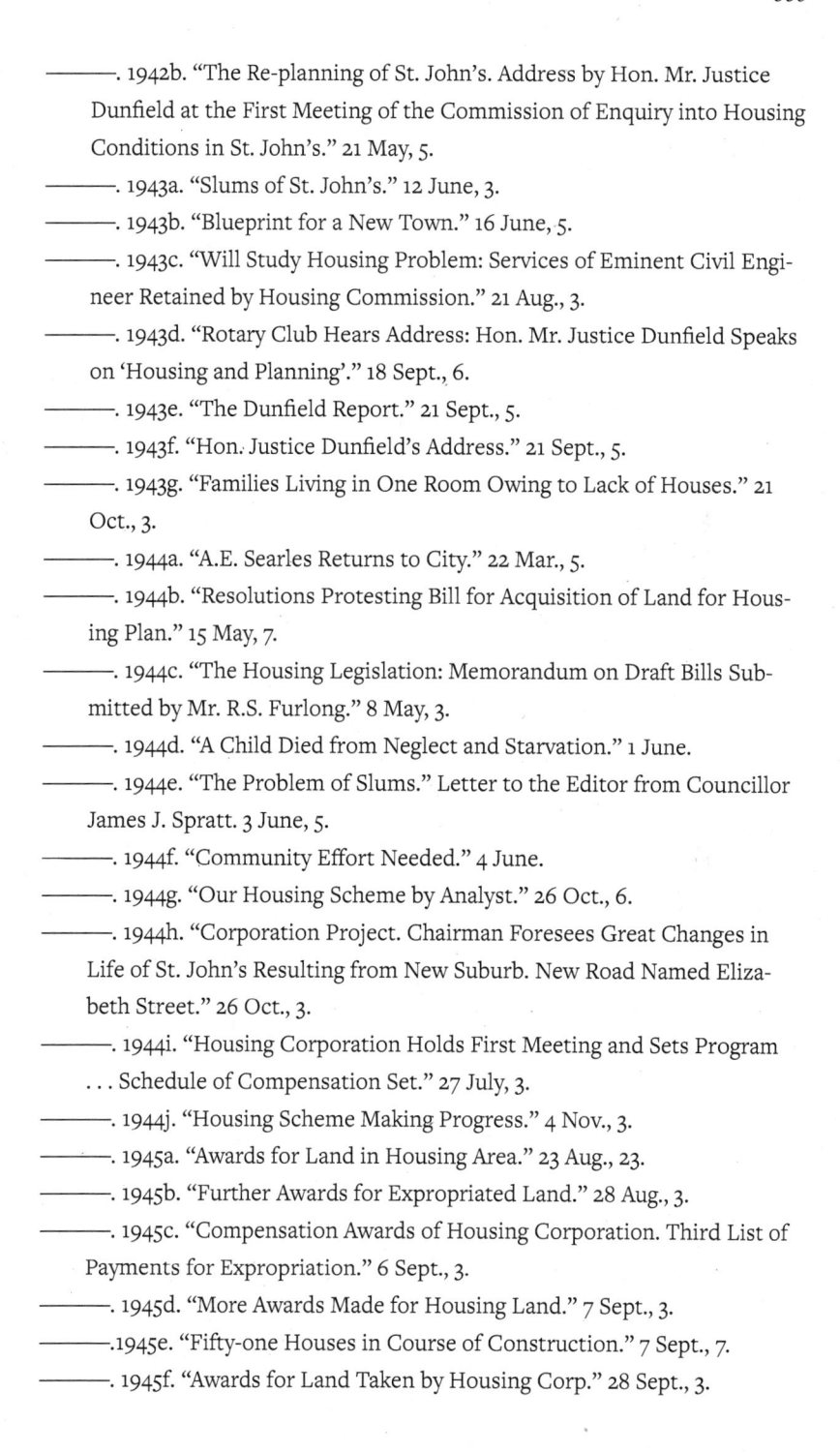

———. 1942b. "The Re-planning of St. John's. Address by Hon. Mr. Justice Dunfield at the First Meeting of the Commission of Enquiry into Housing Conditions in St. John's." 21 May, 5.

———. 1943a. "Slums of St. John's." 12 June, 3.

———. 1943b. "Blueprint for a New Town." 16 June, 5.

———. 1943c. "Will Study Housing Problem: Services of Eminent Civil Engineer Retained by Housing Commission." 21 Aug., 3.

———. 1943d. "Rotary Club Hears Address: Hon. Mr. Justice Dunfield Speaks on 'Housing and Planning'." 18 Sept., 6.

———. 1943e. "The Dunfield Report." 21 Sept., 5.

———. 1943f. "Hon. Justice Dunfield's Address." 21 Sept., 5.

———. 1943g. "Families Living in One Room Owing to Lack of Houses." 21 Oct., 3.

———. 1944a. "A.E. Searles Returns to City." 22 Mar., 5.

———. 1944b. "Resolutions Protesting Bill for Acquisition of Land for Housing Plan." 15 May, 7.

———. 1944c. "The Housing Legislation: Memorandum on Draft Bills Submitted by Mr. R.S. Furlong." 8 May, 3.

———. 1944d. "A Child Died from Neglect and Starvation." 1 June.

———. 1944e. "The Problem of Slums." Letter to the Editor from Councillor James J. Spratt. 3 June, 5.

———. 1944f. "Community Effort Needed." 4 June.

———. 1944g. "Our Housing Scheme by Analyst." 26 Oct., 6.

———. 1944h. "Corporation Project. Chairman Foresees Great Changes in Life of St. John's Resulting from New Suburb. New Road Named Elizabeth Street." 26 Oct., 3.

———. 1944i. "Housing Corporation Holds First Meeting and Sets Program ... Schedule of Compensation Set." 27 July, 3.

———. 1944j. "Housing Scheme Making Progress." 4 Nov., 3.

———. 1945a. "Awards for Land in Housing Area." 23 Aug., 23.

———. 1945b. "Further Awards for Expropriated Land." 28 Aug., 3.

———. 1945c. "Compensation Awards of Housing Corporation. Third List of Payments for Expropriation." 6 Sept., 3.

———. 1945d. "More Awards Made for Housing Land." 7 Sept., 3.

———. 1945e. "Fifty-one Houses in Course of Construction." 7 Sept., 7.

———. 1945f. "Awards for Land Taken by Housing Corp." 28 Sept., 3.

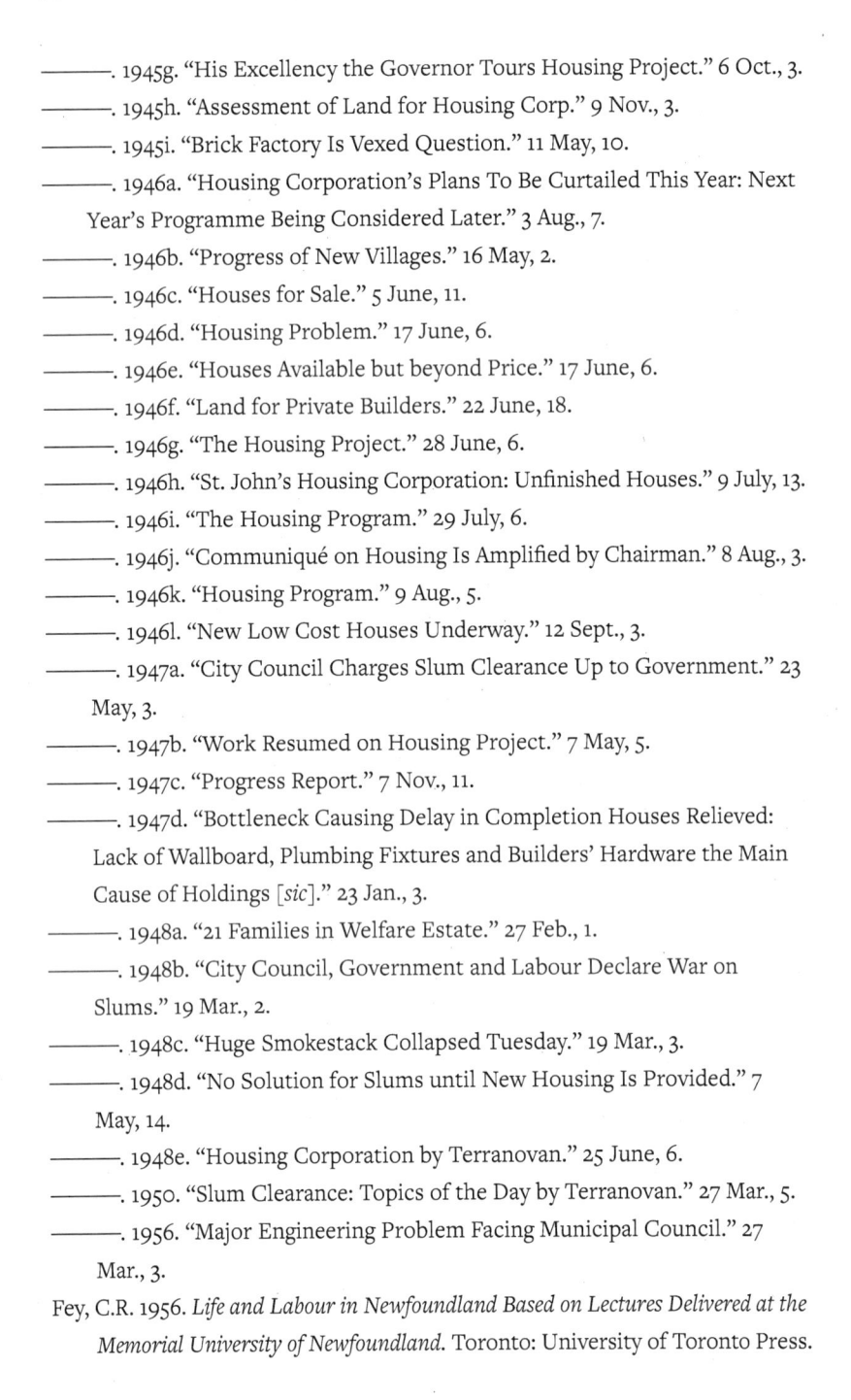

———. 1945g. "His Excellency the Governor Tours Housing Project." 6 Oct., 3.
———. 1945h. "Assessment of Land for Housing Corp." 9 Nov., 3.
———. 1945i. "Brick Factory Is Vexed Question." 11 May, 10.
———. 1946a. "Housing Corporation's Plans To Be Curtailed This Year: Next Year's Programme Being Considered Later." 3 Aug., 7.
———. 1946b. "Progress of New Villages." 16 May, 2.
———. 1946c. "Houses for Sale." 5 June, 11.
———. 1946d. "Housing Problem." 17 June, 6.
———. 1946e. "Houses Available but beyond Price." 17 June, 6.
———. 1946f. "Land for Private Builders." 22 June, 18.
———. 1946g. "The Housing Project." 28 June, 6.
———. 1946h. "St. John's Housing Corporation: Unfinished Houses." 9 July, 13.
———. 1946i. "The Housing Program." 29 July, 6.
———. 1946j. "Communiqué on Housing Is Amplified by Chairman." 8 Aug., 3.
———. 1946k. "Housing Program." 9 Aug., 5.
———. 1946l. "New Low Cost Houses Underway." 12 Sept., 3.
———. 1947a. "City Council Charges Slum Clearance Up to Government." 23 May, 3.
———. 1947b. "Work Resumed on Housing Project." 7 May, 5.
———. 1947c. "Progress Report." 7 Nov., 11.
———. 1947d. "Bottleneck Causing Delay in Completion Houses Relieved: Lack of Wallboard, Plumbing Fixtures and Builders' Hardware the Main Cause of Holdings [sic]." 23 Jan., 3.
———. 1948a. "21 Families in Welfare Estate." 27 Feb., 1.
———. 1948b. "City Council, Government and Labour Declare War on Slums." 19 Mar., 2.
———. 1948c. "Huge Smokestack Collapsed Tuesday." 19 Mar., 3.
———. 1948d. "No Solution for Slums until New Housing Is Provided." 7 May, 14.
———. 1948e. "Housing Corporation by Terranovan." 25 June, 6.
———. 1950. "Slum Clearance: Topics of the Day by Terranovan." 27 Mar., 5.
———. 1956. "Major Engineering Problem Facing Municipal Council." 27 Mar., 3.
Fey, C.R. 1956. *Life and Labour in Newfoundland Based on Lectures Delivered at the Memorial University of Newfoundland*. Toronto: University of Toronto Press.

Finance Committee. 1946a. *Report of the Finance Committee of the National Convention*. GN 10C, Box 4, Folder 8/A1.11 (9).

———. 1946b. *Minutes of the Finance Committee of the National Convention*. 25 Oct. GN 10C, Box 4 Folder 8/A1.11 (8).

Fishman, R. 1977. *Urban Utopias in the Twentieth Century: Ebenezer Howard, Frank Lloyd Wright and Le Corbusier*. New York: Basic Books.

FitzGerald, J.E. 1995. "The Orthodoxy Unchallenged." *Newfoundland Studies* 11: 127–44.

Fitzgerald, Jack. 1997. *Another Time, Another Place*. St. John's: Creative.

Foran, Edward B. 1937. "St. John's City: Historic Capital of Newfoundland." In *The Book of Newfoundland*, Vol. II: 1–25.

Forestell, Nancy M. 1995. "Times Were Hard: The Patterns of Women's Paid Labour in St. John's between the Two World Wars." *Labour/Le Travail* 24: 147–66. Reprinted in *Their Lives and Times: Women in Newfoundland and Labrador: A Collage*, edited by Carmelita McGrath, Barbara Neis, and Marilyn Porter, 76–92. St. John's: Killick Press, 1998.

Forsey, Philip S. 1949. Minister of Provincial Affairs to Gordon A. Winter, Chairman, St. John's Housing Corporation, 13 Sept. PRC 14, Box 15-5-3-3, File K, Vol. 6.

Fraser, Allan F., Peter Neary, and Melvin Baker, eds. 2010. *History of the Participation by Newfoundland in World War II*. Memorial University of Newfoundland.

Fraser, B.A. 1951. Letter from Secretary, Churchill Park Citizens' Association to the Chairman, St. John's Housing Corporation. 30 Mar. Keough Papers, PANL, Box 3, File: St. John's Housing Corporation 1951–58.

Freestone, Robert. 2015. Review of "Paradise Planned: The Garden Suburb and the Modern City" by Robert A. Stern et al., *Journal of the Society of Architectural Historians* 74: 371–73.

Furlong, R.S. 1944a. Memorandum on draft bill concerning housing legislation. n.d. GN 38, S5-2-1, Box 1, File 9.

———. 1944b. Memorandum prepared on behalf of His Grace, the Archbishop of St. John's. 10 May. GN 38 S5-2-1, Box 1, File 9.

Garner, George. 2004. Interview by C.A. Sharpe, 1 Jan.

Garner, Hugh. 1971. *Cabbagetown*. Toronto: Simon and Schuster.

Gereke, Kenty. 1991. *The Canadian City*. Montreal: Black Rose Books.

Gilliland, Jason. 2000. "Visions and Revision of House and Home: A Half-Century of Change in Montréal's Cité Jardin." In *(Re)development at the Urban Edges: Reflections on the Canadian Experience*, edited by Greg Halseth and Heather Nicol, 139–74. Waterloo, ON: Department of Geography, University of Waterloo.

Girard, Michel F. 1991. "The Commission of Conservation as a Forerunner to the National Research Council 1909–1921." *Scientia Canadensis: Canadian Journal of the History of Science, Technology and Medicine* 15: 1–40.

Goddard, Robert. 1988. *In Pale Battalions*. London: Penguin.

Gordon, David. 2018. "Canada Is a Suburban Nation." In *The Future of the Suburbs: Policy Challenges and Opportunities in Canada*, 1–4. University of Calgary, School of Public Policy Publications. SPP Briefing Paper, Volume 11, 23 Aug.

Gorsky, Martin, Karen Lock, and Sue Hogarth. 2004. "Public Health and English Local Government: Historical Perspectives on the Impact of 'Returning Home'." *Journal of Public Health* 35, no. 4: 546–51.

Gorvin, John H. 1939. Memorandum from the Commissioner for Natural Resources to Sir John Puddester, Commissioner for Public Health and Welfare, 17 Aug. GN 38, S5-2-1, Box 1, File 9.

Gosling, A.N. 1935. *William Gilbert Gosling: A Tribute*. New York: Guild Press.

Gosling, William G. 1910. *Labrador: Its Discovery, Exploration and Development*. London.

———. 1911. *The Life of Sir Humphrey Gilbert, England's First Empire Builder*. London.

———. 1914a. "Report of the Executive Committee of the Citizens' Committee." 12 Feb. Quoted in Baker (1981, 46).

———. 1914b. Letter to St. John's Municipal Council, 9 Jan. City of St. John's Archives, RG 01-01, City Clerk, Box 191, File Miscellaneous 1913–14.

Government of Canada. 1998. "National Historic Person, Mary Meager Southcott." Report 1998-013, 2005-072.

Gowans, A. 1992. *Styles and Types of North American Architecture: Social Function and Cultural Expression*. New York: Icon Editions.

Grant, Jill. 2000 "Planning Canadian Cities: Context, Continuity, and Change." In *Canadian Cities in Transition*, 2nd ed., edited by Trudi Bunting and Pierre Filion, 443–61. Toronto: Oxford University Press.

Grigsby, W.G. 1963. *Housing Markets and Public Policy*. Philadelphia: University of Pennsylvania Press.

Hall, Peter. 1988. *Cities of Tomorrow: An Intellectual History of Urban Planning and Design in the Twentieth Century*. Oxford: Basil Blackwell.

———. 2014. *Cities of Tomorrow: An Intellectual History of Urban Planning and Design since 1880*. Chichester: Wiley Blackwell.

Halliday, Robert. 1998. Interview by Christopher Brown. Reported in Brown, "Halliday Place: The Exploration of a Derelict Landscape." BA (Honours) diss., Memorial University of Newfoundland, Department of Geography.

Handcock, Gordon W. 1994. "The Commission of Government's Land Settlement Scheme in Newfoundland." In *Twentieth Century Newfoundland Explorations*, edited by J.K. Hiller and Peter Neary, 123–52. St. John's: Breakwater Books.

Hardy, Marion. 2007. "Terry's Plantation, St. John's." Unpublished manuscript. 6 pp.

———. 2021. "The Teign Estuary Area and Newfoundland and Labrador." Unpublished manuscript. 22 pp.

Harris, Richard. 1996. *Unplanned Suburbs: Toronto's American Tragedy, 1900–1950*. Baltimore: Johns Hopkins University Press.

———. 2004. *Creeping Conformity: How Canada Became Suburban, 1900–1960*. Toronto: University of Toronto Press.

———. 2012. *Building a Market: The Rise of the Home Improvement Industry, 1914–1960*. Chicago: University of Chicago Press.

——— and Chris Hamnett. 1987. "The Myth of the Promised Land: The Social Diffusion of Home Ownership in Britain and North America." *Annals of the Association of American Geographers* 77: 173–90.

——— and Charlotte Vorms, eds. 2014. *What's in a Name: Talking about Urban Peripheries*. Toronto: University of Toronto Press.

Harvey, Sir John. TRPAD, MG 93.

Hawkin, David, Hans Rollman, and Michael DeRoche. 1999. Interviews by C.A. Sharpe.

Heritage Foundation Newfoundland and Labrador. "Rose's Dairy Farm." https://heritagefoundation.ca.

Hiller, James, and Peter Neary. 1980. *Newfoundland in the Nineteenth and Twentieth Centuries: Essays in Interpretation*. Toronto: University of Toronto Press.

Hodge, Gerald. 1991. *Planning Canadian Communities: An Introduction to the Principles, Practice and Participants.* Toronto: Nelson.

Holdsworth, D.W., and J. Simon. 1993. "Housing Form and Use of Domestic Space." In *House, Home and Community: Progress in Housing Canadians 1945–1986*, edited by J. Miron, 188–202. Montreal and Kingston: McGill-Queen's University Press.

Home, Robert. 2009. "Land Ownership in the United Kingdom: Trends, Preferences and Future Challenges." *Land Use Policy* 33, Supplement 1: S103–S108.

Horwood, Harold. 1997. *A Walk in Dream Time: Growing Up in Old St. John's.* St. John's: Killick Press.

Horwood, Sir William. 1944. Letter to Governor Humphrey Walwyn, 29 Apr. GN 1/3/A, File 288.

House, John Douglas. 1964. "Two Lower-Class Areas in St. John's, Newfoundland: A Comparative Study." BA diss., Memorial University of Newfoundland.

Howard, Ebenezer. 1898. *Tomorrow: A Peaceful Path to Real Reform.* London: Swan Sonnenschein. Reprint: *Garden Cities of Tomorrow.* London: Faber and Faber, 1965.

Hulchanski, David. 1986. "The 1935 Dominion Housing Act: Setting the Stage for a Permanent Federal Presence in Canada's Housing Market." *Urban History Review* 15: 19–39.

Hunt, Charles E. 1937. "The Rotary Club." In *The Book of Newfoundland*, vol. 2, edited by J.R. Smallwood, 91.

Hunt, Robert. 2011. *Corner Boys.* St. John's: Flanker Press.

Jackson, F.L. 1986. "The Rise and Fall of the Newfoundland State". In *Surviving Confederation*. St. John's: Harry Cuff Publications.

Jackson, J.B. 1997. *Landscape in Sight: Looking at America.* New Haven: Yale University Press.

Jacobs, Jane. 1971. *The Death and Life of Great American Cities.* New York: Random House.

Jacobs, P. 1983. "Frederick G. Todd and the Creation of Canada's Urban Landscape." In *Landscape Preservation*, special issue of *Bulletin of the Association for Preservation Technology* 15: 27–37.

Jacobs, Ryan. 2010. "From 'Slum Clearance' to 'Revitalisation': Planning, Expertise and Moral Regulation in Toronto's Regent Park." *Planning Perspectives* 25: 69–86.

James, R.L.M. 1946. Memorandum to A.J. Walsh, 21 Oct. PRC 14, Box 15-5-3-3, File L-12.

Job, Robert. 1818. Robert Job Fonds, 1.01 OMF "Properties" with reference to Clapp's Plantation, 24 Oct., Maritime History Archives, Memorial University of Newfoundland.

Johnson, Paul. 2009. "The Commission, the War and Governance." In *God Guard Thee Newfoundland: Searching for Meaning*, edited by Paul Johnson, 14–29. St. John's: Flanker Press.

Johnson, Steven. 2006. *The Ghost Map: The Story of London's Most Terrifying Epidemic and How It Changed Science, Cities and the Modern World*. New York: Riverhead Books.

Johnstone, Kenneth. 1946. "Newfoundland: An Island People Look to the Future." *Montreal Standard*, 23 Nov., 2–28.

Jones, D.R. 2000. "R.O. Jones' Letters from the Newfoundland Coast, 1937." *Newfoundland Studies* 16: 205–26.

Joy, John Lawrence. 1977. "The Growth and Development of Trades and Manufacturing in St. John's, 1870–1914." MA thesis. Memorial University of Newfoundland.

JHA: Journal of the House of Assembly of Newfoundland. 1841. "Road Report." Vol. 2, Appendix: 178.

———. 1843. "Suggestions for Certain Improvement in the City of St. John's Alluded to by the Governor in His Speech": 66.

———. 1845. "Petitions": 52.

———. 1846. "Road Report." Appendix: 228.

———. 1851a. "A Detailed Statement of the Amount of Compensation Awarded to Absentee Landlords under the St. John's Rebuilding Act." Appendix: 232.

———. 1851b. Letter from James Douglas in Reference to Drains, Sewers, Wells, and Tanks in St. John's to the Hon. James Crowdy, Colonial Secretary, 12 Feb. Appendix: 244–46.

———. 1854. Copy of Report from J.P. Nevill, Esq. to His Excellency the Governor on the Subject of Improving the Sanitary State of St. John's by Sewerage and Drainage, 11 Oct. Miscellaneous, Vol. 2: 12–13.

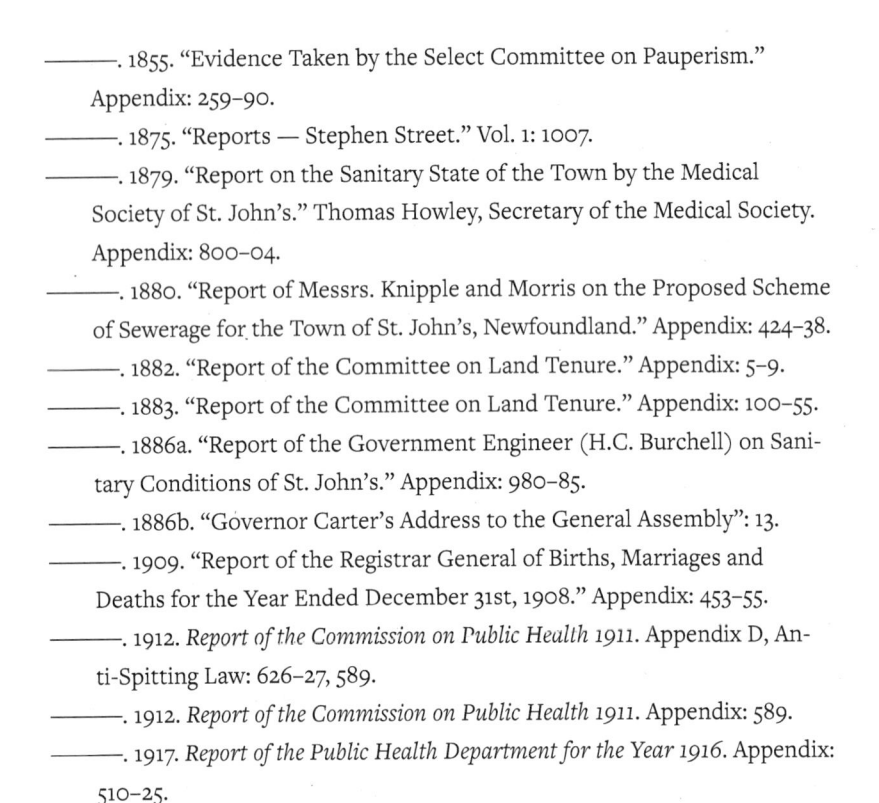

———. 1855. "Evidence Taken by the Select Committee on Pauperism." Appendix: 259–90.

———. 1875. "Reports — Stephen Street." Vol. 1: 1007.

———. 1879. "Report on the Sanitary State of the Town by the Medical Society of St. John's." Thomas Howley, Secretary of the Medical Society. Appendix: 800–04.

———. 1880. "Report of Messrs. Knipple and Morris on the Proposed Scheme of Sewerage for the Town of St. John's, Newfoundland." Appendix: 424–38.

———. 1882. "Report of the Committee on Land Tenure." Appendix: 5–9.

———. 1883. "Report of the Committee on Land Tenure." Appendix: 100–55.

———. 1886a. "Report of the Government Engineer (H.C. Burchell) on Sanitary Conditions of St. John's." Appendix: 980–85.

———. 1886b. "Governor Carter's Address to the General Assembly": 13.

———. 1909. "Report of the Registrar General of Births, Marriages and Deaths for the Year Ended December 31st, 1908." Appendix: 453–55.

———. 1912. *Report of the Commission on Public Health 1911*. Appendix D, Anti-Spitting Law: 626–27, 589.

———. 1912. *Report of the Commission on Public Health 1911*. Appendix: 589.

———. 1917. *Report of the Public Health Department for the Year 1916*. Appendix: 510–25.

J.R. Smallwood Collection 075. Manuscripts and Archives Division, Queen Elizabeth II Library, Memorial University of Newfoundland.

Kelly, Barbara M. 1993. *Expanding the American Dream: Building and Rebuilding Levittown*. Albany, NY: SUNY Press.

Kennedy, Fabian. 1996. "Own Your Own Home: The Railway Employees Welfare Association and the Building of the 'Railway Houses' in St. John's." *Newfoundland Quarterly* 90, no. 2 (Spring): 14–23.

Knott, Christine, and John Phyne. 2018. "Rehousing Good Citizens: Gender, Class and Family Ideals in the St. John's Housing Authority Survey of the Inner City of St. John's, 1951 and 1952." *Acadiensis* 47, no. 1: 178–207.

Kushner, David. 2009. *Levittown: Two Families, One Tycoon and the Fight for Civil Rights in America's Legendary Suburb*. New York: Walker Publishing.

Lamprecht, Barbara. 2004. *Richard Neutra 1892–1970: Survival through Design*. London: Taschen.

Lansing, J.B., C.W. Clifton, and J.N. Morgan. 1969. *New Homes and Poor People*. Ann Arbor: University of Michigan Press.

Latremouille, J. 1986. *Pride of Home: The Working Class Housing Tradition in Nova Scotia 1749–1949*. Hantsport, NS: Lancelot Press.

Legislation (Canada). 1919. An Act to assist Returned Soldiers in Settling Upon the Land. 9-10 Geo V, Chapter 71.

Legislation (Newfoundland). 1833. An Act for the more speedy abatement of Nuisances. 4 William Cap VIII.

———. 1834a. An Act to provide for the performance of Quarantine . . . to provide against the introduction of infectious and Contagious diseases and the spreading thereof in this Island. 5 William IV Cap 1.

———. 1834b. An act for defraying the introduction and spreading of disease. 5 William IV, Cap 1.

———. 1834c. An Act to provide for the Maintenance of Bastard Children. 4 William Cap VII.

———. 1834d. An Act to afford Relief to Wives and Children Deserted by the Husbands and Parents. 4 William Cap VIII.

———. 1840. 23 Victoria Cap VI.

———. 1849a. An Act to prohibit Interments within the Town of St. John's. 13 Victoria Cap 13.

———. 1849b. An Act to Confirm the Acts of the Legislature of Newfoundland respecting the rebuilding of the Town of Saint John's Newfoundland and to enable the said Legislature to make other Provisions respecting the rebuilding of the said Town. 12 Victoria Cap VI.

———. 1851. An Act to extend the time allowed by the Saint John's Rebuilding Acts for the removal of the Wooden Buildings in certain part of the said Town, and for other purposes. 14 Victoria Cap VI.

———. 1852. An Act to consolidate and amend the Saint John's Rebuilding Acts. 15 Victoria Cap IV.

———. 1859. An Act to incorporate the General Water Company. 22 Victoria, Cap VII.

———. 1860. An Act for the prevention of Nuisances in the Towns of St. John's, Harbour Grace, Carbonear and Brigus. 23 Victoria Cap VI.

———. 1863. An Act to provide for the sewerage of the Town of St. John's. 26 Victoria Cap VI.

———. 1864. An Act to make further provision for the sewerage of the Town of St. John's. 27 Victoria Cap V.

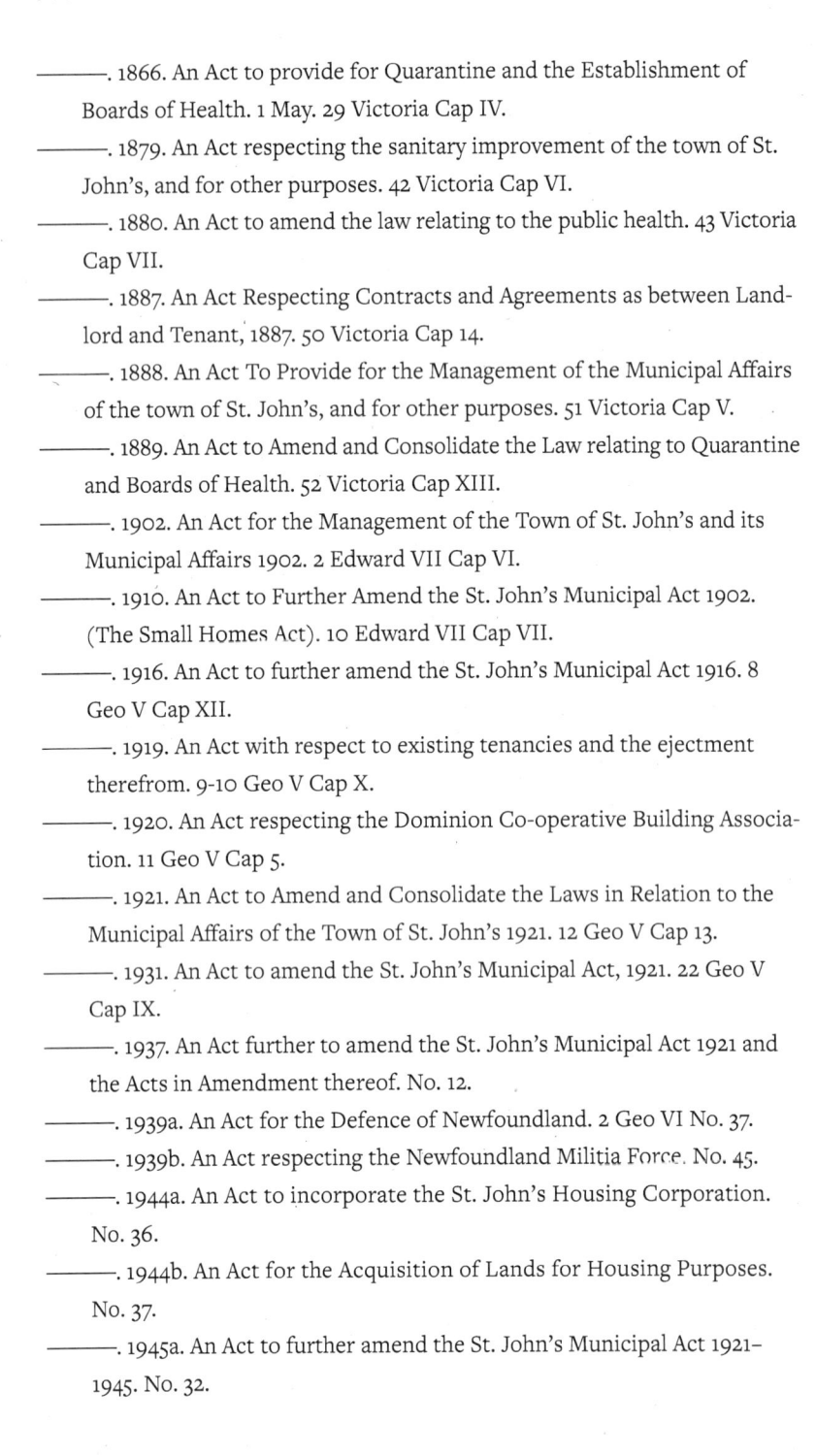

———. 1866. An Act to provide for Quarantine and the Establishment of Boards of Health. 1 May. 29 Victoria Cap IV.

———. 1879. An Act respecting the sanitary improvement of the town of St. John's, and for other purposes. 42 Victoria Cap VI.

———. 1880. An Act to amend the law relating to the public health. 43 Victoria Cap VII.

———. 1887. An Act Respecting Contracts and Agreements as between Landlord and Tenant, 1887. 50 Victoria Cap 14.

———. 1888. An Act To Provide for the Management of the Municipal Affairs of the town of St. John's, and for other purposes. 51 Victoria Cap V.

———. 1889. An Act to Amend and Consolidate the Law relating to Quarantine and Boards of Health. 52 Victoria Cap XIII.

———. 1902. An Act for the Management of the Town of St. John's and its Municipal Affairs 1902. 2 Edward VII Cap VI.

———. 1910. An Act to Further Amend the St. John's Municipal Act 1902. (The Small Homes Act). 10 Edward VII Cap VII.

———. 1916. An Act to further amend the St. John's Municipal Act 1916. 8 Geo V Cap XII.

———. 1919. An Act with respect to existing tenancies and the ejectment therefrom. 9-10 Geo V Cap X.

———. 1920. An Act respecting the Dominion Co-operative Building Association. 11 Geo V Cap 5.

———. 1921. An Act to Amend and Consolidate the Laws in Relation to the Municipal Affairs of the Town of St. John's 1921. 12 Geo V Cap 13.

———. 1931. An Act to amend the St. John's Municipal Act, 1921. 22 Geo V Cap IX.

———. 1937. An Act further to amend the St. John's Municipal Act 1921 and the Acts in Amendment thereof. No. 12.

———. 1939a. An Act for the Defence of Newfoundland. 2 Geo VI No. 37.

———. 1939b. An Act respecting the Newfoundland Militia Force. No. 45.

———. 1944a. An Act to incorporate the St. John's Housing Corporation. No. 36.

———. 1944b. An Act for the Acquisition of Lands for Housing Purposes. No. 37.

———. 1945a. An Act to further amend the St. John's Municipal Act 1921–1945. No. 32.

———. 1945b. An Act further to amend the St. John's Municipal Acts 1921 and 1943. ("Power to Construct Tunnel") No. 5.

———. 1990. An Act respecting certain Leasehold interests within the City of St. John's. Chapter L-10, *Revised Statutes of Newfoundland*.

Legislation (Nova Scotia). 1932 and 1938. An Act to Assist the Construction of Houses. Chapter 58, 1932 and Chapter 49, 1938.

Lewis, J., and M. Shrimpton. 1984. "Policymaking in Newfoundland during the 1940's: The Case of the St. John's Housing Corporation." *Canadian Historical Review* 45: 209–39.

Lewis, P.J. 1944. "Resolutions Passed at a Meeting of Landowners of St. John's East Held at the Board of Trade Rooms. To be submitted to Sir John Puddester, Commissioner for Health and Welfare." 13 Apr. GN 38, S5-2-1, File 2.

Lloyd George, David. 1909. The National Archives, UK, Education Exhibitions 1906–18. https://web.archive.org/web/20080907082934/http://learningcurve.gov.uk/.

Lorinc, John. 2015. "Fool's Paradise: Hastings' Anti-slum Crusade." In *The Ward*, edited by John Lorinc, Ellen Scheinberg, and Tatum Taylor. Toronto: Coach House Books.

Mackenzie, David. 1992. "An Economic and Financial Review of Newfoundland during the Second World War." *Newfoundland Studies* 8: 69–89.

MacKinnon, Robert Alexander. 1981. "The Growth of Commercial Agriculture around St. John's, 1800–1935: A Study of Local Trade in Response to Urban Demand." MA thesis, Memorial University of Newfoundland.

Macpherson, Harold. 1944. Letter to C.W. Chadwick, Dominions Office, London, 11 Sept. GN 38, S5-2-1, File 2.

Mahoney, J.J. 1941. Memorandum to W.J. Carew, 7 Mar. GN 38, S5-2-1, Box 1, File 9.

———. 1943. Memorandum to W.J. Carew, 9 Oct. GN 38, S3-1-1, Box 1.

———. 1944. Memorandum to W.J. Carew, 12 May. GN 38, S5-2-1, Box 1, File 9.

———. 1947. Letter to W.J. Carew, 28 May. GN 2/5, Box 92, File 550.5.

Mahoney, Mr. Justice John W. 2001. Interview by A.J. Shawyer and C.A. Sharpe, 9 Jan.

Major, Kevin. 2001. *As Near to Heaven by Sea: A History of Newfoundland and Labrador*. Toronto: Penguin Canada.

Malone, Greg. 2012. *Don't Tell the Newfoundlanders: The True Story of Newfoundland's Confederation with Canada*. Toronto: Knopf Canada.

Mannion, John J. 1986. "Patrick Morris and Newfoundland Irish Immigration." In *Talamh an Eisc: Canadian and Irish Essays*, edited by Cyril J. Byrne and Margaret Harry, 180-202. Halifax: Nimbus Publishing.

Martin, R.F. 1950. "Report on the Underground Utilities and Streets in the St. John's Housing Area." Engineering Department, City of St. John's.

Massey, J.C., and S. Maxwell. 1996. *House Styles in America*. New York: Penguin Studio.

Matthews, Keith. 1988. "The Irish in Newfoundland." In Matthews, *Lectures on the History of Newfoundland, 1500-1830*, 149-55. St. John's: Breakwater Books.

Mayne, Alan. 1991. *The Imagined Slum. Newspaper Representation in Three Cities 1870-1914*. Leicester: Leicester University Press.

Mayo, H.B. 1949. "Newfoundland's Entry into the Dominion." *Canadian Journal of Economics and Political Science* 15: 505-22.

McAlpine's Newfoundland Directory. 1904. St. John's.

McCann, L. 1996. "Planning and Building the Corporate Suburb of Mount Royal, 1910-1925." *Daily News Planning Perspectives* 11: 259-301.

———. 1999. "Suburbs of Desire: The Suburban Landscape of Canadian Cities 1900-1950." In *Changing Suburbs: Foundation, Form and Function*, edited by R. Harris and P.J. Larkham, 111-45. London: E. and F.N. Spon.

McGrath, James. 1914. Letter from president of the LSPU to W.G. Gosling, Charter Commissioner, 19 Jan. City of St. John's Archives, RG 01-01, Box 191, Miscellaneous 1913-14.

McKellar, J. 1993. "Building Technology and the Production Process." In *House, Home and Community: Progress in Housing Canadians 1945-1986*, edited by J. Miron, 136-54. Montreal and Kingston: McGill-Queen's University Press.

Meaney, J. 1939. "The St. John's Municipal Housing Scheme." 27 Apr. GN 38, S5-2-1, Box 1, File 8; St. John's City Archives, Jackman Collection, file "Property: housing general."

Mellin, Robert. 1995. *A City of Towns: Alternatives for the Planning and Design of Housing in St. John's, Newfoundland*. Ottawa: Canada Mortgage and Housing Corporation.

———. 2011. *Newfoundland Modern. Architecture in the Smallwood Years 1949–1972*. Montreal and Kingston: McGill-Queen's University Press.

Meschino, F.P. 1999. Telephone interview by C.A. Sharpe, A.J. Shawyer, and G.L. Pocius, 24 July.

———. 2000. Interviews by A.J. Shawyer and C.A. Sharpe, 8–12 June.

Meschino, Martha. 2021. Email to C.A. Sharpe, 14 May.

Meschino, Phyllis. 2000. Interviews by A.J. Shawyer and C.A. Sharpe.

Miller, E., ed. 2015. *Ahead of Her Time: Select Writings of Dora Russell*. St. John's: Creative Publishers.

Miller, L. 1981. Interview by Mark Shrimpton, 30 Oct.

Miller, Mervyn. 2002. "Garden Cities and Suburbs: At Home and Abroad." *Journal of Planning History* 1: 6–28.

Morris, Sir Edward. 1907. "The Growth of Municipal Government in St. John's." *Newfoundland Quarterly* 7, no. 1: 6.

Mullins, Margaret. 1989. *And They Stayed: A Selection of St. John's Family Histories*. St. John's: Jesperson Press.

Murray, Hilda Chaulk. 2002. *Cows Don't Know It's Sunday: Agricultural Life in St. John's*. St. John's: ISER Books.

Nader, G. 1975. *Cities of Canada*, 2 vols. Toronto: Macmillan.

Neary, Peter. 1988. *Newfoundland in the North Atlantic World, 1929–1949*. Montreal and Kingston: McGill-Queen's University Press.

———. 1994. "A 'Mortgaged Property': The Impact of the United States on Newfoundland, 1940–49." In *Twentieth-Century Newfoundland: Explorations*, edited by J.K. Hiller and P. Neary. St. John's: Breakwater Books.

———. 1995. "Like Stepping Back: Newfoundland in 1939." *Newfoundland Studies* 11: 1–12.

———. 1996. *White Tie and Decorations: Sir John and Lady Hope Simpson in Newfoundland, 1934–36*. Toronto: University of Toronto Press.

———. 1999. "A Garrison Country: Newfoundland and Labrador during the Second World War." *Canadian War Museum Dispatches* 4: 1–4.

——— and P. O'Flaherty. 1983. *Part of the Main: An Illustrated History of Newfoundland and Labrador*. St. John's: Breakwater Books.

Newfoundlander. 1847. 4 Jan.

Newfoundlander. 1855. 25 Oct.

Newfoundland Express. 1860. 5 Nov.

Newfoundland Law Reports. 1819. Rex v. Patrick Keough et al. Aug.

Newfoundland Law Reports. 1985. *Gill's Estate.* Nov.
Newfoundland Magazine. 1920. "The Homes for the Houseless." Nov.: 7–8.
Noad, William R. 1849/52. "Plan of St John's Newfoundland from Actual Survey." TRPAD, MG 93.
Noble, A.G. 1984. *Wood, Brick and Stone: The North American Settlement Landscape. Volume 1: Houses.* Amherst: University of Massachusetts Press.
Nolan, Stephen M. 2004. *A History of Health Care in Newfoundland and Labrador.* NL Health and Community Services Archives and Museum.
Noseworthy, Frank. 1999. Interview by C.A. Sharpe, 20 Apr.
O'Flaherty, Patrick. 2011. *Leaving the Past Behind. Newfoundland History from 1934.* St. John's: Long Beach Press.
O'Leary, F.J. 1978. "The St. John's Housing Corporation 1944–1978." Typescript.
Oliver, Elizabeth Dale. 1983. "The Re-building of the City of St. John's after the Great Fire of 1892: A Study in Urban Morphogenesis." MS thesis, Memorial University of Newfoundland.
O'Neill, Paul. 2003. *The Oldest City: The Story of St. John's, Newfoundland.* St. Philips, NL: Boulder Publications.
Organ, R.J. 1947. Letter from the Secretary of the St. John's Housing Corporation to W.J. Carew, Secretary to the Commission of Government, 19 Apr., PRC 14, Box 15-5-3-3, File L-2.
———. 1948. Letter from the Secretary of the St. John's Housing Corporation to W.J. Carew, Secretary of the Commission of Government, 18 Dec.
Outer Battery Neighbourhood Association. 2012. "Out to the Battery."
Owens, Gerry. 2001. Interview by A.J. Shawyer, 31 July.
Parker, Elizabeth. 1999. Interview by A.J. Shawyer and C.A. Sharpe, 22 July.
Paton, John Lewis. 1938. Letter to the Rt. Hon. Malcolm MacDonald, MP, 7 Sept. Centre for Newfoundland Studies, Memorial University of Newfoundland, The Dunfield Papers, Coll-006.
Peabody Trust. "Peabody through the Ages." https://www.peabody.org.uk/.
Penney, Gerald. 2010. "Under the Street: Archaeology and the Harbour Interceptor Sewer Project." St. John's: Gerald Penney and Associates.
Penney, Nathan. 2001. Interview by A.J. Shawyer and C.A. Sharpe, 28 Feb.
Penson, L.H. 1939a. F.53-'39. Memorandum from the Commissioner for Finance to the Commission of Government: "Proposed Housing Scheme in the City of St. John's. Referred for Consideration to a Committee

Consisting of the Commissioners for Public Health and Welfare, Public Utilities and Finance," 10 May, GN 38, S5-2-1, Box 1, File 9.

———. 1939b. Memorandum from Commissioner of Finance to J.C. Puddester, Commissioner of Public Health and Welfare, 1 Aug., GN 38, S5-2-1, Box 1, File 9.

Perks, W., and W. Jamieson. 1991. "Planning and Development in Canadian Cities." In *Canadian Cities in Transition*, edited by Trudi Bunting and Pierre Filion, 487–518. Toronto: Oxford University Press.

Perry, Clarence. 1929. *The Neighbourhood Unit*. New York: Doubleday.

Phyne, John. 2014. "On a Hillside North of the Harbour: Changes to the Centre of St. John's, 1942–1987." *Newfoundland and Labrador Studies* 29, no. 1: 5–46.

——— and Christine Knott. 2016. "Outside of the Planners' Gaze: Community and Space in the Centre of St. John's, Newfoundland, 1945–1966." In *Sociology of Home: Belonging, Community and Place in the Canadian Context*, edited by Gillian Anderson, Joseph G. Moore, and Laura Suski, 167–86. Toronto: Canadian Scholars' Press.

——— and ———. 2018. "Schools, Streets and Stores: Childhood Geographies of the Inner City of St. John's, 1935–1966." Paper presented at the Atlantic Studies Conference, Acadia University, Wolfville, NS, 4–6 May.

Pickett, Stanley. 1956. Letter to the mayor and councillors written on the eve of Pickett's departure from St. John's, 8 Sept. Courtesy of Stanley Pickett.

———. 2000. Interview by A.J. Shawyer, Weymouth, Devon, 15 May.

Porter, Helen Fogwill. 2011. *Below the Bridge: Memories of the South Side of St. John's*. Portugal Cove–St. Philips, NL: Boulder Publications.

Pooley, Colin G. 1985. "Housing for the Poorest Poor: Slum Clearance and Rehousing in Liverpool 1890–1918." *Journal of Historical Geography* 11, no. 1: 70–88.

——— and Sandra Irish. 1993. "Housing and Health in Liverpool (1870–1940)." *Transactions Historic Society of Lancashire and Cheshire* 143: 193–219.

Pottle, H.L. 1947a. HAE 165-'47. 11 Dec. 1947. GN 2/5, Box 92, File 550.5.

———. 1947b. Memorandum from Commissioner of Public Health and Welfare to Brian Dunfield, 31 Dec. PRC 14, Box 15-5-3-3, File K.

———. 1948. Memorandum from Commissioner of Public Health and Welfare to Brian Dunfield, 27 Apr. GN 13/1/B, Box 116, File 48.

———. 1949. Letter to Sir Brian Dunfield, 29 Mar. PRC 14, Box 15-5-3-3, File L-2.

Project Planning Associates. 1967. *Blackhead Road, Urban Renewal Scheme*.

Puddester, Sir John. 1941. Memorandum to W.W. Woods, 5 Apr. GN 38, A5-2-1.
———. 1944. P.H.W. 71-'44. Minutes of a meeting on 15 December between a committee from the St. John's Municipal Council and a committee from the Commission of Government, 16 Dec. GN 38 S5-2-1, Box 1, File 9.
Quinton, H.W. 1947a. Memorandum to Brian Dunfield, 3 Mar. PRC 14, Box 15-5-3-3, File K.
———. 1947b. Memorandum to Brian Dunfield, 16 May.
———. 1947c. H.A.E. 114(b)-'47. "Regarding an Act Further to Amend the St. John's Housing Corporation Act." 23 Dec. GN 38, S3-1-2.
Ratcliffe, R.U. 1945. "Filtering Down and the Elimination of Substandard Housing." *Journal of Land and Public Utility Economics* 21: 322–30.
Reeder, D.A. 1961. "The Politics of Urban Leaseholds in Late Victorian England." *International Review of Social History* 6: 413–30.
Riggs, B. 1997. "Biographical Notes." In *The Decisions of the Supreme Court of Newfoundland 1947–1949*, vol. 16, edited by B. Dunfield. St. John's: Law Society of Newfoundland.
———. 2001. "Designer of Bowring Park." *Evening Telegram* 2 Jan., 7
Roach, William M. 1974. *Co-operative Housing in Nova Scotia 1938–1973*. Halifax: Nova Scotia Housing Commission.
Roberts, E.M. 1967. "New Ideas in the New Newfoundland." In *The Book of Newfoundland*, vol. 4, edited by J.R. Smallwood, 102–07. St. John's: Newfoundland Book Publishers.
Rolfson, Andrew. 2003. "Absentee Ownership in St. John's, Newfoundland, 1903–1935." BA (Honours) thesis, Memorial University of Newfoundland.
Rose, Albert. 1980. *Canadian Housing Policies 1935–1980*. Toronto: Butterworth.
Rose, Gary. 2006. Interview by Emily Hobbs.
Royal Architectural Institute of Canada. 1960. Report of the RAIC Committee of Enquiry.
Rutherford, P., ed. 1974. *Saving the Canadian City: The First Phase 1880–1920*. Toronto: University of Toronto Press.
Ryan, James. 2010. "From 'Slum Clearance' to 'Revitalization': Planning, Expertise and Moral Regulation in Toronto's Regent Park." *Planning Perspectives* 25: 69–86.
Ryan, Joe. Interviews by A.J. Shawyer and C.A. Sharpe, 16 Feb. and 2 Mar. 2003, 15 June and 28 Sept. 2006, 8 July 2010, and 24 Sept. 2014.

Ryan, William J. 1944. Letter to Brian Dunfield enclosing "An estimate of the cost of erecting the small home, as shown on the plans and described in my letter of October 26th, 1943." PRC 14, Box 15-5-3-3, Vol. 1, File: Reports.

St. John's City Directory. 1919.

St. John's City Directory. 1924.

St. John's Housing Corporation (SJHC). 1944. *Annual Report of the St. John's Housing Corporation for the Year 1944*. PRC 14, 15-5-3-3, File K.

———. 1951. *Churchill Park: Report of the St. John's Housing Corporation 1944–1950*.

———. 1962. *An Era of Progress. A Review of the St. John's Housing Corporation Activities from July 1944 to December 1961*.

———. 1979. *Report of the St. John's Housing Corporation 1944–1978*.

St. John's Municipal Council Minutes (SJCM). 1892–1946.

Schaffer, D. 1982. *Garden Cities for America: The Radburn Experience*. Philadelphia: Temple University Press.

Schoenauer, N. 2000. *6,000 Years of Housing*. New York: W.W. Norton.

Searles, A.E. 1944. *Engineer's Report to Commission of Enquiry on Housing and Town Planning in St. John's by J.W. Beretta Engineers, Inc., San Antonio, Texas*, 3 Jan. GN 38, S5-2-1, Box 1, File 2.

Sewell, John. 1985. *Houses and Homes: Housing for Canadians*. Toronto: J. Lorimer.

———. 2020. *Shape of the Suburbs: Understanding Toronto's Sprawl*. Toronto: University of Toronto Press.

Shanks, Amy, Victoria Cross, and Richard Harris. 2014. "Doubt about Suburbs." In *What's in a Name? Talking about Urban Peripheries*, edited by Richard Harris and Charlotte Vorms, 89–111. Toronto: University of Toronto Press.

Sharpe, C.A. 1978a. "New Construction and Housing Turnover: Vacancy Chains in Toronto." *Canadian Geographer* 22: 130–44.

———. 1978b. "Vacancy Chains and Housing Market Research: A Critical Analysis." Research Note 3, Department of Geography, Memorial University of Newfoundland.

———. 1986. "The Teaching of Urban Morphogenesis." *Canadian Geographer* 30: 53–58.

———. 2000. "'. . . To Arouse Our City from Its Deathlike Apathy, from Its Reproachable Lethargy, from Its Slumber of Industrial and Social Death':

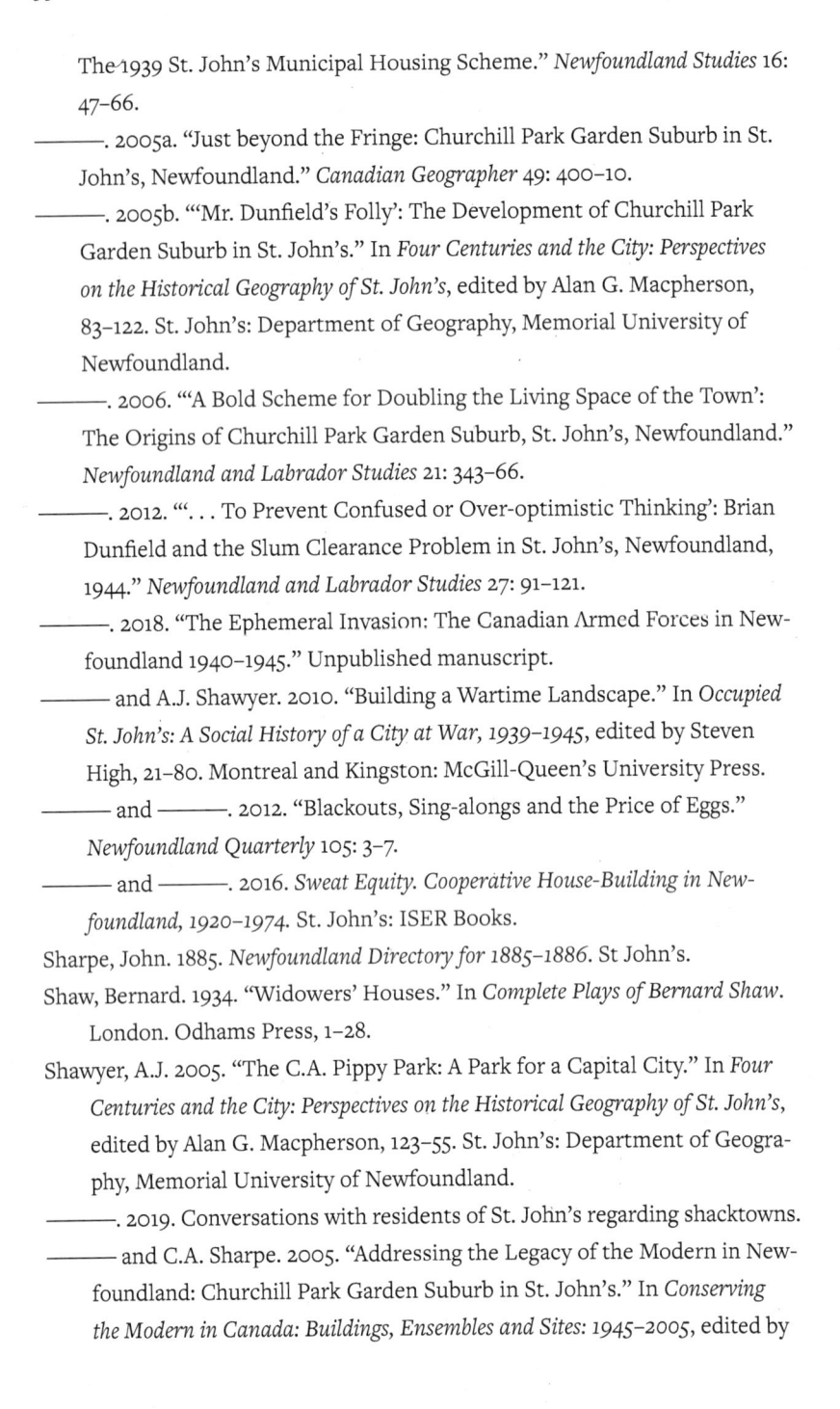

The 1939 St. John's Municipal Housing Scheme." *Newfoundland Studies* 16: 47–66.

———. 2005a. "Just beyond the Fringe: Churchill Park Garden Suburb in St. John's, Newfoundland." *Canadian Geographer* 49: 400–10.

———. 2005b. "'Mr. Dunfield's Folly': The Development of Churchill Park Garden Suburb in St. John's." In *Four Centuries and the City: Perspectives on the Historical Geography of St. John's*, edited by Alan G. Macpherson, 83–122. St. John's: Department of Geography, Memorial University of Newfoundland.

———. 2006. "'A Bold Scheme for Doubling the Living Space of the Town': The Origins of Churchill Park Garden Suburb, St. John's, Newfoundland." *Newfoundland and Labrador Studies* 21: 343–66.

———. 2012. "'... To Prevent Confused or Over-optimistic Thinking': Brian Dunfield and the Slum Clearance Problem in St. John's, Newfoundland, 1944." *Newfoundland and Labrador Studies* 27: 91–121.

———. 2018. "The Ephemeral Invasion: The Canadian Armed Forces in Newfoundland 1940–1945." Unpublished manuscript.

——— and A.J. Shawyer. 2010. "Building a Wartime Landscape." In *Occupied St. John's: A Social History of a City at War, 1939–1945*, edited by Steven High, 21–80. Montreal and Kingston: McGill-Queen's University Press.

——— and ———. 2012. "Blackouts, Sing-alongs and the Price of Eggs." *Newfoundland Quarterly* 105: 3–7.

——— and ———. 2016. *Sweat Equity. Cooperative House-Building in Newfoundland, 1920–1974*. St. John's: ISER Books.

Sharpe, John. 1885. *Newfoundland Directory for 1885–1886*. St John's.

Shaw, Bernard. 1934. "Widowers' Houses." In *Complete Plays of Bernard Shaw*. London. Odhams Press, 1–28.

Shawyer, A.J. 2005. "The C.A. Pippy Park: A Park for a Capital City." In *Four Centuries and the City: Perspectives on the Historical Geography of St. John's*, edited by Alan G. Macpherson, 123–55. St. John's: Department of Geography, Memorial University of Newfoundland.

———. 2019. Conversations with residents of St. John's regarding shacktowns.

——— and C.A. Sharpe. 2005. "Addressing the Legacy of the Modern in Newfoundland: Churchill Park Garden Suburb in St. John's." In *Conserving the Modern in Canada: Buildings, Ensembles and Sites: 1945–2005*, edited by

Susan Algie and James Ashby, 125–33. Papers presented at the Conserving the Modern conference at Trent University, Peterborough, ON, 6-8 May.

Sifton, Clifford. 1914. "Address of Welcome to the City Planning Conference." In *Proceedings of the Sixth National Conference on City Planning, Toronto, May 25–27, 1914*. Boston: The University Press, 1915. Reprinted in Rutherford (1974, 214–19).

Simpson, M. 1982. "Thomas Adams in Canada 1914–1920." *Urban History Review* 11: 1–16.

———. 1985. *Thomas Adams and the Modern Planning Movement*. London: Mansell.

Sir Brian Dunfield Papers. Coll-006, Archives and Special Collections Division, Queen Elizabeth II Library, Memorial University of Newfoundland.

Skinner, Mary and Bill. 2006. Interview by A.J. Shawyer, 21 Feb.

Slattery, John L. 1909. "The British Budget and Land Taxation." *Newfoundland Quarterly* 9, no. 3: 14–15.

Smallwood, J.R. The J.R. Smallwood Papers. Coll-075. Archives and Special Collections Division, QE II Library, Memorial University of Newfoundland.

———. 1937a. "The Work of the Child Welfare Association." In *The Book of Newfoundland*, vol. 2, edited by J.R. Smallwood, 309–10. St. John's: Newfoundland Book Publishers.

———. 1937b. "Sir Leonard Outerbridge." In *The Book of Newfoundland*, vol. 2, edited by J.R. Smallwood, 93. St. John's: Newfoundland Book Publishers.

———. 1937c. "Hawes and Company." In *The Book of Newfoundland*, vol. 2, edited by J.R. Smallwood, 11. St. John's: Newfoundland Book Publishers.

———. 1956. "Statement of Government Policy Respecting the Erection of a New Apartment Building at Churchill Park and the Development of Churchill Square," 21 Feb. PANL, Keough Papers, Box 3, Mines and Resources 1956–58, File: SJHC 1951–58.

Spratt, James J. 1950. Letter to Eric Cook, 12 Aug. PRC 14, Box 15-5-3-3, vol. 7.

Squires, Sir Richard. Coll 250, Archives and Special Collections Division, Queen Elizabeth II Library, Memorial University of Newfoundland.

Stein, C.S. 1957. *Garden Cities for America*. Cambridge, MA: MIT Press.

Stein, D.L. 1994a. "Thomas Adams 1871–1940." *Plan Canada* 34: 14–15.

———. 1994b. "The Commission of Conservation." *Plan Canada* 34: 55.

Stern, Robert, Davis Fishman, and Jacob Tilove. 2013. *Paradise Planned: The Garden Suburb and the Modern City*. New York: Monacelli Press.

Story, G.M., W.J. Kirwin, and J.D.A. Widdowson, eds. 1990. *Dictionary of Newfoundland English (DNE)*, 2nd edition with supplement. Toronto: University of Toronto Press.

Strong-Boag, Veronica. 1991. "Home Dreams: Women and the Suburban Experiment in Canada 1945–1969." *Canadian Historical Review* 72: 471–504.

Symonds, Richard. 2001. *The Architecture and Planning of the Townsite Development, Corner Brook 1923–1925*. St. John's: Heritage Foundation of Newfoundland and Labrador.

Teodorescu, Ioana. 2012. "Building Small Houses in Post-war Canada: Architects, Homeowners and Bureaucratic Ideals, 1947–1974." PhD diss., McGill University.

Tessier, Gerald G. 1951. Confidential Memorandum Concerning Apartments, Legal Secretary of the SJHC to the Board of the Corporation, 9 Feb. Keough Papers, PANL, Box 3, File: St. John's Housing Corporation 1951–58.

Tichelar, Michael. 2018. *The Failure of Land Reform in Twentieth-Century England: The Triumph of Private Property*. London: Routledge.

Tideman, Nicolaus. 2004. "George on Land Speculation and the Winner's Curse." *American Journal of Economics and Sociology* 63, no. 5: 1091–95.

Tippey, Brett. 2016. "Richard Neutra's Search for the Southland: California, Latin America and Spain." *Architectural History* 52: 311–52.

Todd, F. 1930. "Though Slums Are Bad the Cure Is Simple. An Address before the Rotary Club, St. John's, Newfoundland." *Municipal Journal of Canada* 26, no. 4: 3.

———. 1941. Letter to Sir John Puddester, Commissioner of Public Health and Welfare, 28 Mar. GN 38, S5-2-1.

Toopalov, Christian. 2014. "The Naming Process." In *What's in a Name? Talking about Urban Peripheries*, edited by Richard Harris and Charlotte Vorms, 36–67. Toronto: University of Toronto Press.

Toope, Carrie. 2011. Interview by A.J. Shawyer and C.A. Sharpe, 19 Jan. TRPAD, MG 29.49. "James MacBraire."

United Kingdom. 1835. The Municipal Corporation Act 1835. 5 & 6 William IV Cap 76.

———. 1848. Public Health Act. 11 Victoria Cap 63.

Van Nus, W. 1975. "The Fate of City Beautiful in Canada, 1893–1930." *Canadian Historical Association Historical Papers*, 191–210. Reprinted in *The Canadian*

City: Essays in Urban History, edited by G.A. Stelter and A.F.J. Artibise, 176–86. Ottawa: Carleton University Press.

Vardy, O.L. 1967. "The Housing Corporation Success Story." In *The Book of Newfoundland*, vol. 4, edited by J.R. Smallwood, 392–97. St. John's: Newfoundland Book Publishers.

Vivian, Henry. 1910. "Town Planning and Town Housing." *Canadian Municipal Journal* 6: 400–04.

Wagg, Christine, and James McHugh. 2017. *Homes for London: The Peabody Story*. London: Peabody.

Walsh, Sir Albert Joseph. 1944a. HAE 6-'44. Correspondence from the St. John's Municipal Council approving in principle the Fifth Interim Report of the CEHTP, 5 Feb. GN 38, S3-5-3, File 5.

———. 1944b. HAE 21-'44. Drafts of the St. John's Housing Corporation Act and the St. John's Housing Corporation (Lands) Act, 30 Mar. GN 38, S5-2-1.

———. 1944c. HAE 26-'44. Draft of telegram from Governor to Secretary of State for Dominion Affairs, 4 Apr.

———. 1944d. HAE 26(b)-'44. The Municipal Council of St. John's approves the St. John's Housing Corporation bills, 13 June. PRC 14, Box 15-5-3-3, File K.

———. 1945a. Memorandum to Commission for Finance, 22 Feb. PRC 14, Box 15-5-3-3, File K.

———. 1945b. HAE 19(a)-'45. 16 Mar. PRC 14, Box 15-5-3-3, File K.

———. 1946a. Memorandum to R.L.M. James, 14 Oct. PRC 14, Box 15-5-3-3, File K.

———. 1946b. HAE 126-'46. 13 Nov. PRC 14, Box 15-5-3-3, File K.

———. 1946c. HAE 126(a)'46. 3 Dec. PRC 14, Box 15-5-3-3, File K.

———. 1946d. Letter to Brian Dunfield, 16 Dec. PRC 14, Box 15-5-3-3, File K.

Walwyn, Sir Humphrey. 1943. Letter to Brian Dunfield, 23 Aug. GN 1/3/A, Box 52-288, File 253.

———. 1944a. Memorandum to Brian Dunfield, 2 May. GN 1/3/A, Box 52-288, File 288.

———. 1944b. Despatch 42 to Viscount Cranborne, 5 Feb. GN 38, S5-2-1, File 9; PRC 14 155-5-3-3.

———. 1944c. Despatch 92 to Viscount Cranborne, 10 Apr. GN 38, S1-1-3.

———. 1944d. Despatch 218 to Viscount Cranborne, 19 May. GN 38, S5-2-1, Box 1, File 2.

———. 1944e. Despatch 235 to Viscount Cranborne, 31 May. GN 1/3/A, File 288.
———. 1944f. Despatch 240 to Viscount Cranborne, 3 June. GN 1/3/A, File 288.
———. 1944g. Despatch 286 to Viscount Cranborne, 10 July. GN 1/3/A, File 288.
———. 1944h. Despatch 295 to Viscount Cranborne, 18 Nov. GN 1/3/A, File 288.
———. 1944i. Letter to P.A. Clutterbuck, 19 Nov. GN 1/3/A, Box 52-288, File 288/43.
———. 1945a. Telegram 34 to Viscount Cranborne, 8 Feb. PRC 14, Box 15-5-3-1, File: Housing, General, Indigent Persons.
———. 1945b. Telegram 93 to Viscount Cranborne, 21 Apr. GN 38, S3-5-3, File 5.
Weaver, John. 1976. "Reconstruction of the Richmond District in Halifax: A Canadian Episode in Public Housing and Town Planning 1918–1921." *Plan Canada* 16: 36–47.
White, Linda. 2007a. "The Construction of Corner Brook." *Newfoundland Quarterly* 99, no. 3: 3–5.
———. 2007b. "Child Welfare Association." *Newfoundland Quarterly* 100, no. 3: 3–5.
White, Wayne. 2001. Interview by A.J. Shawyer and C.A. Sharpe, 20 July.
Whitelegg, Sir Arthur, and George Newman. 1908. *Hygiene and Public Health*. London: Cassell and Company.
Williamson, T. Morgan. 1971. "Blackhead Road: A Community Study of Urban Renewal." MA thesis, Memorial University of Newfoundland.
Winter, G. 1982. Interview by Mark Shrimpton, Sept.
———. 1998. Interview by C.A. Sharpe, 17 Apr.
———. 1999. Interview by A.J. Shawyer and C.A. Sharpe, 15 Mar.
Winter, H.A. 1944a. HAE 264-'44. Names of persons approved for nomination as members of the St. John's Housing Corporation, 31 Mar. PRC 14, Box 15-5-3-3, File L-2.
———. 1944b. HAE 26(a)-'44. St. John's Housing Corporation Bills. Report of Committee, 11 May. GN 38, S5-2-1, Box 1, File 2.
Woods, W.W. 1941. Memorandum from the Commissioner for Public Utilities to J.J. Mahoney, City Clerk, 12 May. GN 38, S5-2-1, Box 1, File 9.
Wright, Gwendolyn. 2008. *USA: Modern Architecture in History*. London: Reaktion Books.

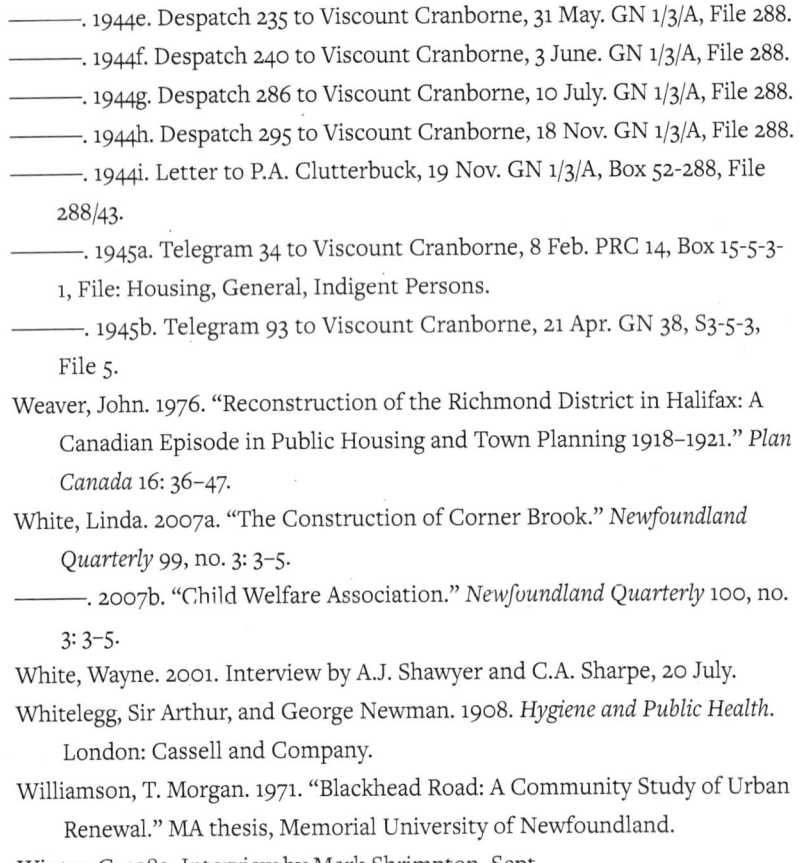

INDEX

absentee landlords, 18, 19, 29, 37, 54
Acton, Brigadier Joseph, 110
Adams, Thomas, 4, 51, 52, 71, 127
Anderson, Hon. John, 64, 108, 230, 237
Anderson, Miss, 68
Angel, F.W., 69, 70
anti-spit bylaw, 9, 42, 44
apartments, 197, 200, 241, 242
Ayre, Lewis H., 162, 225
Ayre's Supermarket, 240
Barter, Jonas, 62, 76
Bartlett, Rupert W., x, xi, 226, 245
Beretta, Lt. Colonel J.W., 118, 140, 172, 297
Bland, John, 140, 147, 204, 297
Bloomfield Farm Dairy, 128, 134
Bonnycastle, Sir Richard, 12
Bowring, Sir Edgar, 75
Bowring Park, 75
Breen, William F., 110, 162
Brehm, Dr. Robert, medical officer of health (1906–36), 40, 41, 43, 58, 88, 229
Brine, Robert, 19
Brookes, Captain Lewis, 194–96

Canadian Commission of Conservation, 50, 52–53
Canadian Manufacturers' Association, 52
Canadian Public Health Association, 52
Cape Cod house style, 174, 175, 176, 176-77, 178, 179, 181
Carnell, Mayor Andrew G. (1933–49), 2, 78, 79, 80, 102, 105, 106, 109, 111, 139, 149, 169, 177, 193, 194, 210, 230, 251, 252
Central Mortgage and Housing Corporation (CMHC), 4, 171, 220, 228, 230
Charity Organization Bureau, 70, 73
Child Welfare Association, 58, 68, 70, 110
cholera, 3, 25, 26, 41, 48
Churchill Square, 3, 186, 200, 201, 240, 241, 243, 244, 317
"City Beautiful" movement, 48–49
City Charter, 55–58, 64, 71, 73
Civic Relief Committee, 75
clearances, 223
Clutterbuck, Sir Peter, 154, 155

357

Cranborne, Rt. Hon. Viscount, 149
Cochius, Rudolf, 75
Colonial Cordage Company, 9, 10, 44
Commission of Government, 1-3, 77-79, 91-94, 104-06, 110, 11, 138, 145, 146, 149, 151, 154, 162, 219, 223, 224, 236, 249
Commission of Enquiry on Housing and Town Planning (CEHTP), 74, 110, 111, 115, 116, 146, 266, 299; Second Report of the CEHTP: new circumferential road for the city is proposed, 117; Third Report of the CEHTP: Review of Housing Conditions and Proposals for Remedies, 118-27; Fourth Report of the CEHTP: Temporary Regulations to Secure Width of Future Streets, etc.,140; Fifth Report of the CEHTP: Engineering Considerations and a Concept Plan,140-45; Sixth Report of the CEHTP: Resignation of Members, 146
Community Nursing Service, 68
Consumption, 27
Cook, Eric G., municipal councillor and deputy mayor (1941-45), 109, 110, 112, 132, 150, 162, 167, 225
Cook, Mayor Sir Tasker, 68, 71, 109
Corner Brook Townsite, 53
Crosbie, Lady Mitchie Anne, 68
Cummings, George, 241
Dalzell, Arthur, 2; trained with Todd,53, 71; invited to Newfoundland, 70; recommends a Town Planning Commission, 72; demolish old houses and replace, 73; and slum clearance, 79, 87, 102, 106, 127, 199
Dominion Cooperative Building Association, 64, 65
Don Mills, Ontario, 4, 5, 142, 235
Doyle, Gerald S., 146
Dunfield, Justice Brian Edward Spenser, chairman, CEHTP (1942-44), chairman, St. John's Housing Corporation (1944-49); chairman, Town Planning Commission (1944-51); character and passion, 111, 112; major speeches, 113, 168, 253; leadership of CEHTP, 115, 123-24, 127; visited Canada to seek advice re land valuation, 132; proposals for housing finance, 136; knowledge of town planning, 138; vision for Churchill Park, 142-45; attitude towards slum clearance, 147, 157; defended leasehold tenure, 159; sod-turning for Churchill Park, 167; touring with the governor, 192, 203; resistance to subsidized housing, 194-96; defending costs, 209-10, 215, 218; questioned by the Finance Committee of the National Convention,211; resigned as chairman of the SJHC, 223, 315-16; daughter Dorothy, 163

Ebsary Estate, 194, 195, 196, 197, 217, 230
Elizabeth Towers, 241, 242, 243
Ellis, Mayor William James, 43
expropriation, 129, 130, 131, 134, 137, 150, 152, 155, 169, 231, 232
filtering, 93, 106, 107, 114, 147, 211, 221, 237, 251
fire hydrants, 24, 31, 32, 33, 51
fires, 3, 8, 11, 12, 13, 22, 24, 25, 27, 34, 43, 45, 51, 55, 84, 102, 140, 237
fishery, 8, 9, 11, 22
fountains (tanks), 22, 23, 24
Frampton, William J., 110, 162
Fraser, Allan M., 110, 140
freehold property, 17, 57, 159, 228, 305
Furlong R.J., 152, 153
Galt, John, 32
Garden City Association, 51
"Garden City" movement, 49, 236
garden suburbs, 53, 75, 125, 127, 128, 147, 246
General Water Company, 22, 30
Gibbs, Mayor Michael Patrick, 36, 37, 229
Gill, Nicholas, 20
Goldstone House, 183, 184
Goodrich, Lt. Harold, 190, 192
Gosling, Mrs. A.N., 56, 58, 63
Gosling, Mayor William Gilbert (1916–20), 2, 41, 46, 47, 48, 52, 55, 56, 58, 59, 61, 62, 64, 69, 71, 73, 74, 79, 102, 106, 230, 231, 237
Grey, Earl A.H.G., 51
Halifax Relief Commission, 93
Halliday, James, 128

Halliday, Robert, 26
Hamilton, Governor Ker Baillie, 26
Harvey, Governor John, 25
Harvey, John, 41, 42, 43, 44, 47
Harvey's Estates Limited, 47
Hastings, Dr. Charles, 40
Higgins, Gordon F., 110, 162
Higgins, Justice W.A., 132, 133
Hope Simpson, Sir John, 88
Hope Simpson, Lady Mary Jane, 63
Horwood, Cyril F., 110
Horwood, Sir William, 152
Housing Area, 128–37, 147, 152, 154, 155, 156, 163, 193, 197, 200, 208, 213, 214, 216, 228, 251
Howard, Ebenezer, 49, 50, 125, 126, 127, 199, 251
Howlett, Mayor Charles J., 2, 74, 75, 77
Hutchings, Mary Ellen, 157, 158
Imperial Order of the Daughters of the Empire, 42
industrialization, 21, 24, 48
infant mortality, 3, 42, 44, 69, 123
Ingpen, Major W.F., 74, 92, 93
Iron Ore Company of Canada, 44
James, R.L.M., 212
Jensen Fresh Air Camp, 42
Jerrett, Eric, 110
Jones, Dr. Robert, 88
Kelly, John P., 109
Kenmount Annex, 133
Kent, Justice James, 74
Knights of Columbus Hall, 140
Knowles, Rev. E.C, 110
land settlement, 94

land speculation, 53, 54, 55, 57, 127, 255, 306
Lawrence, Edward, 109
leasehold, 16, 17, 18, 20, 38, 57, 159, 228
Lench, Thomas A., 110
Letchworth Garden City, 49
Lindenlea, 53
Liverpool Corporation, 93
Lush, F.A.F., 162
Macdonald, Governor Gordon, 200, 203
MacGregor, Governor William, 39, 41
Macpherson, Harold, 128, 154, 155
McGrath, James, 61
malnutrition, 79, 85, 88, 105
Mansur, David, 220, 221, 222
Meaney, John T., 88–92, 89, 94, 104, 106, 107, 109, 110, 111, 125, 139, 193, 213, 230
Mellin, Robert, 185
Meschino, Paul, architect of St. John's Housing Corporation (1944-52), 170–85, 170, 185, 186, 187, 190, 192
Mews, Harry G.R., 140, 217, 227
Mile One Stadium, 79, 234
Miller, Dr. Leonard, 110
Modernism, 113, 170, 173, 251
Morris, Sir Edward, 7, 8, 36, 111
Mundy Pond, 42, 45, 67, 80, 81, 82, 196
National Council of Women, 52
National Housing Act 1935 (Canada), 93
Neutra, Richard, 173
New Jerusalem, 251–52

Newfoundland Association of Architects, 183
Newfoundland Association for the Prevention of Consumption, 41, 42
Noad, William R., 25
nuisance, 21, 23, 24, 26, 39, 57
O'Leary, F.J., 229
Olmstead, Frederick Law, 49, 75
One Mile Area, 57, 68, 80, 102, 103, 157, 159
Outerbridge, Major Leonard C., 70, 73
overcrowding, 21, 43, 57, 156, 263
parks, 30, 75, 96
Peabody Trust, 61, 93, 120
Peet, Charles, 162, 210, 225
Penson, John, 91–93, 106
Pickett, Stanley, 230, 231
Pippy, Chesley A., 162, 210, 325
Pottle, H.L., 146, 218, 223, 227
poverty, 17, 41, 54, 74, 79, 105, 106, 157, 175, 194
Prowse, K.R., 37
Puddester, Sir John, 91, 93, 106, 194, 230
Quinton, H.W., 217
Radburn, New Jersey, 142
Railway Employees Welfare Association, 84
Rendell, Dr. Herbert, 41
Rennie, W.F., 16
Roche, Archbishop Edward, 104
"Roofs and Walls" program, 59
Rotary Club, 2, 69–71, 73, 75, 110, 113, 147, 230, 238
Russell, Doris, 243

Ryan, James V., 210
Ryan, William J., 209
St. John's Housing Corporation (1944-81): need for, 137; funding for, 150; creation of, 162; opposition to expropriation, 152, 156; supply problems and high cost of houses, 187-89, 201-13, 227-30; first houses for sale 5 June 1943, 302, Appendix 7; efforts to reduce cost of houses, 135-36; end of house-building program, 217; new post-Confederation mandate, 215-18; standard form of lease, 270-78, Appendix 3; first meeting, 162; tour of sewer tunnel, 163; employment, 165; sod-turning, 167-68; control of design, 177; disagreement over heating and kitchen cupboards, 180; members of first Board, 225; two mandates, 236-38; maps of houses by cohort, 244
St. John's Municipal Council: lack of Council, 8, 26; municipal incorporation, 28-29; first Council, 5, 29-32; electoral franchise, 58; revenues, 2, 19, 28, 70, 83; lack of revenue, 30, 45, 69-73, 230; debt, 1, 2, 30-32, 71; debt relief, 78; budgeting, 30, 45, 69; taxation, 19, 25-26, 29; resistance to taxation, 26, 45; tax arrears, 31, 45, 56, 102; Municipal Arrears Commission, 56, 78, 102; wartime challenges, 97-100; inspection of houses, 44, 57, 80; housing for the poor, 79, 193; criticism of SJHC, 56, 216-17, 238; Council and the CEHTP 113, 117
St. John's Trades and Labour Council, 139, 156
sewerage, 32, 36, 37, 39, 50, 54, 63, 67, 84, 88, 97, 101, 141, 162, 263, 297, 298
sewers, 23, 25, 26, 30, 33, 34, 36, 37, 56, 145, 163, 216, 258, 307, 310, 311
Searles, A.E. (Ed), 140-42, 141, 144, 154, 162, 164, 170, 172, 173, 189, 220, 239, 245
settlement schemes, 94
Seymour, Horace, 53
shacktowns, 79-82, 157
Sifton, Clifford, 50, 52
Slattery, John, 54
slums, 17, 52, 70, 74, 75, 84, 86, 89, 148, 168, 211, 217, 250, 257, 262
Soldier Emergency, 193, 197, 198, 200, 241
Spratt, James, 104, 109, 110, 158
tenements, 3, 13, 16, 34, 37, 38, 43, 44, 58, 62, 79, 84, 135, 232, 233, 238, 264
Todd, Frederick, 2, 75, 79, 114, 232, 236
Toope, Carrie, x, 249
Town Planning Commission, 57, 73-74, 92, 111, 146, 224, 254
tuberculosis, 27
typhus, 3, 41, 43, 48
Urban Reform Movement, 24, 47, 48, 49, 51

urban renewal, 81, 82, 231, 235
Uthwatt Report 1941 (English Expert Committee on the Composition and Betterment), 131, 152, 155
Vardy, Oliver L., 109, 110, 149, 193, 227, 242
Village "B," 187, 188, 199-201, 201
Vivian, Henry, 51, 71, 75, 135, 199
Walwyn, Governor Humphrey T., 98, 101, 123, 149, 151, 152, 154, 155, 156, 190, 192
waste water, 25, 31, 56
water supply, 8, 21, 22, 25, 27, 31, 32, 33, 40, 119, 123, 164, 271, 296

Whiteway's Grocery, 15
Widows' Mansions, 193, 195, 196
Wild, Ira, 139
Windsor, Newfoundland, 29
Windsor Lake, 22, 31, 32, 164
Winter, Gordon A., x, 102, 224, 225, 226, 278
Woods, W.W., 91, 93, 106, 107
workingmen, 45, 52, 73, 93
workingmen's housing, 61–66, 63, 65, 74, 106
World War II, 5, 95, 96, 97, 230, 239
Wright, Frank Lloyd, 173, 177, 179, 182, 184

ABOUT THE AUTHORS

Chris Sharpe is Professor Emeritus of Geography, Memorial University of Newfoundland. During his 40-year career at MUN his principal research and teaching interests were urban landscapes and housing. He lived in Churchill Park for three decades and knowing that it was an important part of the historical landscape of St John's, teamed up with Jo Shawyer to write its story. This book is the result. He is co-author of *Sweat Equity: Cooperative House-Building in Newfoundland, 1920-1974*.

Jo Shawyer is a retired Associate Professor, Department of Geography, Memorial University of Newfoundland. Throughout her career she has explored the dynamic character of cultural landscapes – their creation, maintenance, and change. Jo has studied landscapes personal and public, urban and rural, historical and contemporary. She is co-author of *Sweat Equity: Cooperative House-Building in Newfoundland, 1920-1974*.